MW00438999

LONG BLUE LINE
Based on a True Story

E. McNew

"I hold it true, whate'er befall;
  I feel it, when I sorrow most;
    'Tis better to have loved and lost
    Than never to have loved at all."
-Alfred Lord Tennyson

Long Blue Line is the coming of age of Elizabeth Jeter. It candidly reveals the provocative and secret world of planned teenage pregnancy and the brutal consequences that follow. The girl next door - popular and driven.

Once upon a time a beautiful teenager looked forward to school letting out and the warm, carefree days to come. But in the summer of her fifteenth year, things would drastically change. After reading a romance book sensationalizing a young woman's perfect life following the hookup with a wealthy prince charming, Elizabeth set out to create her own fairy tale ending. This would become the beginning of the darkest hours in her life: pregnancy, bridesmaids, drugs and jail.

Long Blue Line is Elizabeth's captivating memoir about her descent into addiction. Her obsession with pregnancy, independence, and, ultimately drugs is chronicled in brutally honest Prose that will leave you spellbound. Her journey isn't over - far from it. She still has nightmares, but today she is wiser and lives in reality.

If you are this girl, you will take a deep breath and nod your head knowingly. If you knew this girl, you will rethink your assumptions. If this girl is your daughter, you will finally get an insider's look at what she can't put into words.

Above all, you will be moved - moved to tears, to unity, to action. Elizabeth is one of the lucky ones. She survived. Sadly, many young women and their children are unable to escape the madness and become grave statistics. Not everyone gets a second chance, and she hopes to inspire others with her straightforward honesty.

"I don't know how you lived through that."
"If that happened to my family, I would go crazy."
"I can't even imagine how hard it must be."
"How do you do it?"
"I NEVER would have guessed!"

These are just a few of the responses I have gotten after telling a trusted person my story. Over the years, those who did hear my entire story were people who I least expected to tell. I was blessed to cross paths with a few select people, and some even strangers, who offered a friendly presence, allowing me the courage to speak of what has hurt me the most. I like to think of these people as angels. I don't know why we crossed paths, and I don't know why they were meant to hear such a story from a total stranger, but they were there. They were there to help me release my mind from holding in so much pain. The times and places of these encounters were all unique, but my state of emotional instability was always the same.

A few times I was drunk at a bar. One of those long, deeply emotional conversations on a bar stool, slamming down shots between tears. Another few were after becoming close friends with someone. It took me months to decide if the person could handle hearing my story. I had to decide if sharing the information would be more beneficial than risky. I didn't understand why those kind words were being offered in response to such horrible mistakes I made, and the awful results of those mistakes. I never felt brave. I certainly never felt heroic. I felt grief. If I didn't let this pain out every so often I would notice myself slipping into a path of self-destruction. My angels always seemed to come just in time. They saved me, and they helped me save myself.

CONTENTS

Girls,

I am so blessed to have had you for the short time that I did. Though it may one day become confusing and difficult to think of me as your mother, I'll always hold the irreplaceable memories of your angelic beauty safely locked into my heart and forever hold your memory as my baby girls.

If this book reaches you before I do, I pray that it can offer you truth and an understanding of my eternal love for you, which will be a part of who I am for every remaining breath I'll ever take. The pain of your absence is one that never ends, but the beauty of your memory is one that will always shine strong.

My wish for you is to live your life full, whole and happy. Always chase your dreams and never, ever let anything stand in your way. Remember to love and let your self be loved in return. I know that you'll become the people that most are not - remembering to lend a helping hand and finding beauty in the small things in life. When you feel defeated, stand up strong and refuse to allow defeat to become an option. Remember always that you were created because God has great plans for your life, even if at times they feel out of reach and impossible to understand.

I want you to know, whether you're eighteen or fifty-eight, my heart is yours, my home is yours, and my life is yours. I'm always going to be ready to be the best that I can be, whether it's your friend, mentor, acquaintance or mom. I'll give you everything that I'm capable of, still knowing that it cannot make up for what's been lost. I thank you with the utmost sincerity for coming into my life and showing me what it means to hold and love a piece of God's heaven.

Love,
Mom

Reviews

"I don't read non-fiction books. Now I know why. I become too involved...Real life is much sadder than made-up tales. When I reached the end of the book, I felt like crying. I also wanted to scream out, what will happen next?"
-Susanne Leist, author of The Dead Game

"Wow just wow!! I seriously could not stop reading...it had me smiling on minute and crying the next...and as a mother myself it also broke my heart...I would recommend this book to anyone, but particularly young girls! I gave this book 5 stars because the rating system doesn't go any higher :)"
-Ciara Perkins. U.S Army wife

"The strength and courage it must have took to write this book is unimaginable! Elizabeth really moves you with her words and as soon as you read the introduction, it hooks you in! Absolutely the BEST book I've read in a while!! Look forward to reading more from Elizabeth!"
-Ali, Amazon customer

"Testing the waters is intoxicating :) I can't wait to read the more to come. I completely recommend the book."
-Amazon Verified Review

Disclaimer

This narrative is written to offer information and education to our readers. It is sold/uploaded with the understanding that the publisher and/or author is not engaged to render any type of psychological, legal, or any other kind of professional advice. This content is the sole expression and opinion of the author. Neither the publisher nor the individual author(s) shall be liable for any physical, psychological, emotional, financial, or commercial damages, including, but not limited to, special, incidental, consequential or other damages. Our views and rights are the same: You are responsible for your own choices, actions, and results.

I would like to expressly convey to you (the reader) that if I were to accidentally defame, purge, humiliate and/or hurt someone's person or feelings as a result of reading and/or acting upon any or all of the information and/or advice found in my content, it is entirely unintentional of me to do so.

Acknowledgements

To my family, thank you for your love and support in spite of the controversial events in this story. To my wonderful husband, Steven, and my daughter, Savhanna, who have helped me along the way when it felt like it would never end - you are my motivation, my purpose in life, and the best two people any wife and mother could ask for. I love you both more than life. You have given me a new life. Thank you.

To my readers, and the support from my hometown, South Lake Tahoe, CA, this story has allowed me to reconnect with so many lost friends and colleagues that I thought were gone from my life forever. I value your love and support more than I can explain in words, and it's because of you that this story is here. Your support has played a huge role in turning a very distressing series of events into something that will serve a greater purpose for my children, humanity and for me.

To my amazing Grandmother, thank you so much for sharing your amazingly articulate mind for the sake of this book. I love you more than I could ever say, and I am proud to have such a beautiful and loving Grandma in my life.

Dedication

To my Mom, who has helped me along this road in more ways than I had ever realized until writing this memoir, and I wish that I could have thanked you and shown my appreciation much sooner than today because you definitely deserved my gratitude a long time ago. I am sorry for putting you through so much pain and agonizing years of having to endure the unknown. You have suffered with me, and although this makes me sad, I now understand that I was never truly alone in this journey. I love you so incredibly much, and I am very grateful for your ability to calmly tolerate my frequent dramatic antics and still love me and understand me - all at the same time. I love you Mommy.

I also want to dedicate this book to my Dad. Although we've had our times of conflict and haven't always agreed on everything, you always loved me and wanted what was best. Writing this book helped me to realize this. I am sure that I was a tough teenager for a father to deal with, and I know that you did the best you could. As I have grown older and matured over the years and have had children of my own, I understand why you were upset on more than one occasion. It just meant that you cared. You just wanted me to be safe. Though I was the only person who could have saved myself, I thank you for trying to help me. Thanks for helping me get through some of my rough patches and stepping into my life when I was sad and alone. I love you Dad.

Prologue

Everything is fuzzy. I can't seem to focus. I cast my line out ahead hoping for a fresh salmon dinner doused in lemon and garlic, and the girls always like to eat what we catch. Waiting patiently is always worth the prize. Wondering where they've toddled off to, I peer over my shoulder. The white pickup truck is crookedly parked about 20 feet away. It's too quiet, I think to myself. Something isn't right. Where are the girls? Where is Derrick?

In a panic, I drop my pole to the ground and quickly race toward the truck. The fishing gear is scattered in the bed of the four-wheel-drive, and the only evidence of my girls is a shoe. A blue and white shoe with the laces untied. It's too small to be Chloe's shoe. It must belong to Zoe. Gazing around, I see nothing. Derrick suddenly appears from the side of the truck and asks me, "What's going on?"

He reeks of pot. I could see the heavy smoke swirling out of the passenger side window. "Derrick, where are the girls?" I ask in a panic. "Elizabeth…" he sighs as if we've been through this. "Chloe is in a foster home - don't you remember?" His statement sounds familiar. I must have forgotten. How in the world could I forget about something like that, I ask myself. "Well, where is Zoe?" I demand. "C'mon Elizabeth. Don't get all crazy again. You know where Zoe is." "No! I don't! Where the hell is my baby?" I shriek.

His red eyes look to the ground and the silence returns. As Derrick slowly lifts his head, he glances toward the tailgate, silently urging me to acknowledge the single shoe lying on its side. As I look over, the wind picks up and the laces begin to sway. The silence and the eerie manner in which the shoelace hangs over the tailgate, resting to a slow swing, forces an abrupt vision of choosing a tiny casket for Zoe at the local morgue. The casket suddenly becomes visible. It's in the back of the truck next to the shoe. "ZOE!" I become hysterical. I hurry over to the casket to lift the lid. It's empty. "No, Derrick!" I sob. "What happened to Zoe? Why is this casket in your truck? WHAT DID YOU DO TO HER?"

Oh my God, I say to myself. My stomach clenches as I hurry to pick up the tiny sneaker.

"They told me she didn't die, Derrick!" I yell, as a rush of fear overcomes my body. "This can't be true! Zoe is only 22 months old!"

I cry, more to myself. I begin sobbing uncontrollably as my knees hit the ground.

Dear God, Please let this be a nightmare. Please let me wake up! I want my baby back! PLEASE!

I opened my eyes to the sunlight seeping through my townhouse window. I'm soaked with sweat and still feeling the terror from the nightmare. With tears streaming down my face I sigh, simultaneously with relief and grief. I know that today will be one of those tough days. The lingering feeling of pain and sadness from my dream will follow me around for the remainder of the day, and I'll have nothing on my mind except my babies. I'll also be wondering why my subconscious always seems to bring Derrick into my nightmares as the villain. I sat across the table from him in deep thought while watching him devour his breakfast.

Preface

"Do you think anyone will notice?" I ask my twin sister, Merri. "Liz! You're fine! Quit worrying about it and just be happy that we're getting the hell out of here!" She enthusiastically replied. For as much as Merri and I had fought over the years, and even physically beat each other up as kids, we were still twins regardless, and the idea that we'd be walking down the aisle together on our high school graduation day wasn't a surprising one.

No one else would have wanted to walk with me anyway. I would have felt bad if one of the lonely, partner-less kids who paired up last minute to walk down the aisle got stuck with me. And if it were a guy, he would totally come off as my baby-daddy! What if he was a little scrawny guy half my size? I pondered. Luckily and not surprisingly, my twin and I managed to graduate a year early. It was just a few weeks before my due-date, and I was convinced that I was going to be that kid who passed out on the walk across the field. When we were ordered to stand in line and instructed to prove that we weren't hiding a bottle of jack or a beach ball to disrupt the ceremony, my attempt to conceal my pregnancy with my extra-large gown failed miserably. Those gowns were awesome hiding places. The cat was out of the bag when I opened my gown, revealing my cute polka-dot maternity dress, and the only hidden item I was found guilty of was a baby. The other kids were sly enough to keep their blow-up-Betty dolls and bottles of booze under the radar.

The band began playing that same-old graduation song - whatever it's called. It was our signal to walk, and that's all we knew. We started the walk up the small gravel hill which I had walked on many times over the last few years. We were walking away from the same hill that led to the Young Parents Program. This was the place that I was introduced to as my new school after finding out I was pregnant when I had just turned fifteen. Fat as a whale, at nine months pregnant with my baby, it wasn't exactly a walk in the park trying to waddle my way up to the grass football field to receive my diploma, but I did it.

College was next. I was so worried about everything on my first day of classes. I didn't get to just pack up my bag and speed my way over to the college where my only worry would be of being pulled over by a highway patrol car. I had to wake up extra early to convince Chloe and Zoe to let me get them dressed for the day, brush the knots out of their tiny heads of hair, beg them to eat their breakfast in the least messy manner possible, and try to translate what they were bickering over - which was usually who got to use the Princess bowl for their cereal. What's so wrong with the Minnie Mouse bowl, I would think. After the morning meltdowns had taken their course, it was time to grab my bag, with one kid in each arm, open the front door, somehow turn around to lock it, and stuff their stubborn little bodies into their car seats. I would have to distract them with anything and everything possible just to get them to sit still long enough to get them securely buckled in. At that point, I had sweat dripping from my forehead and wishing that I had brought an extra stick of deodorant to do something about my armpit dilemma. Oh, and this was all in the dead of winter with six feet of snow and all.

It wasn't easy to handle this five days a week at the age of 18 but nothing was going to stand in my way of getting an education. I would one day provide the best for these girls. They deserved the best, and I was determined to give that to them.

Life can sure be one unpredictable roller coaster. If you had asked me then how I felt about drugs and people on welfare, I surely would have laughed as my snooty nose stuck straight up in the air. I would've said something along the lines of, "There is no excuse for being a total loser! We are all responsible for our own actions, and people like that just need to fall off the face of the planet." True story.

Have you ever made an attempt to explain a crappy situation or life event to someone, and instead of actually referring to the events for what they were, you simply called them things? My brain won't allow me to go there, even when I try to go there. Things have a great way of keeping you from falling into that pit of being the person who was living with those...things. Things are the universal word that comes to our mercy when we just can't spit it out. Whoever was awesome enough to come up with things (maybe a pilgrim or one of my great ancestors) forever have my grateful appreciation.

Once again I have to say life is unpredictable and sometimes it takes some pretty rough turns, and eventually if you're one of the unlucky, you'll have zero control over where you'll end up next. One of the most challenging things in life is living through the unknown. Not knowing what will happen next or where the next direction of your life may swerve is usually more frightening than actually knowing what's to come. I lived for four years in this state. Or wait, I existed for four years in this state. I didn't know what would come next. I began to expect that whatever did come next would certainly be bad, and those bad things would always be followed by other things that got worse.

The only explanation that I can think of as to how my mental status is still intact enough to even write my story is the countless nights I spent praying as I fell asleep. I would beg for God to make it better. I begged him to just make it go away. I mentioned to God on several occasions that if my life were to forever continue with this pain, I would rather he just let me die in my sleep. I was too chicken to kill myself. I knew that I could not live like this for much longer. Fortunately, God kept me breathing. He knew that there were better things to come. God knew that I would one day have a better understanding of life, and he knew that I would pass it on to the

3

many others who were still searching. Thanks for that, God. I am thankful that you forced me to endure all of that pain because if you hadn't, I wouldn't be who I am today. And today, because of you, I love myself.

Chapter 1

My scrawny little 13-year-old body was pumping with adrenaline. I peered over my shoulder and through my nerdy glasses to make sure that no one else in the class had noticed my shaky reaction. My G-rated literature days were over. I had never read anything so intense. It was like a first date - so nerve wracking but incredibly thrilling.

After losing my literature virginity, I started spending all of my free time cozied up in my little twin-sized bed obsessing over these novels. The characters were all young, beautiful girls in their teens. They all had a disadvantaged upbringing and faced horrible tragedy. Most importantly, they all ended up living in some immaculate mansion with a rich, distant relative that they never knew existed.

My young mind was incredibly influenced by these books. These stories started to create their own lives, building into my subconscious. I was suddenly and completely infatuated with tragedy as well as thinking up various ways of becoming rich like the girls in the novels. At the age of thirteen, I was going through the obituaries in the local newspaper hoping to find a rich relative that would leave me their estate. I also put together a flip -book of the future mansion I wanted to own in Palm Springs.

If I wasn't romanticizing about death or tragedy, it was money I was thinking about or sometimes boys. The thought of boys would take over about a year later. To say I was a little mixed up would be an understatement.

I was always a sensitive kid. The most minor things would severely upset me, especially unexpected loud noises. I've been told that the vacuum, toilet flushing, and the blinds being pulled up would put me into a panic when I was a baby. On a night back in 1990, my mother was driving us all home from a weekend visit with my Grandma and Grandpa. First, I was already extremely upset over the fact that I had to leave them. They spoiled my twin and me rotten. Our older sister didn't mind leaving as much as we did. She was a teenager and had more important affairs to attend to. My mom must have bribed me with candy of some sort for the four-hour drive home we had ahead of us. The candy was fantastic. The aftermath, however, was disastrous. It left me sticky. Even worse, the napkin my mom threw to me in the back seat was DRY. Little pieces of this napkin broke off as I tried with everything in my soul to get my hands clean. I was bawling my little eyes out.

Not only was I sensitive, I was also very imaginative and compulsive. Let's go back to my very firsts.

My First Crush: We all have a first crush. I was only five years old. Seeing him gracefully fly around on his magic carpet, bravely leap from building to building, was all it took to have me completely in love. I had dreams of flying over the city every night. When I woke and realized that the only Aladdin I had with me was a Barbie doll, it practically broke my heart. I just knew that he would return one day to marry me.

My First Drink: Most all of us experiment with the beverage that so many adults elegantly held in their glasses. They refused to share a taste as they rambled on forever appearing to completely adore life and everything about it. Eventually, I got curious! My mom wasn't much of a drinker, luckily. But other parents were. My best childhood friend, Holly, was just as curious and excited to sample our first drink. I brought a "water bottle" over to her house that night. It was the perfect night for this trial. Her dad was busy working late, and the only company sharing the space was her brothers. The vodka in the water bottle ruined our attempts to be discreet. We were dizzy in the hallway and giggling about how stupid we felt. Holly lectured each and every brother, three total, about the negative consequences of alcohol. They had expressions of fear in their eyes as if she'd gone completely mad. It was epic.

My First Time: How I cringe! I mainly cringe because I was just so young. He was my first boyfriend, and his name was Andy. Even though we were just kids, I still believe to this day that we were truly in love. Clearly, we wanted to move much more quickly than we were really ready for, physically and emotionally. We were together constantly for about a year. He lived with his grandparents, and his grandfather picked up a job out of town about four hours away. Eventually, he had to move. On moving day, my mom dropped me off at his house to help him and his grandparents pack. Another friend of ours, Jesse, was there too. The few hours I spent watching him pack his life away was utter heartache and torture. I had a lump in my throat and it took everything that I had in my soul not to break down and cry. I was too embarrassed at that age to show emotion, and for Andy, it had so much depth to it. We were both each other's firsts - first in everything in the romance department. When my mom returned to pick me up, Andy pulled one of his childhood stuffed animals out from a box about ready to be taped shut. He then doused the bear with his cologne that I loved. Standing in front of his empty garage, with my mom and twin waiting to take me shopping down the hill with them, I had to make the goodbye as fast as possible before I broke down in front of everyone. Andy and I gave each other our last ever hug and a quick kiss with definite plans to be together again. For the next week I cried myself to sleep hugging and smelling the stuffed bear which was all that I would ever have left of my first true love. It took me about three months to realize that we couldn't be together. We were too young, and having to wait for four years is a long time to a teenager.

My first year of high school was a long one. I was quiet and reserved and always thinking that my peers were looking at me and whispering behind my back. I had a boyfriend for most of that year. We were both loners and definitely anti-social. I would have, most likely, enjoyed my first year of high school more if I hadn't been so caught up in being loyal to him. I had a natural desire to be submissive and completely faithful to any boyfriend I had starting when I was only twelve. It was almost as if I was living in another century where women were married off in their early teens and just had to accept their fate. I must have been born with an old and lost soul - not to mention a stubborn one. The last month of school that year was when my wild streak started. I impulsively broke up with the boyfriend who really didn't take it so well as he punched the lockers in the hallway. I suppose breaking up with him after a whole nine months of dating wasn't too nice of me. I decided that I was going to be much more popular than I had been. I started hanging out with more friends and I was feeling more confident than I ever had.

The snow had finally melted, the sun was just right, and the fresh mountain air brought me to the exciting thought of summer vacation! Something about the sun warming up our cold, icy town had the instant effect of waking me up and getting my blood pumping. The winters were always much longer than the summers. It is almost like becoming free after hibernating in a cold, harsh cave for half the year. For most of the school year, we were restricted to staying indoors and wearing snow boots with double layers of socks. Sometimes I would put garbage bags over my socks to make sure that the snow didn't soak my feet as I trudged my way into the heated classroom. No more clanking chains on the tires of cars driving painfully slow down the highway. No more shoveling driveways and suffering through stiff, painfully icy hands, and no more stress over walking to the bus stop with fear of slipping on black ice in front of a crowd of students. Summer had finally arrived. The energy at school was elevated, and every student had an eager and excited anticipation for the last bell to ring. Three months of tank tops and beaches could easily put the most miserable person in a better mood.

On the last day of school, my rebellious group of friends and I thought it would be a great idea to acquire some forty-ounce beers and have a barbeque. I had a small group of friends, and just like me, they were pretty mindless and wild. My twin sister Merri happened to be tagging along. We were really nothing alike. Merri was usually not the type to hang out in a wild crowd. She was quiet and preferred hanging out with her pets rather than humans. Her room was like a jungle. She had a huge, obnoxious bird that I hated with a passion. Every morning at the crack of dawn, this thing would caw like it was being strangled. I wished I were the one doing the strangling. I am convinced it did this just to torture me. Her snakes gave me nightmares on a regular basis. If I were ever forced to share a room with her, I'd probably camp out in the closet.

Merri was not fond of my friends; she thought they were annoying and dramatic. She was usually pretty good at putting that aside for me and faking a smile when she had to. Today was one of those days. The sunshine must have been bright enough to even get Merri in the mood to socialize.

As for my friends, Kate was a girl I had met my first year of high school. She was constantly complaining about some serious life dilemma that she made sound more like a mid-life crisis than an adolescent issue. She and I had a few things in common though; we'd rather skip class on any given day to drink and flirt with boys. Kate was about my height – 5 feet 4 inches. She had the biggest boobs ever and bleached blonde hair. She was curvy with a butt that could knock down a sumo wrestler. Boys loved that about her. Megan was the snotty one. She was funny when she wanted to be,

9

but snotty. She was tall, blonde, and attractive. I had become close friends with Megan in seventh grade. She was new to my home economics class, and I had decided to take her under my wing. We instantly became almost as close as sisters. She had quite an ego and loved to give guys a hard time. Megan also loved to try new things and was always up for almost any sort of trouble. When the three of us got together, the gates of hell opened, and we were out to cause some crazy and thoroughly entertaining trouble. The main stipulation was that the trouble must involve the most recent batch of mostly-innocent boys we were aiming to torture.

As for myself, my name is Elizabeth. At 14, I was a small 115 pounds with long medium-brown hair, and I was frequently given compliments on my perfect lips. I was beginning to comprehend that I had been given the gift of a flawless figure, and when I wanted to, I could easily grab the attention of any guy in my sight. I usually only wanted this when I was drunk and extra conceited. I liked the attention, and even more so, I loved the sense of power I felt every time I caught a guy staring. Even as a young kid, I always looked for reassurance and confirmation that I was worthy of special treatment. This need to feel accepted only became stronger as the years passed. For the most part though, I was bubbly and friendly, but I also had a concealed passive-aggressive personality. I was mostly passive until something annoyed me enough to cause a major meltdown. When I was only five, a little girl asked me about twenty times over if I would be her friend. After saying yes for the nineteenth time, I just couldn't handle it anymore. I started viciously whacking her with my plastic softball bat to shut her up. She ran home crying. To this day, I still feel terribly bad about that. I definitely had my father's temper. I was born pissed off, and I could not tolerate being disturbed with any sort of extra noise or unnecessary chatter. The alcohol took all of this away.

Chapter 2

On the last day of school, we were all talking in a circle in front of the gym about whom we were going to invite to our beer-fest and trying to figure out where exactly this would take place. That's when I met Josh, a senior at my high school. He overheard us talking and invited himself into the conversation. The tall, handsome senior guy confidently informed us that he would be joining the party. Coincidently, he lived about twenty feet from the back of the high school gate. The location became official and now we were all ready to do this. We walked to the location and quickly began smoking, drinking, and laughing hysterically over pathetic jokes that really weren't all that funny.

After chugging half of a beer, I began to feel the liquid-courage pump through my veins. Whenever I caught a buzz, I also caught a case of extremely enhanced self-confidence. In fact, I believed that I was so ingenious that no matter what idea I came up with, it would always turn out in my favor. I was an exception to the rule of consequences. Looking around to try to figure out if Kate or Megan already had dibs on any of these boys, I began to assess which one might be the most attractive and mature. Josh, the handsome and confident senior, caught my eye for the second time. This time, with each glance, I was utterly paralyzed. It must have been his deep blue eyes that were flirtatiously glancing my way every few seconds. It also could have been how I adored the height on this guy, and maybe just his talkative, confident, friendly personality. He was about 6'2", and to me that symbolized protection. His confidence made it seem as if he were in total control. All of the guys my age were just too short. Some of them still had squeaky voices and that just annoyed me.

Josh had such an adult appearance. Of course a youthful one, but it became incredibly easy, and almost natural, to imagine a life with him. As he spoke to the rest of the group about things I still can't recall, my imagination was running wild and his consistent eye contact intensified my ideas with each warm smile. I pictured our new, white, picket fenced home and our little babies playing and laughing. I gladly allowed myself to entertain the idea that Josh just might be the one. Thoughts and fantasies overcame me that I hadn't yet experienced. My trance like state became very specific. I heard myself telling him I was pregnant. I saw him smiling and happy while holding and reassuring me. This vision, however, portrayed both of us as adults and possibly in our mid-twenties. It was so incredibly perfect. I wanted it. Whatever it was that caused this to cross through my mind changed my thoughts on life and growing up - permanently.

The party concluded with Josh and I locked in his bedroom. He turned on one of my favorite songs. He was intensely looking into my eyes as if he were silently expressing his feelings of his instant love.

When the party died down and the light weights passed out, Josh walked me home. I lived about a half mile down the road. I was excited to know that he lived so close to me. That would make it easier for me to pursue him. He led me up the two wooden steps to my front door. It was an awkward moment. I didn't know if he wanted to kiss me goodnight or just see me off like another meaningless girl. Before I could think much more about it, Josh wrapped his long arms around my waist and told me that I had the most beautiful eyes he had ever seen. He called me sweetie before kissing me and saying goodbye. This was the first time a man had spoken to me with such sincerity and respect. To add to my admiration for him, I was delighted to learn that he was a clean, passionate kisser. I could not stand it when a gorgeous guy was a sloppy kisser. It truly gagged me when a date completely ruined the entire outing with a slimy tongue. Definite deal-breaker. I didn't have to worry about that with Josh.

I immediately developed strong feelings for this guy. He treated me as if I were a grown woman - something I had wanted to be for so long. I was sick and tired of other people thinking that they knew what was best for me. I wanted to be ahead of the game. I wanted to have more than any other girl my age, even if it meant finding it in an outrageous way. Josh made me feel like I had a chance to become an adult sooner. I stumbled to my room and fell asleep with a smile.

I woke up the next day to a knock at my door. Josh casually walked in and started chatting away. Ok, good…he still likes me, I thought. I was slightly taken by surprise with his sudden visit, but I wasn't complaining. I was happy to see him, and I was sure that my mom would like him too. I was right. He fit perfectly into our family. Right away Josh was great with helping out around the house when he visited; he raked up pine needles in the backyard, and he loved to cook when anyone in the family was hungry. Josh was very talkative and made a great first impression. He was skinny as well as tall and always dressed in a plain white tee shirt and jeans. I couldn't believe this handsome and mature guy wanted me. No other boy in our grade had facial hair and a deep voice like he did. I was happy to have successfully found a man. Being with Josh lifted my self-esteem and gave me the confidence I had been lacking. He made me feel like I was worth it. Josh made me feel loved and adored and wanted. I felt as if I were finally whole and needed by another person.

Our first serious conversation came after the first time we had sex, which was introduced by him. It was the age factor. I assumed that because he was a senior he would be about 17 years old. He told me he was 19. I wondered if he was a little too old for me, but I quickly erased the thought from my mind. I was nervous about telling him how young I really was. I decided to do some rounding. I boldly told him that I was fifteen. I was still two months away from that but, in my teenage mind, it was close enough. He sighed with relief and said that he was hoping that I was at least fifteen. I ended up telling the truth a few weeks later. By that time, he was already hooked and had said the "L" word so there was no turning back.

We were together every day for every possible minute. Our young relationship never felt young, it always felt mature. I was in love with Josh. The vision that blasted through my mind of the day we met never vanished. It became more vivid, and as we spent more time together, I began to build ideas off of it. He carried himself as if he were my husband - the husband that I wanted. He made me breakfast, gladly catered to my every need, and frequently spoke of our future together. We had our fights, but he wrote me love letters. His spelling was horrible, but I easily looked beyond that. He constantly showed me small acts of kindness, and often, the small acts were what meant the most.

Officially a couple and coming up on our 5 month anniversary, Josh walked me to the chain-linked gate that began the path to my first day of high school as a sophomore. He kissed me and said he would be waiting there for me at the end of the day. As I approached, my friends gave me a look of curiosity and slight confusion. They never thought that I would take a one-night-stand so seriously.

I attended my scheduled classes and could hardly wait for the last bell to ring. Sure enough, Josh was waiting for me at the gate. He had a turkey and cheese sandwich in his hand, knowing how hungry I would be by the end of the day. He always stayed true to his word and had my back, and that made me love him even more.

Later that evening, my oldest sister, Lilah, stopped by the house. She had been cleaning her apartment all day and wanted me to help watch my 2 year-old niece, Summer. Lilah had left home about a year earlier. She and my mother had gotten into some battles over some serious and some not so serious issues. The house had become much more peaceful with Lilah at a distance although I occasionally missed her quirky humor. She had met a man the night before while out with her friends at the casino, and he wanted to take her out again. She spoke of Huey like he was a true keeper. He was even a doctor! Gross. He must be like thirty something! I thought. Why my twenty-one year old sister was attracted to this older man I'll never know. I was later to discover he was in his 50's!

"I have school tomorrow and I have to do homework. I want to hang out with Josh tonight too," I told her. She looked disappointed but was understanding. She called the house about an hour later. "Huey says he'll pay you to babysit, and you can just hang out with Josh at my apartment," she said. "Ok, I guess that works," I replied, trying to conceal my excitement.

I was extremely happy about this new babysitting gig. I knew that Josh and I could spend more time alone, and I wanted to see what it was like to spend time with him in an unsupervised environment. It turned into an every weekend job. Lilah and Huey spent their nights at clubs playing poker. Lilah sometimes didn't return until ten in the morning. I would tell her that Josh had left when it got dark and that he slept at his own house and he would only come by to visit and bring food. Eventually Lilah gave in when I played the "scared" card. Eventually I assured her that Josh would sleep away from me on the floor. That was partially true - at least until Summer fell asleep. As soon as we heard Lilah rustling with her key to unlock the front door, we practically threw each other in the opposite direction. We just couldn't stay off of each other. Josh and I were becoming very serious, very fast, and on a totally new level.

15

Not long into the school year, my health class teacher, Mrs. B., announced that it was time to take home the simulated baby dolls for our 100-point assignment. I had seen other students walking around with these dolls, and I always thought that they looked so pathetic. I thought this would be more of an embarrassment than anything. A week later I was waiting in line at the end of the school day for my doll to be issued to me for the weekend. It was pretty awkward accepting a fake baby and being expected to hold and treat it as if it were real. I was issued the only black baby in the classroom. It was a little boy, plastic penis and all. When I picked up the baby, the first thing that I noticed was that it was actually heavy. The baby probably weighed about eight pounds. The second thing I noticed was that it smelled so good. It smelled like baby powder, clean and fresh. The teachers must have cleaned it and doused it with the baby powder to give it a more real effect. I think I named him too - probably something similar to Josh Jr. I would have to explain to Josh that Jr. was born with a very rare genetic makeup. Nonetheless, he's our precious son! I laughed to myself.

As a child, I had periodically adopted a variety of baby animals so I figured that it couldn't be too difficult to deal with this doll that wasn't even real. One of my first pets was a tiny mouse that I stole from the pet store. I stole Rupert out of fear that he would be fed to a snake and I wanted to spare him. Merri told me that there was no way he would survive because he was just a few days old. I took this as a challenge and spent my last twenty dollars on a small cage and cedar. I set lit candles next to Rupert's small cage every night for the first week to help keep him warm and cozy.

Rupert kept me company for the next six months. After coming home from school one snowy day, he was dead on my floor and torn to shreds. The family cat, Astro, (I called him Ass for obvious reasons) had ripped my little friend to pieces. I became hysterical and ran downstairs to my mother who then

16

asked my pet-expert sister to clean the mess. She did - with no argument. I think she felt bad for me.

Over the weekend, I took care of my "baby" when it cried. I had been instructed to insert a key into its back to calm it down. This baby simulator put ideas into my head that caring for a baby would be as simple as turning a key. I quickly started to enjoy carrying the baby around and pretending that I was a mommy. I wanted to practice, and I wanted my doll to be real. After I turned my doll into class the next week I became much more interested in my health class. I wanted to learn more about babies. However, I failed the assignment miserably. Apparently I hadn't woken up to calm his little butt down on numerous occasions in the middle of the night. Oops. It was freckin' 3:00 a.m.! I thought to myself, as I stared at my big, red "F."

It was about 6:00 o'clock on a Friday night, and as if we were already living together, Josh and I were making my niece, Summer, a grilled cheese sandwich for dinner. Lilah was, once again, heading out with her doctor boyfriend. I had finally met Huey - grey hair and all. He was oddly friendly, but I still thought he was way too old to be dating my sister. It grossed me out, but I loved Lilah and wanted her to be happy. It was just another babysitting night and Josh was getting bored. He invited his older brother, Jed, to come over with his fiancé and their six-month-old baby. I had expected both of them to be at least in their early twenties. Jed was 21, but his fiancé was only 16. Dawn was a really nice girl, and she seemed like a very happy mommy too. Her little baby girl was the cutest thing I had ever laid eyes on.

As I was listening to Dawn talk about the new neighborhood she and Jed were living in, an idea exploded in my mind like a rocket blasting into the night. This was the best idea I had ever come up with! As Dawn was talking, I attentively nodded and smiled while I excitedly thought to myself, I'll have my own baby! My mom will have no choice but to kick me out, and we can be our own little family! Jed and Dawn made it look so easy. It almost looked fun. I didn't really want to be kicked out of my home, and I definitely didn't want to upset my mom. Unfortunately, there was no way that I could have seen that far into the future. I assumed that it would be a minor conflict and forgiveness would surely come sooner than later. My newly acquired vision was that of my new family living together in an adorable little apartment. I saw a happy baby and a husband that worked hard every day to support us. I was a happy housewife wearing a polka dot apron and making cookies with the new offspring. It was the perfect fantasy.

I wanted to be an independent adult so desperately. I wanted to get married and have babies and live in that adorable house with no parent to answer to. I just wanted to grow up. I wanted to make my own choices, and have those choices respected. This new idea quickly became an obsession that would change the course of my entire life. I started spending my days coming up with ideas to expedite my goal of becoming pregnant. I first searched online.

At the age of 15 I learned about fertility and the science behind it. I researched different tips and methods for "TTC," or trying to conceive. I was very secretive and subtle about this mission. I printed out a chart to track my periods so I would know when I was ovulating, and hid the chart under my bed. I started taking my basal body temperature and drinking cough syrup with expectorant that was rumored to help. I had a plan in case I was caught or questioned about anything: the thermometer and cough syrup were under my bed because I felt like I was "getting sick." No one can argue with that, I thought to myself.

I started eating a ton of broccoli. The folic acid in broccoli was supposed to help prevent serious birth defects. I drank extra water and tried to avoid drinking alcohol. I was preparing my body for what I knew it could handle. I was treating this as an adult. This preparation only motivated me to go to any length to make this baby a reality.

I became obsessed with finding more stories about getting pregnant. I found reality shows on television that documented couples having a baby for the first time. My small 14" television set had a timer, and I set it to power on every morning at 9:00. I had to have all of the information I could possibly get. I researched the subject with true diligence. These couples on the reality shows were much older than I, but that was never considered.

I watched a movie on one of those Women's Network channels about a fifteen-year-old girl who accidently became pregnant. I watched the movie intensely; nothing in the world could have disrupted my attention. See, I tried to rationalize that it's not all that bad. It happens all the time! There's a movie about it! It's not like I'm only thirteen or something. I had concluded that fifteen was the earliest acceptable age to have a baby. This movie did not scare or intimidate me; it gave me even more ideas and desires to become pregnant. It was a glamorous thing from what I could tell. I was already mature and grown up enough to make my own decisions. I was sure of it.

After watching show after show and browsing the web for hours on end looking for ways to become pregnant, I went to the storage shed in my mother's backyard where Lilah had left Summer's baby items from when they both lived at home. Lilah had become pregnant when she was a senior in high school. I was only eleven at the time and I was so stunned I could hardly reply to my mother when she announced it.

The only words I could mutter in response were "Lilah had sex?" I was just about insulted. I look back now and realize that I was probably mostly let down. My big sister was supposed to stay perfect forever. She was very popular and had the funniest sense of humor. She also had a true innocence about her, and I was confused how a person could hide such a big thing. Sex, to an 11 year old, is a completely foreign topic that does not have any immediate reality to it. I thought that I would, for sure, wait until I was at least 30, or possibly never even take part in such a thing at all. I honestly didn't even really understand how it worked.

I wanted to see what I could find in the shed to prepare for my baby. I hauled an entire crib and a mattress up the stairs into my messy closet. For days I looked through and sorted bags and bags of baby clothes. My mom and sisters hardly noticed what I was doing. If they did notice and ask, I would explain that I was just doing some cleaning because the shed was a mess. I did tell them the crib mattress was in my room so that Josh didn't have to sleep on the hard floor for the nights that he was too tired or drunk to go home. Josh occasionally spent the night at our home once my family grew to love him. The rule was that my bedroom door remained open and he slept away from my bed on the floor. We were more excited about the fact that we were trusted enough to do this rather than actually spending the night together. On weekends Josh was usually either too drunk to walk home or arguing with his alcoholic mother. We were patient enough to reserve most of our inappropriate contact to times when we knew we would not be caught.

Josh pedaled up on his bike when I was outside folding baby gowns and sorting through items that I didn't want and would donate. I neatly folded up the baby outfits that I found to be acceptable, put them in my purple duffel bag, and hid it in my closet. Josh looked at the tiny pink dresses and socks. "We should have a baby, that would be so cool!" he said, half kidding. That gave me butterflies and encouraged my quest to become pregnant.

By the end of summer vacation, Josh was out of high school and working at an oil-change auto service station. I had not told him my plans. There were times that he mentioned how awesome it would be to have a baby, but nothing direct. I took his indirect comments as approval. Josh was never concerned with using condoms or birth control.

I began to plan our future together as parents. I would occasionally look at the local classifieds to see the rental rates for apartments. I constructed a budget for us but neglected to take into consideration utility bills, auto insurance or medical insurance…pretty much everything important. I took pregnancy tests from the local department store every month for four months. They always came back negative. But I am doing everything right! I would say to myself.

Giving up on getting pregnant after several negative pregnancy tests, I decided that I would not take another one until my period was at least three days late. I was sick of being disappointed when the tests came back negative.

School was tiring, and I was getting sick of waiting to be free to move out of my house. I became desperate for a break. I wanted to spend even more time learning about becoming pregnant, and my forced education was getting in the way of that. I decided that I could probably get at least a break for a week from school if I could find a way to get suspended. To make that happen, I waited for the perfect moment to start a fight. I picked a fight with a girl in my grade. She had it coming though. The night before, she was sending messages to me online. "Your head is way too big for your body. Pick up a fork, stab it with food, and put it in your mouth. Everyone knows your anorexic." She taunted me until I just had to get off of the computer. I didn't even know she hated me in the first place. And yes I was skinny, but I sure as hell ate my food! This girl was now my perfect target and at the perfect time. She called me a bitch in the hallway after the lunch bell rang. I dropped my books and attacked her. From stories I heard after the fact, I pushed her about 15 feet down the hallway. I was mad and ready to be suspended. The fight lasted only a few minutes, but there weren't any school employees who witnessed it. I was bummed. I ended up getting Saturday school once word of the fight spread to the teachers. My plan had backfired and I was pissed. The girl I beat up came to school the next day with a considerably bruised face. I couldn't get myself suspended on purpose, even if I tried. Now don't get me wrong. I'm by no means bragging about this fight. It was stupid. It was a desperate attempt to find my education by other means, even if only for a week.

To change things up and relieve boredom, Josh and I invited a crowd of friends over to Lilah's house on the following weekend when we were babysitting, and we had them bring some beer. Summer was put to bed and the party started. Josh and I were drunk and acting foolish along with everyone else. As I was running up the hallway staircase to relieve my full-of-beer bladder, I suddenly gasped from the terrible pain of menstrual cramps. Ugh. I am definitely not pregnant! Again.

Josh went to work early the next morning. I was nauseous and hung over, but I managed to make it to my last class at school after my older sister gave me a guilt-trip and convinced me to go. Fifteen minutes in, I decided that I was too sick to focus. I walked home and crawled into my fluffy, comfortable bed.

Lying there I thought about when my last period had been. I pulled the chart from underneath my bed. In shock, I realized that I was already four days late! I jumped out of bed and hurried into the bathroom.

I pulled out a pregnancy test that I had been reserving. It was blue and white, and holding it gave me an adrenaline rush. I read the directions for the tenth time and tried to avoid peeing on my hand. When I sealed off the test, I turned my head away hoping that when I locked the cap in place it wouldn't spray me in the face. I took the test back into my bedroom. Sitting on the floor in front of the mirror, I put my make-up on and fixed my hair into a ballerina-style bun. I always tried to look my best for when

22

Josh got off of work. I waited about ten minutes before I nervously looked back at the test.

What if it's actually positive? No, don't get your hopes up. But what if it's positive? This could be a big deal – so much more than I thought. Oh no. I don't know if I'm ready for this. Nervous thoughts ran through my head as my adrenaline picked up more and more. Finally, I knew that no amount of nervous self-chatter would change the result - whatever it may be. Reaching for the test with my right hand, I avoided looking at the result until I had a firm grasp on it and it was in crystal-clear sight. Holding my breath, a second blue line stared back at me, telling me I was pregnant. This blue line signified more than I was able to comprehend. It was going to be a long, uncertain road ahead.

Shaking and gasping on the floor of my bedroom, I was afraid and confused. I had so many fantasies about life as an adult and doing whatever I wanted any time of the day. But they were just that - fantasies. This was real. There was officially a life growing inside of me. There was no turning back. The reality of the situation suddenly brought upon me a dark cloud of guilt and fear. I began to wonder how my family was going to react. I had a feeling that I wasn't going to be as in control of my life as I wanted. Staring at myself in the mirror, I quickly understood that this was permanent and I could not go back. This was the moment that changed the direction of my heart, mind, soul, and spirit. I was now following a new path that was going to be far more advanced than I ever could have known.

Chapter 3

Once I calmed down from the shock of the positive pregnancy test, I casually asked my mother to drop me off at Josh's work so I could walk home with him when he got off. She said that would be fine. She was extra nice to me on the ride there. Watching the road and not knowing that her fifteen-year-old daughter was holding in her pocket a test confirming the existence of her second grandchild, my mother chatted about mundane, everyday things. I started to feel sad and guilty. I knew that she was going to be hurt and let down when I told her. There was nothing worse than seeing my mom upset. I hated to see her cry. It rarely happened, but when it did, it broke my heart. I would soon have to face telling my mother that I was going to be a mother.

Josh was busy working when we pulled up. Covered in black shiny oil as usual, he looked over and smiled when he saw me. He asked his boss for a five-minute break to walk over to the gas station with me for some cigarettes. My face must have been saying that I was upset, and he asked me what was wrong. I cautiously pulled out the positive pregnancy test and held it up for him to see. His expression wasn't happy, but he wasn't upset either. He shrugged as if he almost expected it. It didn't seem like he was too afraid or worried either; I think he may have been in shock. I waited at the picnic bench that the guys at the shop used for lunch breaks until it was time for Josh to clock out.

Derrick, one of his co-workers, was making me wish I had waited to tell Josh the news. Derrick was in his mid-twenties and always hitting on me. I could never tell if he was joking or serious, and it made me uneasy. I had a brief flashback to a few months earlier when Josh convinced my mother to let me go fishing with him and Derrick and Derrick's brother, Donnie. My mom asked Josh for all of the details and the exact location. Since Josh did not have a car, Donnie picked us up on the sunny Friday afternoon. Derrick would follow later in his own car. Donnie had a small one-seat pickup truck that we all had to squeeze into. It was a bit awkward sitting between Josh and an older man whom I barely knew. Donnie had long hair down to his jaw and looked like a mix between a hippie and a hobo. He seemed like the stoner type but was always nice and personable. The thing about Derrick and Donnie, was that they both knew how to make astounding first impressions. They were very engaged in conversations and always made sure to add in some sort of humor. Donnie was about 10 years older than Derrick although Derrick looked older than Donnie. They were an interesting pair.

After making it to the fishing spot and getting the gear out of the truck and set up, Josh and Donnie opened the cooler right away and started drinking beer. Derrick arrived shortly after and was diligently focused on his fishing instead. He brought his obnoxious friend, Jimmy, along. Jimmy had already been drinking when they arrived. I wanted a beer too but didn't want to ask Donnie because I didn't know him well enough. Josh saw the longing look of thirst on my face and handed me a beer, knowing Donnie wouldn't mind. I was still fourteen at this point. I was excited that these older men were so accepting of my age and didn't mind me drinking with them. It made me feel like I was a part of the "grown-up" club.

26

While the four men were drunk and I was more than buzzed, we started to pack up because it was getting dark. Donnie said that if he had any more to drink he would not be able to drive. Goofing off and having silly, drunk conversations while packing up, we were all gathered around Donnie's truck before parting ways. Jimmy was openly hitting on me in front of Josh. I never took it seriously knowing that he was in his mid-twenties. He couldn't possibly be serious, I was thinking. The topic of boobs was somehow brought up, and Josh began bragging about how perfect mine were. "She probably doesn't even have tits, she's only fourteen," Donnie proclaimed. Offended that a person was challenging my womanhood I replied, "Oh please; you'd be surprised." Not knowing that I had placed myself into a vulnerable situation, Jimmy excitedly challenged me. "Yeah, right. If they're so awesome then prove it!"

Standing in the dark, surrounded by four men who were all much older than me, I looked up at Josh to defend me. "Show 'em," he confidently said with a drunk, pathetic slur. They rambled consistently about me exposing myself for what felt like hours, and they were not about to let up.

I purposely postponed the challenge as long as I could because it was getting dark and the darker it got, the less they would be able to see. My liquid courage was not serving me so well this time. It was finally almost completely dark, and my buzz was wearing off and making me tired. I just wanted to go home. After the hundredth time, I finally lifted my shirt as if I were a confident showgirl from Vegas performing a routine. "Yep...those are brand new," Donnie casually said as he was exhaling his cigarette smoke. "Damn! Junior has it made!" Jimmy practically yelled. (Junior was the nickname given to Josh by his coworkers because he was the runt of the group.) Derrick looked annoyed and almost mad. "Macy is making lasagna tonight, and I'm outta here," he said as he got into his car and drove off. With the flash show over, I was pleased to be accepted into this "grown-up" crowd, but my stomach ached and I knew that God was very sad with my decision. My youth and innocence were further tainted by this choice. I later blocked it out of my mind and pretended that it was just a bad dream.

Millions more thoughts raced through my mind while I sat on the wooden bench at the tire shop. There were even more conflicting emotions. I did not know if I should be happy or if I should be devastated. However, the more I thought about my child the more I grew attached with each passing minute. I knew who this person was, and I knew that this person was necessary to the world. This person was going to be beautiful, perfect and needed. I was not the only one that would need this person. My child's purpose was much more powerful than that.

As a mostly mature adult, I have learned that what is meant to exist will exist. It will find a way to embrace this world if God decides that it needs to be here. Through this process, I felt God was with me. I heard God's whisper of encouragement to move forward and to not allow any force to stand in my way. I felt safe and cared for even when I was at my loneliest moments.

When the next morning arrived, I knew deep down that I was going to keep this baby. No person or force would have the power to change my mind. I had a vision of what my baby was going to look like. She would be beautiful, tall, and skinny, with stunning blue eyes and a big, bright smile. And, of course, she would have long, dark hair. Yes, that would be her. I knew who she was long before I met her. I knew who she was from the beginning of her existence. I held off telling my mother the news for as long as possible. I just didn't want to face it. I was worried she would be mad.

I was exhausted by the time the last school bell rang within a few days after finding out I was pregnant. I was enrolled in Driver's Education class after school for the next few months and having to sit and watch documentaries on the consequences of drunk driving was no picnic. That was when the seriousness of my age was brought to light. I began to feel uneasy thinking about the fact that I was pregnant, and I wasn't even old enough to get a driver's license! I was no longer feeling confident about anything or secure with what I thought I wanted. That day I drove myself home with Mr. Morris in the passenger seat. He stomped on his brake pedal every time I went too fast or didn't look over my shoulder. I was already feeling sick, and the bumpy ride was not helping. I walked into the house and slouched on the couch. I was happy the day was finally over.

Idly watching a talk show discussing cheating husbands and their lies, I barely glanced up when my mom came through the front door. She quickly looked at me and spoke. I was surprised by what came out of her mouth: "Are you pregnant?" Well, shit. That was a pretty straight forward question, I thought. I used my usual topic-avoidance-technique: I rolled my eyes. "No. What the hell? Where did you hear that?" I said, trying to sound offended. She then explained to me how she had received a phone call early in the day from one of my teachers who had overheard other kids talking about it. I was confused as to where that came from. I hadn't told anyone except Josh!

My mom sighed with relief and walked back to her bedroom to do her usual nighttime ritual of watching the news in her pajamas and eating ice cream. I knew I could no longer hide the truth from her. I had to face what was happening.

The next morning I woke up feeling sick and nauseated. I came to the conclusion that I wasn't going to school...my life was over anyway. I would spend the day at home trying to figure out how to tell my mom the truth. Josh came by the house on his lunch break to see how I was feeling. We mutually decided to spill the beans to my mom. Both of us were much too afraid to tell her in person. We decided to write her a letter. Later, after spending an hour carefully finding the right words to scribble down, Josh was brave and took the letter down to my mother's bedroom. He came back up to me, and we waited in fear for her reaction. My room was directly above hers, so we could hear most of what was happening below.

"Gosh, damn it!" She was so mad that she didn't come up to talk to us for what felt like a lifetime!

Finally, she came up to notify us that we better figure out what the hell we were going to do and how we were going to take care of this. I had no idea what she meant by "take care of this." Neither did Josh.

The next morning I decided not to go to school again. I slept until about 10:00, and when I woke up, I still didn't get out of bed for a while. I started to think about my options and how sad it would be to choose abortion. I knew that nothing could ever make me do such a horrible thing, but the thought of it still made me cry. I heard my mom coming up the stairs and I buried my face in my blanket. She walked in and sat on my bed. The second she started to lovingly twirl my bed-head frizzy hair the floodgates opened. It was as if the Hoover Dam had collapsed. Something about sympathy from a parent makes it much more difficult NOT to cry. She explained to me that I still had to go to school. She asked me what I wanted to do about the pregnancy. I told her that I would rather choose adoption over abortion. I told her that I did not want to feel guilty for the rest of my life for killing an innocent being.

"Well, if you and Josh are that serious, maybe we can look into you two getting married." That statement brought me peace and comfort. I just needed her support in this. I knew that without her help I would be lost.

The events of the next few days changed the feeling of the situation. I finished up my Driver's Ed but refused to attend my other classes. I did not want to deal with people talking about me every time I walked into a room. My mom scheduled an appointment with my school counselor to discuss my options.

The counselors told me that I could keep attending my regular classes, get started on independent study and do work from home, or attend the Young Parents Program.

I wanted to stay at home. I had this idea that it would be safe to hide away from the world. What I did not know was that the world, and the people in it, could not be avoided.

Later that day a detective from the police department came to my door looking for Josh. One of my high school counselors had called the police.

Chapter 4

A loud knock on the door startled me as I lay on the couch. I had just gotten home, tossed my backpack on the floor, and fell on the couch. I was tired and definitely not in the mood to deal with those annoying churchgoers wanting to invite themselves in to talk about ways of avoiding going to hell. According to a Mormon family I was acquainted with, I was already there. About two months pregnant, I felt bloated and just wanted to unbutton my jeans permanently. I walked through the atrium to the front door to see a tall, dark silhouette standing behind the blurry glass. I had no idea what this person wanted or who it was. I slowly and cautiously opened the creaky door to be greeted by a man wearing a badge that read Police Department. Great. What did Josh do to get himself into trouble last night? I thought to myself. Josh had been out drinking with a few friends the night before to "celebrate" our future baby.

The police officer looked to be in his late 30's with dark hair and a kind smile. He announced that he was there to speak with a Ms. Anna. "That's my mother and she's in school right now," I replied. He asked me for my name. Upon introducing myself, he took a small notepad out and located his pen to scribble down notes. I was confused and starting to become worried. A rush of fear made me weak when I heard the words "How old is your boyfriend, Miss

Jeter?" I stuttered as I attempted to think of a way out of telling the truth.

I am a horrible liar when I'm nervous. For that reason, I just spit it out. "He is 19 sir," I said. I realized that the only way to fix this potentially terrible situation was to become extra sweet and appear to be mature. I wanted the police officer to see me as a 19 year old; I did not want this man to see the situation for what it really was and have Josh arrested. Josh was only 4-1/2 years older than me. I really did not think that it was that bad. People would just have to understand. After all he is stepping up to the plate and supporting me, right? Why would anyone believe it to be necessary to take away the father of an innocent child and maybe soon to be husband?

The officer replied with a series of questions: "So, how did you meet Josh? Is he supporting you through everything? How does your mother feel about this? Did you ever feel pressured into sleeping with Josh, Miss Jeter?" I answered every question simply and in a way that I thought would only be beneficial enough to keep Josh out of jail.

The officer was very nice about the entire matter, and as he retreated down the driveway, he announced that as long as my mother did not wish to pursue criminal charges, the case would be dropped. Later in the day, I overheard my mom on the phone with the officer.

She was speaking as if she was upset and confused, but she did not mention anything about agreeing to have Josh thrown in jail. I did not expect that she would; she loved Josh like a son, and she knew that his intentions had always been right. I was happy that the dilemma was over. I did not even fathom the fact that this particular dilemma was only the first out of hundreds to follow.

I discovered that I was pregnant in the beginning of September 2002. It took about two weeks to get the guts to tell my mother, and then it took another two weeks to officially tell her my decision to have the child. I played it off as if it was just another simple issue and life was to carry on as usual. I did not want to talk about the subject because I already knew what my decision would be. I knew my decision would stir up some anger in my friends and family members. My innocence was entirely gone to them. What was done was done. There was no way in hell that I was going to agree to have an abortion. Most every person I knew was attempting to convince me that if I kept this baby my life would be over. These people had no clue that I wanted this baby; they had no clue that I became pregnant on purpose. I was being harassed about having an abortion almost every day. I was almost to a point of frustration that I just wanted to agree to shut everyone up.

A bright Saturday morning blazed through my bedroom window and made a mean attempt to ruin my slumber. I thought Thank God for my thick purple curtains, as I stretched. As I was painfully trying to open my eyes, I was startled when I heard a knock on my bedroom door. "Who is it?" I groaned. "Hi Elizabeth, it's Huey," my older sister's boyfriend called from the hall. "Can I talk to you for a minute?" I was pretty irritated that, out of all people, Huey was at my door. Jeez, does he want to put a move on me too? Maybe Lilah's last birthday really did him in and it was time for a newer model. Dirty pervert. Why the hell is he at my door? I told him that he could come in, and I was relieved to see that Lilah was following behind him. At least with Lilah there it wouldn't be totally creepy and awkward with him in my bedroom.

The second he started talking I knew what his intentions were. He talked about a former colleague of his who used to perform abortions. "It's quick and painless. Most Doctors will use metal instruments, but Dr. Smith only uses leaves from a seaweed plant. He soaks the leaves in a saline solution before the procedure, and he uses it to scrape out the contents of your uterus. It won't cause cramping or pain because the seaweed is soft."

35

I wanted to vomit as he was holding up his fist, as if his wrinkly hand, with grey knuckle hairs, were my uterus. He was trying to show me how a seaweed abortion worked, and I was lucky enough to get a reenactment to go along with it.

Seriously, what in the hell was that all about anyway? Seaweed…abortion…? Seriously dude, you're an idiot, I affirmed. I gave him my attention but never confirmed to him what my decision would be. I thought it was incredibly insensitive of him to refer to my unborn child as "contents." I could not understand why terminating a pregnancy was so freely accepted as an option, almost to the point of being favored.

This was my child we were talking about. I consciously chose to give this child life. It should be no person's decision as to who lives or dies, especially such a pure and perfect creation of God. Our world needs more innocence, more purity. This baby would forever be a part of me, who I was, and what I stood for. I knew this child's soul. I could envision the face of this child. I saw the smile, heard the laugh…and felt the embrace. These feelings were so intense that they could not be classified as only feelings. It was more than that. It was more than a natural inclination to protecting the human species. It was more than a teenage girl with baby fever. It was meant to be and supposed to happen. She was meant to be. Unable to see past the next year, I did not quite understand how important this small angel would eventually become to the world, and some of the desperate people in it.

I was getting sick and tired of people being so adamant about this abortion thing. They were acting like it was just another common thing to do and that it was perfectly okay. I chose to become pregnant! Making that decision followed by an abortion would be completely senseless, and it would ruin me forever. I had to find a way to get people off my back. I knew exactly what I needed to buy some time.

"Thank you for calling the Women's Clinic, this is Chelsea, how can I help you?" the receptionist said. "Yes, I need to make an appointment to have an abortion." I confidently announced. The receptionist asked me a series of detailed questions, and I noticed that her voice sounded very caring but somber. That must be a really horrible job; making appointments to schedule the killing of innocent babies, I thought. After answering all of her questions, she confirmed that it would be four hundred dollars. "That will be fine," I stated, knowing that I would not need to worry about coming up with the money. After she collected all of my information, it was time to schedule the appointment date. I told her that my schedule was open, so she could just choose the day. "Will October 6th be okay, Elizabeth?" she asked. "Sure! Go ahead and book me," I said. Chelsea must have thought that I was a whack job with how enthusiastic I sounded about this abortion. I just wanted to hurry up and get off the phone so I could announce the fictitious death of my baby and have a moment of peace.

This particular scheduled day was not just any day. This was my mother's birthday - a day that I would recognize for the rest of my life.

I took this as a clear sign. This was not a coincidence. This was God trying to show my mother that this baby was meant to live. When I informed my mother that I scheduled my appointment to have an abortion, she seemed relieved. She did not seem to care much about the fact that it was on her birthday. She even said that she would give me a ride to Reno where the abortion was to be performed. After talking with me about my options and having some time to realize that I was truly pregnant, I think she just wanted this problem to go away. She was going through the stages of grief: shock, denial, bargaining and anger. I was eagerly awaiting the acceptance stage. I knew that I would have to be very patient.

What my mother did not know was that I had only scheduled this appointment to get everyone off my back. There would be nothing left for anyone to say if they thought that I had accepted the decision to terminate the pregnancy. What could they say? "Congratulations" or "I'm sorry." I was outsmarting them. I was way ahead of the game, and for a moment, I felt a small twinge of control again.

Over the next few weeks I was able to live in peace without any harassment. The few days before my appointment arrived, I felt the tension arising once again. The day before, my mother confirmed that she was giving me a ride to the clinic in Reno the next morning. I just couldn't beat around the bush any longer. "I am not having an abortion, and no one is going to change my mind. I will never be able to live with the fact that I took an innocent life, and I would rather choose adoption if it comes down to it. I would be reminded of the fact that I KILLED my baby every year, for every birthday you have," I boldly told her from the door of my bedroom.

The screaming match began. She had prepared herself to get rid of the dilemma and forget about it, she did not expect that this "dilemma" would be permanent and not go away so easily. "When my baby is older I will tell it that you wanted me to kill it!" I angrily yelled at her. "Good! You're an idiot," she screamed back. "You have no idea what you are getting yourself into!" The yelling back and forth lasted about ten minutes before it was over. Neither of us heard much of what the other was saying. My ears were ringing. Not too long down the road, my mother apologized sincerely for things that were said. I ended up apologizing back. I have learned that it is never wise to make any statements based on emotion. You only end up hurting the people you care about, and even worse, yourself.

I was sad, but I was also relieved to know that my decision was strong, firm, grounded, and exposed. I was sad because I knew that my family was disappointed in me for the decision I had made. At least now, life could carry on without questions up in the air. I did not even bother calling to cancel my appointment.

I thought that the clinic deserved to lose money from my no-show. I thought it was an evil place that killed innocent beings on a daily basis. For all I cared, the entire building could burn.

Chapter 5

Finally having made the clear decision that I was going to have the baby, it was time to decide how I would finish school. I received a phone call one Friday afternoon from a woman with a very friendly and cheery voice. I had no idea why this woman asked for me. I was so down in the dumps that others who seemed extra happy just pissed me off. I wanted to be happy too. I wanted to be excited and brag about my future baby. The excitement went out the window entirely when I realized that because of my age, I would not have support from my community for this pregnancy. It was shameful in their eyes. I desperately needed an adult to as least act like they cared.

"Hi Elizabeth, this is Mrs. Snow! I am calling to find out if I can work with you to help you finish your high school education. I understand that you want to do independent study for your pregnancy, but we have a really great program here. It is called the Young Parents Program, or YPP. You'll come in for half of the day, we'll feed you breakfast and lunch, and we have a great daycare along with parenting classes for the remainder of the day to help you get ahead. Can I meet you in person?" she pleaded. Mrs. Snow genuinely sounded thrilled about this program.

It also seemed as if she might have had several teen parents turn the program down based on the hopeful, yet uncertain, tone that I sensed. I did not know much about the program, but I knew that it was in the building down the street from the football field and away from the main campus. I always thought that the kids who went there were the troubled drug addicts. "Um…sure, I guess I'm willing to come take a look at the place," I unenthusiastically said. I told her that I could come in on the following Monday to give it a test run. I had no clue what I was getting myself into, but deep down I really needed the extra support, and I was hoping that I could find it there.

Once the shock of my decision started to fade, my mother slowly got back to normal with our relationship, and the old conversations that we usually shared seemed to level out. When this happened, it was like a breath of fresh air. It had made me sad and stressed to have negative vibes and unspoken anger consuming our home, and it honestly had put my life and happiness on hold.

When I explained to my mother the conversation I had with Mrs. Snow, she seemed happy about the whole idea and agreed that it would be best to give the Young Parents Program a try. As far as becoming a teen parent was concerned, I needed all of the advice and education that I could get. When I was planning this entire pregnancy, my vision of actually being pregnant was way off from what reality proved to be.

I did not see myself as a teen mom. I saw myself as an adult with her first baby on the way in a society that had no objections to it. I now understood that I would face criticism and the disapproving turning of heads, probably on a daily basis. I came to the realization that if this was going to work in my favor in any way at all, I was going to have to become the best teen mom that I could possibly be. I was going to need to rise above and beat the statistics. The first step that needed to be taken was to graduate high school.

I was painfully tired on the morning of my first day. I remember feeling so overwhelmed from just moving to get out of bed.

From the time that I was a baby, I have always hated mornings. Any small disturbance quickly set me off like a Mentos dropping into a Pepsi - fast, intense, and sizzling over the edge. I recall getting ready for kindergarten on a distant October morning.

Talk about a terrible morning. I was only five, and all I knew was that I had to hurry up and put my socks and shoes on. We didn't want to be late for the bus. In a hurry, I found my sneakers tangled up on the brown carpet in my bedroom, grabbed a pair of socks and carried my stuff to the bathroom where I plopped down on the floor. I had recently learned to tie my own shoes, so I wanted to make sure I had no interruptions as I was focusing on this delicate process. I never actually made it to the shoe part. THOSE SOCKS! They were plain white socks; I thought I would have no grief with them. My heart sank the second my tiny little piggy's attempted to snuggle to the end of these particular socks. "THESE ARE THE WRONG ONES!" I was hysterically trying to explain to my mother that the seams at the end of my toes felt funny. She was dumbfounded. For the life of her, she could not comprehend why an almost microscopic seam would bring me to such hysterics. I later learned that I sat on that bathroom floor for an hour twisting the socks around my feet, over and over again, because I could not get it right. One way or another those obnoxious seams would, very rudely, bombard the cracks of my toes. My mother, at that point, was at a loss. We missed the bus, we were late for school, and I was at the maximum meltdown point that any five-year-old could possibly be.

Finally, as if the good Lord sent down a guardian angel to guide her, she pulled both socks off of my feet, yanked them inside out, quickly put them back on my feet, and all was well. The day was free to resume as usual.

As we were driving a short distance down the street, which was less than a mile from my new school, I became nervous since I had no idea what to expect. She was dropping me off for the day and I was hoping that I wouldn't have to be stuck in a room with a crowd full of annoying and immature screw-ups. I walked into the portable classroom building and was surprised that it looked like a regular classroom. Mrs. Snow greeted me, and she was warm, friendly, and enthusiastic.

She had short, grey hair but her skin appeared youthful and her personality even more youthful. I liked her right away. She asked me a few questions and had me fill out some forms, and I never felt any sort of judgment coming from Mrs. Snow. Her heart was no doubt in the right place.

There were only three other girls in the class. They were all Hispanic and speaking to each other in Spanish when I walked in. I was worried that they might be talking about me. One looked to be about six months pregnant, and the other two did not appear to be pregnant at all. I assumed their babies were at the daycare Mrs. Snow had told me about. After I was introduced to the class, I found out that the girls were all older than me. Great. I really am an idiot for getting pregnant. I could have at least waited a freaking year, I was thinking to myself. The girls were 16, 17, and 18. I didn't think that I was going to fit in very well. I didn't see how I was supposed to make any friends if they wouldn't bother to speak English to me. I felt left out.

After finishing the paperwork and getting acquainted with my new surroundings, I sat down at one of the tiny chair-desks that were lined up in a row and facing the whiteboard. I wondered how in the world I was supposed to wedge my pregnant body in one of these things once I got big. It was inevitable. I just hoped that my boobs would stay preserved.

A few minutes after taking my seat, one of the cafeteria kids wearing a dorky looking hair net entered the classroom pushing a cart full of trays. Oh, joy. It must be breakfast time. Mrs. Snow handed each of us a tray and a carton of milk. Breakfast included

44

a cinnamon roll and an apple. I devoured the cinnamon roll. It was amazing. It made me thirsty, but I was always thirsty in the mornings anyway. I opened the carton of milk, which I normally didn't consume as a beverage alone, and chugged away. I drank the entire carton in about ten seconds. This is when I realized that along with being pregnant, I would be forced to suffer through the crappy symptoms. It felt like the milk was about to come back up.

My fear of throwing up came to me full force. As I was feeling an adrenaline rush and hot flashes racing through my still tiny body, I decided that I could not throw up in front of the class on my first day. I would never be able to live that down. I would be known as the girl who puked. I tightly closed my eyes and mouth, slightly dropped my head, and focused on my breathing. I meditated my way out of throwing up. Thank God! That was definitely a close one. I was only ten weeks along, and this was clearly only the beginning of the horrible symptoms.

After Mrs. Snow issued my books and assigned my first homework assignment, it was almost lunchtime. "For lunch we will head down to the daycare and spend the rest of the day in groups doing projects or sharing our concerns as teen mothers," she announced. This had me thinking: Great, now I get to spend the next few hours listening to pathetic pity stories. We all walked to the Daycare Center as a group.

It was away from the main classroom and down a gravel road. The building was hiding behind trees at the end of the football field, and to get there we had to walk down an extremely steep hill. I thought it was pretty ridiculous that they had pregnant girls make this walk. Maybe they secretly wanted us to slip and fall. It was obvious that this daycare was hidden away from the rest of the school. Of course, the school and the town wanted to hide this shame. South Lake Tahoe is a tourist town - a town that caters to outsiders by offering them brightly lit casinos, boat rentals, shopping, and concerts. The facade, put on for the tourists, annoyed me. Beauty can be deceiving.

Finally arriving at the daycare, we walked through the front door. The building looked old and beat up. There was what appeared to be finger paint on the windows next to the door. I wasn't sure if this was artwork that had been done by the kids being cared for, or if the kids-with-the-kids had done it. Either way, it made me feel like I was in first grade again...except I was pregnant. I hoped I wouldn't be asked to contribute to it. It was just strange.

Lunch was served but I really did not want to risk the possibility of throwing up, so I just picked at my tray. There were a few babies in the room and a few more young mothers as well. Some of the mothers chose to study at home and take only their parenting classes at the school. When Vanessa walked in, I was relieved. At eighteen she was six months pregnant, and she spoke English and appeared normal. She was cute and seemed to be much more mature than the other girls. I immediately made conversation with her and asked her questions about morning sickness. Meeting Vanessa definitely perked up a day that had been long and confusing.

After everyone finished lunch and the mothers tamed their screaming babies, a public health nurse walked in. She was going to lead the day's group activity and ramble about the importance of breastfeeding. I couldn't tell if the chubby nurse was naturally nasally or had a cold, but her loud breathing got on my nerves, and I wanted to chuck a box of tissues at her head. I did end up learning some valuable facts on breastfeeding though, and I had already decided that I would probably nurse my baby for at least a year. That's what Lilah did with her daughter so I figured it was the right thing to do. She actually nursed her daughter until she was almost two and, at that time, my snotty preteen-self gave her hell for it. I thought it was gross. Anyone with a baby, who could walk and talk, should not be able to dine on your boob just anytime. I was completely merciless to her.

Before it was time to go home the nurse, Valerie, pulled me aside and asked me some really detailed questions about my pregnancy. I was polite and answered to the best of my ability, but became irritated when she made the most unnecessary statement I had ever heard. "Well, you're still under twelve weeks gestation, so you could still have a miscarriage.

Oh, but don't worry- it's just a little clump of cells right now." I wondered if she was thinking that I wanted to have a miscarriage. Why else would that statement ever have any sort of value? I disliked that nurse from that point forward.

The day was just about officially over, and I was finally free to walk home. The walk was not very long, but some days I was incredibly lazy and easily became irritated if my mother or sister couldn't give me a ride home.

Walking through the front door of my home, I was sweaty and short of breath, but I was actually excited to tell my mom about my day. She was in the kitchen making something that smelled amazing and I began to blab away. Even though I was super tired from my long introduction to my school life as a teen parent, I still felt that I should attend the Teen Parents Program on a regular basis. It would be the only place that I could turn to where my situation was completely accepted, and the instructors had such a positive outlook.

It would be a while before my mom started to fully support me, and my sisters were just as confused with the whole thing as I was. Although my mother was clearly in shock over the situation and trying to find a way to process what was going on, she did her best to put on a smile for me and encourage me to stay in school. That made me happy.

Chapter 6

Over the next few weeks Josh continued to work at the oil change place making minimum wage, and I got myself into a routine with my new school. Now that I was now pregnant, as I had once so desired to be, Josh and I naturally wanted to spend even more time together. I wasn't babysitting Summer as much and I thought Lilah must have been getting worn out from all of her outings with her boyfriend. Babysitting had really been the only time that Josh and I had privacy and the chance to spend our nights together.

Considering the circumstances, a couple of unusually uneventful months went by. I was about four months along. I could still easily hide my condition if I wanted to, but I didn't need to bother. It was a small town, and everyone talked. I knew that hiding the situation would only prolong my anxiety about people's reactions to it anyway. Having to tell friends why I suddenly left school was bad enough; I dreaded telling my extended family. Most of them lived a couple hundred miles away, and it was going to have to be a phone call that broke the shocking news. I knew it would be difficult because I loved and respected them so much.

My grandparents on my mother's side spoke with my mom frequently, so I knew that she must have told them already. Any time I heard her talking on the phone, I would intentionally hide. I either went to the back yard where it was easy to hide behind a gigantic pine tree that must have been hundreds of years old, or I would run

49

out the front door and go on an aimless walk down the street. I hated confrontation. On one occasion, I heard my mom coming towards the stairs with her clanking heels tapping against the hardwood floor. I heard her reply "Hang on, let me see if I can find her." It was time to move fast. I rolled off my bed in a hurry, almost landing on my face, and somehow performed a stunt-man style leap into my huge closet. I hated my closet. I always had evil spiders creeping in the dark corners. This was a situation where I had to suck it up and hide, as if my sanity depended on it. I was just not ready to talk to my grandparents, for the fear that they would be extremely disappointed in me. I loved them both so much, and became so sad thinking about how I must have let them down. Walking through the door to see an empty bedroom, my mother was in and out. I am never going to be able to handle this, I thought.

Finally, about a week later when my mother was on the phone with my grandparents, I gave up on my fight to hide and I forced myself to become available to talk. Handing me the phone, my mother could see the worry on my face. "Hello?" I nervously said.

Immediately followed by my shaky greeting, their all-too familiar voices were like music to my ears and helped to put me at ease. "Hi honey! How is our girl?" My grandparents always sounded enthusiastic when I spoke with them. They always made me feel very loved. I was thinking that our conversation was off to a good start by the way they were maintaining their normal conversational style. I carried on and spoke as if I wasn't thinking about the pregnancy, as if nothing had changed. I desperately wanted to keep our relationship as stable and happy as possible and as innocent and loving as it had always been.

There was only one statement that my grandpa made that brought an immediate lump to my throat: "Honey, I am really disappointed - Really disappointed." I had to fight to hold back my tears. I never wanted to disappoint my grandma and grandpa. That was just about the only negative comment I had ever received from either of them and, to this day, this still remains true.

My grandparents always uninhibitedly gave us twins the kind of treatment that only royal princesses receive. This started the day we were born. Not only did they spoil us with presents and chocolate pudding; they offered us their constant attention every minute that we were together. They were much younger than most grandparents that I knew and only in their early 40's. Our grandpa was technically our step-grandpa. He never had any biological children with our grandma, and I suspect that could partially explain their love and attention to Merri and me. My grandpa even named me when I was born and still in the hospital. When I was little, I would obsessively brag about this. They truly cared as deeply for us as any parent would care for their own children. Out of every member of my extended family, my grandparents have always had the tightest grip on my heart.

I had let them down, and it broke my heart. Getting off the phone and saying our goodbyes, I set the handset on the kitchen table and ran upstairs. I didn't want my mom to see me crying. I was crying out of guilt for feeling like such a disappointment to two people who always took such good care of me and loved me so very much.

I waited until Thanksgiving to tell my dad. I wanted to wait as long as I possibly could. I knew it wasn't going to be a pleasant conversation. I really did not want to hear his criticism. Even my mother avoided telling him. We avoided him for about two months, so I was sure that he suspected something strange was going on. When he called on Turkey Day in the morning, my mom answered the phone. It was, at first, a normal 'Happy Thanksgiving' conversation. It turned bad the second she told him. "What the HELL Ron! Maybe if you ever showed an interest in her life she wouldn't be in this situation!" I heard my mom scream. The two of them were like fire and ice. They just did not mix. I have no idea

51

how they were ever together long enough to create me. For the record, I really try to avoid thinking about that.

Our parents split when Merri and I were just babies. When we were little, our dad would come and pick us up on the weekends. We were only about three years old, and he had a small apartment across town. I remember that I would always get excited when I saw him pull up. I loved it when he picked me up and gave me attention. He was tall, and I thought it was so cool to be so high up in the air in his arms. My twin was the opposite. She was never very thrilled about leaving our mother for the weekend. The story we were told is that he threw a sandal at her forehead and she, being angry as hell, locked him out of the house.

Our mother is not a person who you want to make angry. She can definitely hold her own and is not afraid to show it. Apparently our dad came back to the house a few hours later begging for the can of soup he had left. To this day, Lilah still talks about how bad she felt for him that night. I'm guessing that he didn't really return for just a can of soup. He probably wanted to resume his normal family life and seek forgiveness for that sandal shot. Needless to say, their relationship was over.

Lilah has a different father. She didn't get to meet her father until she was seven. Gabe was with my mother from the age of thirteen. He later joined a church that was strong in his beliefs. For some reason, Gabe disappeared and decided to marry another woman from the church. I could never understand why any man would ever do that to a woman as beautiful and loveable as my mother.

As I grew older and met my older sister's father and his family, I realized that everyone involved really seemed to have good intentions, and things just turned out the way they did because they were probably supposed to be that way. Every person lives through a unique experience and through a totally different reality. I try not to draw conclusions about other people or situations unless I'm directly involved.

After Gabe left, my mom was on her own at 20 with a small baby and not enough help. At that time, she was living in a mid-sized California city that was pretty much a ghetto. She was only there because of our great-grandmother, whom we called grams, as she was one of the only family members able to help her at that time. After living in a pretty disgusting city for a few months, she just couldn't handle it any longer. She hopped on a bus with her last twenty dollars. The one-way ticket took her on a 4-hour ride to Lake Tahoe.

My mother went straight to a casino to see if she could find a job. She was hired on the spot. It was going to work out for her after all. My mother took a huge leap into the unknown to offer her baby girl, Lilah, a better life. In turn, she offered all of her daughter's a better life.

Even after living in Tahoe for 21 years, I could easily still sit and stare at the lake and admire the beauty that the deep blue, sparkling water permanently imprinted in my memory. That sparkling imprint would soon transform into a deep, black, suffocating scar that would follow me around for the next 6 years.

On the phone with my dad, the criticism started. "What the hell have you been doing, young lady?" my dad questioned in a deep, matter-of-fact tone. I was silent for a few seconds. I had predetermined that if my father was not going to offer me any comfort, love, or support, I was simply going to hang up on him.

"Elizabeth, are you there?" he growled. "Yes, I am here. It is what it is, dad… I can't go back, so I am going to work on finishing school early," I attempted to confidently say. "The only thing I can say that you're doing right is not getting an abortion. God doesn't approve of that," he reminded. I explained to him that an abortion would never be an option for me. "So, what the hell do you think is going to happen? How are you going to support this kid? Do you really think that this Josh guy is going to give you what you need? You have really screwed up big time." I was done with his negative scolding. It was Thanksgiving, and he was ruining it. "You know what?" I finally screamed. "I'm not going to put up with your shit! If you can't be supportive then I'm just not going to speak to you anymore!" Tears began to roll down my face. I pushed the red button on the phone and it was over. I attempted to hold back my tears as my mom and sisters came into the hallway to see why I had been yelling. They all comforted me and gave me hugs to try to calm me down.

I didn't know if I was crying because my dad was a jerk or if I was crying because I was a jerk for hanging up on him. Regardless of the reason, my heart was aching. This particular incident did prove one positive thing - it showed me that my mother and sisters really did care. They were there to support me for the long haul. Once I dried my tears, I stuffed my face with my mother's amazing Thanksgiving dinner. For the moment, all was well. Except that Josh was nowhere to be found.

Chapter 7

My mother and sisters were lifelessly lounging on the couch with me – we were totally satisfied after stuffing ourselves to no end with turkey. Suddenly I heard the squeaky front door of the house open. Joy. Josh must have decided to finally join the family I thought. Sure enough, he stumbled in with that all too familiar, glossy look of disorientation on his face.

He was drunk…again. I was definitely upset. I could not figure out why, of all days, he decided to get trashed on this day. He'd been drinking at his mother's house, or his second-house, I should say. He went back and forth from my home to his mother's in a bit of a lost, transitional limbo for quite a while. I knew that at any given time he was with his mother for longer than an hour, he was drinking.

Josh's mother, Hilda, was an alcoholic. Although a functional drunk, there was no hiding her addiction. It fit her perfectly well. She was loud and obnoxious and overwhelming to be around even when she was not drinking. Her alcoholism, however, can be somewhat sadly justified. When Josh and I first got together, we were spending time together at his mother's house when she and her new fiancé were on a short vacation.

I noticed that on the floor was a small brown chest with a few toys neatly displayed on the top. Josh noticed me looking at the chest and took this as an opportunity to share with me a very sad piece of his family history.

His name was Beau. It was a bright, sunny Friday, and the boys were all excited and getting ready for their first trip to Disney World. Beau was about three years younger than Josh and Jed was about two years older than Josh. Hilda had three boys, all with the same man, and it sounded as if the family was intact and happy. After a normal six-year-old tantrum, Beau was instructed to spend time in his bedroom to calm down. After getting everything together for the trip, Josh went to get Beau. Opening the bedroom door, he realized that Beau was gone. In a panic, nine-year-old Josh searched the room high and low only to notice that Beau's fishing pole was missing and the window was wide open. Without thinking twice, Josh leaped out of the window and ran down the path that led to the boy's favorite fishing spot.

When Josh arrived, he discovered his little brother face down in the river. The hills, rocks, and water had been too much for a six-year-old to safely maneuver through. Josh screamed and found someone who called 911. The rescuers were able to transport Beau to the hospital, still breathing, but otherwise lifeless. After spending days on life support, Beau was gone. His brain endured severe and irreversible damage.

I was saddened to hear this story. I wondered how Josh still remained to be such a happy and kind person. I was shown pictures of the sad experience, and one particular picture broke my heart. It was a last goodbye picture of the big brothers by Beau's bedside, broken and in tears. The wooden chest was all the family had left of their youngest member. It was filled with toys, stuffed animals, and cards from Beau's classmates. I vividly recall Josh sharing this experience with me. Maybe it was the universe preparing me for the uncertainty to come, or maybe it was a sign for me to hold on, fully and completely, to everything I held dear.

Although Hilda angered and annoyed me, I now had an understanding of what had shaped her into the person she had become. What bothered me most, though, was that she had most likely been a negative example for Josh from the time that Beau had passed away. In Josh's world, getting wasted on a nightly basis was normal. It was what his mother did, and naturally, he sought her approval.

Rising from the couch where I had been with my mother and sisters, I moved toward Josh who was standing inside the opened front door. Josh looked at me like a deer-in-the-headlights, and I instantly knew what he had been up to. Naturally, I wanted to take care of him and just fix the situation. After closing the front door, I grabbed his hand and attempted to drag him up the stairs and away from my family. He was so incredibly inebriated that he was grabbing onto anything and everything along the way to keep his balance. At the bottom of the staircase he grabbed my mother's wooden hutch, knocking off every valuable piece of glass with a loud shatter. I heard my mother yell something as I continued to lead him up the stairs. We managed to make it to the top without incident. Before he could make his way into my bedroom, he fell flat on his face in the hallway and broke his nose. Gushing blood and breaking expensive items along the way, he lay in the hallway as my mother raced to see what was going on upstairs. This is where everything took a plunge.

"What the hell is going on, Josh?" My mother yelled. "Shut up you dumb bitch," he slurred. "Yer just jealous you can't have me." My jaw dropped and I almost burst out laughing. That was very out of character for Josh to say. My mom was so mad that her lips tightened, and the look that I usually ran away from was there instantly. "That's it. I'm calling the cops," she stated. She followed through with her threat and called the police. On one hand I couldn't blame her, but on the other hand, I was extremely afraid and unsure if this was the right thing to do. I tucked my drunken boyfriend into bed. He made a horrible attempt at taking off his pants to sleep in his boxers. His boxers came off with the pants. I hurriedly tried to get his pants back on so the poor cops wouldn't have to deal with a naked drunk, but I failed. He was nothing but dead weight. This is where my sympathy for Josh ended. He was about to embarrass us, including my family. Accepting our fate, I gave up and walked out of the room.

The police sobered Josh up enough to get him in cuffs and escorted him down the stairs and into the patrol vehicle. Josh went to jail for vandalism.

That night I felt very lonely and let down. I felt betrayed by Josh, and I felt as if my mother simply didn't understand. I didn't know why Josh felt it was necessary to ruin Thanksgiving, and I didn't know why it was necessary for him to be arrested when I depended on him so much. The only thing I could do for comfort was to write in my Journal.

Dear Josh,

I have never felt so empty and sad. Right now I am lying in my cold, lonely bed and you are lying on concrete in a jail cell. I don't know why things had to turn out so bad tonight. It was supposed to be Thanksgiving. Out of all days, why would you ruin a holiday? I'm at a loss and don't know what to do. The drinking has to stop. I can't allow this to continue. We have a baby on the way and that is no environment for a child to ever be in. I don't want to break up, but I think you need to stay at your mom's for a while. I know that you are probably just as nervous as I am about having a baby, but there is no excuse to binge-drink every day! You're not the same person when you drink. You break my heart every time you stumble in the door drunk. Either way, I still love you and I always will. I can't imagine having to do this without you, but I am going to have no choice if you can't get sober. Please, just do it for me? And if not me, then get sober for your baby.

Love always,
Hoping to be your future wife.

I did not intend on giving Josh this letter. I just had to release my pain. I was unsure of what the future would bring. I was unsure if he could truly handle the responsibility that would soon be bestowed on him. Finally at around 3 a.m., I fell asleep. I fell asleep sad that Josh was probably sleeping on a cold concrete floor. I fell asleep sad that our semi-stable circumstances had just been slammed down over a dark and cruel bottle of whiskey.

Chapter 8

The storm from Thanksgiving died down and life returned to a somewhat stable routine. Josh learned a lesson - for a while anyway. He still drank, but not as much as he had been drinking.

My pregnant belly was changing as fast as the seasons were changing. Christmas morning arrived and deep down I knew that it would be my last Christmas as a child. This would probably be my last Christmas living with my mother and sister. This would be the last time that I would be woken up at 4am by my twin sister to sneak down the stairs to retrieve the beautiful stockings that our mother had always carefully and thoughtfully put together. Every year, she would spend so much time finding us gifts that were perfect for who we were. The gifts, from books to chocolate and diaries, were always wrapped and tied with an artistic touch that only a perfectionist could master. They were beautiful. The most beautiful part was the love and energy that she had put into them.

After excitedly (but also somewhat sadly) going through my gifts on my unmade bed, I stuffed four truffles into my mouth and lay down to go back to asleep. Merri woke me up a few hours later as Lilah and Summer arrived. As a family, we opened our gifts, cracked jokes, and unknowingly enjoyed our last Christmas together that would resemble a normal family and childhood. We didn't know it at the time, and would not have wanted to.

A short time later, Josh came over. I had a stack of gifts for him. I had really gone all out. After learning the story of Beau's death, I had a deep sympathy for Josh and I wanted to make up for his loss and sad childhood memories. I wanted to make better what his mother could not. This was a big factor in how I treated our relationship from that point forward. I just wanted to love and help him. I wanted to show him what a safe and happy family was like. I wanted him to someday see how poorly the lifestyle his mother was leading and how horrible it could be for him to follow her. Everyone can hope. I hoped until there was none left.

After Christmas break I resumed school as usual. I had finally made friends with the Hispanic girls that I thought hated me. They were really nice and usually pretty damn funny. They made it easy to laugh at the small things that would normally bother me. I had a great sense of belonging, and I knew that no matter what obstacles were in my way, the Teen Parents Program offered plenty of resources. They even had a counselor come once a week to talk with us individually for a half hour. Her name was Rosa. She was in her early 30's and I loved her personality. She reminded me of a hippie as well as a responsible and concerned mother. I could talk to her about anything that was bothering me without worry of judgment. I usually was able to do the same with my mother, but it was nice to have a person that was not in my immediate life. Between the support from school, my immediate family, and Josh, I was doing exceptionally well. I was going on 7 months. My body had changed, but I wasn't too concerned. I knew that was the sacrifice of my choice.

One day, out of the blue, my mother announced to me that she wanted to throw me a baby shower. I was initially unsure about the idea. I was wondering to myself, who in their right mind is going to want to attend a baby shower for a 15 year old!

62

I was embarrassed. It was okay for me to be openly excited about my baby while I was at school or when I was with Josh, because everyone else was in a similar situation. I was worried about what friends of the family and even my friends would think.

The following week during Josh's lunch-break, he took me to my final ultra-sound appointment. We were both excited and betting on a boy. There were so many girls in my family already, and I wanted to be the one that broke the dramatic cycle of nail polish and pre-menstrual mood swings. However, deep down, I did not think that we were having a boy. I just played along to keep Josh's spirits up. As we were walking down the long hallway to sign in at the hospital, Josh was talking about what he would teach his son. I only had one thing on my mind: I had to pee - bad. My doctor had instructed me to drink as much water as I possibly could before the appointment. He said this would cause my bladder to push my uterus up into a favorable position for the tech to take measurements. I was gagging through episodes of severe acid reflux, and I was sure that I would pee everywhere.

The male technician squeezed ice-cold gel on my pumpkin shaped abdomen. He firmly pressed the probe directly on my bladder. I grimaced in pain but decided to tough it out. After fifteen minutes of torture, the part we had both been anticipating arrived. "You kids want to know the sex of your baby?" he casually asked in a monotone voice. It was as if he had been trained to ask the same questions and was bored with it. "Yes, please," I said in the calmest tone I could. I was extremely eager and excited, but I didn't want to annoy him with my teenage giddiness. He already seemed annoyed.

After scanning for about two minutes, we were given the news - sort of. "I am not 100 percent positive because the legs are crossed... but if I had to bet on it, I would say it's a girl." Josh and I looked at each other and smiled. I was worried that he would feel let down if his dream of having a son was shot down, but the look on his face told me that he was already completely in love with this little girl. I was excited to confirm the vision I had earlier in the year of a beautiful baby girl. I had known it from the very beginning.

Pulling into my driveway, I noticed a few strange cars. I had no idea who would be at our home. It wasn't until I walked in and noticed a stack of bibles on our table that I knew what was going on. My mother had recently started attending a church down the street. She went to Bible Study on a regular basis, and she had confided in the pastor about my situation. That night the Bible Study was being held at our home.

I was introduced to the pastor, along with a handful of other middle-aged locals. They were all very nice. I really liked the pastor - Pastor Gene. He was an older man and maybe in his late 60's. He had a slight resemblance to Santa Clause. His personality fit the character well. Something about this pastor made me feel safe. I felt like I was speaking to a very positive and clean force, almost one of an angel. "I was speaking with your mother, and I wanted to ask you if I could host the baby shower at my home. There is plenty of room and I would really love to help you get things set up," he said. I was surprised that a person who must be so morally and spiritually intact would want to help me. "That would be awesome! I was worried about how many people would show up, and I just wasn't sure how to go about it all," I said, trying to contain my relief. It would be easier to accept a baby shower if it were held by a third party. It wouldn't make me look so stupid and desperate if another person was hosting it for me.

Two weeks before the baby shower I was 8-1/2 months along. My mom handed me a stack of invitations to send out. I had not thought about whom I would invite and was afraid that it would turn into proof that nobody cared when nobody showed up. After battling with my self-esteem taking a plunge and my hormonal brain being extremely emotional and indecisive, I decided to follow through. I sent out an invitation to every person I could think of. I made some phone calls to get missing

64

mailing addresses then sealed and stacked the envelopes. I was expecting the worst but truly hoping for the best.

The next week I had trouble focusing at school, and I became somewhat overwhelmed. Between being extremely pregnant and having to show the reality of this fact by attending my baby shower, I was not getting much sleep. I would stay awake until two in the morning reading the novels I had once obsessed over - hoping to distract my busy mind from my fears and worries. After sleeping for only 4 hours, I would wake up again at 6:00 in the morning to waddle down the stairs to the kitchen. I found a particular cereal to be extremely pleasurable. I would drench it with honey and waddle back up to my bed. My insomnia was normal for third trimester fatties to deal with. It was nature's way of preparing for the soon-to-come sleepless nights of caring for a newborn.

Chapter 9

"What the hell, Merri!" I angrily screamed. I was so mad that I felt tears streaming down my cheeks. The warm, and clearly fresh, dog shit must have been waiting specifically for me. It was in the perfect place, at just the right time.

"What's wrong Elizabeth?" my mother asked with a concerned tone. "Merri needs to clean her dog's shit off the floor! I just stepped in it and it's stuck between my toes!!" I hysterically announced. This time, waddling with a limp, I rushed to the bathroom and awkwardly lifted my leg to get my foul smelling foot in the sink. The warm water gave the dog crap an enhanced, steamy smell, like it was being boiled for dinner or something. I gagged and, almost throwing up, quickly squeezed the entire contents of the bottle of hand soap onto my violated foot. Standing with my foot in the sink for about fifteen minutes, I hoped that all of the microscopic, disgusting particles of bacteria were gone. I forfeited my quest for cereal and waddled back up the staircase and into my bed (which I hoped wouldn't become contaminated with any hiding feces I surely missed).

The day of my baby shower had arrived. It was a bright and sunny day. Spring was teasing me with the melting snow that always had a beautiful sparkle. My mother and I headed to the pastor's home early. We needed to get things set up and make appetizers that my mother was determined to serve. It was the first time I had been to the pastor's home. I imagined that it would resemble the typical old person's home with that brown Tahoe-style shag length carpet with orange and green appliances from the 1970's. This home proved my imagination wrong. It was big, beautiful, modern, and very clean. It was located in a part of town where the well-off usually chose to reside. Actually, it wasn't too far from Dr. Huey's house. I learned that the home was provided to the pastor and his family by the church for the duration of his work.

I nervously paced around trying to come up with some sort of helpful task, but I was probably just in the way. Pastor Gene must have noticed my anxiety. As the time for guests to arrive neared, my stomach was in knots and I felt seriously ill. Pastor Gene approached me and asked if everything was all right. I casually explained my nervousness, and he handed me a plate with cheese and crackers. He told me that eating would help my nausea and things were going to be just fine. As I was choking down the dry crackers, my first guests arrived.

"Hi guys!" I excitedly said. I was more than happy when I saw that Merri had brought along some friends we had made during our first year of high school. They were all boys, but I thought that it was so sweet of them to show up considering that most men have egos in the way of allowing them to attend a baby shower. I was instantly relieved that anyone had shown up at all. As the next fifteen minutes passed, more people were ringing the doorbell than I could keep up with. There were so many beautiful gifts on the dining table, and the big living room was nearly filled to capacity.

Chapter 10

I hated the clinic that my doctor had forced me to make an appointment with. It was a community clinic, and it was smelly and overcrowded. My options to see a specialist were slim since I was forced to enroll in state insurance to cover the expenses of the pregnancy. When the state had asked for my mother's personal information (because I resided with her) she just about burst a gasket. She was irritated and insulted that the same office that disbursed welfare payments wanted information from her. She eventually got over it and gave them her social security number to get me on the coverage. Growing up, we did not have a regular insurance plan; any time we were sick or needed any sort of medical care, our mom would always make sure that we were promptly taken care of. She had a way of being classy and resourceful all at the same time. I look back and admire her for this.

The nurse called me, and I was greeted by two male doctors. I felt uncomfortable and was glad that I had my mom come into the office with me. One doctor was an intern and the other was clearly a veteran. When he introduced himself, I realized that he was the father of a boy I went to school with. How freaking embarrassing, I thought, as he was checking to see if I had dilated. It was mild torture. "You are about three centimeters, and with your permission

I would like to strip the bag of waters to help your labor progress. We can't really allow a woman with preeclampsia to remain pregnant for very long," he said. "Sure. Do whatever needs to be done," I replied. This procedure wasn't supposed to hurt, but because I had not finished growing, it hurt like a bitch. Luckily, it only lasted about thirty seconds. I was happy to get dressed and out of the clinic. I didn't feel any different, and I assumed that whatever he had done was probably not going to make anything happen yet. I had never even heard of that procedure and thought it was probably just an old wives' tale.

Waddling my way back into our home, I started to feel sick and tired. Mrs. Snow had left a message on the answering machine wanting me to go into school to take an important state test that all of the students would have to take. I had scheduled to do my work at home for the last month of my pregnancy, but I thought that I would just stick it out and go in the next morning to prove my dedication to graduating high school.

I had it in my mind that I would graduate early so I could start college. I did not know what would become of my future when I began to live away from home. My mother had not mentioned anything to me about moving out, but I knew that eventually we would have to get our own place. Josh, going back and forth from our house to his mom's, was frustrating to me and it would be difficult to feel like a responsible parent if I was still living with my parent.

I walked into the portable classroom the next morning at nine. I was surprised when I realized that the classroom was completely full. It was not just pregnant women or mothers - there were regular students in the class taking the exam as well. One of these students was a boy I had hooked up with the previous year. He was a popular kid, and I felt like a complete idiot when he gave me a second glance. I was sure he was thinking: "go figure...she's knocked up." I tried to ignore my insecurity and focus on the exam. The first hour I was doing just fine. When I began the next part of the exam my nausea overcame me to the point of searching for a trashcan. I again meditated my way out of humiliation and quickly guessed on the rest of my answers. I left early, and Mrs. Snow didn't put up an argument.

My mom picked me up in the hidden parking lot by the football field, and I explained to her that I was feeling pretty crappy. "You're probably in labor, Elizabeth!" This was the first time that I knew for a fact that she would love this baby. She was as anxious to meet this baby as I was. "I am not having contractions though. It's probably just a bug or something," I stoically replied. As confident as I was, I was forced to rethink my statement when I sensed how confident she was. After all, she did have three children - two in one shot. She should know. When we returned home I spent the rest of my day on the couch. I was unable to eat because I was still sick to my stomach and it was definitely not letting up. Josh came home from work and I forced him to rub my feet. When 9:00 o'clock hit, we were both too tired to finish our movie and headed up the stairs. He grabbed his portable twin sized mattress out of my closet and kissed me goodnight. Looking back, it was pretty silly that we both had our own twin beds and his was on the floor. It was like a really screwed up slumber party or something. Curled up in the fetal position, as best as my stomach would allow, I fell into a deep sleep. I was dreaming about giving birth to baby kittens. It was so realistic, but I knew that there was no way I was a cat.

Chapter 11

Opening my eyes, I had to squint to see the clock across the bedroom. It was already three in the morning. I was confused from the dream I was having, and I wondered why I had woken up when I had been sleeping so well. I felt a little bit sick. It was coming in waves, and it was more of a sharp pain than nausea. I realized that these pains must be contractions. They started to come every fifteen minutes, and the intensity was a little harsher each time. I quietly wrote the times down on a piece of paper. I didn't want to wake anyone up until I knew for sure what was going on. I thought it was strange that these contractions didn't hurt; they were just uncomfortable. I was extremely calm, and I lay in bed thinking about how bad it could possibly be to give birth. A strange calm came over me.

Finally, when 6:00 a.m. rolled around, I needed to get out of bed and do something to relieve my discomfort. What was worrying me the most was that the contractions were now only five minutes apart. I didn't want to put up a fuss and panic though. I didn't want to startle or worry my mom or Josh, mainly because I wanted to take a shower before I went to the hospital. I thought it was very important for me to be clean and primped. This was a special occasion and I was not about to show up in pajamas. I knew that family would be invading the hospital room and snapping tons of pictures, and I did not want my baby to one day see these pictures and how horrible I looked!

"Josh, can you go ask my mom if it's okay for me to take a bath and also tell her I am having contractions every five minutes," I quietly, yet firmly, requested. I didn't want to be mean, but in order to get Josh to fully wake up I had to display a serious side. He was a deep sleeper. "Yeah, sweetie, I'll be right back," he said as he bounced up from the floor, flew out of my bedroom and down the stairs.

Only thirty seconds went by before he came back up. "She said as long as your water didn't break you can take a bath." Thank God. I just needed to change my position and do something to distract myself. The pain still wasn't too bad, but I felt the increasing intensity with each contraction. I submerged myself in the bath and it was heaven for about five minutes. The contractions were coming much closer together. The relaxing bath may have triggered this. I quickly stood up and dried off. I sat in front of the mirror and quickly put my makeup on. I really wanted to dry and style my hair, but I knew that I could not spend that kind of time at the moment. I twisted my wet hair up into a bun on the top of my head and changed into a comfortable sweat outfit. Josh followed behind me as I walked down the stairs. My mom met us at the bottom. "Elizabeth, do you want to ride with me to the hospital so I can hurry up and get you checked in while Josh packs up the overnight bag for the stay?" she asked. "Yes. I was going to ask if we could do that anyway. But we should go because they are kind of close now." I tried to say casually, but my strained voice gave me away. On the drive to the hospital the contractions were more intense, and it was miserable sitting in the upright position that the passenger seat forced me to be in. I really had to focus on my breathing at that point. These contractions were just too strong. If I hadn't focused on my breathing, I could have panicked.

At last we pulled into the hospital parking lot. I hurried (almost sprinted) into the entrance. I had to go to the admissions office first, but once I sat in the waiting room, I just couldn't handle waiting around. The older lady holding my stack of records kindly instructed me to go ahead and get over to labor and delivery while my mother finished up for me. She must have recognized the look of agony on my face that appeared every few minutes. I was thankful that I was free to go.

"You're six centimeters dilated and fifty percent effaced," the nurse excitedly announced. I was expecting to be maybe two or three centimeters at the most. I have heard numerous stories from women about how long and tedious their first labors were. Lying on my side in the hospital bed, I looked at the clock and it was eight-thirty. I didn't understand where all the time had gone. It felt like I had been in my bath five minutes earlier. Maybe the inability to keep track of time is nature's way of helping women deal with pain. Pain alone is already difficult; having to endure pain with a sense of time to accompany it could be a recipe for disaster. I was quite the pro at meditation by this time. I had plenty of practice from all the times I avoided throwing up. I transformed myself into a deep trance toward the end of my labor. I closed my eyes, and as each contraction peaked, I envisioned myself standing barefoot on the beach as the waves rose, peaked, and crashed down. The waves eased my anxiety immensely. My subconscious did not know what to expect with the foreign, yet natural, forces of labor, but I very well knew what to expect with the waves of the ocean. There was a break every time, like my contractions, and a rhythmic movement but never continuous.

Flashing back to the beach, some of my favorite memories were running barefoot and free as my grandparents tried to keep up. My Grandpa sat me on the counter in the motorhome as the first rays of sun glistened from the crashing ocean and helped me drink a small cup of orange juice. I must have only been three years old. Falling asleep to the peaceful waves and reacting to the forces of our planet is an experience I'll never forget. That sound carried me along my journey of bringing a new life into the world. It was nature working within itself. Even at fifteen years old, I wasn't afraid. I felt like it was okay and it was supposed to be happening.

Josh and my mother were the only family in the room. I had a group of friends, along with my twin, sitting in the waiting room. Lilah was still at work, but she had called my mother to say she was heading our way. The clock on the wall said ten-fifteen as the doctor walked in to assess my progress. Rolling onto my back for the exam was horrible. As I was contracting, it was nearly impossible to meditate my way to relief. After all, the doctor was intrusively breaking my water. "Holy shit! That is so gross," I whined in shock. There had to have been over a gallon of liquid that came crashing onto my legs and bed! Doctor Howard was trying not to laugh. He was about my mother's age and was very well known in the small town. He carried himself calmly and confidently, which was exactly what I needed to see. I needed a certain, unspoken reassurance and it was as if he could read my mind. "Rub my feet!" I screamed to Josh. I needed something, anything, to distract me from the pain. "I think I feel the head," I said, with panic in my voice.

"You're ready to have this baby," the nurse said.

Chapter 12

Completely unaware of what to expect, I welcomed the idea of finally bringing my baby into the world. Pain was no longer the dominating thought. Getting to meet my baby for the first time was far more important. For the entire pregnancy I planned to be tough and deliver my baby "naturally" without an epidural. My mother had twins naturally, so of course I could handle the pain of just one baby. At fifteen, I had no way of even slightly predicting the pain of a natural birth. Of course, I knew somewhere deep down that it must not be pleasant. I also did not know the extent of this unpleasantness.

Josh was holding my right leg, my mom was supporting my head, and a young nursing assistant was holding my left leg. I was more concerned with down south (uh-hum) being groomed enough to avoid my peer to the left becoming grossed out. Sure, I was thinking about the pain, but this girl looked familiar enough to the point that I wondered if she had recently graduated from my high school. I was thinking about how embarrassing it would be if she came to the realization that she knew me outside of the hospital room. I hope I remembered to shave, I was thinking, as I was having a thirty second break from the nearly continuous contractions. My fear of embarrassment quickly vanished as the next contraction forced a pressure on me that I had never known to be possible. As much as I wanted to stay calm and push this baby out while still maintaining my dignity, the pain forced a moan from my mouth that was even foreign to me. This moan was not voluntary, it was nature taking its course by whatever means necessary, to keep my body and mind from going into total shock from the pain. The moaning was a minor release of the overbearing pressure. I remember thinking that if I were to grip my mother's fingers tight enough and hard enough, maybe I could transfer the painful energy over to her instead. Focusing on my forceful squeeze was also a slight release to my pain.

Besides my discomfort and the awkward, completely foreign, sounds that emerged from me, the room was peacefully silent - as silent as it could safely be with medical personnel communicating.

The doctor's voice broke my inner silence. "Now this is what we call the ring of fire, Elizabeth. It's going to be very uncomfortable, but it is the shortest part, okay?" "Sure," I responded through clenched teeth. Like I had a choice anyway! The only fix to this pain, which felt more like a soccer ball making its way out, was to deliver this baby. After Dr. Howard explained that he was going to be performing an episiotomy and first had to numb my perineum with a local anesthesia, I rolled my eyes and slammed my head back onto the hospital bed. What the hell is a perineum anyway? It sounds like one of those gross words - like "Volvo," a car I will never drive because of its resemblance to "vulva." I almost laughed to myself. The medical terminology was getting annoying. Out of an unexpected nowhere, a great relief came over me. The pressure was still there, but it was lifted up from the deep, torturous hell I had previously been feeling. "Umm…did you just cut me with those scissors?" I shamelessly asked. I was truly curious. It seemed like a mutilation of such

78

extremes would be horribly painful, but was actually quite the opposite. I'll put it plain and simple: it felt good. Okay…I said it.

Lilah made her way into the hospital room just as I was about to deliver. She looked scared as she ran to the other side of the room, being forced to cross paths with my gaping vagina. I couldn't handle any more of this drama with my legs up in the air and everything completely exposed. I hated feeling vulnerable. This was definitely the most vulnerable I had ever felt in my entire fifteen years of existence. With another contraction coming full force, I took a deep breath and pushed with all the strength of my existence. This was the last push before I felt my baby finally exit my body.

I felt as if I would float off of the hospital bed at any moment. It was the most enormous feeling of relief I had ever experienced. This baby, that we had all been waiting so long to meet, was finally here. As the nurse wiped the blood and white greasy stuff off of her little body, I was finally able to look at my baby's tiny face.

"Oh my God, I'm going to cry!" Lilah exclaimed, choking back the start of a sob. My mom was at the baby vital station with my new baby snapping as many pictures as she could with her newly purchased disposable camera.

The nurse set her on my now un-pregnant belly, and for a few moments I was in shock. I could only rub her head and make sure that she did not fall off the bed while I was attempting to absorb what was really going on. I noticed that she smelled funny, and I wondered if anyone else in the room noticed this.

A little cry finally emerged from her hard-at-work lungs, as they were trying with all their might to offer her the first few breaths of her life. In a daze, my memory still remains blank except for noticing that she had my lips, a head of beautiful, soft hair, and the sweetest cry I had ever heard.

Before I knew what was happening, my hospital room was flooded with visitors including Josh's family, my high school friends, and my twin sister, Merri. I was even shocked when Josh's mom and her fiancé both gave me a hug and kiss on the forehead. It made me happy to know that so many people actually cared enough and wanted to be a part of this precious experience. A short time later, my mother and Lilah returned with a lunch of fresh strawberries and lasagna from a bakery that I so dearly loved.

After the visitors left, Josh went to announce the news to his buddies and coworkers who lived down the street. I finally had time to be alone with my baby in silence. As she was peacefully sleeping in her bassinet next to my bed, I reached over to gently rub her head. Tears began rolling down my face. I allowed myself to sob with joy.

Chapter 13

Just looking at my new baby girl brought tears to my eyes that were completely uncontrollable. I was so grateful to have this little angel who looked exactly like me. She made little creaky-door noises and was so perfect. I had no idea that I could possibly love something so deeply. I had no idea that something so small could fill my heart with so much happiness. She was beautiful and perfect, and I had no doubt in my mind that she had come from heaven. God had sent her to me, and my faith was given strength and certainty because of this. She was mine.

I picked up my little girl and brought her close to my chest. Chloe Lynn would be her name. Weighing seven pounds and 19 inches long, she was perfect in every way. It was so hard to imagine who she would become as she grew older. For now, I didn't care. I wanted everything to stay just as it was right then, in that very moment forever. I had never felt such a rush of euphoria in my life. I held onto my baby girl until I was ready to fall asleep. I gently put Chloe back into her bassinette. I realized that it was nearing eleven o'clock at night and I wondered why Josh hadn't returned yet to get to know his new little girl. As the clock continued to tick I was becoming angry and sad. I fell asleep with a bittersweet feeling in my heart. The bitterness was because the father of my new baby was nowhere to be found.

About an hour after dozing off, I was rudely awakened by the sound of Josh stumbling through my hospital room door. A strange woman followed behind him. I felt rage come over me. My face must have been turning a deeper red with every passing second. Confused, disoriented, and flat-out pissed off, I could not understand for the life of me why Josh had decided to get wasted tonight and why he thought it would be okay to allow some strange woman to follow him back to the hospital room. Trying with all my might to contain my mounting rage, words still spilled out of me, "What is going on? Where have you been? I have been waiting here by myself for hours." The way Josh looked at me as I was speaking clearly told me that, once again, he was totally trashed.

The woman behind Josh suddenly stepped into the room and started speaking even faster than I had moments earlier, "I'm sorry I didn't introduce myself right away, my name is Devalin. I'm a friend of Josh's mom - isn't she great by the way? Anyway, I gave Josh a ride because I didn't think he should drive. Oh yeah, I also wanted to ask - do you want me to sneak you a margarita? I mean it must have been some hard work you just went through, huh? There's nothing like a cold refreshing drink to take that pain away!" This hideous woman began hysterically cackling. No wonder she was a friend of Hilda, I thought. Birds of a feather...

Her obnoxious laugh woke up Chloe. I practically lunged at the bassinet to retrieve my daughter before one of these drunks attempted to touch her. I was so incredibly tired and dealing with them more exhausting. "No, thank you. I am actually pretty tired and need to get back to sleep. Thanks for dropping Josh off though." I said with a short and strong tone. The strange lady got the hint and left. I had never been so irritated. Josh always seemed to ruin special moments with his drinking habit.

I attempted to explain to Josh why I was upset and why my feelings were hurt, but he was too drunk to comprehend. It was useless talking to him. It was like talking to a pet rock! He curled up on the chair in the corner of the room and passed out. I fell asleep staring at my baby girl, trying to sooth my deep fear that Josh and I may not work out. This baby was nothing but innocent and pure and Josh's behavior was the complete opposite.

The next morning I woke up to the nurse bringing in a tray of oatmeal and juice that reminded me of the breakfasts I was served at school. I was ravishingly hungry: much more than I had realized. It was nice to have the freedom to eat as much as I wanted without having to worry about it coming back up.

Chloe had been a perfect angel throughout the night. She woke only twice to a dirty diaper, which was extremely awkward for me to handle. Her little legs were so tiny that it was borderline scary trying to change her diaper. I was afraid of hurting her. The first time around, to my luck, the nurse came in to check my vitals. She must have noticed that I was struggling because she graciously stepped in to show me that changing a newborn's diaper was more of a mind-over-matter issue. The second time around was still scary, but I managed to get it done. Josh, of course, was no help as he was lost in his drunken slumber.

It was about 8:30 in the morning and, with my luck, the mean nurse from my school walked in. Nurse Val. I put on my fake smile and greeted her as I usually did. "Congratulations," she said, practically speaking through her nose. "Are you going to breastfeed?" She was so damn nosey all the time, and I really did not want to deal with her at the moment.

"Thanks, and yes, I plan to nurse her." I replied, emphasizing the word "nurse." I was so sick of terms involving anatomy that were spoken so medically correct. It was annoying, and I just wanted my world to be back to normal - as normal as it could possibly be with a new baby.

Nurse Val asked me to show her how I would nurse Chloe while she sat on the edge of my bed. I thought it was odd and totally uncomfortable, but I agreed. She was trying to make sure I had the technique correct, but I couldn't possibly focus on technique when a woman in her forties that was not even close to me was staring at my boob! After dealing with Nurse Val for half an hour, she finally left me in peace. Thank God that's over, I thought to myself. At that point I was ready to go home. I wanted my own bed, my own jammies, and my own space. I wanted to bring my baby home for the first time, get her settled, and just maybe, get back into some sort of normal routine.

The only problem I had to face at that point was Josh. If he thought getting wasted on the night of his daughter's birth was okay, he would surely be getting wasted whenever he wanted from that point forward without a second thought.

"Josh!" I demanded his attention, not caring he was hungover and looking pathetic in the corner of the hospital room. He looked my way confirming that I had his attention. "Choose - it's Chloe and me or alcohol. I am not kidding. You haven't even spent any time with us, and I just gave birth to your baby! If you refuse to stay sober, we are done. It's over. So choose and I want an answer now."

I was worried about making Josh choose the booze or his immediate family, but it had to be done. I was scared of what his answer was going to be. I really did not want to do this alone. I knew that I could not do this alone. I wanted Josh to be in our lives forever, but the excessive drinking just had to stop. There was no question in my mind.

To my surprise, Josh got out of the chair with a concerned look on his face. For the first time, he actually looked as if he felt bad for what he had done. Walking to the side of the bed, he grabbed my hand and apologized. "Sweetie, I am really sorry. I am an idiot and I don't know what I was thinking," he said with a voice full of regret. "I don't ever want to lose you. I love you so much, and I love our beautiful daughter too." "Well, Josh, you're on thin ice. I am really getting frustrated with your crap, and I don't know what to do anymore," I said - trying not to display the ounce of empathy I had left for him.

Out of nowhere, I heard a startling explosion.

Chapter 14

Josh and I simultaneously turned our heads to the corner of the room. Chloe began screaming. I think the explosion startled her too. It was Chloe with a dirty diaper. With no further discussion of Josh being in the doghouse, we knew we must act quickly. Chloe had been so quiet throughout our stay. Suddenly, she was screaming and I didn't know what to do. She was so incredibly tiny that it was scary changing her diaper. I was scared that any wrong movement would damage her for life. I looked at Josh with total uncertainty. "Josh, just go get the nurse," I pleaded. Josh's face formed a crooked grin as if he were truly proud of what his baby girl had just accomplished. "Sweetie, I'll change her; it's not a big deal." he stated.

As confident as ever, he took charge and changed the green mess like he knew exactly what he was doing. Great. How am I supposed to be mad at him now? Our newborn baby would depend completely on us to give her a safe environment to live in, free of alcohol and fighting. However, Josh had done nothing to prove his intentions were to grow up and stop drinking. On the other hand, if Josh and I did not stay together, I would be forced to do most of this teen parenting stuff on my own. I would have to live at my mother's house until I turned eighteen, and even though things at home were great for the time being, I knew they could quickly change back to catfights and bickering to no end. After a thirty-second battle with my own mind, I decided to stick it out to see if he was capable of growing up. After all, he had just made a small amount of progress.

The clock was nearing noon, and I was ready to spend time at home with my new baby. I was excited when my mother returned from the nurse's station with the news that I could go home. Josh and my mom helped pack everything up, and Chloe was safely tucked into her car seat and ready to go on her first car ride. I could not believe how tiny she looked in her seat. She was so delicate, and every movement with her was slowly and cautiously carried out. On the way home, my mom stopped by our local grocery store to get dinner and a prescription for me. I thought it would be fun to take my new baby into the store with me and show her off to the envious women who were past their childbearing years.

I thought young mothers were so much better than older mothers. At least we were pretty and still youthful with enough energy to play with our kids. This parenting thing is going to work out just fine, I was thinking to myself as my mom and I were checking out at the store. The Clerk, who had interacted with our family frequently from several years of our local shopping, was looking at me strangely. She looked confused. Finally, after purposely stepping away from the counter to get a good look at my new prize, she said "Oh my! How old is the baby? I was hoping it was one of those fake plastic babies the kids get from school! I'm sad to see that it's not a school assignment!" This ticked me off, and I felt the blood rushing to my face in anger. I gave her no reply. What would I say anyway? "I'm sorry I had a baby," or "Yep, my baby is real!" Luckily, my mother did the talking, and I got out of explaining my situation. I was sad after this encounter because I knew that the negative remark would not be the last one I heard.

We pulled into the driveway of our home eager to carry our new family member in and get her acquainted. As I began to climb the stairs, I noticed that there were scattered garments lying around. I knew that this was an indicator that Josh had made another horrible mess. He was notorious for this. I walked into my bedroom and was once again immediately pissed. It was one thing for him to get wasted the night that our daughter was born, but it was a whole different playing field to mess up my personal space. I was livid. I screamed at him from the top of the staircase, and told him that he needed to watch the baby so I could clean up his disgusting mess. He obediently complied.

Still recovering from the strenuous process of childbirth, I was on my hands and knees wiping the dirt off the bathroom floor. I gathered all of the trash he had left lying around and was finally able to vacuum. When I was finished getting my bedroom back to normal, I was tortured with painful cramping, followed by gushing blood running down my legs and ruining my new pajama pants that my mom had gotten me just for my recovery. I wanted to have a meltdown, but I was too tired to battle with my OCD any longer. Josh brought Chloe back up to me as I crawled into bed, exhausted. "I wanted to come back and clean up before you came home, I just forgot," he said with worry in his voice. "Whatever, Josh. Just have some respect in the future. I just had a baby. You never consider important things like that." I was happy when Josh finally quit babbling apologies and left me alone. By this point, I had learned to turn off his uncontrollable rambling.

Josh had a true case of ADHD, and his most obvious symptom was speaking nonsense for hours on end. Sometimes he just didn't make sense. I was the one in control, and as long as Josh did as I asked, I truly did not care if he made sense. I did, however, frequently get comments from our peers regarding his conversation style. I knew where people were coming from, but I chose to disregard their input. Josh had good intentions; he was a hard worker and a nice person. As long as he didn't embarrass me in front of important people, I could deal with it. Josh wasn't crazy, just often confused.

The first night home from the hospital with my baby wasn't the easiest. Chloe took four days to learn how to nurse properly, and this meant that I was waking up every few hours when she became frustrated and hungry. After finally getting the hang of it, on both of our ends, caring for my baby quickly became more of a pleasure than work. Chloe was a very calm and content baby. She hardly cried, and when she did, it was always for a feeding or diaper change. Our routine became natural and perfect - that is, as long as Josh was behaving. He had a few nights of trouble, but for the most part, he was on track.

Chapter 15

My mom and I were counting the days to my sixteenth birthday as she was driving me home from my last day of summer school. I wanted to graduate early, so I had hauled Chloe along and raced through my required courses. As the summer nights passed, our home felt smaller and smaller with our new addition taking up more room. Josh also had a new addition of his own. His best friend, James, was devastated about having to leave Tahoe when his parents moved out-of-state for a new job. I hadn't really seen much of James during my pregnancy. Once Chloe was born, I was more mobile and motivated to get out of the house. The boys became best friends all over again, and James pretty much became a part of the family. We had a spare room in our home, and both Josh and I thought it would be fun to have James around permanently. We offered him the room with my mother's hesitant permission. He gladly accepted and moved in.

Not long after James moved in, I could tell that my mom was getting tired of putting up with a house full of kids. She wanted and needed her own space back. She asked us what our long-term plans were. Josh and I looked at each other and gave her a shrug. She brought up the marriage topic again. I thought it sounded fun, and Josh was on board as well. Legally, because of my age, I could not move out of my mother's house to live with Josh unless I married him. With the marriage, I would be emancipated. That meant freedom! Plus, I was really beginning to feel like a loser with a baby and living under my mother's roof. I knew that I wouldn't have any sort of respect from the community if I remained just another statistic. Josh and I began casually talking about getting married, and the more we spoke of it, the more excited we became. We decided to get married as soon as good ole' Uncle Sam approved. That would be the day after I turned sixteen!

We realized that we only had six weeks until I would legally be permitted to marry in the state of Nevada, which was just a short five miles away. After looking through a calendar, we decided on the official date. The day after my birthday landed on a Saturday. It was going to be just perfect. First, we had to start planning the details. Unlike my baby shower, I was eager to come up with a guest list and send out the invitations. It was the perfect summer to plan a wedding. It would also be the perfect opportunity to prove to my peers and family members that I was actually kicking ass at the whole teen mom thing.

The first person I wanted to invite and be my bridesmaid was Megan. When I was pregnant, she ended up moving away to stay with her mom for the remainder of the school year. It was about four hours away, and I had gotten used to her coming and going. She loved living with her dad, Neil, but just needed some time away from him. For the most part, he was a good guy with good intentions. Because he was six-foot-four and clearly had too much testosterone pumping through his veins, he was easily angered, and I mean fast. There was a summer when Megan and I were considerably bored out of our minds most days. Neil didn't know what to do with us, but I think the fact that I had pretty much moved in for a few months to stay occupied had made it easier for him to keep his daughter occupied. There were a few days that summer when Neil was unusually angry and getting upset over any little thing that went wrong. One day, Megan's long lost great-aunt stopped by for a surprise visit. This put Neil into a state of rage, but he was forced to contain it because he was obligated to be nice to his aunt. This woman really must have had ESP. She came at the perfect time, just as Megan was considering moving back to her mother's home. When Neil had to go to work unexpectedly, his aunt pulled a white tackle-style box out of her bag. She began to present us with small pills to use as a remedy for Neil's violent outbursts. She reassured both of us that the pills would dissolve immediately so Neil would not know.

We spent the remainder of our summer drugging Megan's dad with holistic remedies by putting it into homemade Kool-Aid. We loved studying the effects of his response so we'd know if he needed his dosage upped. It gave us both a sick pleasure to know that we had more control than he knew. He was so easy to trick. This, however, was by far one of the less sneaky antics we had gotten into in our early teens.

I could easily write an entire novel covering our rebellious shenanigans - especially the ones we put over on Neil. The selling point of this novel would most definitely be the incident where we had a naked man hiding in the attic crawl space of my sister's apartment. Neil came to check on us while we were babysitting, and this, of course, was a good judgment call on his end. When we heard him coming up the staircase to the front door, Megan's victim for the night, Marcus, bolted out of the spare bedroom so fast that it took a second for his nudity to register in my brain. He clambered into my sister's closet, knocking things off the shelves, and pulled himself up into the crawl space. I wondered about what the itchy insulation was doing to his naked body. Trying to keep from laughing was excruciating.

Megan still ended up living with her mother. I called to ask her for her address so I could get her invitation mailed. She excitedly announced "Guess what? I am coming back for good in two weeks!" Relieved, I responded "Good! Now you can be in my wedding!

Josh has a friend that we both think you should meet. He started renting the extra bedroom a few weeks ago. He decided not move out of state with his family." "Oh!" she squealed with delight followed by "Is he cute?"

"I think he is pretty cute. I really think you will like him. Our boyfriends will be best friends, and we are best friends so it is just perfect!" I plotted. We ended the conversation in an excited fashion. I was so thrilled to start living a life with friends again. It wouldn't be the same as it had once been, but maybe that was a good thing.

Once again, I put together a guest list for my wedding, drawing off of the baby shower guest list, but with much more confidence this time. I already knew who my bridesmaids would be; I just had to get enough men who didn't appear to be twelve years old to balance it out. This was going to be an exciting summer.

As promised, a few weeks later Megan was on her way home. I forced her and James to talk on the phone for a few minutes every time I talked to her just to find out if they would even like each other. I figured that they must. Opposites usually attract, and their personalities were like night and day. James was pretty calm and laid back. He was a little bit on the passive-aggressive side and only got mad at me one time when my bath tub water leaked through the upstairs pipes and onto his bed. He acted like I did it on purpose! It wasn't my fault that Chloe and I loved to splash! Megan was not quiet or easy-going at all. She was loud, exciting, obnoxious, snotty, and a complete blast to be around. We could say or do anything, literally anything, in front of each other and laugh about it. The most fun we had was usually laughing over some sort of torturous prank we were inflicting on someone. Megan and I had fun together every day until an unspeakable tragedy occurred a few years later.

Chapter 16

Four other girls were to be in my wedding. The first was Merri, (obviously), then Kate, Holly, and Jessica who had been best friends with us since we were eight. Holly had almost been our stepsister at one point. Our parents dated for about a year and our young families were like the freaking Brady Bunch. We had a blast going to Disneyland in a humungous suburban and torturing other drivers because we were in love with the Hanson Brothers and we were blasting bop down the freeway. That really makes me cringe. The Hanson Brothers – ugh!

Holly was not only a friend growing up, but she was also like a mediator for twins and a loving sister trying to keep the peace. She made it hard for me to hold on to grudges. She always laughed at me or said some hilarious nonsense statement. After inviting Holly to be a part of my wedding, she secretly and cautiously whispered over the phone to me that she was pregnant. "Shut up! NO WAY! Holy shit!" I was throwing the poor girl shocking reactions instead of advice. I knew she wouldn't mind though. The only problem was that the dress I wanted her to wear for my ceremony was surely going to reveal her pregnancy. I felt her pain; her father was coming to the wedding. We agreed that she should wait to tell him out of fear that he wouldn't allow her to be part of the wedding.

Once the guest list was settled and we had found just enough men to stand in, I was relieved that I was still important to other people. My mother and I spent several days, without rest, planning all of the details. It was really fun doing this with her. I knew that I could always trust that she had the best taste and class when it came to decisions for me. She knew who her little girl was, and she chose the most beautiful dress for me. However, the first time I tried it on was discouraging. My boobs were implant-huge from nursing Chloe who was only about six weeks old at the time. My mid-section had some serious flab I needed to lose, and my stretch marks were horrendous. We also went cake tasting which was a blast. I had a strange craving for lemon that entire summer. I chose lemon icing for the cake and obsessed over lemonade on a daily basis.

We searched the town for a location that would be a happy medium - not too fancy but not dumpy either. One of our favorite restaurants at the time was a place connected to the tiny local airport. We would swing by there for lunch often, and the Cajun grit cakes were fantastic.

After picking up our engraved champagne glasses (to be filled with bubbly cider, of course), we stopped for our usual gumbo and grit-cakes and it clicked. This would be the reception location! It was big and bright inside, with huge windows facing the airport runway and the beautiful meadow beyond it. The owner offered to reserve the space and cater a buffet for an extremely reasonable price. On top of my mother's savvy and class and resourceful talent, Pastor Gene offered to help out once again. I believe he contributed $2000 and that was a big help. I still don't know how my mother did it, but she truly planned the most elegant and beautiful wedding a sixteen-year-old could ever want. With all the details taken care of, it was time for the countdown.

Almost forgetting that I wanted to invite Derrick and Donnie (Josh's co-workers), we stopped by their house to deliver an invitation and show off our little Chloe. Hesitantly walking into a typical bachelor pad with barking dogs, Derrick greeted me with extra positive energy. I set Chloe on a stool in her carrier so I could sit down while the guys talked about nonsense. Derrick looked my way and asked me how I was recovering. "I am doing pretty good but still waiting for my fat to go away - other than that, I'm good!" I was surprised that he was taking an interest in something that wasn't leading up to a flirtatious remark. Who was I kidding… he couldn't help himself. "Did you get that weird line down your stomach from bein' pregnant?" he curiously and oddly inquired. "Yeah, I got it a little bit, but I think it will fade," I said. "Well, lemme see!" he politely demanded. "Uh…okay…" I responded, as I hesitantly lifted my shirt to just above my belly button. "Ah nah, that ain't shit. You're all good," he enthusiastically said. I was definitely having a flashback of that horrible mistake I made while we had been fishing last summer. I thought it was strange of him to be interested in the progress of my returning figure. I grabbed my precious cargo and said goodbye. It was time to get home and call Megan and have her hurry over. She had just gotten into town, and I couldn't wait to see her.

James was home being lazy on his bed and babysitting Merri's snake, which we kept far away from baby Chloe at all times. I thought it was so creepy how it strangled its dinner and swallowed it whole - only to crap out bones that seemed like it would hurt! When Megan's dad dropped her off for the night, I ran to the front door excited and screaming. She looked pretty, as usual, but was still her snotty and sarcastic self. "It's time to meet James!" I sang, dragging her down the hallway and practically launching her into his room.

Immediately the awkwardness kicked in and both of their faces instantly turned bright red. They eased their way over to each other for a shy hug. It was only a matter of minutes before Megan was bossing James around, and he clearly didn't mind. Megan came over to the couch as I was nursing Chloe to sleep. Goggle-eyed and puppy faced, she had that all-too-familiar mischievous twinkle in her eye.

Oh crap, I thought, Megan has an idea. This is bad. This is very, very bad.

Chapter 17

"What, Megan?" I asked her, with a smirk on my face. "This is so much fun!" she loudly whispered. "You freaking love James, don't you?" I accused. "Sort of!" she giggled. I knew that this was not the only thing on her mind. I didn't want to pry too deeply into it with the boys in the next room. Plus, I knew that we would have plenty to talk about later.

The wedding was inching closer every day; it was only a week away! My mom picked up a full-time summer position at a local golf course. Josh, James, Megan, and I would frequently visit during her lunch break. They served good food and it was nice getting out of the house. By this time, Megan and James had fallen in love as I had predicted. It was cute seeing them together, and it was good for us to have another couple to hang out with. They loved being with our daughter as much as we did.

"Lizzy-Beth…" my mother reminded, "You and Josh need to go to Carson City today to pick up your rings. Here is the money, and make sure you get it done because it's right around the corner!" Lizzy-Beth was one of the nicknames that only a few select family members called me. I didn't mind. The only names I did not like were "Liz" or "Lizard." They were so unfeminine, and I just hated it. Since I was a teenager and, of course, didn't understand the value or concept of earning money, I excitedly and willingly took the bundle of cash from her. In the back of my mind, however, I did understand that she had been working pretty hard for that money. The singles and fives were evidence of tips, and tips usually signify hard work. I was lucky to have her.

James and Megan decided to go on a romantic drive around the lake after lunch, and Josh and I headed down the mountain to Carson City. Tahoe was a small town, and any real shopping had to be done off the hill. No matter how many times we did it, the thirty-minute drive was always stunning and gorgeous. There is nothing that can be compared to driving through the Sierra-Nevada Mountains. I highly recommend it. Pulling into the JC Penny parking lot, Josh took Chloe's carrier out of the back seat, and we excitedly walked into the department store. Three weeks previously, I had decided which ring I wanted to be mine. Peering through the glass, I had instantly spotted my bling. It was only a couple hundred dollars, but it was gorgeous with white gold and it had a touch of diamonds. Josh picked out his ring after trying several sizes on. They were boxed up, paid for, and we were ready to go grab some burgers.

Snapping my seatbelt before the car even started, I was surprised that Josh wasn't eagerly burning rubber as he usually did. He looked at me with a stupid grin on his face. "What are you goggling at, weirdo?" I teased. He pulled the box out of the small plastic bag and held it up to my face. "Sweetie, will you marry me?" he asked. "Josh, you are such a dork, but of course I'll marry you!" I laughed. He gave me a quick peck, and we were off to chow down. It wasn't the proposal of my dreams, but it certainly would do.

After we stuffed ourselves mercilessly with lunch, we drove back up the summit while I listened to my favorite country tunes. Chloe was totally content, as usual. When we got home we noticed that James and Megan were already back from their drive.

We unloaded our precious baby cargo for the hundredth time and walked in the house. We were excited to show off our rings. James had his door closed, and my mother was nowhere around. I heard an odd squeaking sound. Oh my god, they're doing it!! I thought. I knew it was going to happen eventually, but it was awkward that it was in a bedroom in my family's home. At least Josh and I had always been very discreet about it. We decided to wait upstairs in my bedroom until they were done. Finally, when I heard the downstairs door open, I knew that it was safe to resume downstairs activities.

Megan was in the bathroom fixing her hair. It was a wreck! "Holy crap, what happened to you?" I questioned. "Nothing." she giggled slyly. "Oh PLEASE! I'm not dumb! Look at the beautiful product of my dumbness," I said, pointing to Chloe. "I know! She is so adorable too!" Megan said in a squeaky baby-talk voice. "Oh no! I know what you're thinking! You have baby fever - don't you?" I accused. "Hehehe - Nooooo! Well, just a little bit. Wouldn't we have the cutest little baby?" she affirmed.

After this conversation, I got the gist of where her thoughts were headed. She saw how easy it was to care for Chloe (who was an exceptionally easy baby) and assumed that it would be just as perfect for her. I was somewhat excited about her statement. It would be so awesome to have a friend (my best friend) have a baby too. That way, we would always be on the same page, and we would have plenty more to talk about. Our babies would be best friends too, I was thinking.

"Well, if you want what I think you want, I have some things you can have," I offered, as I led her up the staircase. Josh and James were out back smoking their cancer sticks (which I hated). From under my bed, I pulled out a folder and handed her the stack of papers in it. "What the hell is all this?" She shockingly asked. "Go through it and you'll see," I claimed.

Upon opening the folder, her eyes grew big and her smile was ear-to-ear. "You did it on purpose? I knew it! I don't know why, but

I knew it!" I replied with nothing but a shoulder shrug. She read through my once obsessive material as I changed Chloe. It was official. Without James knowing, she was going to attempt to get knocked up. We talked about it every day after this secret conversation while hiding it from the boys.

My sixteenth birthday had finally come, and the wedding was less than twenty-four hours away. To celebrate our birthday, Merri and I had several friends and family (even from out of town) show up at our home with gifts. My uncle and grandparents bought us a brand new queen size bed for our wedding present. I was so excited because Josh was way too tall to share my twin size bed with me. Also, it was lame sleeping separately after we had a baby together. After setting up our new bed, my uncle and grandparents announced that it was almost time to head down the street to the church where we would be doing our rehearsal. Luckily, the whole wedding party was there and everything would go as planned.

Pastor Gene would be the one to marry us, and I was really happy about this. He came up with a great idea of also doing a baptism for the three of us after the vows were completed. I wanted to be baptized. I already felt guilty enough for being so rebellious and reckless at such a young age, and the Good Lord knows Josh needed it too. Standing in the church near a set of pews, a fly was harassing me as Pastor Gene was going over his words for the next day. The fly landed in just the right spot for me to give it a good crunch. I swiftly, like Jackie Chan, stomped on it with my foot, not realizing that I should not have made such a ruckus in a beautiful and calm church. The stomp echoed, and I truly looked like an idiot with Tourette's syndrome, or something. "Liz!" my mom quietly growled. "I am so sorry! I just didn't think! It was a really annoying fly!" I defended.

The pastor finished his beautiful vow compilation, we all shared pizza and cake, and the day was over. The next day was

102

going to be one of the biggest days of my life. I wouldn't let myself think about all of the details; I was already far too overwhelmed. Going to sleep for the first time with my husband and our baby girl in a big, fluffy and comfy bed was absolute bliss. I finally felt like we were on our way to becoming a normal family. We just needed to find our own place. As I was dozing off, I was fantasizing about what our married life would be like. I pictured Josh and I growing old together but wondered if he would even live long enough to grow old. He was just so reckless when he was drinking. It had slowed down a little bit for now, but I knew it would come back. I just hoped that I would somehow find a way to help him make a permanent change. Chloe was cuddled up between us, and I was blissfully uneasy.

Chapter 18

I woke up to my sister, Lilah, frantically banging on my bedroom door. "Liz! Oh my God! You aren't up yet? The wedding is in an hour!" She was a notorious nag. It drove me crazy. I was just so comfy in my bed. As I slowly inched my way out of bed, Josh opened his eyes and did his usual ADHD pounce to the bathroom to get ready. We were actually going to have two weddings that day. The first one was just to make it legal, and the second would be a bigger ceremony with family and friends. Nevada made it legal to marry at sixteen with a parent's permission. The Officiate that my mother hired would meet us for the legal part at ten-thirty. I honestly didn't even know exactly where it would be, but I hoped it wouldn't be awkward to just have a few important family members there to witness.

When Josh was through showering, he quickly got dressed and grabbed his bag of clothes that he would be wearing for the wedding. He gave me a quick peck on the cheek and raced down the stairs to have James help him get ready so I could have my space. The second I stepped out of the bathroom after showering I was hurried down the stairs by my mother and sister out of fear that I would be late to my own wedding. I am always late! I was born that way. It actually took my mom an hour and nine minutes to deliver me, twin "B."

Usually with twins, that sort of thing only takes a minute or two. I take my time with everything - especially important occasions.

I felt like a queen being pampered. My mother, also an aesthetician, was doing my makeup, and my older sister was incorporating beautiful tiny flowers into my long hair. When my hair and makeup was finished, I looked in the mirror and was very pleased. Next, I had to quickly strip down to my underwear so they could tightly wrap a corset around my abdomen and chest. It was perfect for squeezing in the extra baby flab. I called it my flat tire. I stepped into my poufy slip and then eased my way into my strapless dress. I did not remember my dress looking so beautiful when I tried it on a few weeks earlier. Finally, I was ready. I looked at my reflection in the full-body mirror in my mother's room, and I truly felt like royalty. I had never felt so beautiful in my life. This completely erased any worry or doubt that had been lingering in my insecure mind.

My mother and Merri, along with Megan and the other girls who were still too young to drive, all rode together to the destination. James and Josh rode together, and I rode with Lilah in her truck. My dress was poufy on the bottom, like Cinderella. There was no way I could have sat in a car with other people without causing some sort of damage to the dress.

The drive felt like it was taking forever. It was a bright, beautiful sunny day and that meant the highway would be full of tourists making their way to the casinos and the beaches. However, this wasn't anything new. Passing the strip of casinos, I knew that we were almost there. We pulled into a local recreational area and for a minute I thought that my mom was making us get married on a soccer field or something crazy. We parked the truck and Lilah hurried around to the passenger side to help me get out of the car so I wouldn't get dirt on my dress. The small group of friends and family were walking at a distance toward the official spot. I assumed it was safe to follow.

106

As Lilah and I neared the crowd, I began to see how beautiful the location actually was. I walked up a small grassy hill and looked around at the surroundings that suddenly offered a beautiful panorama of the turquoise lake surrounded by tall mountains in the distance with perfect, yet modest, icings of snow on the very tops. It was like a secret location that had the most beautiful view I had ever seen. The beauty was suddenly able to confirm my anxious and nervous feelings of growing up so fast. It gave me a complete sense of peace and serenity. I knew that I was supposed to be doing this. I knew that every person there loved me and Chloe and even Josh. I felt as if I was in heaven, and God was standing right behind me.

As Josh was holding my hands and gazing lovingly into my eyes, the minister spoke of our brave choice to bring Chloe into the world. I don't recall what he said word-for-word, but I do know that it was beautiful. Right as tears were about to ruin my makeup, I felt an intense, horrid, overwhelming itch. It was under my diamond necklace. Freaking bugs! The sparkle from my bling must have been the white light to heaven for those little suckers. They are called no-see-ums, and they dig their pointy little noses into your skin and it's torturously miserable. Trying with all my might to avoid spastically slapping myself on the neck, I was forced to sink into my meditation zone. Towards the end I was able to casually smear the nasty things into my skin, and I was officially the bug-gut bride. It was still a beautiful ceremony regardless of the dilemma. By the time Josh was permitted to kiss his bride, my itchiness had calmed, and I was able to enjoy the best part.

Josh and I held hands as we walked back to the parking lot to race to our next wedding where EVERYONE would be waiting. My grandparents had been toting Chloe along, but on the way to the car I just had to see her for a minute. I told her that she was my "little princess" and that I loved her so very much. She gave me a little split-second smile, and I knew that she was aware of the joy. Chloe was a quiet and reserved baby, but she was always aware of her surroundings. The drive back into town had a celebratory vibe. As Lilah and I pulled into the full-to-the-max parking lot of the church, I was extremely horrified. I was scared of the fact that Josh's entire family from all over the state, and even their friends, were going to be sitting in that church watching ME.

I stepped out of Lilah's truck and told her that I would be right in and I just needed to talk to Megan for a minute. Megan and James pulled into the parking lot at the perfect time. I knew that they were carrying the goods. "Thank God I found you before you went in!" I frantically said to Megan. James locked his car and announced that he was going to go in to see if Josh needed help with anything. "Where is my promised present Megan?" I begged. "Dude! There are so many people here!" she replied with wide eyes. She dug to the bottom of her purse and pulled out a small bottle of Bacardi. I crouched down next to the car, looking like a freak in my wedding dress and took two good swigs. There was no way I was going to be able to get through this without fainting unless I had a few drops of liquid courage. It was just the right amount.

Five minutes later I was in the lobby of the church, hearing the quiet chatter of the guests. One of my mother's good friends that I had known since I was five, Lena, was kind enough to bring me a gorgeous bouquet of flowers to carry down the aisle. My bridesmaids looked beautiful, and Summer was the cutest little flower girl. Before I knew it, I was alone with my uncle, waiting for the music to start. I hurriedly grabbed onto his arm. I am sure I had a look of pure terror on my face. He clearly realized how frazzled I was. At six feet, four inches tall and wearing cowboy boots, he smiled down at me. Just before stepping into the church, he said something that I'll never forget, but certainly didn't expect; "Ah man, I have the worst wedgie! Great timing." I nearly screeched with laughter, but I managed to get a grip on myself in time to avoid looking like a looney.

108

For the second time that day, I met Josh in the presence of the minister, Pastor Gene. We held hands and exchanged vows; I was pleased that it was relatively short. It was then time for my mother to hand baby Chloe over to me for our family baptism. I didn't know how the process worked, but as long as Pastor Gene didn't spray a hose of holy water in my face (which he would have had the merit to), I would be just fine. It became another peaceful and calm moment. It was comforting to hear his words and know that God forgave me for my sins, and he always would as long as I asked. I needed that. After Chloe came into my life, my view on rebellion and mischief changed entirely. She proved to me that we are all born completely innocent, and if she grew up to do the same sort of things I had, it would break my heart.

Since Chloe was still so young at only six weeks, it wasn't always easy to get a smile out of her. Beyond a coincidence, the moment that Pastor Gene sprinkled the holy water on her head, she contently smiled the most beautiful and innocent smile I had ever witnessed. I was so touched and excited that I actually turned around to announce this to my mother, who was sitting just feet away. "She smiled!" I said excitedly, forgetting that I was in a church partaking in a life-changing ceremony. All I had eyes for, at that moment, was my precious little girl. She now had an even tighter grip on my heart, which I did not think was possible.

After the ceremony, we all went outside to do the traditional marriage photo shoot. I loved taking pictures with my family, whom I did not get to see as often as when I was younger. This was the last time I can remember having the entire family and close family friends together in the same room. Following the photo session, the large crowd piled into their vehicles to drive to the reception.

At the reception I gave a toast to my mother, bawling my eyes out and telling her how much I loved her and how I would be "so screwed" without her. Normally, the word "screwed" wouldn't be appropriate at a wedding, especially in a toast, but I was only sixteen, so it was to be expected. After eating from the buffet and some of the guests getting tipsy at the bar, we sliced our gourmet (and mouth-watering) cake and opened our mounds of gifts. For the budget that my mother was on and trying to get her mortgage paid on time, she somehow managed to give me the most beautiful wedding ever. She even got us a suite on the lake for the night. Of course Chloe came along because I was still nursing. That was just fine. We were exhausted and overjoyed all at the same time and definitely looking forward to having a peaceful, relaxing night.

The next day Josh and I were eager to get back home and go through all of our gifts. I was also eager to study for my driving test. I knew that with a baby I would no longer be able to walk to school, especially in the harsh winter conditions.

Settled back in at home, we enjoyed redecorating my bedroom to look more like a married couples' bedroom. We had a great time obsessing over the wedding photos that were arriving in small increments. Chloe was growing every day, and Megan and James were happy as ever, cuddling, almost non-stop, in the tiny bedroom downstairs.

About a month before school was going to start back up, Megan and I were joyriding in her car and on the hunt for some greasy, super unhealthy food. She mentioned that she was irritated when her period had started a few weeks before. "I really, really want a baby. It would be perfect! I am so sick of my dad bossing me around. He probably has a GPS in my car!" she whined. I was excited. "Yeah, it would be a quicker way to get out of his house, and it would be so much fun, too! But don't listen to me because every baby is different. Just because I got lucky with an easy one doesn't mean you will. You have to make sure that you really want this. You aren't going to be able to go out and party whenever you want. Any time you do anything you will have a baby with you. You don't get any free time to yourself, and a lot of mothers don't get much sleep either. Just sayin'." I sat in silence thinking about what I had just said.

"Oh I know. I have thought about all of that!" she affirmed. We were going through the drive-through as she ordered James a burger with no onions. After she paid, I decided to have her drive down to my school so she could see what would really happen if she got pregnant. She wouldn't want to go to regular school anymore. The other students would talk too much. As I predicted, she got excited about the school and even the hidden away classrooms down the hill. I knew that she had her mind made up - just like I had mine made up not too long before.

Chapter 19

"Whoohoo! I did NOT think I was going to pass!" I childishly screamed as I skipped down the line of the Department of Motor Vehicles. "Good job, sweet pea!" my mother said. She was carrying Chloe in her car seat as we walked out of the once-horrifying place that would determine my outward appearance as a responsible teen mother. I was desperate to start my junior year with the convenience of driving myself. I was a married woman and a mother, and I needed to look like it. School was only a week away.

After picking up one of my favorite lunches from a little diner, we arrived back home and the phone was ringing off the hook. I answered in my usual monotone. "Hello," I said - it was Megan. "Elizabeth! Get over here, now!" She was breathing heavily like it was a huge emergency. "What is going on? Why?" I asked. "Just hurry up!" she screamed and hung up on me. Since I had just gotten my license, I thought it would be fun to take myself across the highway to Megan's house. My mom said that it would be okay to use her car and she even offered to watch Chloe. I grabbed my bag and excitedly headed out the door, forgetting that my friend sounded like she was dying.

"Let me see it!" I excitedly demanded. She practically threw the thing at me, and I was happy the cap was on. "Yep, that is definitely

113

a line. You are totally knocked up!" I announced. Megan was still in shock. We sat on the couch and discussed how she was going to break the news to James and even more worrisome, her dad. After coming up with ideas, I realized that it had been about an hour and I had to get back to Chloe. Now Megan would definitely be my study-buddy at school. I also had to make sure that Josh enrolled in the home-study option at the Teen Parents Program, since his ADHD had interfered with his ability to graduate high school. He was a father now, and he had to have his diploma.

That afternoon, after eating my mother's delicious pasta and putting Chloe down for her nap, I laid on my bed and started thinking about how sad it would be to not have a traditional High School graduation. I was still determined to graduate this year, which would be a year early. I knew that I would probably end up not walking down the aisle with all the other students because the traditional Senior Project was always a requirement. Oddly though, I still had a vision of myself walking down that grassy aisle on the football field with my family all gathered, clapping and proudly screaming my name. Only pipe dreams, I thought to myself.

The first day of school had finally arrived. Megan was all set to attend the Teen Parents Program, and her dad was still as outraged as he had been the previous week when she broke the news to him. He put a very tight leash on her and she was restricted with everything that she did. James took the news well although his parents were upset. They thought that it would be best for the baby if they got married. Megan was begging her dad on a daily basis to sign the paperwork to let her tie the knot. He just wouldn't budge. The morning that I was getting ready to show off my new baby to the girls I had made friends with at school the previous year, an intense blaze of sirens went off. It sounded as if it were just down the street. It made me wonder if

Merri was ok, as she had just left for school in her beat up Camaro that she dearly loved so much. After about thirty seconds, I heard even more sirens. There must have been at least three police cars and first responders. Feeling sick to my stomach, I hoped for the best and began to pack up Chloe's diaper bag. On my way out, I met my mother in the driveway as she was pulling in. She had gone to make sure the emergency had nothing to do with Merri. Luckily it didn't. She did say that it looked like a black car had flipped over onto its roof near the entrance of the Keys. The Keys is a neighborhood on the lake with beautiful and expensive homes.

"Elizabeth! How are ya?" Mrs. Snow asked as she welcomed me. I gave her a smile and told her that I was ready to graduate this year. "You still have tons of credits to earn; let's just take it one day at a time, okay?" I hesitantly nodded. In my mind, I was determined to graduate no matter what the obstacles would be. Mrs. Snow sat at the circular table with the group of girls including Megan and myself. She got a somber look on her face and asked if anyone had heard about what had happened earlier that morning. "I heard some really loud sirens, but that was about it." I responded. Mrs. Snow took a deep breath before she spoke. "There was a fourteen-year-old girl, and I think her name was Melissa. She was skateboarding to her bus stop. Some guys, heading home from a night at the casinos, were speeding and hit her. She was flown to Sacramento, but they don't think she's going to make it. So sad..." She looked down. Hearing that was incredibly sad, and it bothered me probably more than anyone else in the room. The rest of my day at school was somber because of this, even with Megan cracking her typical jokes. The poor girl did not survive. Even though she was a little younger, I hung around the same crowd with her. Her older brother was my age. Merri had a crush on him in the seventh grade, which consisted of holding hands and a peck on the lips. My heart was aching for him and his family. When things like this happened in Tahoe it was usually a big deal, and everyone knew about it. It reminds me of the song, "Everybody dies famous in a small town."

School had been in session for about a month, and I was nose-deep in my books and assignments. Megan was gone again. She and James had gone to live with James' parents. Megan had taken her father to the Court House on a day that he was loopy from pain medicine because he had somehow broken his leg. He signed for her marriage certificate, but the next day decided that he was pissed again and didn't want to consent. He hid the marriage license only for Megan to hunt it down while he was at work. Josh, Chloe, and I followed James and Megan down the hill to Reno where we met up with James' parents who had driven in from Utah. If Megan was going to get away from her father to be with James, the marriage had to happen quickly. Megan had a last minute meltdown that almost stopped the wedding, but I convinced her that she had no choice. I had written "Congrats Megan and James!" on the back of their car. I didn't have the official car-friendly paint for this, so I figured that my lipstick tube was good enough. I was bawling my eyes out when it came time to say goodbye.

For the next month or so, Josh and I had a hard time adjusting. We had grown attached to living with our best friends. They had become family, and we were very upset that they were gone. Coming home from a long day at school, I walked into the house with Chloe in my arms - she was about four months old already. Josh was sitting on the couch talking to a man in an Army uniform. It took me by surprise, and I was hopeful that Josh was doing something drastic to get our lives going. The recruiter gave me a friendly smile and shook my hand. He began going over different career options for Josh and all of the benefits that our family would have if he joined. It sounded beyond perfect. The next step would be to take a test in a few weeks to see what he qualified for. After that, we would schedule his date to leave for basic training. Josh became overly excited, probably more for bragging rights. He told every person he knew that he was joining the military. Everyone was excited for him, and I was dreaming up a whole new life in my head. I envisioned a small white house in a safe military neighborhood. I could see myself taking care of babies - yes, BABIES... and being the housewife that I wanted to be. The whole idea was romantic. I would have a husband in the military that would come home every day in a uniform. It couldn't be more perfect.

Since Chloe was so easy to care for and Josh was joining the army, I thought to myself - this is the perfect time to have another baby! I want to get pregnant before he leaves so he knows that I won't cheat on him, and he will be able to focus on his training.

Looking back, I probably subconsciously wanted to get pregnant again to put more pressure on Josh to be more responsible. Although he worked, it just was not enough to support us. Josh's job only paid him a quarter over minimum wage. If it hadn't been for my mother, we would have been in big financial trouble. I don't know where we would have lived or how we would have fed ourselves without her. I wanted to give my mother a break, so I spent more time with Josh at his mother's house. She was happy to see more of Chloe and didn't seem to drink as much with Chloe around. Josh's test was only a few days away, and the results would determine our future.

I was getting ready to leave Hilda's house to go to school. Josh had just left with the recruiter to take his test in a town about two hours away. I was nervous for him, mainly because I knew that his untreated ADHD was the reason he did not graduate High School. I worried that it would affect him during the test. I went about my day staying close to my new cell phone that I had recently bought. Finally, right after I finished my disgusting cafeteria lunch, it rang. It was Josh. "Did you pass? What was your score?" I impatiently asked. In a casual and not very concerned tone, he replied, "No, I was three points off. I can't take it again for another two weeks. Sorry sweetie." I was so upset that I couldn't immediately respond. I was let down, worried, and completely disappointed. The test could not have been that hard. "I guess you will just have to study and try again," I said dryly.

I began to doubt Josh and what he was really going to accomplish with his life. I knew that he had potential, but it didn't seem like he was trying very hard. Another week had passed, and I had resumed staying at my mother's house. Josh went back and forth between houses, as usual. After finishing up my homework one night, I finished Josh's homework too-which he refused to complete. As I was putting both assignments away I started counting back to the day that I had my last period. After realizing that I was four days late I knew that I would have to get a test in the morning.

I did not announce this to anyone, not even Josh. It was just a suspicion, and maybe it was stress from school, work, and the whole Army ordeal. Before heading to school the next day, I stopped at the grocery store to purchase a pregnancy test. I wasn't about to steal another one like I had before. I had a baby who depended on me now and I just wasn't that person anymore. Once the test was in my possession and Chloe was buckled into her seat, the anticipation was just too much to handle. I went home and decided that Mrs. Snow would forgive me if I were late to class. Anxiously awaiting the results, I once again stared at myself in the mirror. My reflection was much different than it had been the first time. I had a new appreciation for life, and a new respect for what it really took to be a mother. I was happy with what I saw and who I had become. I was growing up. Glancing down to the counter, the pink line stared back at me and told me that Chloe would be a big sister.

Announcing this news did not have nearly the same effect as it had the first time around. Josh was the first to find out,

118

responding with an "I love it when you're pregnant!" and a hug. "So you love me when I'm fat, cause I could have just gone on a Twinkie diet!" I teased. I wasn't sure how I felt about this pregnancy. I was excited but also nervous. Josh wasn't holding his end of the bargain as much as I had hoped he would. Lilah found out next. I had told her that my period was late, and she excitedly went to purchase me another test thinking it was my first. I took the test and handed it over, knowing what the results would be. "Yep! You're pregnant!" she said. "Hey, Mom! Liz is pregnant again!" she yelled down the hallway. "Is she really?" My mom responded. My mom wasn't mad, just surprised. The only questionable reaction I received was from one of my teachers at school. She sort of cringed as if she were thinking, "What the hell is wrong with you?" All in all, I had a good amount of support. This also meant that I would really have to come up with an alternate living arrangement. It would be asking way too much of my mother to support Josh and I with a second baby. My mom was busy with her own life, and I didn't want to hassle her any more. She never implied that we were an annoyance, but it was just time to grow up.

Josh and I put our name on a waiting list for a low-income apartment complex. They only took thirty percent of your income for rent, regardless of what it was. The wait, however, would be about six months. Our other option was a townhouse community that always looked so clean and cute. It was relatively new and I liked how it was so close to school. We put in our paperwork and got a call a few days later. We had been accepted and told that we could move in right away. The only problem was that it would cost $680 a month. With Josh's job, we were only able to pay for diapers and car insurance. My mother had given me her old car when she got herself a new one. My mother had given me everything so far. She paid our first month's rent too.

Chapter 20

While I was continuing my schoolwork and suffering through terrible bouts of morning sickness, we were getting ready to move into our little one-bedroom townhouse in a few days.

The holidays were coming up, and there was so much going on all at once. I had been consistent and diligent with not only racing ahead with my schoolwork, but also altering my handwriting just enough to pull off doing Josh's homework as well. I had finally gotten to his last few assignments when Mrs. Snow announced to me that Josh was all set, and would get his diploma in June with everyone else. She wanted him to wait to get his diploma because she thought that his hard work deserved to be celebrated with a formal graduation ceremony.

Oh jeez, you have no idea lady that I did his homework, I thought to myself. As I had expected, Josh avoided the Army recruiter and did not even attempt to study for the test that he had to retake. As far as he was concerned, those exciting and hopeful days were over.

He seemed happy with working his meager job and getting nowhere. It was hard for me to accept this, and I easily blocked it out of my mind, telling myself that he was still young and would eventually grow up.

Moving day had arrived and it was time to say goodbye to the childhood bedroom that had given me many years of comfort and content. I had many life-changing moments in that room and had grown from a child to a teenager to a mother. Every happy, scary, uncertain, and beautiful day had with me falling asleep in that room. I had spent many evenings staring out of my second story window while the sun went down just thinking and dreaming of what my life would be like in ten years. From getting into sneaky trouble with my twin after our mother had fallen asleep to getting into some knockdown fights with her (and her evil bird), I was truly sad to leave, and deep down I knew that this would never be my bedroom again. I turned around with my arms full of my last straggling belongings to take a last look, and I knew that it would sink into my memory forever.

Walking into our new home for the first time, I was pleased with the cleanliness but I was displeased with the smell. It had that musty "apartment" smell. It definitely didn't have the smell I was accustomed to. We immediately began putting things away, knowing that Chloe would determine our schedule. As ten o'clock at night neared, we were just about done. I hadn't realized how many belongings we actually had. We somehow managed to acquire everything that we would need to be independent. My mom peeked in through the front door to check on me and ask if there were anything else that I would need. "No, I think we have everything." I said quietly, trying to hide the fact that I was already homesick. "Ah, Lizzy-Beth, I know you're going to miss home, but you'll be ok!" she said and rubbed my head. She almost opened the floodgates once more. I knew that this time I had to be strong and tough it out. I was devastated deep down although I had wanted this so badly only a year earlier.

Waking up in our new home the first morning was confusing for a few seconds. I knew where I was, but it didn't register that it was permanent. I had a feeling that any minute I would be back in my old room, and my life would be as it always had been. It took a week for me to adjust to my new surroundings. I tried to stay busy by going to school on time, every day, and I even took an extra college course with Lilah to help ensure that I would graduate early. Lilah was a big chicken and didn't want to face a class titled "Human Sexuality" on her own. I thought it was funny, and it would probably be interesting.

Chloe was nearing ten months old, and my belly had once again blown up on me and much quicker. I was about five months pregnant and feeling every little pain that came along with it. Josh started drinking even more, and it did not help that he was friendly with a neighbor who was his age and also drank. It frustrated me, and I wanted him to grow up so desperately. There was a night where I had chest pains so intense that I had to go to the emergency room and take Chloe with me. Josh, of course, was passed out drunk and completely useless. The on-call doctor gave me a cocktail of medications claiming that I had heartburn. I had a horrible reaction to this and ended up hallucinating in the hospital for the next six hours. I was scared and alone; my own husband didn't even try to sober up to be by my side. This made me wonder what else I would have to worry about in the future.

As school continued, I tried to continue to avoid thinking about what a loser I had married. I was still on track and getting very close to completing my last few units to graduate. It was actually going to happen a year early, and I was incredibly excited. As Mrs. Snow was going over my completed work, I spoke up and told her what I wanted. "So, my twin sister, Merri, is going to be graduating a year early too, and I thought it would be really cool if I could walk down the aisle with her. What do I need to do to make this happen?" Mrs. Snow looked somewhat surprised that I was so serious about this. "Well, Elizabeth, you would need to do your senior project. It is a lot of work, and you will have to get started right away. With you caring for Chloe and your pregnancy, are you sure this is something you want to take on?" she asked, looking concerned. "Absolutely! I really want to make this happen, and I know that I can," I reassured her. It was official. I was going to tackle my senior project and make my vision come to life. Everyone would be proud of me, and more importantly, I would be proud of myself. I was ready to prove to the world that I was more than just a statistic.

After living in our new home for only about two months, Josh and I received a call from the manager at the other complex we were interested in that offered low-income families a realistic solution to paying rent. We had finally reached the top of the list and could move in the next week. I was thrilled knowing that we would have two bedrooms. We managed to break our lease with the townhouse management and began packing for our next move right down the highway. I was six months pregnant, and it was perfect timing considering our new addition would be making an entrance soon. As I brought Chloe up the stairs to our new place, I excitedly showed her to her new room. "It's your own room Chloe! Aren't you excited?" I babbled. She gave me an adorable grin and clapped her hands. Our family unpacked in about two days, and it was exciting to settle into a place that could be more permanent because of the extra space it offered.

Our neighbors were all very friendly senior citizens, and they were very curious about Chloe and my new pregnancy. They never openly questioned my age, and I truly felt as if I were an accepted part of their small community. The downside was that Josh knew quite a few people living in the neighboring building. This encouraged his drinking habit even more. It felt like the more pregnant I became the worse his drinking became. There were several nights when he did not come home until four or five in the morning if not later. I would stay up and silently cry wondering if he was okay and wondering if he still even loved me. I could not understand why he felt it was so important to be

124

out, getting wasted, instead of being at home with his wife and daughter who loved him.

In the classroom of the senior project presentation, I was a nervous wreck. "Who in their right mind does a senior project on soup?" I asked myself. My mother had been my required chosen mentor that I worked with for the completion of the project. She was a great cook, and we thought it would be fun to experiment with soup and make a cookbook to give to the Judges when my presentation was finished.

They were all adults, and they were all successful members of the community. Most of them were business owners. They were very friendly to me despite the fact that I was eight months pregnant. After asking me what my future plans were, I replied "I am going to take college classes full-time to get my degree in nursing. I love to help people, and I have always loved the hospital environment." The Judges all seemed very impressed with my drive, and they were probably surprised that I wasn't another statistic, thus far.

I passed my project with a 95 percent, and I was thrilled that it was almost time to live out my vision of having a normal graduation. Ironically, for the graduation ceremony, all of the graduates were instructed to wait down the hill where I had attended school for the last few years. They would signal to us when it was time to start walking to the football field. I was so pregnant and so hot that I thought I might faint. Luckily, Merri was right there with me and would most likely make an attempt to catch me if I did. The band started playing the popular graduation song and in a line and standing next to our walking partner, we started moving. Once the green field came into view, my fears calmed. I began to feel proud of myself and truly in awe that I had made it this far. Sixteen, married with a baby, and another one on the way, I knew at that point that I was officially not a statistic. With our entire family in the crowd, I knew that I had met my goals and even more. Following Merri, the principle called my name and shook my hand as I happily accepted my diploma. I had officially graduated from High School and could now start my young life as an adult who would do great things. One day I would be an inspiring example to other young parents.

Chapter 21

The summer after graduation was hot and miserable. I was ready to pop and desperate to have this baby. My mom had been spending a lot of time at my apartment knowing that I needed help with anything she was willing to do.

It was a normal, hot, boring Saturday, and Josh decided to ditch the family and go fishing with Donnie. I honestly didn't care, because he was getting on my nerves anyway. My mom, Chloe and I went on a little shopping spree, and she got me my favorite combination of the pregnancy-preferred snacks that I was currently obsessing over. Once we got home and blasted the fan, I practically fell back onto the couch, ready to chug my soda and indulge in my Kit-Kat bar. It was already late afternoon, and of course, I had no update from my husband or his whereabouts. This was sadly typical behavior to be expected from him. As it started to become dark outside, I did begin to become worried and I quickly became angry knowing that he was probably just too drunk to remember to update me...again. I was extra upset because I was so pregnant and expecting to go into labor at any moment. It hurt my feelings that he just didn't care.

"RING...RING...RING..." my phone blared. It was nine o'clock at night. I had a bad feeling. Josh typically either called me by six or just showed up the next day. Rarely did I get a peak-party-hour update. Picking up the phone, I could not believe what I heard.

"Hello, is this Elizabeth? My name is Nurse Mary and I am with the Enloe hospital emergency room in Chico. Your husband, Josh, was in a roll-over car accident and flown here because he was periodically going unconscious." The nurse gave me this information as if it were an everyday conversation. I guess it was to her.

"Oh my gosh. Okay... is he going to be all right?" I asked with a trembling in my voice and my hands shaking as I gripped the phone. "Oh yes! He is doing well now. We are waiting on some simple test results, but other than that, he should be free to go home tomorrow."

After getting off the phone and calling my mother to tell what had happened, I was in a panic to get to the hospital that was five hours away to be with my husband. My mother was the only one who could take me because I had no idea where this place was and was too pregnant to go that far on my own.

"Honey, it's almost ten at night and Josh is fine. We need to wait until morning to go get him, Liz. Maybe this will teach him a lesson," my mom affirmed. She was right, and if no one rushed to his rescue, maybe it would force him to think about it even more. I felt like I was reliving that Thanksgiving night that he went to jail, except I felt a different kind of sympathy. It was an exhausted sympathy that was running out. The one thing that these two incidents had in common was alcohol.

The next day we made the long drive to get Josh. He looked beat up and hung over. I was glad that he was at least alive. I forced an explanation out of him once we got home. Apparently a tire on Donnie's truck just suddenly "fallen off" causing them to flip. That was total crap, and I knew it. I also knew that he

128

would stick to this lie to protect Donnie. He wouldn't admit that the two of them had been drunk and speeding.

The accident caused Josh to slow down on his drinking for a couple of weeks. It was good timing. I was really pregnant and really needed him to just grow the hell up.

In a desperate attempt to put my body into labor, I went on five-mile walks with Josh, gagged down castor oil and orange juice, had miserable sessions of sex, and made a pathetic attempt at jumping jacks. This baby was going to come when it was ready, and there was nothing I could do to change it. After taking a long cool shower one hot afternoon, I dried off to realize that my leg continued to stay wet. I dried it again, and it was soaked again. My water was leaking. Happy and nervous, I called my mother to come pick me up, and I called Josh at work instructing him to head over to the hospital. The nurses admitted me and ran a test to make sure I was correct, and sure enough, one of them announced "Let's put it this way; you aren't leaving this hospital without your baby in your arms."

I let out a sigh of relief. Although I knew that it would never be the same, I wanted my body back. Chloe's birth was painful, but I was confident that I could deliver Zoe without an epidural. I would be induced the next morning at 7:00. I tossed and turned the whole night in anticipation with Josh by my side. My mother spent the night so she could be with me in the morning.

Seven o'clock finally rolled around. I explained to the nurse that I just wanted to go with the flow, and if I ended up needing medication I would let her know, but I could probably do without. My mom had dropped Chloe off with Hilda, which didn't happen often because Hilda was seldom sober. When she was sober, though, she was a good grandma.

Merri was hanging around the hospital room pacing nervously. She somehow got stuck with my mother and had no way to get home. She wasn't the type to be a part of anything that was gruesome involving humans. Pets yes, but not humans. She helped out with surgeries on animals for her senior project, but that was a different story for her. By ten o'clock the pain was nearly excruciating. The pressure, once again, was overbearingly nauseating. At that point, I couldn't handle any more. "I need the epidural, like now!" I demanded to the nurse. "Well, you are already eight centimeters. I will call the anesthesiologist, but don't get your hopes up because he may not arrive in time." You have got to be absolutely kidding me, I angrily thought. I was so disappointed that it was borderline heartbreaking. The memory of the intense pain was all coming back to me full-force.

Unlike the last time, I was in a full-blown panic and scared to death of what I knew was to come. I fought it pretty hard. I really wanted no part in this ordeal - not to mention the nurse's lack of caring enough really fueled my fire. Merri became so scared of the screams coming out of my mouth that she had to face the wall and plug her ears. I later learned that she was actually in the corner of the hospital room having a full-blown panic attack.

"AAAAAAAAH!! Get this thing out of me NOW!" I wailed. I was in so much pain that screaming was the only way to release it. Finally, the Dr. had to get in my face, force me to make eye contact with her, and tell me to push instead of scream. I came to my senses and understood that she was right. On the next contraction I pushed as hard as I possibly could, and that familiar and beautiful sense of relief overcame me. It was finally over. Our new baby, another girl, was a beautiful little screamer that looked just like her sister. Her face was a little swollen from the quick entrance she made into the world, but she was gorgeous, and I was immediately in love. We had decided that if we had another girl, her name would be Zoe.

After the doctor tested my patience with stitches, and who knows what else, I was finally able to sit in a normal position and hold my baby girl. Visitors came and left, and the night fell. This time, Josh was by my side the entire time. He helped me when I asked, and he said nothing about leaving to go anywhere that surely would have led to alcohol streaming down his throat.

For once, I actually felt like we might be okay, and he might have just grown up a little bit. In the middle of the night, Zoe started to cry out of hunger. I was happy to have more confidence than I had had with Chloe. I picked the sweet, little life up from her bassinette and brought her to my chest. "I love you so much little girl. I am so happy you are here and part of our family." I whispered, as I welcomed her cuddly embrace. The most innocent creature to ever greet the planet is, without doubt, a newborn baby. A newborn is incredibly innocent and helpless. Unlike Chloe, Zoe didn't make many creaky door noises. I noticed that she had a frown on her face, and a lightning-fast thought came and left my mind all in an instant. What if she knows something that we don't? What if she foresees a sad future? The thought of anything sad that might happen to my precious little girls' lives hurt my feelings. I quickly erased it and fell asleep with her on my chest.

The next morning my mother brought Chloe to the hospital just as we were getting ready to check out. The sweetest sight that I had ever witnessed and the most symbolic sight as well, was when Chloe, with assistance at only fourteen months old, held Zoe on her lap. She became so excited that she laughed out loud. Chloe was thrilled to have her baby sister. It was almost as if she knew that her best friend had finally arrived. They were meant to be in each other's lives for more reasons than anyone will ever understand.

Bringing Zoe home was a new experience. I was lucky to have my mom's help with Chloe when Josh was working because without my mom around, I was alone with my two babies. It became a blur, but I remember asking myself, at one point, if I could handle it. Physically, I only had so many arms! Mentally I felt okay, just unsure if I would be able to keep up with the demands. My day was diaper change after diaper change, nursing Zoe, feeding Chloe, battles over naptime, and meltdowns over competing for attention. Bedtime didn't even provide any relief because I was too nervous to keep them in their own rooms. I was afraid of a variety of scenarios: someone might break in, the house would catch fire, or one of them might stop breathing...you name it and I worried about it. When Zoe had her first birthday, I finally started to feel like I was adjusting to having two babies in diapers. I had lost most of the baby weight and I started to feel like I had more energy and a better grip on the routine.

I was excited when I learned that Megan would be moving back. Apparently she was sick of Utah and couldn't stand James' mother bossing her around. I was interested to see how we would go on our joyrides with three babies in the back seat. In order to be a happy mother I needed to have a routine of getting out of the house once in a while. I was enrolled in community college courses full time, and my goal was to transfer to nursing school after two years. I was a bit nervous when college started, as I hadn't done much socializing in what felt like forever. I managed to get the girls enrolled in daycare part-time, and I had my paperwork turned in for school and my schedule set. I was approved for financial aid as well, and I knew that would help tremendously.

On my first day of school, I was nervous and sad about dropping the girls off at daycare. I was worried that the girls might flip out and think that I was abandoning them. It was definitely more difficult for me than it was for them. Chloe wandered off infatuated with the mounds of new toys and other kids, and Zoe had no idea what was going on, but she didn't cry and that is all that mattered at the moment.

My classes were laid back, and after going through each syllabus, I realized that I could easily get through them. The more I did my homework and aced my tests, the more confident I became. I was completely driven and motivated to get into

132

nursing school. I knew that I loved to help people, and I had a way of putting myself into other people's shoes. My first round of final exams had come and gone, and, eager as hell to know how I had done, I pulled up my grades online. Three As, and one B! I was so excited that I let out the most high-pitched, girly scream that was totally foreign to me. "Sorry...!" I said to Josh. He was startled and looked my way, annoyed. I had proven myself right once again and beaten the odds. I was a mother, a housewife, and a full-time student and doing all of these tasks exceptionally well. Life couldn't be better. Except for Josh. I knew deep down that if I ever wanted to offer my babies a good life, I was going to have to do the hard work and become independently successful. Josh didn't have the drive that it took, and his drinking problem was getting worse by the day.

Our marriage felt childish, and fake. The more he drank and the more he failed to come home at a decent hour, the more respect I lost for him. Josh was still a boy. By no means was he ready to be a man and really be around to support his family. I was not ready to leave Josh, but it was fun to daydream about other options. Maybe I let myself daydream too much. Each time Josh brought the bottle to his mouth, I fantasized even more about finding a person to be with who could genuinely take care of me and the girls. I wanted a normal family environment, and I was so sick of worrying each night whether or not Josh was going to come home, or if I would get a knock on my door from authorities stating that he was dead. If he had ended up joining the Army and dying in combat, at least it would've been an honorable death and his girls would grow up proud, knowing that their dad died a hero. Dying from the resulting damage of getting behind the wheel while drunk was the absolute opposite of heroic. It was shameful and selfish.

I began to realize that it was becoming more and more unfair for the girls and myself to base our lives around his drinking and the stupidity that came along with it. I called a local recovery center to inquire about treatment for Josh. "You can't force your husband to come to treatment, and unless it is Court ordered, there is nothing we can do. He needs to come in himself and agree to stay." I sighed and thanked the lady for the information. There was no way in hell he would agree to stay in treatment. It was so easy for me to just want to give up on him. It would be one less thing to worry about if he wasn't in my life. Of course, I would always want him to be a part of Chloe and Zoe's lives, but I was tired of babysitting a now twenty-two year old man. He was clearly not going to grow up any more.

Chapter 22

The holidays came and went, I was in my second semester of college, and Megan, James, and their daughter, Kylee, had moved into the apartment complex a few buildings down from us. We were happy to be neighbors and began hanging out like the old days. It was good for Josh to have a friend that wasn't a raging alcoholic. Megan and I managed to squeeze all three of the girls into the back seat of the car any time we wanted to go somewhere. Kylee was between Chloe and Zoe's ages. It was adorable lining them up from biggest to smallest. We no doubt resembled a teenage version of the Desperate Housewives.

We were bored with the same stuff happening on a daily basis and our husbands became boring. We got out of the house and left them together as much as possible. Eventually we thought it would be entertaining to find some guys to flirt with. We didn't intend on moving an inch past flirting. One sunny (but icy) afternoon, Megan needed to stop at the tire shop to get a flat tire repaired. Sure enough, Josh was working his usual shift. Of course, Donnie and Derrick were also working. Donnie instantly started to flirt with Megan. It was obvious that she was entertained by the attention of a thirty-two year-old. I assumed she was just playing along. And go figure, Derrick, whom I had written off as a total pervert, was attempting to get any reaction out of me that he possibly could. "So Elizabeth, how should I break up with Macy? She is just too dumb for me. I need someone smart like you." he said. "I don't know, just tell her she is a total idiot and you never want to see her face again." I said, annoyed. "Daaaamn girl, ouch!"

I wanted Derrick to think that I was not a nice person, even though I was. I wanted him to not like me and to not hit on me. It backfired and made him want me even more - now I was a challenge to him, and he would be on an intense mission to make me his. "I'm married with two kids." I pointed to the back seat as he was loitering. He smiled, then laughed and walked away. "Come see me when you're eighteen!" he yelled. This man had no shame! With my husband directly behind us, and knowing that he wouldn't say anything, Derrick blabbered on. I felt bad for Josh, and I knew that it really took a hit to his self-esteem. On the drive home, I said to Megan, "I don't know... Derrick is cute and everything, but I just have a bad feeling about him that I can't quite pinpoint." "Really? That's weird. I don't think he's that bad," Megan said.

As the winter months dragged on, Megan and I had a bad case of cabin fever. Eventually she and Donnie exchanged numbers as friends. This led to us making secret stops at their house on a daily basis. We never got out of her truck; the guys were beyond happy to come outside and hang on the car doors and chat. Their house was a dump. It was on a dirt road that shared the same property as an abandoned trailer. I later learned that they were growing massive amounts of marijuana in the trailer. Megan and I ditched our husbands when we could get away with it and snuck to their house as much as we could. I hated Derrick hitting on me like a sick pervert, but subconsciously I liked the attention. Josh didn't know how to make me feel that way. Josh wanted sex and dinner and that was it. He would never have a serious conversation with me.

136

Finally, one night, after Josh had been drinking for eight hours, I just couldn't take it anymore. If you can't beat 'em, join 'em. I gave in, opened a wine cooler, and sat down at the kitchen table to play cards with his friends. I was willing to go to whatever extent it took to either give Josh the wake-up call that he needed or just get it over with. I caught a buzz and became flirty. I figured this would result in one of two things - Josh would man up and ask his friends to leave so we could have a serious talk, or he would feel sorry for himself because of the drunken mess that he had become and do nothing to help the dilemma. Josh noticed my harmless flirting and embarrassed us both. He sat in the corner and dropped his head, slurring profanities at me, and then caved in to a drunken sob. He couldn't possibly have been aware of what he was doing or saying with how intoxicated he was. Chloe and Zoe were in bed asleep, and I knew that if I bolted out of the house before he could catch me, Josh would have no choice but to stay home until I returned. Slightly drunk, I did just that. Because it was 1:00 in the morning, I was really unsure of exactly where I was going. I suddenly wanted to go to Derrick's house to see what would happen if I showed maybe a tiny bit of interest, but I didn't think he would be awake.

I slowly drove past his house, and I saw the reflection of the glaring TV - someone was awake! Thrilled, I pulled in and drove down the bumpy dirt driveway. I assumed that it would be Donnie that was awake as well as wasted, which was his usual routine. After knocking on the sliding glass door, Derrick opened the curtains, and with his eyes wide in shock, he smiled and told me to come in. Looking me over, he said, "Look at you, hottie, what are you doing awake right now? Isn't it past your bed time?" I shrugged. "Josh is a total idiot, and I just can't stand it anymore. It's just not going to work. He is a full-blown alcoholic, he never helps with the girls when I need to do homework, and it is like having a third child. He just won't grow up!" I ranted. "I knew this all along," he gloated. "I knew that one day you wouldn't be able to handle it and you would show up at my house and knock on the door in the middle of the night!" I socked him playfully on the arm. As much of a pervert as he was, I was impressed with his ability to hold a serious conversation. He actually had some knowledge and insight. He was starting to grow on me with each passing minute.

We sat on the couch as he finished watching his movie. It was some sort of a boring action movie. Testing the waters, he decided to get complacent as he laid his head on my lap. I put my hand on his head as a green light. Before we knew it, we were making out with him on top of me on the old, beat up couch. I just wanted to feel like an adult, being loved by an adult. Now THIS was a man, I thought - physically and mentally.

One thing led to another, and it happened. I officially cheated on my husband whom I vowed in front of God, family, and Chloe, to always be true to. The sign that it was really over for me was that I didn't feel bad. I was more excited that I had the chance to see what else was out there, and in my mind, at that moment, Derrick was much more than I thought him to be. I instantly fell in love with him.

By now it was around four in the morning. We were hungry and decided to take a drive and get breakfast at the casino. Now eighteen and in my pajamas with pigtails, I fearlessly sat down at the Wheel of Fortune game and tried my luck with a twenty dollar bill that Derrick gave me. I thought that it was so cool that he could just spare an extra twenty dollars. To me, in my world, that was a lot of money that could go pretty far. Lucky me; I won $220. I thought this was an awesome sign and offered to buy breakfast. After dropping Derrick off at home so he could get ready for work, I headed over to my mother's house where Josh had dropped the girls off. I was very tired and feeling hung over. As I was lifelessly lying on my mother's living room floor, Josh knocked on the door. I had nothing to say to him. I began to feel guilty, and it was too much to handle. I just ignored him.

"Elizabeth, I know what you did last night," he accused. "This is your last chance to talk to me because I have someone else who wants me and will treat me better." I still did not respond though adrenaline was pumping through my veins. I had a feeling that I knew who he was referring to. It was a fifteen-year-old girl named Alena whom Megan had been hanging around with.

As soon as Josh left, I called Megan and demanded to know what was going on. To my surprise, Alena answered the phone. "What do you want, you stupid whore? Oh, and by the way, your kids are ugly. My baby is way prettier!" she childishly sang. "Oh please, little girl. Where is Megan?" I heard Megan scolding Alena for answering the phone. "Megan, what is going on?" "They were flirting earlier today, but nothing serious," she said, Why would you care anyway - aren't you with Derrick now?" she accused. "I don't know what is going on, but regardless, you are supposed to be my friend! I guess I really have no idea who you are!" I screamed, hanging up the phone with tears streaming down my face. I had a million emotions going on all at once, and I didn't know how to process them. I went outside and lit up a cigarette. I had not smoked up until then. The nicotine made me happy, and I went down the street and bought a carton.

Later that evening, while battling with Josh over the phone, I was tormented by sex noises coming from the background. I assumed it was to give me unmanageable grief. I was at a loss, and there was no bargaining. There was no way to make it better with Josh. We had both done each other wrong, and the damage was too severe. I had reached the point of just wanting to go home and work it out for the girls' sake. Josh was not being reasonable and could not even bite his tongue for one second to let me talk. I could hear Alena and Megan egging him on. I was sad that my best friend had suddenly turned on me and I really didn't know why. She was the one constantly wanting to go flirt with the brothers, and now she was stabbing me in the back.

I was close to a meltdown when Derrick called me at the end of the day. "What's up? Are you okay?" He genuinely asked. "Not really… just a bunch of drama." I said. "Well, hey, let me buy you dinner tonight. Do you want to go down to Route 395 Grill in Carson?" "Hell, yeah!" I replied. Getting off the hill and away from all of the mixed emotions sounded like heaven. I packed up Chloe and Zoe and picked up Derrick. He was clearly already comfortable around me and talked about work and life at home with his brother. We arrived at the restaurant, and without hesitation, Derrick got out of his seat and opened the back door where Chloe was sitting. He helped her out and held her hand to cross the street. As I was carrying Zoe, who was about thirteen months old, my heart melted and this made me want Derrick even more. It seemed like he naturally knew what to do, and that would be necessary if I were to have another relationship.

Chapter 23

Our barbeque dinner was delicious and sitting with Derrick and my girls felt natural. He took initiative and helped chase down the girls when they began to get bored at the table and stray. He even shared pieces of his dinner with Zoe. Either he had experience with children or it was a big show to melt my heart -and of course it did. "How are you so great with kids? I had no idea you had this side!" I said, teasingly. I squeezed Chloe's adorable two-year-old cheeks "Derrick is so good with waddle ones isn't he?" I said in a baby voice. "Yeah!" Chloe responded. She was my girl and always vouched for mommy. We had dined outside on the patio, and although it was a little chilly, the heat-lamps above us were soothing and romantic. After eating until our stomachs hurt, we had to head back up the hill to get the girls put to sleep. It was getting late and at that rate, they wouldn't be in bed until eleven at night.

I had Derrick drive us back. I hated driving in the dark, and I didn't have my glasses with me. He drove cautiously, and I respected that. Josh always drove wild and free just like his ADHD. Driving in the dark, the girls passed out, and I started wondering out loud how I would get into my apartment. "Josh somehow stole my only key, and I know for a fact that he isn't going to give it to me." I said. "Just stay away from Megan's apartment!" he warned. "You know Josh is there and screwing that little fifteen-year-old. You're going to wind up in jail if you don't listen to me." I figured he was probably right, but it was not fair for Josh to take this out on his innocent daughters. They needed their jammies, diapers, and wipes; I had nothing for them to wear at my mothers' house. It was the whole principle of the matter that bothered me.

After driving for thirty minutes, we pulled into Derrick's driveway so I could switch places and get the girls to bed. When I got out of the car, he met me at the hood and grabbed me by the waist. Quietly, he whispered, "Girl, don't make me fall in love with you just to hurt me. If you're going to hurt me, just get it over with." He lifted my chin and slowly kissed me. It was a long, passionate kiss, one that I had never experienced. It was a true kiss; a kiss that he put his feelings into. "I'm not going to hurt you." I promised. "Trust me, I've made my mind up about how I feel. I wouldn't be throwing my marriage away if I was questioning how I feel about you." He kissed me again. This time, longer, harder, and more passionately than before. He kissed me like he really meant it. I kissed him back even harder. Before it got too out of hand, he gently pushed me away. "Now go get those girls in bed, and don't go to jail or I'll be pissed." he demanded. "All right, I won't. Call me tomorrow. Okay? And thanks for dinner." I smiled sensually and walked back to my car.

Pulling out of the driveway, I knew it was game time. No guy was going to screw me, or my daughters, by denying us our basic needs. Without thinking twice, I headed straight for my apartment complex, knowing that I was getting that damn key, no matter what it took.

As I pulled into the parking lot, I dialed Josh's cell number. The lights were on in Megan's apartment, and it was obvious that a good time was going on. "What do you want, bitch?" Josh answered. "Josh, I don't want to fight with you. I want to stay civil, and I just need you to let me into the apartment so I can get diapers and clothes for the girls," I pleaded. "I'm busy with better

142

things and a better girl. You ain't getting anything!" He slurred. As I had anticipated, he was drunk. No surprise there. I pulled up in front of Megan's apartment and turned my bright lights on. When no one came out, I began flashing the lights. My adrenaline was pumping full-force. My heart was racing with rage. Alena walked out in her fifteen-year-old pigtails wearing fluffy slippers. She stopped on the grassy hill and put her arms in the air as if she were a gangster from the hood. "Your man would rather be with a real woman! You don't deserve him. He's mine now, bitch!"

I laughed to myself and came to my senses. If I were to accept her invitation for a fight, I would surely go to jail. I was legally an adult, and she was still an idiotic kid. If I were going to end up in jail, I was going to at least do it with a bang. I had the common courtesy to keep my affair quiet. I knew that making a statement and rubbing it into Josh's face would surely be far too hurtful. As angry as I was, I wouldn't have wished that kind of pain on anyone. Even though we were fighting and it was over, I still loved Josh. I knew that a part of me always would. He gave me the most beautiful gifts that any person could ever ask for. For that, there will always be a sense of appreciation.

Josh finally walked out of the apartment and down the grassy hill. I knew right away that he would not have the ability to reason with me especially because he had been drinking. Defeated and praying for an ounce of empathy, I calmly asked him, "Josh, the girls are sleeping, I just need their things. You don't even have to let me in - will you just get me their things, please?" Almost in tears, I looked him in the eyes. "Nope! You screwed up, and I'm not doing shit for you!" he yelled. I made a third attempt, then fourth attempt, and just like the time I hit the girl with the plastic softball bat my patience ran dry. Alena came closer to the parking lot and started to yell. "Josh! Get away from that nasty hoe! Let's finish where we left off, do you know what I mean?" This little girl was a terrible instigator.

Whether what she was saying was true or not, it cut me like a knife. It cut me deep. Josh looked over at her, "Hang on sweetie, I'll be there in a minute." Sweetie? SWEETIE? This is the value he places on that word? The first pet name any man had ever given to me? HELL NO! I raged to myself. Completely losing any sense of time or place, I slammed my car into reverse and backed up about five feet. Josh was standing against his car, and I aimed my front bumper right toward him. "Give me the key for our girls and give it to me now!" I screamed. Josh stood there unphased. I inched my way toward him and his precious car slowly but aggressively.

I was so close he almost didn't have room to make his way out of the metal gap. "I'm giving you a fair warning, Josh! If you don't give me that key RIGHT NOW, I am going to hit your car!" I devilishly yelled. "You're not getting the damn key!" he screamed. He must not have truly known what I was capable of at that moment. Out of his own anger, he kicked my side mirror so hard that it flew off and was hanging by the wires. "Go to your mother's house, you stupid bitch!" he violently yelled. "That's it, you stupid, lowlife piece of crap! I gave you a chance, and I warned you!"

Slamming the car into reverse even harder this time, I backed up about ten feet. I sat for a moment, giving him one last chance to hand over the key. When he clearly didn't expect me to do what I had threatened, I released the brake. I gassed the car just enough to make it lurch forward, but not enough to cause a rough impact. I was able to put a nice dent in the side of his car, but it just wasn't enough. I wanted his whole car to be completely shattered, just as my feelings were. I backed up again and gave it another whack, a little harder. I still wasn't satisfied, but I knew that I had to get out of there because someone was probably calling the cops. I reversed my car one last time, knowing the last time would be the best. I slammed my front end into his

144

passenger side door, and gave it the damage I was hoping for. When I was finished, my heart was pounding and my entire body was numb with adrenaline. I pulled out onto the quiet highway, expecting to be pulled over any moment. I laughed as I saw the police drive right past me and turn into the apartment complex. I was hoping that I would at least make it to my mother's house before being arrested. I was so outraged that I had completely forgotten that my sleeping babies were in the back seat of the car. They stayed sleeping and quiet the whole time. Fear rushed through me as I pulled into my mothers' driveway. I had officially been a bad mother that night. I lost my mommy innocence. I royally screwed up, and I fully knew it.

I turned off the car and unbuckled the girls from their seats. When I walked inside, my mom was just getting ready for bed. "What's up, sweet pea?" she asked. "Is everything okay? It's pretty late." The girls heard their Grandma's voice and became alert. They both loved her, and wanted to wake up to play. I was exhausted, mentally and emotionally. I set them down, and took my sweater off from the heat of my boiling blood. "Oh, nothing. I went to dinner then tried to get the key from Josh. He wouldn't give it to me and we got into a really bad fight. He messed up my car, and the cops might be coming." I calmly lied. I didn't want to give her all of the details in case the cops didn't show up. I could possibly get away with it, but I doubted it. "Well, if he messed up your car, why would the cops come for you?" she questioned. "That's true. You know what? I think I am going to call the cops on him right now." I decidedly announced. "Liz, are you sure it is that bad?" she asked. "Yes, it's that bad," I replied.

I had a great plan - I would call the police on him, and they would have to believe me. I would simply tell them that I thought my car was in reverse when I drove into his car. I was so scared and frazzled from his yelling that I just wanted to get out of there! My plan was going to work like a charm. Fifteen minutes had passed and I was wondering if the police were even going to show up at all. I was able to find some pajamas for the girls in the diaper bag and got them cozy and ready for bed. I was tired and just wanted to get the police interview over with. My mother was waiting up with me but she looked exhausted and unsure.

"BANG, BANG, BANG! It's the police! Open up!" a man with a deep, authoritative voice demanded. "What the hell? They are seriously rude. It is late and I didn't do anything wrong!" I whined. Fixing my hair before opening the door, I took my time to unlatch the lock. "Hi, come in!" I sweetly said, in an attempt to butter them up. Only two men walked in, although I knew that more were out there assessing my car. Immediately upon entering, the taller officer demanded to know "Are you Elizabeth Jeter?" "Yes sir." I replied, with the highest attempt of maturity that I could. "So, what kind of drugs are you taking?" he immediately and coldly asked. "I'm not..." I began. "Just cut the bullshit and tell me what you're on!" he interrupted. Tears began flooding from my eyes. I was so offended that he accused me of using drugs that I had always stayed far away from. "I am not on any drugs! Drug test me RIGHT NOW!" I screamed at him. I must have been convincing, as he quickly changed his tone.

"Okay, well I believe that you're not on drugs. Any person who is on drugs never offers to take a drug test." I nodded to affirm his statement. "I am Officer Michaels and this is my partner, Officer Herald. Now, we need to ask you some questions. But if you lie to us, we'll know it, and you will go to jail right away. If you just tell us the truth, we can work with you. Okay?" he stated. "Yeah, of course. I'll be glad to tell you the truth," I said, gaining a small bit of confidence back.

Officer Michaels went to the back of the house to speak with my mother and to inquire about Zoe and Chloe. Officer Herald would be the one to question me. We sat down on the stools near the kitchen breakfast area. He took out his notepad and began to question me about the entire incident, start to finish. I recalled

146

the events truthfully until it came to the demolition derby that I had initiated. What I didn't know was that I had already incriminated myself with a statement that I assumed to be innocent. "Where were Zoe and Chloe when you pulled into the parking lot to get the key?" he sympathetically asked, playing a definite "good cop" role. "Oh, they were sleeping in the back seat. They didn't wake up at all through all of the yelling, and I was so happy for that!" I idiotically replied. As we progressed into the interview, I answered his questions confidently with the innocent lie I had concocted to save my ass. "Elizabeth, I like you, but that is total bullshit. Just tell me the damn truth so we can get out of here and resume our night!" He begged. He sensed my stubbornness. He knew that he had to get me to trust him and get to my level if I were to fess up to anything.

Tears began rolling down my face. I refused to admit that I was that stupid. I was even afraid to admit it to myself. "When Josh was between you and his car, did you want to run him over - because he thought that you were going to kill him," he asked. "Of course not! I would never kill a person!" I said. I saw the look on his face. BINGO. He had all of the information that he needed. Oh God. Dear God. I prayed, silently. Please don't let me go to jail. I'll never do anything bad ever again. Please, please, just one more chance! I was not that kind of person. I didn't belong in jail. I was not a bad statistic. Everything would be fine, and like the officer promised, if I just told the truth, they would be moving on with their night. I didn't think that would include taking me for a ride in the back seat.

The taller officer came into the kitchen area and when Officer Herald gave him a nod he said to me, "Elizabeth, I need you to stand up." Well, what the heck. Maybe it's just a sobriety test. Don't you get tackled to the ground when you go to jail? I pounced up and flipped my hair, "Okay, can I help you?" I asked. He looked at me like I was a total retard. "Turn around, and place your hands behind your back." Oh shit. This is not happening. This is one of those scare tactics you see in those boot camp shows.

147

They are totally going to let me go. They just want to teach me a lesson. I bargained. As I felt the heavy, metal cuffs tighten around my tiny wrists, the floodgates opened again. "You are being charged with felony vandalism and felony child cruelty. You have the right to remain silent. Anything you say can and will be held against you in a Court of Law..." Child cruelty? Isn't that a bit extreme? What the hell! They were SLEEPNG!!! I screamed, inside my head. As the police officer finished reading me my rights, my mom looked at me helplessly. "It's going to be okay honey; just do what they say," she said as she attempted to offer me reassurance. "But what about Chloe and Zoe? My babies need me!" I said while sniffling between each heartbroken word. "They'll be fine, Lizzy; I'll take care of them," my mom promised in a broken voice and also on the verge of tears. Helplessly, I walked ahead, with no shoes on, and no faith remaining in myself as a person, a daughter, and most painfully, a mother. I was not going down without a fight. I had an idea.

Chapter 24

Before directing me over to the patrol car, the officers lead me to my vehicle, which was parked under my mother's carport. "We just need you to sign this to verify that we have made a report on the damages to your vehicle." "Um...okay. What does signing this do exactly? In case you're wondering, I am not okay with what he did, and I am not going to let him get away with these damages. He is just as guilty as I am!" I practically yelled. I was trying hard to fight back the tears so the officers would at least take me seriously; the only other way I could express my emotions was to raise my voice. "What are my options? I want to press charges against him." I thought back to when Josh was drunk on Thanksgiving, not too long ago, wreaking havoc in my mother's home. "I want to put a citizen's arrest on Josh. Can't I do that?" I pleaded. The police officers shrugged their shoulders with the realization that I was legally allowed to do this.

As they radioed in my request to the other officer who was across town investigating Josh's side of the story, I was happy that at least he would go to jail too, and the girls wouldn't be stuck with him or his alcoholic mother. That was my main motive for the request. I knew that Chloe and Zoe would be much less traumatized over the ordeal while I was gone if they could be with their Grandmother whom they loved and trusted... for who knows how long. My naïve brain was thinking that I would be out in no time. A quick process, finger printing, and maybe a mug shot would send me on my way.

The drive to the police station was a quiet one. The officers didn't try to make small talk, and I was wondering how many intoxicated idiots had puked in the same seat that I was uncomfortably sitting in. The seat was completely plastic, no cushion or anything! What if I had a broken tailbone? These cop cars should really be better equipped for their detainees, I thought.

Pulling into the police station wasn't a big deal. I began to get nervous, though, when a big, metal garage door opened, and the car slowly rolled in. The officers stepped out of the front of the car and opened my door. They reminded me to go slow so I didn't hit my head on the edge of the door above me. I had to balance my way out. I was immediately grossed out that I had no shoes on and was walking on concrete floors that had probably endured the worst of the worst. About twenty steps later I was escorted into the booking room.

To my left there were two desks with officers sitting at them, and straight ahead was a wall with blue padding on it. The officers played a generic recording for me to listen to about fessing up if I was hiding any kind of weapon or contraband like needles or anything that could potentially hurt the officers while they were searching me. There was nothing in my pockets so I didn't attentively listen to the static-sounding recording. Feeling somewhat humiliated, a female officer asked me to face the wall and stand with my arms wide out and my legs apart. She thoroughly searched my pockets and all other nooks and crannies that could have been hiding anything illegal. She even searched my hair. Obviously, she didn't realize that I had no idea what was going on. When the search was done, I was asked to remove my earrings, my belly button ring, and the hair tie wrapped around my wrist that I kept for bedtime. They put my belongings in a little plastic bag and had me sign a form with the inventory.

I was led to one of the desks where an officer asked me several questions about my identity, sexual preference, race, gender (well, duh), and religious affiliation. I was also asked if I were a part of any gangs. I almost laughed, knowing that any gang in Tahoe was a ridiculous attempt to be hard, and it must suck walking around with guns and spray paint in fifteen degree weather. After about fifteen minutes, my interview was over and the officer explained to me what I was being charged with and what my bail was going to be. "Okay, Miss Elizabeth. You are being charged with child endangerment, a misdemeanor, and vandalism, a felony. Your bail is set to fifteen thousand dollars. You think you'll bail out tonight?" the officer asked. When he spoke the words child endangerment" my heart sank and I felt the most disappointing feeling I had ever experienced. "I really don't think that anyone I know can pay that kind of money to get me out of here." I thought out loud. This is when it hit me that I was definitely going to be stuck spending the night in jail. The place smelled like urine, and I desperately wanted this to be a nightmare. I somehow managed to compose myself and go through the booking process with as much dignity as I could muster while being respectful to the officers with secret hopes that they had the authority to set me free.

After the police had finished their welcome ceremony with me, I was put in a holding cell to make an attempt to find a way to bail out. I did not know that the holding cell was for this reason only. I figured it was where I would stay the entire time. Walking into the cold room, and hearing the heavy metal door slam, I quickly came to realize that jail was exactly what I imagined it to be - minus the bars you see on television. I was surrounded by a beige-colored 8x10' cell with walls that appeared to be painted bricks. The wall to my left had a built-in concrete bench that extended into an L shape, reaching

151

the wall in front of me. I guessed that this was made to accommodate more than one offender. In the right corner was a toilet area with a small wall of bricks to just barely block the officers from having to see someone use the toilet. On the wall on my right was a pay phone with a cord that was about five inches long. I was annoyed that I had to keep my face so close to the keypad, which was surely previously poked at by some messed up people who had their grimy hands on who-knows-what beforehand.

"To make a collect call located in the United States, dial one," said a generic recording of an operator. Even the operator sounded depressed. I dialed the number to my mother's house. I had only three minutes to find any sort of comfort possible. "Are you doing okay, Lizzy-Beth?" she worriedly asked. "I'm okay. I only have three minutes, and my bail is fifteen thousand dollars. They are charging me with child endangerment and vandalism. I don't think they are going to let me out tonight," I cried. "Just hang in there. The girls are doing fine and they are asleep. We'll figure it out. It is just temporary, okay? The Judge will probably let you out in a few days." She was trying to assure me. I started crying harder - to the point of doing that irritating sniffling and gasping thing that interrupts your speech and makes you sound like a desperate child. "I don't have a few days! Chloe and Zoe need me! This is such bullshit and they need to let me..." "Your call has ended, goodbye," announced the operator. I silently finished my sentence.

There was nothing left to do but wait. I stared at the sign above the phone. It was a list of hundreds of bail bondsmen and their phone numbers. I was too embarrassed to give them a call. Not that I could afford it anyway. It was 2:00 in the morning, and I was physically and emotionally drained. My hands felt sticky from holding onto the pay phone as if it were a lifeline. I wondered where the sink was - if there was one at all. Cautiously

152

inching toward the metal toilet, I was stunned to see that the sink was a part of it. The toilet and sink were the same entity, with the sink in the place where the top of a toilet would normally be. I was utterly disgusted. The faucet wasn't a faucet, either. It was a drinking fountain. This was the most foreign and intimidating fixture that I had ever encountered.

I once learned that feces particles have the ability to fly up to twenty feet if the toilet is flushed with the lid open. This toilet had no lid so I had no doubt there was feces on the drinking fountain. There were no paper towels either, so I had no way of pushing the button to wash my hands, one at a time, without re-infecting them. I carefully held the button down with my pinkie finger and tried my best to clean up.

I walked over to the bench, as I would have on a formal occasion, to sit. My posture was straight; I was at the edge of the seat, hands in my lap. I really didn't want to have to touch anything more. It was just so dirty. It made me feel contaminated. The cell was already bright, and the hallway was even brighter. I closed my eyes. I heard the echoing voices of the officers making small talk. When I opened my eyes I noticed the unwanted leering of two ugly male inmates peeking in my cell window to get a glimpse of a young girl. I was already frightened enough. The two men had mops and buckets and were cleaning the other holding cells. I was surprised that they were ever cleaned.

"Jeter!" a correctional officer demanded, as he poked his head in my cell. "Yes?" I stood up anxiously like a sad puppy wanting to be adopted from a shelter. "Do you want a hygiene kit?" he asked. "Yes, please. Also, is there a way to get my sweater or something? I am really cold in here." I begged. "Yeah, I'll toss you a blanket." he mumbled.

My hygiene kit was confusing. It was a big plastic cup with a lid. I peeled off the plastic lid and pulled out a toothbrush and the smallest tube of toothpaste I had ever seen. There was also a bar of soap, a razor with one blade, a two-inch pencil, a piece of paper, and a quarter-sized stick of deodorant. I had no use for any of that. The only thing I wanted was my freedom and a way to go back in time. Just a few hours back was all I needed. I prayed as I dozed off under the itchy wool blanket.

What must have been about an hour later but felt more like five minutes, a female officer unlocked the cell door and double-checked to make sure I wasn't going to bail out. Half asleep, she instructed me to step out of the cell and follow the blue line down the hallway. I stayed as much on the line as I could. I didn't want to get in trouble if I accidentally inched off of it. The officer was extra nice, and asked me if it was my first time there.

She brought me into a room with piles of clothing and two big bins. She had a clipboard with my information on it and copies of my charges. "What size are you?" she asked. I was confused again because I did not think I would have to wear some other clothes on top of everything else. "Probably a medium" I half whispered. She walked behind a glass window and pulled down piles of clothes. She brought back a big green bin with a folded blanket, a sheet, and a towel. She handed me a small stack of clothing that included bright orange pants, a bright orange shirt, a white t-shirt, a pair of socks, a sports-bra with the size drawn on it, a baggy-looking pair of granny-panties, and a pair of bright blue slipper-shoes that looked similar to the clown shoes used for bowling. I prayed that the underwear was not used.

She instructed me to remove all of my clothing and put it into a green net-fabric bag that was hanging on the wall. She offered me the respect of looking at her clipboard as I undressed and awkwardly navigated my tiny body into the baggy shirts, and evidently recycled underwear. The clothes were stiff and definitely didn't smell like my beloved laundry soap. All that was left to put on was my issued socks and shoes. I slipped on the

154

socks, which were a straight tube shape. They did not have a designated space for my heel. THOSE SEAMS! Again, my childhood pet peeve was back to torture me! I laughed at the idea of sitting on the floor and spinning them around my toes for an hour but thought that I might end up in a padded room if I repeated that behavior here.

All dressed in my lovely new attire, the female officer had me walk into the hallway and follow the blue line all the way to the end of the building. We arrived in an oval shaped, dome-style area with eight blue metal doors, each with a letter painted on them. The door that was painted with an H was the door I would be walking through. It automatically unlocked when we walked closer, and I wondered where her remote control was or where the spy was that knew to let us in.

Walking into H pod was a blur. It was the middle of the night so the lights were dimmed. On the first floor were several metal tables with built-in metal stools. To my left I noticed blue rubber-looking chairs lined up in front of a small, thirty-inch T.V. mounted on the brick wall. I was surprised to see a television set at all. There was a row of more blue doors on the first floor marked with numbers seventeen through thirty-two. The officer informed me that I would be getting my own cell, which was up the stairway. At that point, I didn't know what a luxury it was to have my own cell.

I hiked up the metal stairway, holding my bin of nothing, and was led to room number two. Again, the door automatically opened. I walked in and set my bin on the metal desk to the left of the concrete bench with green padding on it, which would be where I would sleep. I was wondering where my pillow was, but I was too scared to ask. She kindly, and somewhat compassionately, explained to me that breakfast would be at 6:30 a.m. and the on-duty officer would announce it over the loudspeaker. She told me that the first announcement, 5:45 a.m. was only for inmates who took medication, so I didn't have to wake up for that. The last thing she did before

155

leaving me on my own was hand me an orange inmate manual which carried the rules and regulations of the jail. My cell door closed and locked, and I was left in silence.

I searched through my bin to see if there was a pillow under the other linens. No pillow. I discovered an extra set of clothes and a teal colored nightgown. It was huge, and I really didn't want to change again. I took my orange shirt off and decided that I would just sleep in my new outfit because I would be getting out soon anyway. I made my so-called bed and stared at more bricks. The light in my cell was on, and I really wanted it off. I looked everywhere for the light switch, but it must have been hidden somewhere because it was nowhere to be found. I lay down again and kicked my shoes off. As I pulled the blanket over my legs, I stared at the ceiling, dumbfounded. I first thought about Chloe and Zoe and cried because I was supposed to be with them to make sure they were cozy and asleep. I was supposed to be there when they woke up in the morning. I was supposed to get them ready for daycare and put their hair in pigtails. I was their mother, and I was in jail! Tears rolled down my cheeks and I silently cried, my heart aching with guilt. I thought about Josh. It was sinking in that our four-year relationship, including two years of marriage and a beautiful family, was over. I cried harder. I cried because I had tried so hard. I cried because I still loved him. I cried because he broke my heart. I cried because I broke his.

Chapter 25

"Pill call! Everyone up for pill call!" said a stern sounding officer over the intercom. When I opened my eyes and comprehended that I really was in jail, my heart sank. Again. I was so incredibly exhausted, and I just wanted to block everything out of my mind. I quickly fell back asleep. After what felt like three minutes, the same voice was back to announce breakfast. I was supposed to get up.

As fast as I could, I rose off the padded concrete bed and made sure my hair wasn't frizzy or sticking up. I peeked out of the tiny 4"x2' window built into the door to see nothing but a guard rail. I guessed that I should walk out when I saw whoever was in the cell to my right walk past me. I heard the echoing clicks of the doors unlocking all at once, then loud chaos. I did not think that this H pod would be so full of inmates. When my neighbor left her cell, I opened my heavy door and walked down the upstairs walkway. Almost instantly, a woman on the first floor yelled at me to go back into my cell and put my orange shirt on. I ran in and did as she instructed. I really didn't think that it would be a big deal to not wear the ugly thing, but I guess it was part of the rules. Making a second attempt to walk down to the first floor was also a failure. Another inmate informed me that I had to go back into my cell and put my shoes on. Still half asleep, I walked back to my cell and followed her advice.

I finally made it to the first floor and picked up a tray full of mush and burnt sausage links that resembled cat poop. I timidly stepped over to one of the metal tables where three other tired and miserable looking women were sitting. I noticed that they had forgotten to put a fork on my tray, and I was fed up. I asked the woman sitting across from me if she knew where the forks were. She laughed and said that we don't get forks. "The only eating utensil allowed is a plastic spoon. And make sure not to throw it away either, or they will make the whole pod dig through the trash and you'll have a bunch of people pissed off at you." "Good to know," I replied, without looking up. I swirled the mushy hot cereal around the tray with my spoon. "Do you know if we are allowed to have pillows? And where are the light switches in the cells?" I just had to know what was going on. The woman laughed again. "We don't get to have pillows in jail, and they never completely turn the lights off. They have to do count in the middle of the night and need to be able to see that you are in your cell." "Oh..." I replied with a blank stare on my face. Clearly, I was a rookie. This is probably why the other inmates were extra patient with me - and my ridiculous questions.

I suddenly became aware of how thirsty I was. Breakfast came with a carton of milk, but I never drink straight milk. It was a cereal thing, and that was about it. I looked around and asked where I could find water. A woman pointed over to a big metal sink. I asked her where the cups were. "You have to use the plastic cup that your hygiene stuff came in. It's going to smell like soap for a few weeks too." Once again, I just couldn't believe what I was hearing. Jail wasn't how I imagined it to be. It was worse!

After eating breakfast and before falling asleep again, I was pondering the irony of my situation compared to Merri's. I thought how it was odd that, at that very moment, both twins were going through hell only in very different ways. Merri had joined the Air Force. She had been training and planning for basic training for about six months before our eighteenth birthday. She had left for Texas only a few weeks earlier. My mom brought her to my apartment so she could say goodbye to me, Chloe and Zoe. Josh was working so she didn't get to say goodbye to him. I remember how she seemed a bit nervous. After all the trips she had made to the gym every day, this was finally it. She gave Chloe and Zoe hugs and kisses, and I gave her a long hug and told her she would be okay. That was the last time Merri would see her nieces. None of us could have known that at the time.

I was stripped of everything, from my clothing to my dignity and basic necessities that we take advantage of on a daily basis. I now had a new view and appreciation for freedom, forks, and pillows. After each meal, I slept. Sleeping was the only escape out of that place. I hardly ate. I was too upset with my actions and the actions of my soon to be ex-husband. I was hurting for my babies and thinking about what was going to happen next. I wondered if Derrick would still want me after ignoring his warning. Thoughts of the time we had spent together brought a smile to my face, even sitting in a jail cell. It was only Saturday, and I would have to wait until Monday to see a Judge and ask about being released. That flat out sucked.

What was to be a couple of days felt like eternity. I called my mom as much as I could. The conversation on Monday morning, right before I was called to my Court Hearing, delivered another shock that I was unprepared for. The police had left my daughters with my mom when I was arrested. Her home was clean and she clearly loved them and was more than capable of caring for them. In fact, she was the only person I trusted to take care of them.

"It's just unbelievable!" she told me over the phone. "I had child protective services knocking on my door wanting to know what happened between you and Josh. I guess the police must have called them. The guy that showed up said they're opening a case, and I have to go do a fingerprint check to keep Chloe and Zoe with me. It's a total nightmare, Liz!" she tiredly explained. "Ugh. I am so sorry they're hassling you," I told her. "We have to keep the girls away from Josh and his mom. They would not be taken care of, and they know you the best out of the family," I worried. She agreed and wished me luck as we said our goodbyes before I walked down the hallway to meet my fate.

Over the intercom an officer loudly announced "Jeter! It's time for Court!" I made sure that my new fabulous orange wardrobe was tucked and pressed where it should be and eagerly walked to the exit door. It magically unlocked again. I was surprised to hear other women wishing me luck as I walked out. "Follow the yellow line down the hall, Jeter!" the same voice echoed. I followed the line as best I could, wondering to what extent they meant. If I were to walk perfectly along the line, it would look like I was doing a sobriety test. I awkwardly limped and shuffled, trying not to veer too far from the line.

As I came to the entrance of the hall where the holding cell was that had greeted me into the world of jail life a few days earlier, I saw a few other inmates also getting ready for Court. By "getting ready" I mean they were being shackled. "Stand on the blue tape and face the wall!" a female officer demanded. "Lift your arms up and out to your side!" she said. She thoroughly patted me down again to search for contraband. She wasn't gentle about it either. She wrapped a long chain around my waist. The two ends met in front of me and locked around my wrists. It hurt, because my wrists were small and bony. She then had me face the wall again and lift each leg, one at a time, to secure more cuffs around my ankles. Everything about this place was awkward and humiliating. All shackled and ready for Court, I was curious as to why they thought it necessary to go to such extremes. I can understand being handcuffed, but was cuffing my legs necessary? I wondered if it was more for the humiliation factor or for true security reasons.

I sat in another holding cell for about five minutes until a bailiff opened the door and instructed me to follow another line down a hallway I hadn't yet seen. I overestimated my ability to casually walk at a steady pace and tripped, almost hitting the ground on my third step. "Be careful Miss! Those things will get ya!" he kindly said. He was older - maybe in his sixties. He had a kindness about him that felt compassionate and non-judgmental. He treated me like I was a real person. I needed to feel that treatment to bring my sanity to a reasonable level.

I walked ahead, as instructed, and arrived at a regular looking door. The bailiff held the door open for me and instructed me to walk ahead not looking at anyone sitting in the Courtroom, especially the other offenders. I didn't want to look at anyone anyway. I had too much of a sense of embarrassment and shame. I was especially embarrassed when I sat in a row of chairs and, out of the corner of my eye, realized that the Courtroom was full of free people. They were locals in my community. The size of my town made it very possible that someone in the audience was a person I personally knew. Some of these people were offenders themselves out on bail or on Probation, and others seemed to be possible Social Workers, family members and who knows whom else.

A short, professional looking woman walked toward my row of chairs holding a stack of files and introduced herself as my Public Defender. When she announced her name, I was relieved and pleased to know that I had luckily been assigned one of the best Attorneys in town. Laura Lamour was her name. She was actually Neil's Attorney at one time. I remember Megan saying something about how her father gave Laura a free tune-up because she was able to get a Judge to remove a restraining order against him. Neil was notorious for having restraining orders against him. He had a hot head. Women initially loved Neil, but once they saw his moody side they got revenge with restraining orders. At least that's the story I was told.

"I'm assuming you know what your charges are?" she asked in a matter-of-fact tone. "Yes, I do," I replied. "So how do you want to plead? I'll need to talk to you in my office later, but usually, unless you want to admit that you're flat-out guilty, I enter a plea of not guilty until I can go over your case with you in private." "That is totally fine," I said. The Judge called my name and case number about five minutes later.

I stood up and was terrified to walk from my seat to the desk where the Attorneys represented their clients. It was only fifteen feet away, but I could hardly walk with the shackles. I looked at the floor and steadily did my best without tripping this time. The Judge was an old man who looked to be in his seventies. I was afraid of him. Once he began to speak, though, I sensed that he wasn't as scary as I thought he might be. He read some laws and my rights to me, and as he asked me if I understood what he was saying, I made eye contact with him and politely replied that I did. I wanted him to see that I was taking this matter very seriously. I wanted him to know that I had respect for authority.

"Ms. Lamour, how does your client want to plea?" I was getting nervous because I had a feeling that in only a minute or so my fate as an inmate would either stay the same or dissolve. "Not guilty, Your Honor" Laura stated. I liked her. She had confidence and a no-nonsense approach. She was the kind of person that could see through the bullshit, and I had every intention of telling her the truth about what happened. That is, of course, if what I told her was private and wouldn't get me into even more trouble. I had a feeling that she dealt with some class-A idiots on a regular basis. I wanted to show her that I wasn't like that - maybe a class C or D idiot but definitely not an A.

As I was silently praying to God in my head and asking for forgiveness, as well as admitting my sins and begging for mercy, Laura was explaining to the Judge that I was a first-time offender, and I had never been in trouble before this. She explained that it would not happen again if I were to be released on my own recognizance and that I was in the middle of college courses that I needed to complete. I thought that she was doing pretty good defending me, considering she only knew the very basics. The Judge was silent for a few seconds before looking up at me. "Ms. Jeter, do you understand that if I were to release you on your own recognizance, you would be expected to appear at every Court Hearing, follow all the rules on your minute order and not have any contact with your husband?" He paused, but I could tell that he wasn't finished. "You are also not permitted to leave the state or country without the written permission of the Court. You must completely refrain from drugs and alcohol, including marijuana, and you must surrender your person to the El Dorado County Jail at any given notice. You are subject to search and seizure at all times and must comply and obey all law enforcement, including peace officers. Do you understand this, Ms. Jeter?" He looked directly at me. I almost wanted to shout "I DO!" with fireworks going off in my head, and butterflies flapping around my stomach. I sweetly replied with the happiest "Yes" that ever came out of my mouth. I was finally getting out of there, and I was so happy.

I scheduled a meeting with my Attorney for a few days later. She handed me some paperwork and, poorly containing my excitement, I limped toward the door as instructed. After being unshackled, sent back to H pod to gather my green tub of crap, and mop out my cell for the next poor soul, an officer opened the door and called my name. An older inmate hugged me and gave me congratulations. She wished me well. In her eyes I saw that she was sad that it wasn't her getting to go home. I felt bad for her.

I practically skipped through the blue metal door and down the hallway, annoyed that I still had to follow the yellow line. I called my mom from a payphone in another holding cell while I waited for my normal clothing to be given back to me. I was so excited to get dressed in my own clothes! My mom had the girls so Lilah was going to pick me up outside the visitor entrance. The officer at the front desk returned my earrings and belly-button ring in a plastic bag, along with a form I had to sign to confirm receiving them. I scribbled away…and that was it. "Okay, good luck. Just walk through that door over there," she said, pointing toward my freedom. The door unlocked as I approached, and I stepped outside for the first time in four days. It was so sunny that I had to shade my eyes. The air smelled like fresh pine - a smell that I usually only noticed after leaving town for extended periods of time and then returning. It was the best breath of fresh air that I had ever inhaled. The grass was so green and everything was so beautiful. Lilah pulled up screeching her breaks and driving like a mad woman, as usual. I got into the passenger seat of her truck to hear her say "Oh my God! You look so hot for just getting out of jail!" I shook my head and had to laugh. I felt like I was seeing the world for the first time ever. It was amazing.

Chapter 26

It was so nice to be able to finally give my girls a hug. I almost cried seeing them run toward me as I walked into my mother's house. I was only able to stay for a few minutes. My mom was advised by C.P.S. to keep Josh and me away from the girls until they did an investigation. I had a custody hearing regarding this matter in just a few days. I was hoping that the Judge would see my side and dismiss the case.

I knew that I was a good mother. Josh knew that I was a good mother too. I was hoping that he would be reasonable and realize that the girls were better off being with me. I had no idea what C.P.S. really was, and I didn't feel as threatened by them as I probably should have. I just needed to figure out a way to get Josh to agree to let me keep the apartment where the girls were comfortable and secure. Lilah had her apartment in the building next to mine so I drove back to the complex with her. Since I didn't have a key I had to stop in the office. I told the complex manager the situation and they were nice enough to give me a key and make sure that I was able to get into my apartment. When I walked through the front door it was a complete disaster. Things were missing and stuff scattered all over the place. I was stressed because I didn't know if Josh was staying there or when he would be back. Lilah offered to let me stay the night at her apartment until I figured out what was going on. I was relieved because I really didn't want to be alone that night anyway. I packed an overnight bag and we headed over to her place. I took the most amazing shower of my life and did my hair. I desperately needed some normalcy.

Lilah and I chatted for a while, shared some snacks, and joked about me going to jail. When she got tired, she and Summer headed to bed. I had never been so excited to sleep on a couch before. It was so comfortable, with fluffy pillows and a warm, fuzzy blanket. I was tired, but I was also thinking about Derrick. I was nervous about calling him. I wanted to update him and let him know that I wasn't in jail anymore, if he even knew about it in the first place. I just wanted to hear his voice and get some reassurance that he still liked me before I fell asleep.

"Hello?" said Donnie. "Hi, Donnie, it's Elizabeth. Is Derrick there?" "No, he's over at his friend's house right now but he wanted me to give you their phone number in case you called. He really has a thing for you and it's his birthday so I'm sure he would love to hear from you." Donnie said. I jotted down the number and thanked Donnie for the information. He laughed and congratulated me for getting out of jail, which I thought was pretty funny.

Crap, I thought to myself, it's his birthday today and I am way too tired to go anywhere. I felt super bad...I guess I definitely need to call him now, I affirmed. I nervously dialed the number. The phone was answered by a friendly female voice. I asked if Derrick was there, and she asked me to hold on for just a second. He got on the phone and immediately sounded excited to hear from me. I explained to him what happened and that I was out of jail and exhausted, but I would make it up to him for missing his birthday. Derrick told me not to worry about it and said that his birthday present was that I was out of jail.

We agreed to meet the next day to grab lunch or maybe even dinner. I hung up the phone with a smile on my face. I was happy to know that he hadn't forgotten about me. I fell asleep that night with a hundred mixed emotions - I missed my babies, I was sad yet relieved that Josh and I were over for good, and I found it hard to stop thinking about Derrick and how much I liked him. He had the whole bad boy thing going on. This was a new concept to me, and I was eager to find out if he was really a teddy bear deep down. He was older, in shape, attractive, and extra masculine. It was the first chance I had to know what it was really like to date a man. I once thought that Josh was a man, but that all changed when he started spending his minimum wage paychecks on booze instead of bills. He was an alcoholic and an adolescent who would probably never grow up. Being let down time after time ruined the respect that I once held for him.

The next day I met Derrick for dinner at a local restaurant. We picked up right where we left off and everything was great, if not better. He was opening doors for me and treating me with respect, as well as showing a true concern for what was going on. That night I ended up staying at his house. We quickly fell in love, and I was at his house all the time. He shared his house with his brother Donnie, but Donnie didn't seem to mind having me there. The Court granted temporary custody of Chloe and Zoe to my mother and had ordered me to complete a few things before I could get them back. I had to begin taking anger management courses once a week, and I also had to do an assessment to make sure that I didn't have any sort of addiction problem that Child Protective Services didn't know about. Going to Court for my daughters was, by far, more stressful than going to Court for the criminal proceedings. Derrick offered me comfort, and I felt like I could turn to him when I was stressed out.

Somehow, I ended up forgiving Megan for completely going behind my back. When she found out that I was staying over at Derrick and Donnie's house, she suddenly began to show more of an interest in hanging out with me. I think it was because she just wanted to be part of the excitement that was clearly created by Derrick. Plus, I knew she always had a thing for Donnie; she just never openly admitted it to anyone.

I could only see my daughters on a schedule so I had more free time than I had in a long time. I decided to check on my apartment and see if Josh had removed any more of our items. I wanted to clean it because I kind of missed being home, and I needed my place to be clean and ready for Chloe and Zoe when the Court gave them back to me. As I was scrubbing the kitchen floor the apartment manager walked up and knocked on my door. "I am just here to give you this notice," she said nicely. "You have thirty days to move out or you will be evicted. Your husband put in a notice to cancel the lease and because he is the Head of Household listed on the lease, he has the right to do so." I took the form out of her hand and glanced over it.

This was actually quite devastating, and I honestly had no idea what I was going to do or where I would live. I shut my door and began to cry. My whole family was separated and nothing was ever going to be the same. I was sad that our home was no longer our home. I was sad that the person I married would never get better and would probably die a drunk. I was sad that Chloe and Zoe no longer had parents as a unit but as rivals. None of this was their fault, and I never wanted them to suffer or be sad. They were still very young, and I wondered if they knew what was going on. My mom frequently told me that Chloe, in particular, was asking for me on a regular basis. This broke my heart. I just wanted to get back to normal.

I took some belongings out of my apartment that I thought were most important, and I loaded them into my trunk. I remembered to grab my books for school. I called my father and he offered to box up the rest of the items and store them for me. My dad and I had started speaking again just a few months prior.

He met Chloe and Zoe and clearly forgot about how mad and disappointed he was in me. He even started coming to visit more often and was there to help any time I needed it. At least I wouldn't have to worry about where my furniture would go. I couldn't go to my mom's house because she had the girls there. I had no choice but to stay with Derrick and live out of the trunk of my car until I got the girls back. I was only able to visit my daughters each day for short periods of time.

Josh started spreading rumors, and his mother joined in too. They said all sorts of nonsense to the Social Workers assigned to the case. They accused Derrick of being a full-blown drug dealer and beating his ex-girlfriend. They accused me of being on drugs, being the most negligent mother ever, and of being a compulsive liar. When I saw these accusations in the reports that I was handed from the Social Worker, it made me sick. I was furious that they would actually put such things in the report before investigating enough to get the clear facts. Derrick calmed me down and had a ton of good advice. His ex-girlfriend, Macy, went through the same thing with her ex. He was an important resource for me.

My mom knew where I was staying, so I finally decided to bring Derrick over to meet her. As my luck turned out, a CASA worker was visiting the house to see how everything was going with Chloe and Zoe. She was Court-appointed to be a "non-biased" advocate. I initially liked her and thought she was nice. Later, I would find out that she would become my worst enemy.

I was initially scared of what she would think of Derrick. He had tattoos up his arm and looked like the typical bad-boy. He turned on the charm with both my mother and the CASA worker, and they seemed to truly like him. The CASA worker even stated, "Well, you're not the monster you were made out to be!" This pleased me and gave me a sense of freedom to continue our relationship without having to worry so much. After this meeting, the Court case slowly got better, and I was allowed unsupervised visits just a month later.

I was thoroughly exhausted when I had the girls again for the first time. They were getting older, smarter and ever so clever. They were best friends, and every time they held hands it made me so happy. I don't recall them ever fighting.

When the girls were placed back into my custody just two months after the whole ordeal, my mother was getting serious with her boyfriend (who would later become her husband) - a man she had met when she was just sixteen. She and Don determined that the only option was for me to initially move into her home to care for Chloe and Zoe. In the meantime, I was to look for my own apartment. However, shortly after I moved in, she moved out to be with Don. The night before they left and after I put the girls to bed, Don got on his high horse and gave me an unexpected lecture about men. "Liz, guys with tattoos and shaved heads are bad. I guarantee he'll end up pimping you out or getting you hooked on drugs." I laughed, half-sarcastically and half-seriously. I had no idea what he was talking about or where he had come up with this ridiculous conclusion about Derrick. After smiling and nodding my head for an hour, he finally went to sleep. He and my mother would wake up early the next morning to move her things.

My mother made it clear that the girls and I were to be the only ones living at her home. She was out of town now, and Derrick and I couldn't stay away from each other. She said he could visit, so I took that as a green light for him to move in. I did not know how the girls would react, and I didn't want them to be confused without their dad. I agreed to allow Josh to take them on weekends. I had gone back to attending classes, and I needed a little break for homework now and then.

One Sunday afternoon Josh dropped the girls off at my house. When I got them inside and took their jackets off, the first thing that Chloe said when she saw Derrick was "You're not my daddy!" "I know I'm not your daddy" he replied. "I don't want to be your daddy." I thought it was a bit insensitive of him to say that to a two-and-a-half year old. It hurt my feelings, too. I avoided talking about it then and didn't say anything to him. A few days later, Derrick was sitting on the couch with Zoe, sharing his ice cream with her. Chloe had just calmed down from one of her tantrums, which had been happening more frequently since her father and I had split. She toddled up to Derrick, looking for a bite of what her sister was obsessing over. "Say sorry first, or I'm not sharing with you," Derrick demanded. Chloe had her mother's stubborn streak, and I could tell that she was hoping he would get off his power trip and just share. He refused. She sat on the side of the couch, watching her sister happily eat ice cream with a sad look on her face. I never gave my girls unfair treatment like that, ever. "Derrick, just give her a bite! That's not cool, she's only two!" I snapped. "Nope. I stick to my word. She's not going to walk on me like she does you, sorry." I was furious. I got my own spoon and stabbed it into the pint of ice cream, scoping out a bite for Chloe. That was that. He spent the rest of the night giving me the silent treatment. I didn't care. He was going to need to learn where his place was in MY family or leave.

The next morning I got up and dressed as usual to drop the girls off at daycare so I could get to my classes. On the way out, Derrick made a strange request: "You should leave Zoe here to hang out with me; I get bored sitting here all day." His work, which was a seasonal job, was slowing down because of the coming winter weather. He spent half the year on unemployment. "I'm not going to let Zoe stay home and make Chloe go to daycare, that's not fair to her," I replied. "If you want to watch both of them, that's fine, but not just one." "Nah, never mind." he said. My instincts were whispering to me that something just wasn't right. In a hurry, I rushed them out the door. I didn't want to be late to class. When I spoke to Megan later in the day, I laughed about how I thought it was funny that Derrick wanted to babysit. "Yeah, that is funny," she answered. I wanted reassurance that it wasn't anything to be worried about, and she gave it to me.

Chapter 27

Over the next few days, as the snow melted, Derrick was able to find a few jobs, but this meant that he would be hanging out with his friends and co-workers more. They were known as party animals. I stayed busy with school trying to get through the most difficult course required for nursing. I was nervous, but I knew that I could do it. The following Saturday I was all caught up on my school work, and I wanted to hang out with Megan to catch up with her on gossip. She had kicked her husband out because they were fighting so much. They were like fire and ice. After their initial honeymoon phase, they just didn't get along, and it was clear that they never would.

I called Megan and she sounded extra hyper. I laughed and asked her what was going on. "I have some diet pills that are making me really, really wired. Ha ha! You should bring the girls over, and we can hang out. I'll give you one, and we'll just watch funny shit on TV." Derrick had made some coffee, so I poured myself a cup and then went to get Chloe and Zoe dressed. Derrick was never fond of Megan, but I invited him to come along anyway because we had nothing better to do. When the girls were dressed and ready I realized that I had left my coffee in the kitchen. I quickly found it and chugged it so we could leave.

We got to Megan's house and the girls were excited to play with her daughter. Megan handed me one of the diet pills she had been talking about, and I broke it in half and gulped it down. About a half hour later I was insanely wired and had never felt so aware of my surroundings. I was acting like a hyper idiot with Megan, and Derrick just sat there shaking his head. He frequently told me that I acted like an immature idiot when I was with Megan, and he thought I was better than that.

After spending a few hours hanging out and doing nothing, we decided to bring the girls back home because they were getting tired and needed a nap. There wasn't much else to do, so I did a little bit of studying while Derrick watched TV and ate ice cream. The day went by and I fed the girls dinner, gave them a bath, and put them to bed as usual.

Later, Derrick and I were cuddled up on the futon in front of the TV, watching one of my favorite scary movies. "Thanks for being so patient today. I was surprised that you didn't get mad at me for getting all hyper and annoying," I said.

Derrick looked up at me with a strange look on his face and replied, "I have something to tell you, but you're going to get really mad at me." "What is it?" I asked. "Well, this morning when we were drinking coffee, I think our mugs got mixed up. I don't know for sure, but I think you drank mine." "So, what's the big deal?" I asked. "Don't hate me, and I'm really, really sorry, but I was extra tired today so I put a little rock in my coffee to help me wake up," he cautiously said. "What's that supposed to mean? What's a rock?" I demanded. I had no idea what he meant by "a rock." "You know...a small rock of crystal." "Crystal meth? Are you kidding me, Derrick? I've never done that in my life, and I didn't think you did either! What the hell is your problem? Why would you do that when you know that I have two small girls that I need to take care of, and I just got out of the Court System! Do you have any respect for me at all?" I began to sob.

I was so disappointed that I just didn't know what to do with myself. He apologized again. For the rest of the night, I was extremely sad and confused with the emotions that I was feeling. I had such strong feelings for Derrick. I didn't really know why, but I just did. I also felt betrayed, and I knew that I couldn't trust him if he was going to do something like that.

To me, crystal meth was the worst of the worst. It was the one drug that I had always heard horror stories about. I eventually got over it, hoping that it really was an accident and made it clear to Derrick that if he ever did anything like that again, or if I ever found out that he was using it, it was over between us.

Over the next week things were back to normal again. I got back into my school routine, and Derrick was working. I think he felt bad about what he had done. He was extra nice to me and extra helpful when it came to the girls. He helped buy diapers when I needed them and helped put food on the table, which I had a hard time doing with only working a part-time job and getting random financial aid payments from school.

Eventually Derrick started to spend more time over at his brother's house. He would go straight there after work and wouldn't come home until late in the evening. I started to notice that his behavior, and everything else about him, seemed off. He was demanding more sexual favors. He always had a stern look on his face and it seemed like he was in deep thought. He was also always intently focused on one thing at a time. He was either on the Internet, downloading music, or working on some electrical device. This continued for the next two weeks, and I started to pay attention to the patterns of when he appeared normal and when he didn't. He acted normal in the mornings and if he came straight home from work. He acted strange if he went to his brother's house after work before coming home. After I was sure of what was going on, I couldn't handle it anymore. I didn't want to be treated like I was an idiot who knew nothing.

Derrick walked in the door on a Tuesday night around nine o'clock. "What the hell is going on with you?" I demanded, "You think I'm dumb? You think I don't know what's going on?" I practically yelled as he walked in the front door. He began to laugh and act like it was me who had a problem and not him. He played dumb for about an hour, refusing to give in. When he finally realized that I was not letting up until I had answers, he caved.

"Okay, I'm sorry about what's going on. It's just that my co-worker got a hold of someone who had some class-A cocaine from Mexico. It's something that doesn't ever come around, and I just couldn't pass it up. We all went in on it together and bought more than we originally planned on. Plus, it's so strong that we don't have to do very much for it to last a long time. Coke is something that everybody does at one point or another. It's not addicting like everybody claims it to be. I'm just having fun. Don't worry about it!" he said with a cocky arrogance. Once again I was stunned and disgusted that he was being such a moron and completely disregarding everything I had said a few weeks earlier.

The previous week we had taken the girls to my niece's birthday party at the ice skating rink. Derrick was helping me chase the girls around, and my stepdad, who gave me those warnings about men with tattoos and bald heads, was actually impressed with Derrick's participation with the girls. My stepdad and Derrick even talked for a few minutes, so I assumed that I had approval from my stepdad and my mom. I had told my mom that Derrick was helping me with everything financially, and I desperately needed that help. She understood, and she knew how hard it was to be a single mom.

Suddenly none of that mattered. My stepdad was proving to be right. I, again, began to cry out of frustration and anger. "That's it Derrick. You need to make a choice, and you need to make it right now! Choose between drugs or me. I have babies

176

to care for and that can't be in our lives. If you can't do that, I'll understand. But that means that we need to part ways and you need to move on. I won't have any hard feelings; it's just how it has to be. I'm not that kind of person and I never wanted to be." I looked him in the eye, and I asked him, "Can you live the rest of your life drug free and be okay with that decision? If not, you just need to go. I'll never be okay with drugs, and I refuse to be with someone who is doing drugs."

He sat down next to me on the porch step as I was puffing away at a cigarette, in tears. "Honestly, I love you, Elizabeth. I've never felt like this with any other person. But I don't think I can stop, it's just too fun." He started to laugh. The stupidity of his statement made me laugh. He had a good way about changing the subject and trying to turn serious matters into funny conversations. The conversation became serious again when I wiped my eyes and looked at him with desperation. "Derrick, I truly do love you, and I think that we could have a good life together. If you can't make this choice now, and make it with confidence, we just have to go our own ways." He stood up. "I'm sorry, I just don't think I can stop, and I don't want to put you through so much stress."

I decided to be strong and stop my tears so he knew how serious I was. I was not going to change my mind or back down on this. He packed his bags and walked out the door. I could tell he was in tears. I sat down on the couch and, as the girls slept peacefully, I cried openly.

At the age of eighteen I had no sense of time, nor did I know the possibilities that the future could hold for me. I was convinced that, because I was only eighteen and already a single mother of two, no one else would want me because it would be too much baggage. After sitting on the couch and crying for an hour, Derrick walked back through the front door without his bags. "Elizabeth, I just can't do it."

I don't want to be without you, and if it means giving up cocaine and everything else, I'll do it." "Well, where are your bags?" I excitedly asked. "They were too heavy, and the walk is too far, so I just left them at my brother's. Can you give me a ride to go get them?" he said, laughing again. "Just take my car. You're such an idiot, the girls are asleep." I said, laughing. He came back with his things and put them away. We were now back to the honeymoon phase after the drama settled. He always had a reason for having some kind of sex, and tonight he wanted to have "make up sex." I just dealt with it. I didn't want another fight to happen after the exhausting drama I had already gone through.

Over the next month Derrick stayed true to his word and always came straight home after work. I was proud of him and my trust in him slowly returned. He started to treat the girls a little bit better too. Although he was usually good with Chloe and Zoe, I figured that he didn't really know much about kids since he was never around them, so he had to get used to it.

Zoe began to put up a fight every night when it came time for bed. She never wanted to go to sleep, but I could tell she was exhausted. I always caved in and rocked her for a short time to calm her down and reassure her. After she put up a fight for about the fifth night in a row, Derrick said confidently: "Just let me handle it. You'll see, I'll put her to sleep at night until she knows how to go to sleep without a fight." "How do you know anything about kids, Derrick?" I asked. I've changed more diapers than you'll probably ever change in your lifetime. You have no idea how many diapers I've gone through with the two girls," I replied.

Giving Derrick the benefit of the doubt, I let him take the reins. I was curious to see if he really knew what he was talking about. He picked up Zoe and put her in her crib. I walked out of the room because I knew that if she saw me, she would not be

178

able to stop crying. She knew that I would always cave. As I walked out of the dark bedroom Zoe started to scream. I had never heard her scream so much in my life. I panicked and peeked in the bedroom to make sure that everything was okay. Derrick was hovering over her crib and making sure that she remained laying down. Every time she stood up, he would gently lay her back down. He was calmly whispering to her, go "night-night." I didn't interrupt him because I didn't want all that crying to be for nothing. I just wanted her to understand that bedtime meant sleep. He was in her room for about twenty minutes, and she finally calmed down and went to sleep.

The next week, during a lunch break at school, I decided to give Megan a call because I was bored as usual. She had that familiar tone to her voice. She was excited about something. I had a feeling I knew what it was. "Donnie and I are official," she excitedly announced. "I'm not surprised Megan, I knew that you guys liked each other a long time ago but just weren't in the right circumstances to have a relationship. Do you think your dad is going to be upset because he's an older guy?" I asked. "I don't know, hopefully not!" she laughed. We got off the phone, and I started to ponder. I thought that it was so odd, and kind of funny, that we initially dated best friends (and eventually married them) and now we were dating brothers. I was excited because that meant that we could all hang out more and do couples stuff.

Megan and I always had big influences on each other. We were immediately best friends from the day we met, and we had so much in common that it was insane. On a free weekend when I had no homework and Derrick was at his brother's house helping him work on a car, Megan called me. I asked her what she was doing, and she replied with a mischievous tone to her voice. "Oh, nothing," she said, secretly wanting me to question her further. "Come on Megan, just spit it out," I said. "Okay, but don't get mad," she said. "I promise, I won't. Tell me what you're doing you, weirdo!" "Well, the other night Donnie was doing coke, and I was just too curious so I tried it. It is so much fun! Seriously, it's not that bad - it just makes you hyper and gives you a bunch of energy. You have no idea how much I got done around his scummy house!" she enthusiastically said. "Gosh, what is this hype with everyone and cocaine?" I was kind of curious. Megan knew me best out of everyone, and she knew that I was paranoid when it came to putting anything strange into my body. Even with her diet pill, I just took half to be safe. "All right," I said. "I'm coming over there. I'm too curious now, and I want to see what this stuff looks like." "Okay," she said. "I'll see you in a few minutes." I drove down the street to her apartment with the girls in the back seat who were excited to play with her daughter. The three of them had become best friends.

As soon as I walked through her front door I could clearly see that she was on something. She was in her pajamas vigorously scrubbing her bathroom floor. I thought it was kind of funny because she didn't typically scrub like that. I remembered how she used to make James do all the cleaning.

She showed me what she had, and it just looked like baking powder. When she did a small line in front of me, and I saw that she didn't have a heart attack, I was even more curious and wanted to try it. I was thinking to myself once again - if you can't beat 'em, join 'em.

"Just make me a tiny, tiny line." I said to her, a little bit paranoid. "You know about those stories where someone tried coke once and rolled over and died? That better not be me!" She laughed and announced to me, "I know how you are, and I wouldn't give my best friend something if I thought it was going to kill her." She took a card, chopped it up and made me a line. It was only about half an inch long, but I still thought it was too big. I told her to cut it in half because I was nervous. She did, and handed me a cut up piece of a straw. I hovered over the line that was laid out on a plate on her stove for about twenty minutes. Every time I went to snort it, I got scared and backed out. Finally, she was frustrated and said to me, "Look, if you don't want to do it, just don't do it. It's not that big of a deal." After she made that statement, I picked up the straw and just got it over with. It didn't hurt my nose like I thought it would. The only thing that bothered me was the taste dripping from the back of my throat. It was really disgusting, and I had to sip on a soda to wash it down.

Before I knew it I had more energy. I didn't feel weird or disoriented; I just felt like I could get a ton of things done that I normally wouldn't feel up to. We were laughing and joking about Donnie and Derrick, and after about a half hour it started to wear off. I wanted more, but she was out. "Do you think that Derrick is over there doing cocaine right now since Donnie has a bunch?" I asked her. "Probably." she said. "Let's go over there and bug them, but don't tell them that I did it with you. I don't want him to get mad for doing it behind his back," I requested. Sadly, I wasn't surprised that she thought Derrick was probably still doing cocaine, despite his promise not to. Deep down, I felt like I contradicted everything that I held valuable to myself. First, I made him promise not to ever do it again. Then, what did I do? I went behind his back and used cocaine for the first time. I knew that it was wrong, but I didn't foresee any consequences. I felt like having more energy could only do more good than harm, especially when it came to taking care of two babies.

Megan and I pulled into the long dirt driveway. The guys were outside working on a car. There were more people there than I had expected and they were blasting music. It was clear that there was a party going on. I walked up to Derrick with a big smile on my face. He asked me why I looked like a doofus.

"I officially want to try it!" "What are you talking about?" he asked. "I want to try coke! Megan said that she tried it, and it's really fun. I trust her judgment because she knows me. She knows how paranoid I get over things. I know you guys have some." After playing dumb for a few minutes, he gave in. He knew that I was stubborn and I wasn't going to let up. He led me into the back room where the plate was, stacked with lines and lines of cocaine. I couldn't believe how much there was. It was kind of exciting. This is where it all began...

Chapter 28

It was a Thursday afternoon and my shift at the Community College Bookstore was just about to end. Normally, getting off of work was a good thing. It signified the end of my busy day of classes and hours of putting price tags on tons of textbooks. Thursdays, however, were different. The Court had ordered me to attend an Anger Management course every Thursday, for one year. It wasn't that bad because, ironically, Megan had also been ordered by the Court to enroll. She had kicked her ex-husband in the groin, and he called the police. That was when their marriage ended. I had known all along that it wasn't going to take much. Things change when couples have children. We all like to have this delusion that having a baby will solidify a marriage or relationship, but if your marriage isn't already solid it's just going to cause even more stress and break it down further. In the case of Megan though, it seemed that she was with James for the opposite reason - to have a baby, whether it affected them as a couple or not.

It was like being back in school again for us. We always sat next to each other and made fun of the creepers who were in the class with us. On top of that, we always had something to say about everything. That's because we were now adults. We were eighteen years old and knew everything. We had life all figured out and then some. We thought that we were hot because we had older boyfriends, and using cocaine on a semi-regular basis was nothing but innocent recreation in our eyes. We always seemed to somehow cause a scene no matter where we went.

We both had agreed that we had a mini crush on our Anger Management teacher. His name was Mickey. There was also another man named Marty. He had been friends with Megan's father and was around his age. Megan and I always tried to kiddingly seduce him. We liked to see what we could get away with and thought it was funny that every guy we encountered would have some sort of weakness for us. We were a disaster waiting to happen. When it happened, we would hysterically break down laughing because everything was just so incredibly funny. Growing up in such a small town, we had no idea what the real world was like. Even the most rundown neighborhoods in Tahoe would no doubt seem like a heavenly escape to the most poverty-stricken families from the big cities. Before leaving Tahoe, I never truly believed that it could be unsafe to walk down the street alone. I didn't even know what it really meant to "watch your back." Perhaps being surrounded by complete beauty for the first twenty-two years of my life instilled a false concept in my mind that the world was beautiful and safe, and it would always remain that way.

I clocked out of my job at the bookstore and realized that I still had an hour before my class started. I hated it when that happened because I didn't have enough time to go home, but there was way too much time to just sit in my car smoking until the class started. I called Megan to see what she was up to, and find out if she wanted to grab a smoothie before class. She answered the phone and instructed me to head over to our friend Byron's house. He lived just a few blocks away from the Women's Center where the Anger Management class was held. She told me Derrick was over there. Derrick and Megan hated

184

each other, and it had always been that way. I figured only one thing could be going on. Normally this didn't happen until Friday because Friday was payday. By Sunday, every little speck of cocaine had been sucked up our noses or rubbed on our gums as if our survival depended on it. I walked through the front door. Byron and his girlfriend were sitting on the couch, and Derrick was on a chair beside them. Of course, there was a glass coffee table with a white, shiny dinner plate displaying that wonderful pile of excitement that I had grown to adore.

I had never previously liked to alter my sense of reality. That sort of thing made me feel out of control, and when I felt out of control, I started to panic. Cocaine, however, didn't make me feel that way. It gave me a feeling of renewed energy that I had not known or felt in my entire existence. I had felt abnormally tired for as long as I could remember. In elementary school I would have a hard time staying awake to get through class until lunch. My eyes would water so bad from yawning that it would look like I had been crying. I even remember having my first feelings of fatigue when I was only seven. I never wanted to play sports in school like the other kids, because I knew that I didn't have the energy to be competitive enough to win. This new energy I found made me feel normal for the first time in my life.

Megan and I had fun at Byron's house "powdering our noses" and headed over to the Anger Management class. We were lucky that the instructor didn't call the police on us. He never directly said that he was suspicious, but he kept giving us weird looks.

The next day while I was at work I got a phone call. It was the lady that managed the townhouse complex that I was trying to get into. "Congratulations Elizabeth! I just wanted to let you know that in spite of your misdemeanor in vandalism, my manager approved your application and you are all set to move in." I was so excited to get this phone call because I honestly didn't think that I was going to get a place there. After several Court dates, the District Attorney agreed to reduce my Felony Vandalism charge to a misdemeanor and completely removed the Child Endangerment charge.

These townhomes were very well kept because management was more on the picky side. She asked me when I wanted to move in, and I asked her if next week would work. I didn't say it out loud, but I was worried about how I was going to come up with the $1700. I knew that if I could at least have a few extra days, I could find a way to get the money together and get Derrick to pitch in. I told Derrick that I got the apartment and he said that he would help out. He also said that he just got a pretty good paycheck. I was also supposed to be getting paid the following Monday, so I figured that between the two of us we would be able to move in on Tuesday. I should have planned my weekend a little bit better.

After getting off work and picking the girls up from daycare, I was excited that it was the weekend and I could take a break from school. When I got home it was already six o'clock in the evening. Derrick's cousin dropped him off right behind me. Derrick didn't have his own vehicle because his driver's license had been suspended over a domestic dispute with his ex-girlfriend, and he hadn't finished his required Anger Management course.

Whenever I asked him about what happened, he explained it as if his ex-girlfriend were to blame. He said that she was spun out on cocaine and acting like a psycho. He pushed her away, out of self-defense, and she ended up falling down a set of stairs. The way he described it sounded pretty believable, and he had never acted violently toward me. I didn't think much about it. Derrick walked into the carport to help me get the girls out of the car. "Let's hurry up and get these girls fed. We're going over to chill with Lance and Tara tonight." Lance was his cousin and Tara was his cousin's fiancé. They also had a young daughter together who was about three. Byron was also going to be there. We all knew that meant – party time.

We walked through their door around seven. There were a few people I hadn't met before. All of the kids were playing together, and the adults were in the kitchen. I had never seen so much cocaine before. Derrick snorted a huge line and still had a bunch left. He offered it to the other people, but I think everyone else was already too high. "I'll take it!" I announced, trying to come off as hot shit. Derrick didn't oppose, and I grabbed the straw and prepared to snort the biggest line I had yet to snort.

I did it too fast. I had to sit down immediately. I managed to play it cool, walking over to a chair in the living room. I sat down and, as each second passed, my heart raced a little more. My heart was pounding even faster than it did when I was forced to run a mile in middle school. I started to worry. Composing myself, I started to pace my breathing, taking in long, slow breaths and slowly releasing them. After about five minutes, my pulse started to slow down. Derrick announced that he was ready to take the girls home and put them to sleep because it was getting late. We drove home, put the girls in bed, and finished our party. Derrick had a lot of cocaine, and I was wondering how much money he had spent on it. I didn't want to ask.

Normally Derrick would lay a line out for me about every thirty minutes, but that night he was being extra stingy. I also noticed that each time I snorted it, instead of giving me the numbing effect, it gave me a sharp pain in the side of my head. I wasn't coming down as fast as I normally did either. I started to become suspicious. I paid close attention the next time I snorted a line. I noticed that it looked a little more chunky than usual and it was also clearer. It resembled small shards of glass. High out of my mind, I grabbed my laptop and started to do research. By the end of the night I concluded that my cocaine was laced with crystal meth. Nobody had told me this.

g I called Megan and told her about my
appened to be over at her house, and they
ff of the same batch. "You didn't know that
al?" she asked. I started to cry. I was so pissed!
I really neve͟ted to do that. Yes, it was stupid of me to be
doing cocaine, but the addiction that results from crystal meth is
a more dangerous one. Everyone knows that. Cocaine is also
highly addictive, but I thought it would be much easier to recover
from it. I felt betrayed. I was mad and feeling overwhelmed. It
hurt my head to think about it. I didn't know why Derrick was
sneaky about the crystal meth. Why was he forcing it on me? I
wasn't sure.

To make myself feel better, I began to have second thoughts
about it. I did like that it was so much stronger. It only took one
line to keep me high for six hours, compared to twenty minutes!
I thought that it would probably save money too. Feeling mixed
up, I let myself cry some more after getting off the phone with
Megan. I found Derrick and yelled at him. "Well, Derrick, if
you're going to play games like this, you better come up with
some more shit because now I'm coming down and I am
miserable and I have to pack to get ready to move into my
apartment. Figure it out." He was a little dumbfounded. I was
too. After crying again, I realized that I had better start packing.
I didn't have time to sit around crying if I was going to get into
my new townhouse on schedule. I didn't know what to think or
feel, but I did know that I had to get things done, and I couldn't
let this drama get in the way. I started packing so I could move
on Tuesday.

Derrick got more meth, and I snorted and snorted and packed
and packed. Luckily Josh had picked up the girls before it all
started. I felt bad for them. I knew that I was not being a good
mom. Although I loved them with all my heart and provided
them with what they needed, I wasn't being fair to them. For

188

being the only person they had to rely on to keep them safe, being spun out on drugs was just totally wrong.

I had just a few hours of sleep when Sunday morning arrived. Hours earlier, my body couldn't handle staying awake any longer, and I had started to hallucinate. Derrick had been talking about some little girl in the house that was really a ghost. I had to go to bed. He was losing it even more than I was.

My eyes opened to sunshine glaring through the curtains and the sound of Derrick in the shower. I stared up at the ceiling wondering if Chloe and Zoe were having fun with their dad. I had a sudden flash before my eyes. It was Chloe and Zoe. They were drifting away from me and slowly flying towards the sky. They were holding hands, laughing, and wearing angel wings. They were waving "bye-bye." I snapped my head up. I didn't know what this sudden vision meant, and I didn't want to know. I had the chills and couldn't shake it off. I got out of bed and started cleaning the house. I had to block this from my thoughts.

From that Sunday morning to the morning of moving day, I did not sleep one second. I packed, got high, and packed some more. At that point I was mainly snorting meth just to stay awake and keep the downer effects from defeating me. Tuesday morning Derrick had to get the girls ready for daycare. I was so tired I couldn't function. Before leaving the house, he had McDonalds breakfast at the table. "I don't want to eat - thanks though," I said. "You need to eat right now. You are all sucked up, and I don't go for that kind of girl!" he demanded. Whatever, I thought. The girls were happily eating at the table. I sat down and took my first bite of a breakfast sandwich. It hurt my mouth to eat. My mouth had been so dry for so long, and it wasn't used to having food in it. It felt like the skin on the roof of my mouth was peeling off with each bite.

Derrick started yelling at me. "Dammit Elizabeth! Quit doing that; you're scaring me!" "Quit doing what?" I asked, totally confused. "You keep falling asleep while you're sitting there! Wake up so we can get this move done!" I didn't even know that I was falling asleep. I began to cry. I was scared and upset that I was getting yelled at for being overly tired. "You need to drive the car," I said. "Obviously if I am falling asleep it isn't safe for the girls." He refused. He didn't want to get pulled over because he would go to jail for driving on a suspended license. "I'll keep you awake, don't worry." he replied. We put the girls in the car, and I tried to mentally prepare myself for the five-minute drive to their daycare. We made it safely, dropped them off in their classrooms, and got back into the car. We headed to the college to pick up my paycheck then back to finish packing what was left.

Later at the townhouse complex and in the manager's office, I was praying to God that I could make it through signing the lease. I looked horrible, with dark circles under my eyes, and probably a look of disorientation on my face. As I sat down, I was secretly pinching my forearm the entire time. I knew that if I fell asleep during the lease signing, it would raise a red flag. I told the manager that I was really sick. She seemed to believe me. After the lease was signed, she handed me the keys and I was free to check out my new home. Derrick was waiting for me in the car. He couldn't be on the lease because of the domestic dispute from his previous relationship. I walked up to the car and flagged for him to get out. We found my apartment and unlocked the door. I was so exhausted but really pleased with how nice it was. Everything was new and clean and that was all that I wanted for my girls.

Driving back to my mother's home to get the last of my belongings, I started to panic when I saw someone lying in the middle of the road. "What the hell!" I screamed. "What?" Derrick asked in a panic. "Is that a...dead...body?" I panicked even more. The closer I drove to this figure in the road, the more real it looked. "What the hell are you talking about?" Derrick asked. As I passed the figure, I realized that it was only a black trash bag.

"Oh…just a…trash bag," I panted. This was the first vivid, drug-induced hallucination that I had. I was sure that it was a dead body. Of course I was relieved that it was not. When I arrived at my mother's house for the last trip, I called Josh and got him to agree to take Chloe and Zoe for the night. I didn't tell him why, but I knew that it would be dangerous for me to be responsible for the girls during the move. By 11:00 that night everything was moved. We fell asleep on a futon and slept hard for fifteen hours.

Chapter 29

This is by far the most difficult chapter of my life. This is the first time I have ever sat down to recall every painful moment and memory. I am not doing this to simply tell a story. I am not doing this for self-therapy. I am doing this to send a message to as many people as possible. A message that says "Yes, it CAN happen to you." You are never completely safe. The world, and life in general, is very unpredictable. Love yourself first. If you don't care for yourself as you would a small child and protect your health and well-being first and foremost, you will be of no use to anyone else.

It's 6:21 a.m., January 31, 2014. I'm sitting outside on my back patio in the dark and sipping coffee. After a couple weeks of procrastination, I decided to be brave and write this as thoroughly and accurately as possible. This was the life changing tragedy that determined the direction of the rest of my life, the lives of my family, and the lives of my precious little girls. They were only 19 months and 2-1/2 years old. It's still incomprehensible to me today that there exists such evil in our world. It is something so terrible, yet society rarely hears about it when it happens. It's even painful for complete strangers to hear about.

Nature amazes me. Although I was just a young girl when I gave birth to my daughters, I instantly grew a bond stronger than any other force a woman can possibly feel. I knew that I would do anything to keep them safe even if it meant losing my own life. I would imagine scenarios of possible dangers, and I would come up with a plan of how I would keep them out of harm's way. They showed me the beauty of true innocence, and ironically, kept my childhood alive. I remember tucking them in at bedtime and letting them fall asleep to Charlotte's Web. Then I would sneak in a couple hours later to make sure that they had their blankets wrapped tightly around their little bodies to stay warm. I would give them one more kiss and whisper "I love you, forever." Chloe's hair was so soft, and her little cheeks were so kissable. Zoe's sweet face was angelic as she slept in a deep, peaceful sleep. Something deep in my heart held onto these memories more intensely than others. Something was telling me that these moments should be remembered and cherished. They are the most vivid and beautiful memories that I have. If I take myself back to those nights, I can still feel the warmth of Chloe's cheeks as I nuzzled her, saying goodnight. I can still feel the soft touch of Zoe's cheeks and recall how I could have just stayed in that moment forever.

Have you ever hurt so bad that your entire body and every inch of your soul ached with rushes of pain, tingling through your extremities, chest, and head? Or have you ever cried to the point of wanting to throw up, fall to the floor, or jump through a window just to make the pain stop - then suddenly everything goes numb? Your natural instincts know to protect you from further pain because your life depends on it. Then the tears come streaming down your face because you lost something you can't replace. When you love someone so dearly and then you lose that person(s)...could it get any worse than that? "Lights will guide you home and ignite your bones, and I will try to fix you." God played this on the radio many times for me.

The only time I recall being sober for any number of consecutive days during my time on drugs was over Christmas in 2005. The girls and I went with Derrick to his Aunt and Uncle's home in Quincy, Ca. His parents made the trip from Texas, and I was going to meet them for the first time. Derrick was eighteen when his father's place of employment relocated to Texas, so they had no choice but to move if he was going to keep his job. Derrick went with them but missed California too much. He went back to the Bay Area where he was raised but really had no place to live. His brother was living in Tahoe so Derrick moved in with him. From what I could tell, he seemed like a pretty good kid before moving to Tahoe. I met his friends earlier that year when he took me on a weekend trip to the Bay Area. They were all honest and nice people, and they all seemed like they had good jobs and were drug free. It was a fun trip and it brought us closer. Over Christmas, the girls behaved like angels and were adored by everyone in Derrick's family. We stayed for four days, and it was nice being clean and just doing normal family stuff. His cousin had given us her room for the trip since I had the babies, and at night I would put them down and let them watch Finding Nemo. When the movie was halfway through and the girls had fallen asleep, Derrick put his arms around me. "You're gonna marry me one day, right?" My heart melted. He was sober, normal and sincere. That is when I knew that he truly loved me. "Of course I'll marry you, what kind of question is that?" I playfully replied. Everything about that Christmas trip was promising and romantic. It gave me a glimpse of the person that he had the potential to be. The problem was, he didn't know how to get clean. Neither did I.

After moving into our townhouse, everything took a downward spiral. Everyone had a way of justifying their actions and making excuses for it being okay. It was all a delusion. Quickly, we were all high more often than not. Ally, one of my friends that I had met from my biology class when I was seventeen, had been coming over periodically with her husband and their new baby. I didn't tell her that we used drugs, because she wasn't into that sort of thing. Derrick didn't like Ally and Brennen, and I assumed that was why. I recall having them over for dinner. I barbecued burgers and we all sat around joking about random stuff. I had to run out to my car to grab my cigarettes, and Ally walked with me to the parking lot. "Dude, is everything okay?" she asked looking worried. I was not doing drugs that day, so I didn't understand what she was thinking. "Yeah! Everything is good! I am actually really happy," I responded. I thought that I was happy. Deep down I was lost and trying to find my identity. My heart knew that my identity was not meant to be a drug addict, but my mind fought it. "I just have a weird feeling. I can't explain it, but I have a feeling that something bad is going to happen." she said. "Don't worry! I promise I'm fine. If anything goes wrong, I will totally call you." I lied. Everything was already wrong; I just didn't recognize it yet.

On the day that Derrick got his tax return, we wanted to go to Reno to buy some new electronics and some toys for the girls. It was on a Friday and I was still working. I asked Megan if she could pick up the girls from daycare for me so Derrick and I could quickly go to Reno and get back before it was too late. She agreed to pick them up, and I was going to get them from her at Donnie's house as soon as we were done. Derrick and I had our fun little shopping spree and hurried back up the hill with a car full of stuff we wanted but really didn't need. When I walked into the house, the girls were all playing and Megan and Donnie were on the couch watching TV. I noticed that it looked like gum was stuck in Zoe's hair. I walked up to her and tried to pick it out. It was really, really stuck. It was stuck to her head and looked like gum that you see run over by a tire on the road. "All right, which one of you idiots gave Zoe gum?" I asked, sarcastically. Megan looked at me like I was dumb. "We didn't give her gum. For Christ's sake, you think I want to deal with three little devils playing with gum?" she laughed. "It's weird. There is something seriously stuck in her hair." Megan called Zoe over so she could inspect. She picked some of it out. "Dude, I don't know if this is gum," she said. "Well what is it?" She inspected further. "It looks like a really bad scab."

The guys were in the kitchen talking about work. I pulled a key chain flashlight out of my purse. It was looking more like a scab. I was totally confused because I didn't understand how a monstrous scab would suddenly appear out of nowhere. Zoe was in daycare every day, and they hadn't mentioned seeing any scrapes or marks on her head. "How would a humongous scab like that just appear? She didn't have any scrapes or fall or anything, I don't get it," I thought out loud. "You know, burns will do that. They are just red at first and then crust over after the blister pops. You could have not seen it because her hair was in the way." I started to feel nauseous. "How the hell would she get a burn on her head?" I asked. "The stove in my kitchen has a glass window, but any time anything is in the oven I keep the kids out of the kitchen," I said. "Derrick!" I yelled across the room. "What?" he said - annoyed that I had interrupted him. "Did Zoe accidentally fall back on the stove when you were cooking last week?" I asked, trying not to jump to conclusions. "I don't know! When she's in there I usually tell her to leave. When I'm cooking, I'm not gonna babysit too!" he said.

The next day I asked the lady at the daycare if anything had happened to her that I didn't know about. I asked if she fell back and hit her head on anything. "No, not that we are aware of. But yesterday I saw that in her hair, and like you, I thought it was just gum, so I was just going to leave it up to you to pick it out," she said, laughing. I told her I didn't blame her for that one.

This scab was a mystery. It healed up pretty fast, but the more I thought about it, the more it bugged me. It was about the size of a fifty-cent piece, if not a little bigger. Even if she fell back on the oven, I couldn't see how it would be such a big burn because she would have jumped and moved away from it once she felt the pain. It was big to the point that it seemed that someone would have had to literally hold her head on the oven glass for a long enough time. I was always in the house when Derrick made dinner. I don't remember Zoe screaming out in pain and surely she would have. Once her scab healed, I didn't think about it as much because I wasn't going to figure it out anyway. I started to look for signs that would put up a red flag for abuse, but Derrick didn't display any. Eventually I let it go and resumed life. I thought that if I was taking care of the girls and keeping them happy, that what I was doing was okay because it was a phase that would pass. I didn't get the chance for the phase to pass. It was already too late.

It was a cold, snowy night in early March of 2006. I had gotten off work and was happy that it was finally Friday. I was hung-over from using cocaine the night before, and knew that the only way to recover was to use more - or sleep. I went home and took the girls inside. As I dusted the powdery snow off, Megan was calling my phone. "What 'cha doing?" she asked. "Nothing. I just got off work and I'm freakin' tired," I replied. "Does Chloe want to come for a sleep-over? Kylee needs her friend!" "Heck yeah!" I said. I needed a break - even if it was only a half break. Megan was already out so she came by for Chloe five minutes later. Chloe was excited and I knew she would have fun. "Don't you want to take Zoe too?" I asked, only half-kidding. "Who do you think I am? Mary Poppins?" Megan joked. I kissed Chloe goodbye and Megan drove off.

I walked back into the townhouse and told Derrick that I was going to run to the store to stock up on some food. My hunger was seriously catching up to me. Using cocaine and methamphetamine always caused me to go days without eating. It took my appetite away, and the dry mouth it caused made it very difficult to swallow. My body was weak and tired, and it felt as if my chest were caving in. "All right, go get some groceries and I'll watch Zoe." I walked back out to my car and drove ten minutes down the highway. The grocery store was packed. I grabbed a basket and tried to be quick, but it was impossible with the ridiculous number of people blocking every isle. Was the whole town there?

After grabbing some of the basics, I took a stroll down the frozen isle to get some junk food. I had already been gone about thirty minutes so I called Derrick to see if he wanted anything in particular and to make sure Zoe was okay. "Just get whatever you want. She's fine. I gave her pizza and put her to bed." he said. I finished my shopping and drove back home through the whiteout blizzard. I was excited to just get home and binge on food and then go to bed! I put the groceries away and, as Derrick was playing video games on the couch, I walked upstairs to check on Zoe. I always had to be the last to check on the girls. No matter how good their dad or Derrick was with them, I didn't care. I knew what they wanted and needed the best. Zoe was in her bed, swaddled in a blanket. An extra blanket was piled on her. I thought it was a little extreme so I pulled one of the blankets off, trying not to wake her, gave her a kiss and went back down to make a frozen dinner for myself. After scarfing down my food I announced to Derrick that I was going to bed. "Don't I get some lovin' first?" he demanded. I was not about to humor him. "No, you don't want to go there anyway, I'm on my period." I walked up the stairs as he whined. "Gross!" I was happy to gross him out. I got under the covers and that is the last thing I remember of that day.

"Mama!" Zoe called. She toddled into my room. Her light brown hair was a mess but the cutest mess ever. "Hi pumpkin! You have bedhead!" I said in my obnoxious baby voice.

"D-r-ess-ssed!" she replied. "You want to get dressed?" "Ya!" she said, enthusiastically. "Okay, sweet pea, mommy will help you get dressed." I rolled out of bed after looking at the clock. It was already ten in the morning. I felt like I had only slept for an hour. I woke up in the same position as when I got into bed the night before. Picking Zoe up, we walked five feet across the hallway to her room. I asked her what she wanted to wear. She had a really cute new jean outfit with a purple vest. I set her on her bed and walked over to her closet to get it. I heard loud, annoying laughter from downstairs. I could smell sausage too. Derrick must have had some guys over. I had no idea how long they had been there, but it sounded like they were thoroughly entertained. I heard the obnoxious sound effects of the Xbox. I was pretty irritated that there were so many people over and it was so early in the morning!

"Let's get dressed." I said, smiling back at Zoe. She wasn't putting up the fight that she typically gave me. She didn't like to stay still for long periods of time so getting her dressed could be a task. I grabbed the cute, new outfit out of her closet and started to dress her. In the process, I had to look again. Wait a minute - I've never seen this before. What the hell? I got dizzy, the room was spinning, and I knew that I had to wake up because this was a nightmare. "What happened baby?" I asked, as I was shaking and feeling queasy. "Owe!" she announced, pointing to the injury.

"DERRICK! GET UP HERE! NOW!" I wailed. It was a scream I didn't know I was capable of. "What?" he casually asked. "GET UP HERE RIGHT NOW!" I shrieked. I didn't care who heard me, or if anybody thought I was a psycho bitch of a girlfriend. If he had allowed my baby to get that hurt in the little time I was at the grocery store, he was in really big trouble! He took his time, and appeared about a minute later. I showed him what I was hoping would not be a nightmare and asked, "What the hell is this?" I was trying not to scare Zoe any more than I probably already had. His response was one that twisted my stomach. It was vague and nonchalant. He shrugged his shoulders, his lips tightened up in an awkward way, and said, "I don't know. Do you wanna go to the emergency room?" I didn't like the way he was acting. He wasn't concerned enough. If I went to the emergency room, I was not going with him by my side. I told him I had to think about it and that he should go back downstairs. I had to gather my thoughts and try not to panic.

I dressed Zoe in her outfit and thought about what I should do. What if one of the guys downstairs had done something to her? I wanted every person in the house to be questioned and tortured until there was an answer. Should I just call 911? That way, while everyone is here, the police can report it on record. Is this really happening? This is a parent's worst nightmare. Why me? Why my 19 month old baby who is completely innocent and doesn't deserve any sort of pain, torture, or abuse? It suddenly sunk in. I was lying on her bed with her on my chest. Hot tears streamed down my cheeks as I rubbed her head. "I'm so, so sorry." I whispered. She was falling asleep. "I love you so much Zoe. Mommy is so, so sorry she didn't protect you." I quietly cried. I looked up at the ceiling, hoping for a miracle. I started to beg God. I begged him to take it back. I begged him to let me wake up from this bad dream. I held my baby, who may have gone through the most terrifying thing ever and prayed. I don't know how long I was with her, but right as she woke up Derrick came back into the room. "Everyone left. What do you wanna do? You know if you take her to the hospital they will probably call CPS and the kids will be taken away again. I'm not saying you shouldn't, but I can fix this up myself and she'll be fine in a few weeks."

I couldn't believe what I was hearing. Just as drugs are normal in his world, he was attempting to eliminate the severe nature of the injury that my daughter had somehow sustained. I didn't reply except for a nod and a mumble. He left again to resume his video games. After putting Zoe's shoes on and zipping up her coat, I told him I was going to get Chloe and walked out the front door. Maybe I was seeing things. Maybe it wasn't as bad as I was making it out to be. I needed Megan to tell me what I didn't want to hear. I needed her opinion.

"Um…yeah. Kylee has had rashes before but never anything like that." she said. She was high. She had foil on her table and had been smoking meth. Why was she not panicking? If my 19-month old baby had been assaulted, why was no one else panicking? I didn't understand. I was confused and scared and heartbroken for my child. I didn't think I could get through it.

Zoe was excited to see her sister, and toddled her way toward the toys. She seemed fine. They all ran back to Kylee's bedroom. I sat down at the kitchen table and smoked with Megan. I don't know why. The very thing that had been a factor in my daughter's assault was in complete control of me. I just couldn't say no. If it was in my face, I was ingesting it. It tricked me. It tricked me into thinking that I was superior and only good things would be in my future. It tricked me into believing that Derrick, his brother, and their friends were "cool" people to be around. It stole my perception of reality, and it made me like the distortion.

After getting my energy back, I called my sister. She was still dating Huey. He was a doctor, and he would be able to tell me for certain what was going on. Lilah answered her phone, "Hey Liz, what are you doing?" she asked. I told her what was happening, and she also responded casually. "Liz, I'm sure it's fine. Just bring her over and I'll have Huey tell us what he thinks." I left Chloe to play with Kylee and drove to Huey's house. I told them what had happened at my house when I woke up to get Zoe dressed. Huey looked for only a few seconds. "It looks like the injury is maybe twelve to twenty-four hours old." I knew what he was implying. I put Zoe back into her car seat and we went to the hospital. Lilah and Huey were following behind me.

Chapter 30

Nothing will ever justify my actions and make them okay. Yes, I was young, had a severe lack of judgment, and very poor decision making skills. I have yet to find a psychiatrist to help me understand why I made so many mistakes. I think about it every day. Just like you, I also want to know why. I want answers that I may never have. I want the justice that was never served. I get so mad at myself. I took for granted the precious time that I had with my children - my gifts from God. They could have only come straight from heaven. The devil stole them from me. Drugs had taken over my life, and bad people gloated about my grief. Demons were laughing as I was signing a no-suicide contract. The devil was whispering over my shoulder that this was all just pretend.

The local hospital confirmed the nature of the injury and directed me to transport Zoe to the U.C. Davis Medical Center. They said that if I didn't take her they would have her go via ambulance. Megan brought Chloe to the hospital and offered to take me. Before leaving the hospital in Tahoe, I called my mom to tell her what was going on. It was late, and she was already asleep. "Hello?" she answered, sounding disoriented. "Mom!" I began to cry from hearing her voice. "Derrick hurt Zoe!" I sobbed. "Gosh damn it, Liz! That's why you stay away from screwed up guys like Derrick!" she yelled. She was shocked and angry. "Dan and I found drug paraphernalia when we were cleaning my house after you left. You guys trashed the place. I don't know what's gotten into you lately, but it's not you!" she angrily said. I guess she had been suspicious for a while but just didn't want to make me mad by bringing it up. It would have made me mad but only at myself, because she was the last person I wanted to disappoint. "I'll come to the hospital tomorrow. Keep your phone on." She hung up.

The drive was dark and long. The first night at the hospital I was grief-stricken. I was asked if I wanted to talk to the chaplain. I declined. Extensive testing was done on both girls. It gave me hope that answers would be found. I didn't think anything could possibly get worse. I held my baby as she was injected with anesthesia and collapsed in my arms for surgery. The emotional pain was agonizing and relentless. I held Chloe until she fell asleep on the second night. Then I held Zoe when she woke up crying in the children's hospital bed resembling a cage. I couldn't handle this. Megan went to her mother's house, which was an hour away to clean up. The girls and I were alone in the intensive care unit filled with very sick babies, but I still felt like we were alone.

I saw a crowd of medical professionals rushing a baby across the hallway in a wheeled cage, while performing CPR. It was a sad place, and the energy was wrong. I had to call Josh. I needed him. The girls needed their daddy. I was crying as I explained what was happening. Although the drive was two hours, he walked into the hospital room only forty-five minutes later. Zoe was sleeping and Chloe was restlessly sleeping on the tiny fold out chair we were sharing. He came in and sat down next to me. He held me and just let me cry. He told me it wasn't my fault. He told me that he loved me. "I love you too," I replied, choking up. He told me that I was a good mom. When the girls woke up they were excited to see their daddy - the only man that should have been in their life.

The on-call doctor walked in. She was a short, black woman wearing all white and holding a clipboard. "I have some bad news. I'm sick to my stomach for you. I have a two-year-old son, and I can't fathom what you're going through. We found traces of methamphetamine in her system." "WHAT?" I grabbed my stomach and keeled over. "What the hell is going on?" I cried. I couldn't take any more of this. Why, why, WHY? I had been abusing drugs, but I always made sure that the girls weren't close enough to be exposed, and I always kept any paraphernalia out of their sight and reach. The doctor made it seem as if someone had deliberately fed her the drugs. My baby had been tortured, and I wasn't there to save her!

My first instinct told me that Derrick had done it. I began piecing things together. I had to have an answer immediately. I couldn't endure this without knowing whom to blame. It all made sense, but it didn't matter anymore because it was too late.

In an instant, I went from being treated with sympathy and dignity, to being looked down on and questioned by the hospital, child protective services, and the police. I wanted to get back to Tahoe immediately to speak with detectives so they could arrest Derrick. I hadn't made any contact with him since I last saw him. He had left at least a hundred messages on my phone, wanting to "check in" and see how we were doing. That made me sick. I had to go home and confront him. Josh agreed to stay at the hospital with Zoe the entire time I would be gone. I was hoping to be back the next day.

Josh had an aunt that lived nearby, and she offered to come to the hospital to take Chloe to her house so she would be out of that horrible environment. I was happy to see her walk in before I left. Her young daughter was with her and I remembered seeing her at our wedding. They had gifts for the girls - baby dolls and books. I felt even better about leaving the hospital. I kissed the girls goodbye and gave Josh a hug. I regretted leaving him. I wondered if he would ever be able to look past that. I wondered, for a moment, if we could ever realistically work out again. Josh made me feel safe. I had a new respect for him, and I knew that he would never, ever harm our beautiful babies.

Megan drove me back home. We stopped at a gas station so she could get gas. I went inside to get a drink. "How are you today?" The polite cashier asked me. How am I supposed to answer that? She really doesn't want to know, I thought.

When a tragedy is in your path, the world still goes on. Life continues whether we want it to or not. The world keeps spinning, the seasons keep changing, and the sun continues to rise and set. I cried and cried and ached.

My first meeting with the detective wasn't what I expected. It was more like an interview or an interrogation. He played the good cop at first. I walked into the police station eager to cooperate in any way possible. I trusted him. His name was Detective Olden. He was a tall, skinny man. He initially spoke to me with respect and let me speak without interruption. The tables turned quickly. He was now the bad cop. Once he realized that there was drug use going on, he turned against me and he went hard. I cried and fessed up to doing drugs - hoping that even if my honesty put me in jail, it would at least solve the crime. The first interview was over, and I was even more heartbroken.

That night I was planning on driving back to the hospital. There was a blizzard, and my car didn't do too well in the snow. When Josh called me and said that Child Protective Services were taking Chloe from his aunt and that Zoe would also be taken when she got out of the hospital, I panicked and got in my car. I wanted to get there to be by Zoe's side as much as I could. If they were going to take her, I wanted to tell her I loved her first. I just wanted to be there. As I began driving through the terrible storm, Josh called me again. "Josh, have they given you any sort of paperwork or anything? How do you know for sure that they are taking them?" I asked. "They haven't done anything except tell me they are taking Chloe and Zoe. I didn't even do anything wrong. They need to let me take them home," he said. "Take Zoe home then! If they don't have a Court Order they can't possibly just take her!" I cried. "Just stay there and we'll figure it out when I get there okay?" I concluded.

We got off the phone just in time. There was a chain stop ahead, and I had to find a way to get chains put on my tires. This was the only way I could get to my baby. I pulled into the gas station and walked up to a door that read CLOSED. I saw a woman in the store counting her register. I had arrived five minutes too late. I didn't care. I was getting in that store and getting chains to make it over the summit. I knocked loudly on the glass door. The woman looked at me from a distance. "I'm sorry, but we are closed." I began crying. "Please help me! I need to buy chains to get to the hospital. My baby is at U.C. Davis and I need to get to her. I would do whatever it took to be by my baby's side to help comfort her. The woman must have had sympathy because she unlocked the door to let me in. "What do you need ma'am?" she asked. "I need chains to get over the mountain." She ran to the back of the store and brought out cables because they were all she had left. I paid and she wished me luck. As I was headed toward the hill that would eventually lead me to Sacramento, I saw that the road was blocked off with chain control. Everything was white. The big digital emergency alert billboard was right above the chain control.

As I got closer, I realized that it wasn't displaying a road condition warning as I had expected it to. It was displaying a bright, flashing Amber Alert. I instantly knew what it was. Josh had taken Zoe out of the hospital. I pulled up to chain control and told them that I had no idea how to put chains on. I tried to compose myself and not act paranoid. The man was very nice, and he put the chains on for me as I sat in the driver's seat. "You know ma'am, keep an eye out for a green Subaru. There's an Amber Alert. A little girl went missing from U.C. Davis hospital." "Oh, wow," I said, trying to stay calm. "Where are you heading?" he asked. "To Sacramento. My daughter is in that hospital, sick, right now," I replied. By the look on his face, I think he knew something was up. He didn't say anything else and wished me luck as I drove off. I called Josh's cell phone repeatedly to no avail. Finally, as I was driving to the steep and dangerous part of the summit, he called. "Josh! What happened and where are you?" I asked. "They put a tracking device around Zoe's ankle. It pissed me off. I took it off of her and walked out. I started driving, but I'm out of gas so I am parked behind a gas station." "Is Zoe okay?" I asked. "Yeah, she's sleeping right now. We are lying down in the back seat." I started to cry as I pictured my baby contently cuddled up with her daddy - knowing that she would soon be torn away from him. "I am going to try to find you. I'll call you when I get closer to your area, okay?" We hung up.

As I started to climb even higher up the mountain, thousands of feet above sea level, the weather got more and more intense. I could not see five feet in front of me. Fatigue was kicking in, and I started seeing things that weren't there. I thought I saw the road turn into an intersection, but it did not. If I had gone left, I would have driven right off the mountain. God was telling me that the girls would be okay and I should turn around, go back and rest. I had been with Megan at her house the entire time I was in town, so I had not gone home to rest. I turned around and went back to Tahoe.

I continued to try to get ahold of Josh on the phone to explain why I didn't make it to Sacramento and to make sure he and Zoe were okay, but he never answered his phone. I figured that the police had found him, arrested him, and took Zoe back to the hospital. I later learned that Josh was in jail over the "kidnapping," and he would possibly be released in a day or two.

208

When I found out that he was placed in the Sacramento county jail, I worried about his safety. He is not much of a fighter, and if he were to talk too much (his ADHD always caused him to ramble) he might have some trouble. I hoped he was okay, and I felt really bad for him.

I pulled into my driveway praying that I wouldn't find Derrick and his brother lounging around like they owned the place. I quietly walked up to the glass sliding door where I could see into the house before entering. The door was unlocked and all was quiet. I cautiously walked in and saw that the kitchen was a disaster. I investigated further and noticed that my brand new computer was gone. Everything was trashed. "Why, God? Why does this have to be happening?" I cried again. I broke down, feeling completely defeated. I fell to the kitchen floor and just sat there crying. I couldn't breathe. I was so overwhelmed, worried for Josh, worried about who would be comforting Zoe when she was taken back to the hospital, and worried about Chloe and where CPS would be taking her. I couldn't handle this! It was late, cold, and dark.

I suddenly realized that this was the perfect way to get Derrick put in jail - from now until the crime was solved. I picked up my phone and called 911. "What's your emergency?" the operator asked. "Yes, my house has been broken into, and I need an officer to come and make a report." Two officers showed up less than five minutes later. They were very nice. I told them what had been going on and how I was suspicious that Derrick was the one responsible. The officers made me feel like I was a person and not a piece of trash.

As I was searching through the desk for the computer manual to determine the make and model for the police report, I came across a small bag with white residue. I did not recognize this bag, and I knew it was not from my use because I always threw them away. I gave it to the officers for evidence. As I went into my downstairs bathroom to pee, I noticed that Derrick had spit in my sink. It was tinged with brown. Derrick knew that this was one thing that highly upset me and grossed me out. It was disrespectful and lazy of someone to not just rinse it down the drain. He must have done this on purpose. I pointed it out to the officers and said that I knew for certain it was not there before I initially left. They took a sample of it for further evidence. They left my house to try to retrieve my computer, which would be held for evidence.

About thirty minutes later I got a call saying that Derrick had been arrested for burglary, and he did have my computer. I was so relieved. At least I wouldn't have to worry about him trying to show up at my apartment. It was around midnight, and there was nothing left to do except try to sleep.

I went up to my room wondering what I would use to replace my bedding that he had also slept in. I wanted every trace of him out of my house and far away from me, forever. I decided that I would sleep in Chloe and Zoe's room. As I got into Zoe's bed, I noticed an old tube of ointment that I had used for my tattoo on her dresser. I knew for a fact that I did not put it there; I would have no reason to. I picked it up and snapped the lid open. It was tinged with blood. Oh my God. He tried to fix her injury with ointment for Christ's sake! This was evidence, and I would take it to the detective tomorrow. I now regretted picking it up because I was afraid I smeared the fingerprints that would surely name the suspect. I hoped that traces of whatever happened would surely be prominent on the blood-tinged lid. I tried to fall asleep, but I couldn't stop picturing what might have happened to Zoe. I wondered if it happened in the very room I was laying in. I grabbed Zoe's stuffed animal and went to Chloe's bed. I fell asleep, tightly holding Chloe and Zoe's stuffed animals, soaking them with my tears. I could smell both my girls, and I could almost feel their sweet, innocent presence. I ached for them so badly. I ached, knowing that they did not understand why I wasn't there with them. Small children have only one thing that their world revolves around and that is their parents. They don't understand much of anything else but the fact that their parents are always there to bring them comfort and make them feel safe. I wasn't there to do this for them, and the fear that they were suffering was ripping my heart out. I eventually fell asleep. I periodically woke up, crying throughout the night.

Chapter 31

The next morning I woke up and slowly opened my eyes. I was hoping that things would be back to normal. I so desperately wanted this to just be a nightmare. In my reality world something like this would never happen. I noticed that I had a voicemail from the detective. He wanted me to come in again for a second interview. He said that he had spoken with Derrick and that Derrick had not been very cooperative through the glass window of the jail. I called him back immediately and asked him what time I should be there. "Just come in around four o'clock," he said. I got up out of bed feeling just as tired as I had the night before. The grief was completely wearing me out. I had no energy, and decided that I should stay distracted until it was time to meet with the detective. I started to clean my house. Usually, when I feel stressed, I clean. I also wanted every little speck of anything that reminded me of Derrick to be gone. I was ashamed of myself and in complete disbelief that I had allowed such a person to be in my life and around my children. In the back of my mind I was hoping that the person responsible for what happened to Zoe was one of the other people that had been in my home that night. In reality, I knew that Derrick was the person who was most likely responsible.

I would ask the detective if it would be okay to scrub my house when I went to see him. I was surprised that my house hadn't been raided and they hadn't tried to take more evidence. I assumed that they would certainly be back later. When I went into my bathroom, I noticed that the trashcan had a lot of garbage in it, and it was unusually heavy. I investigated further because I always took the trash out at least every other day, and I was wondering what could be in there. I found items that were wrapped up, along with some foil and other paraphernalia. I was afraid of what I would find. I never put this kind of trash in that specific trash can. I always put it in the trashcan in the kitchen. My heart started racing, and I became very anxious. The items in the trashcan supported the possibility of an assault. This gave me a horrible visual of what was brought upon my daughter, and hot tears were quickly running down my cheeks.

I firmly believed that this trashcan held the key to the crime and would be what helped to solve this horrible crime. I put the items back into the trashcan and raced out my back door. Driving down the highway and trying not to speed, I called the detective from my cell phone. I told him what I had found in my bathroom and said that I was bringing it over to him. He told me to drop it off at the front desk of the police department.

As I walked up and rang the bell to unlock the front doors, he poked his head out and grabbed the can from me. He rolled his eyes, and I was surprised that he wasn't taking this more seriously. I was highly disappointed and I started to lose faith that he even cared about solving the case. A few days passed, and I was astonished to learn that the police would not be further searching my house for more evidence.

Looking back, I wish that someone had told me not to talk to the detective without my Attorney. I thought nothing of it, though, since I had done nothing wrong to Zoe. All I wanted to do was help get this horrible crime solved. I was willing to talk to anyone that I needed to in order for this to happen. I went back to the police station at 4:00 p.m., and walked through the hallway following the detective. He took me into the same room as before. At that time I didn't know that it was an interrogation room. I thought it was weird how he would periodically get up and ask me if I wanted something to drink. He said he was thirsty and was going to get something anyway. I always declined; I really could care less about anything to drink. I just cared about getting this crime solved. Every time I talked to him he always played the good cop first - probably trying to get me to trust him. Of course it worked because I was eighteen, very naive, and confused.

"I spoke with Derrick yesterday. It took me about five times of questioning him before he started to cooperate, but once he did, he gave me all the information that I needed, and I'm really good at reading people." "Okay," I said, a little unsure of where he was going with this. "I think that he's innocent. I think that he is being truthful with me. Unlike you, he immediately admitted to using drugs." "What is that supposed to mean?" I asked. I was starting to get upset with what he was implying. I already offered all of the information that I possible. For him to think that I knew more felt extremely betraying. "Come on Elizabeth, I know that you know more than you're telling me. You were on drugs and you were binging and something happened. Just tell me what happened." "Excuse me? You're kidding right?" I was stunned. I began to cry out of frustration. "I have no idea what happened! That's why I'm sitting here. You can search my car, you can search my house, you can get all of the evidence necessary, and I actually would prefer that you did. Give me a lie detector test right now!" I demanded. "I have a guy coming up from Placerville, and I'm going to have you both take a voice-analysis test." "Good, I'm eager to take this test since you think that I know more than I do," I said, steaming mad. The interview was over.

I was too upset to talk to him anymore and he knew it. Before I left, he asked me to take a drug test. I agreed. I hadn't used anything since that horrible day anyway. A female officer escorted me to the restroom and stood there while I peed in a cup. At least she let me close the stall door. After the drug test, the detective told me that he would call me with a time to come in for the voice-analysis stress test. I had never even heard of that before. I was hoping to take the traditional polygraph, but I was willing to do whatever it took. I called my Public Defender after the interview and told her about the way he was treating me. She told me not to speak with him unless she was present. I told her about the voice-analysis, and she asked me, "Well, do you want to take it?" "Yes! I have nothing to hide, and if this proves that then I'm all for it." I answered, firmly. "Okay, then I suggest you definitely take it."

I went home and tried to call Megan. She hadn't answered her phone for a few days now. Normally, she would call me right back. I assumed that she either wanted to stay away from me to cover her own ass and keep her drug use discreet, or she had sided with Derrick because she was dating his brother. I told myself that it would be my last attempt to contact her. If she was going to ditch me when I needed her the most, she was never really my friend in the first place. My mom lived three hours away so I was basically alone.

A week after the horrible tragedy my twin sister was coming to town. She had graduated from her Advanced Individual Training from the Air Force and had orders to go to Germany for the next three years. I was so happy that she was coming. I was also sad and afraid of what she would think and if she would be disappointed in me. Lilah and Merri met me at a local Thai restaurant. She immediately hugged me, and of course, I started to cry. She was crying too. She felt my pain. Although we're

216

fraternal twins and look nothing alike, we still had that twin connection.

I hadn't realized how much I missed having her around. She was certainly a different person. She was mature and responsible. I was so proud of her for getting through all of that difficult training. She decided to stay with me for the remainder of her stay, which was only another few days. My older sister, Lilah, came over to see Merri. After they hugged each other, she wanted to know how I was doing. I was not doing well. The thought of my girls being away from me, possibly forever, was killing me. "If I don't get Chloe and Zoe back home, I WILL kill myself. I will have no reason to live, end of story. I don't want to do this," I said, crying. "I can't handle it all, and I just don't understand why something so sad had to happen to my family, especially my little baby!" I said, sobbing more.

My sisters both began to cry, and Lilah began to panic. She was truly worried that I would hurt myself. I didn't mean to scare them. It was just a clear fact in my mind. If I didn't get my girls back, I would no longer have a reason for living. Trying to survive would just be too much of a struggle.

After lunch, Lilah drove me to the mental health facility down the street to talk to a crisis counselor. She was an older lady. She was nice but didn't really say much. I think that she was expecting me to do most of the talking. What was there to say? I was shattered and in a deep, dark, evil hole. I was in the darkest place that life has to offer, and it had brought me down fast. I didn't have the energy to pull myself out. I just wanted to lie down and sleep and only wake up when my babies were back in my arms. Nothing that any person said or did made it better. Nothing took the pain away. The counselor pulled out a piece of paper for me to sign. She called it a "no-suicide contract." I almost laughed. I was shocked that such a document existed.

That night Ally came over with her friend and all of the girls helped me get rid of Derrick's belongings that were still in my closet.

We all started laughing when Ally jumped and screamed as I threw his vest down the staircase and it landed on her. We were treating his things as if they were toxic waste. That night of support has always stuck with me. During the worst moments of my life, I found out whom I could count on through the good the bad. The next night, the night before Merri had to leave for the airport, I came down with a horrible sore throat. I didn't know if it was from chain smoking or crying so much or what. I was also devastated that my twin sister had to leave. I wanted her to stay with me forever. She made me feel as secure as I could feel at that time. I lost my whole family and now I had to say goodbye to her too. I broke down on the bathroom floor, sobbing. "Liz? What's wrong?" She rushed over. "I just can't...take...this!" I said between sniffles. "I know. I love you. I'm sorry you're having to go through this." She hugged me. She drove me to the hospital later that night for some antibiotics. The next morning at 4:00 a.m., I woke up and drove her through another blizzard to the casino so she could get on the shuttle headed to the airport. I hugged her and told her I loved her. I cried on my way home. I got back into my clean bed and went back to sleep.

I woke up a few hours later to a phone call from CPS. They told me that I could schedule a visit that day with the girls. They finally found a foster home in Tahoe where the girls could stay together. I was so incredibly happy that they were together and would be staying close to me. They were born to be best friends and to always stay together and keep each other safe and happy. My visit was at 3:00 o'clock. I was so anxious to see them but sad at the same time because I knew I couldn't take them home with me. I got dressed, put on makeup for the first time in a week, and headed down the highway.

Walking into the office, there were three Social Workers. One was holding Zoe. Chloe was in the corner playing with toys. I immediately grabbed Zoe, hugged her, and rubbed her head, so grateful to be holding her tiny body in my arms. I was so grateful that she was alive and seemed happy. "I love you so much little girl. Mommy has missed you!" I said, after kissing her forehead. Chloe ran up to me. "Mommy!" I knelt down with Zoe in my arm and put my other arm out as Chloe ran in for a hug. I was finally holding my babies again. It was natural for them to be in my arms - not in the arms of strangers. The visit was only an hour long but it felt like ten minutes. The Social Workers stepped out but they were watching me through a glass window. This made me timid, and I felt like they were just waiting for me to say or do something wrong. I talked to the girls, and asked them how they were. Chloe asked, "Where's Derrick?" Ugh, I was hoping she wouldn't bring him up. "I don't know honey. Show mommy how you color!" I said, changing the subject.

The female Social Workers walked in, all three of them, and the one with long red hair announced that the visit was over. "Okay," I said, trying with all my soul to fight back tears. I picked up my handbag and tried to move slowly so the girls wouldn't notice that I was leaving. Chloe immediately knew what was going on. She rushed over to her puffy, light blue coat and hurried to put it on. "Mommy! I want to go in your car!" She begged. I knelt down to her. "Can mommy have a hug?" I asked, with tears running down my face, landing on her soft head of light brown hair. "But I want to go in your car!" She cried. This time, she was crying out of pain. She didn't want me to leave her there with those strange people. We were both crying and hugging each other tightly. She wasn't even three years old but we had such a strong and loving bond. She felt my pain, and I felt hers. Zoe toddled up, confused. She began to cry. I hugged both of them. Chloe continued to beg to go home with me. "I'm so sorry honey, but they won't let me take you home right now. I promise, I am going to do everything I can to get you home very soon…okay?" I sniffled.

The woman with red hair came up to us. "It's time for you to leave now. You're just making it worse for them." she said. "I'm not allowed to cry because they can't be with me?" I almost yelled. "You are the most inhumane person I have ever met!" My voice rose even louder. She shrugged. I had to go, but I felt like I couldn't physically let go of my daughters - my flesh and blood, my perfect angels. I was forced to walk out of that room without my babies, and it was one of the saddest, most heartbreaking moments I've ever experienced.

I walked out of the building crying. I felt pain shooting through my body. My heart ached as if it were begging me to go back and get my girls. I was not whole without them. I called my father. I was hysterically crying. He listened and told me to pray. I knew then that my dad really did love me. I realized that he had always loved me.

Chapter 32

That visit truly ripped a chunk of my heart out. I went home, wondering what to do with myself. I wanted to stay busy and distracted, but every small thing was a reminder of my daughters and how they weren't at home where they were supposed to be. I had to close the door to their bedroom. I couldn't handle seeing their toys, their little beds, and their stuffed animals. I decided to go to the Court and file for a Restraining Order in case they let Derrick out of jail. I didn't think he would be going anywhere for a long, long time, but I wanted CPS to know that I would never allow him to be near me or the girls again. After filing the paperwork, I went down the street to the college to talk to my boss at the bookstore because I was sure she was probably wondering where I had been. I hadn't called her to let her know what was happening, but I figured that the small-town gossip had already started and she must have heard something. I walked in but my boss wasn't there. She was probably on a break. One of my favorite co-workers, Michelle, was working. She got off the phone shortly after she noticed me standing there. I didn't know what to say. What could I say? "What's wrong?" she asked, seeing the evidence of stress and heartache in my eyes. I tried to talk, but the words wouldn't come out. I tried to hold back my tears so hard. I wanted to be in control of my life. Nothing was under control. I started crying. "Baby, what is it?" she asked again, hugging me. "My...boyfriend...hurt my baby!" I cried. "Oh no, I'm so sorry Elizabeth!" she consoled. I explained in further detail about the events that had taken place. She sat in the back office with me and just listened. The bookstore was pretty empty, so she didn't have any customers at the moment.

She called our boss on her cell phone, and she said that she would be back in a few minutes. Before I knew it, she walked in to find out what was going on. I explained the situation while trying to hold myself together as best as I could. "Well, I'm so sorry you're having to go through this. If anyone wants to talk to me, I'll be glad to tell them that from what I've seen you have always been to work on time and responsible, and I've never noticed any drug use." "Thank you," I sniffled. Of course, I hadn't told her about my drug use. I didn't want anyone to know about that. It was humiliating and had led to tragedy. I felt like everything was my fault. I never, in a million years, would have expected anything that horrific to happen to one of my children. If I had been clean, those men would never have been in my home in the first place. I would have kicked Derrick out at some point along the way and everything would have been okay. I would have struggled financially, but my daughters would have been safe and at home. My boss scheduled work for me, and we agreed that keeping busy would only be a benefit to me. I was alone and my co-workers were just about the only non-biased support I had.

After I left the college, I went to the gas station to get myself a pack of cigarettes. They were just about the only thing that kept me from passing out or vomiting when I had one of my many breakdowns. When I was paying the cashier Jesse, a friend that I had known since third grade, tapped me on the shoulder. I was so surprised to see him. I hadn't seen him since before I was pregnant. He dated Megan for a while, and his best friend, Andy, had been my very first official boyfriend. Andy moved away a year after we dated. We were only twelve and thirteen, but we were definitely in love with each other.

"Holy crap! It's been forever!" I exclaimed. "I know, I know. What have you been up to?" he asked. "You don't want to know. Things are really bad right now." He saw the look on my face and became concerned. "What's going on?" he asked. "I can't tell you right now, but you should stop by my place later on and we can catch up," I said. I gave him my address and left the gas station. I didn't think that Jesse would actually come by, but later that night he knocked on my door. "Hi!" I said, gesturing for him to come in. I gave him a long overdue hug and told him I was glad he stopped by. He had grown from an obnoxious little kid, shooting spitballs through straws at other girls (me included), to a handsome young adult. He had a contagious smile. He always maintained a positive attitude no matter what kind of crappy situation he was in. I remember one day when I was fourteen and before I met Josh. My first boyfriend had unwillingly left me, and Jesse was one of the few left of our once-upon-a-time little group. I had a group of friends over including him. We were all jumping on the trampoline while listening to Britney Spears. I was dancing to one of her classic songs. My mom didn't like that. She thought that I was dancing like a slut. She yelled at me about it in front of everyone and told me to stop. I got off the trampoline and said some smart-ass remark. She slapped me across the face in front of everyone. She hardly ever did that. I was so upset that I felt tears running down my face. I didn't want to cry in front of everyone so I left.

I started running down the street. I didn't know where I was going, but I knew there was a trail in the mountain a few blocks away from my house. I hiked about half way up the small mountain. It was starting to get dark so I finally stopped. I knew that I wouldn't be found there. I had gone a long distance in a very short amount of time. I sat on a log, crying, thinking about my life. The trees, the fresh air, and the silence of the mountains always brought me into a meditative state. I calmed down and my thoughts began to ease. I was in sync with my surroundings, and I didn't ever want to leave. If I were attacked by one of the many bears in Tahoe, I figured it was just meant to be. "Elizabeth!" I heard a yell from a distance. I didn't immediately recognize the voice so I didn't respond. I didn't want to give my mom the satisfaction of remorsefully running back home to her.

"Elizabeth!" another echo sounded. I heard a loud whistle. I knew that my mom didn't know how to whistle like that. It was Jesse. "What?" I responded loudly. He showed up less than five minutes later. He somehow knew where to find me, and I still have no idea how he knew. I had never hiked that mountain before. "What are you doing crazy girl?" he asked with that silly grin he always had on his face. I couldn't help but smile. "I hate her. I am so sick of her! I am so sick of the bullshit!" I said, holding back the tears. "I know, but she said she's sorry and she wants you to come home." he relayed. I rolled my eyes. He reached out his hand. "Let's go, it's getting dark and I'm going to have to carry you down the damn hill if we don't hurry, crazy girl." I grabbed his hand and he helped me up. We made the hike down the hill, and when I would start to slip on the steep pine needle covered slopes, he would always make sure to catch me. He walked me home. "Do I at least get a hug for saving your life?" he joked. "Of course." I said, as I hugged him. He held onto me and told me to go in and work it out with my mom. I did what he suggested. At that moment I was just a kid who didn't realize how much he must have cared about me. After writing this, I now see it. A typical fourteen-year-old kid wouldn't go out of his way to hike two miles to convince his female friend to work her drama out with her mother. He did. So, thank you, Jesse. You possibly could have saved my life. I never officially thanked him for this.

224

He sat on my couch and before I told him about my horrible situation, I asked him how he was doing. "I'm good. My ex-girlfriend had our baby two weeks ago. He's so cute," he said, pulling up a picture on his phone. "Oh my gosh, Jesse! He is adorable! But I'm confused - how is she your ex if you just had a baby?" I asked. "She's mean, and we just don't get along at all. We decided that it's best for us to not be together because all we ever do is fight. We have an agreement that I will be there every day and pay for whatever they need, but we aren't ever going to be a couple again." he said.

I thought that was really mature of him. Most guys his age would run, and I told him that. I then told him about what had been happening in the previous weeks. I cried periodically, still stunned that I had to tell such a story. He listened and said what he could to comfort me. I told him about the detectives accusing me, too. "Don't worry, they lie and say anything to get any kind of information. They just want to see how you react." That helped me feel better. We ended up getting a pack of beer that night. We invited his friend over, whom I also knew. Jake was super laid back and non-judgmental. It felt so nice having friends with me that I had known forever who would always have my back no matter what. We got a little buzzed and determined that the guys would crash downstairs on my couches so they wouldn't have to drive. Jesse was passionate and sensitive with me. He cared.

The next day we spontaneously got in his truck, and the three of us made the six-hour drive to Santa Cruz. I just wanted to get away and stand in the ocean. I wanted to feel the windy, salty ocean breeze on my face. I wanted to go back in time to when I was little with my grandparents. The ocean reminded me of them. After the long, long drive, we arrived at a hotel around two in the morning. We hardly had any money but just enough to get the room. It was a suite with a separate bedroom. It was a romantic room, with white curtains tied to the side displaying the ocean. We fell asleep to the sound of the waves crashing, and I was given a night of peace and comfort. I felt secure with the ocean and Jesse and just being away from the pain.

The next day we woke up at 11:00 a.m. to the phone ringing. The hotel told us we had to pay for another night or kick rocks. We had about twenty dollars left. We packed our things and headed to the boardwalk. The sun was blazing and there were hippies with dreadlocks skating around everywhere. It was the side of California that I loved - carefree, happy and sunny. We all shared a $5 pizza for lunch but weren't quite sure how we would make it back home. None of us seemed to care though. We started to drive. After a couple hours, the gas tank was getting low. We stopped at the next gas station knowing that fifteen dollars would, in no way, get us home. I tried a trick with my debit card, and it ended up filling the gas tank - $60 worth. We finally made it home, and I was instantly depressed again because I knew that I had to face reality. I hated it. I had another visit with the girls the next day and Court the day after. The Judge would determine if the girls could come home with me, or if they would remain in foster care for another six months.

Chapter 33

I wasn't always so weak. I once had a strong sense of the person I was - a mother, daughter, sister, and young woman with my whole life ahead of me. When I was a seventeen-year-old mom of two, I didn't put up with crap from anyone. And people knew not to mess with me. I was a college student dedicated to providing my daughters and my husband a better future. We were living in a tiny apartment, and I knew that we all deserved much better than that. I was studying to pass the required courses to apply to a nursing school in Carson City. It was a competitive two-year program, but I knew I could do it. I wanted to work in the maternity ward at the local hospital as a labor and delivery nurse and eventually become the head nurse. I figured that the only thing that would prevent me from recklessly popping out another six kids would be to make a career for myself.

As I moved on and became seriously involved with Derrick, those goals were becoming less important to me. I stayed in school but had a hard time keeping up with the classes. The crazy all-nighters were starting to wear on me. The girls were eventually in daycare for twelve hours days. I had to find time to study at school because I knew I wouldn't get a chance once I got home.

Derrick had a group of friends he liked to hang out with. A few were more on the normal side but most were not. They had a way of making drinking binges and parties seem normal. They were all older than me; I was definitely the runt of the group. The first time

I saw them smoking crystal meth, I had no idea what it was. They sat in a circle and passed around a glass pipe filled with boiling liquid. The smoke was extremely thick and white. It had a slightly sweet smell to it. I knew that it couldn't have been anything good, but other than that, I was lost.

I was always paranoid of that sort of thing. I had never tried illegal drugs before. Well, besides marijuana, that is, when I was a freshman in High School. It was a bad experience. I assumed that if I couldn't handle pot, I would probably not be able to handle anything of a stronger nature.

The night I chose to leave Josh to be with Derrick was the night I chose my fate for the next four years. That night I chose not only my fate, but also the fate of Zoe and Chloe, and the fate of their relationship with my family. My spiritual and moral struggle was just beginning.

I woke up the next day and got ready to visit my daughters at noon. I made sure I grabbed a copy of the signed restraining order to give to the Social Worker when I arrived. Immediately after walking through the door, a Social Worker asked me to follow her back to her office for a moment. She handed me paperwork and said that I needed to sign it before the visit could take place. I read the paperwork and it said something along the lines of "I agree not to cry during my visit with my children. I further understand that I am not allowed to make any promises to my children and any inappropriate behavior will lead to the termination of my visitation." I absolutely could not believe what I was reading. I was completely disgusted, and I wondered if this was even legal! I thought that the Court could only make decisions like that. I never thought that being emotional over the situation would lead to threats of not being able to visit my girls. This made me angry, and I had a very difficult time showing respect for any of those people from then on. I knew that I could

228

not trust anyone and had to constantly be aware of my surroundings and who was watching me.

I was finally able to see the girls for the measly hour-long visit. It was bittersweet because I knew that I was being watched, and I didn't know how to interact with my girls under that kind of pressure. I wanted to just be normal, as I always was, but I knew that they were taking notes about everything and I was afraid. I sat in a chair and talked to both of the girls as they rambled on about what they had been doing for the past week. I also had them show me how to put together a puzzle and asked them what their favorite toy was. I always made sure to tell them how much I loved them and missed them. I wanted to make promises but wasn't allowed to. I was absolutely defeated. The girls cried this time when I left, but it wasn't as bad as the first time because I think that they were expecting it. Of course, I cried as well, but I was better able to conceal it because I didn't want to risk my visits being cut off for good.

I just had an hour before I had to go to the first Court Hearing for CPS. I went home and found something decent to wear. I tried to fix my hair because I just wanted to look like my normal self - before I had ever gotten involved with Derrick or drugs. It was hard to look presentable. I had lost so much weight. My grief had caused a serious loss of appetite. I had dark circles under both eyes from crying so much, and I just looked unhealthy in general. The proceeding was really quick.

The Lawyer for Social Services gave the Judge a petition to keep the girls in the Custody of the State, and the Judge signed it. I was given a copy of this report. We would begin a Court trial to determine the cause of the injury and who caused it the following week. I think that the Judge wanted to make sure that I had absolutely nothing to do with the injury. There were also drug-abuse accusations in the report, so the Judge ordered me to take regular drug tests. I just wanted a list of whatever it was that they wanted me to do so I could hurry up and do it and get my babies back home

229

with me. Right after Court, the CASA worker that had met and approved of Derrick asked to talk to me in an empty conference room. I sat down next to her, facing a long meeting table, not expecting to hear what I did. "How could you, Elizabeth? I am disgusted! You should have known what was going on in your home! And drugs? I thought you were clean! You should be seriously ashamed of yourself." I sat silently as she continued "It's going to take a lot of work for you to get those girls back. I won't recommend them to return home until you really work long and hard on yourself." She spat at me everything that I did not want to hear. I knew that I was stupid, and I had made bad choices. I had let freaks into my life and home. She had kicked me hard when I was already down. Once again, hot tears were rolling down my face, and I couldn't even respond to her. I knew that I had completely let down every person that I had ever known. I already knew everything that she said. I walked out of the conference room with my head down.

Before leaving the building, my Public Defender pulled me aside and informed me that Derrick was upstairs in Court at this moment. The District Attorney wanted to know if I would be willing to testify against him. "Of course!" I said. She told me that she wasn't sure if the Judge was going to let Derrick out of jail or not, but either way, if Derrick didn't take a plea, the case would go to trial. I waited outside in the lobby until my Public Defender came back out to inform me of his custody status. About fifteen minutes later, she came out shaking her head. "Well, they let him out in his own recognizance." "What?" I replied. I was in disbelief. I did not understand why they let him out. I thought that they were supposed to keep people like him locked up for a very, very long time. I thought that they would do anything to make that happen. I didn't understand. I returned home, exhausted from the day and just wanted to go to sleep and never wake up. Jesse came over later that night to keep me company. He had been coming over almost every day.

A Detective called me the next day asking if I could go in for a voice-analysis-stress-test that afternoon. "I would be happy to," I eagerly said. My dad called to check in on me, and I told him about the test I was going to take. He advised me against it. "I know you want to prove that you have no knowledge of the incident, Elizabeth, but I had a good friend who took that same test and failed it. He ended up spending time in prison, and, to this day, he says he was innocent. Those tests are a bunch of crap; they are just used as a tool by the cops," he warned. "I know, but I just have to take it because I know I'll pass. I have nothing to hide!" I replied. My dad offered to go with me and said he would start driving to Tahoe in the next hour. He was only forty-five minutes away. I was happy to have him go with me. I was so tired of being treated like a horrible mother and a criminal, and maybe if they saw my dad there they would give me just an ounce of respect. My dad picked me up twenty minutes before it was time to take the test. He drove me to the police station and walked me in. A police officer that I did not recognize opened the door and called my name, gesturing for me to follow him to the back. "I'll be right here, Elizabeth. If they make you uncomfortable, just walk out." my dad said as I walked to another interrogation room. The officer was nice to me, initially. I couldn't help but wonder if he was playing good cop as all the others had done. He said that he was going to clip a microphone to my shirt so it could record the levels of stress in my voice. He pulled out his laptop and started going over how the test worked. I thought it was pretty pathetic that I was taking a test that was supposedly 100% accurate from a laptop! I questioned the validity of this so called "test" that I had never even heard about.

He started out by asking me simple questions, with only yes or no answers. "Is the wall in front of you blue?" he asked. "No," I replied. "Do you know who is responsible for the injury to your daughter, Zoe?" he asked. "No," I replied. "Okay, you did well on this question." he announced. I wasn't surprised, because I knew I would. "Are you responsible for the injury inflicted on your daughter, Zoe?" he asked. "No," I replied, trying not to envision what could have really happened to her. The vision of her injury appeared in my mind as it frequently did. "Elizabeth, it looks like you are not being truthful here. Just tell me what happened. You can't lie to a machine!" he pressed. "What the crap! Are you kidding me! I do not know what happened to my daughter, which is why I am here right now!" I yelled. "Let me take it again, NOW!" I demanded.

He went back to the first question - the same question I already passed. "Elizabeth, you are failing this test miserably. The lines are spiking with your answers. You can't lie to a machine!" he said once again. This time with rage, anger, and pure fury, I got up, "You know what, this is total crap! I am sickened by the way you all are twisting everything around to be my fault. Do your jobs and figure out what happened to my daughter! I should have just listened to my dad." I stormed out the door and back to the lobby. My dad saw that I was clearly upset. "They...are saying...that I know what happened! I don't know or I wouldn't be here!" I managed to say, between sniffles and sobs. "I was worried about that happening, Liz, but you know that you are innocent, and as long as you maintain that, God will take care of you." He hugged me and drove me home. I was so upset that I started to have a panic attack. I was wondering if I was crazy. These law officials were supposed to catch the "bad guys," and they weren't doing that! I had always had trust in the justice system. Not anymore. I had no faith in the system and that was truly scary. If I couldn't trust in those who are supposed to protect us from danger, could I trust in anyone at all?

Chapter 34

I told Jesse about what had happened that day. He offered to come over after he got off work, but I just wanted to seclude myself and be alone. I was so anxious, angry, and stressed out. I simply did not know what to do with myself. I was so sad. I was let down and I felt betrayed. The police were betraying me! They didn't give a shit about what had really happened. They wanted a quick answer; a confession, and they didn't care who it came from. If I could go back in time, I would lay into them and make them feel like the criminals, neglecting to do their job, which I imagine, they were sworn to do when they took the job. To protect and serve…don't think so!

Every visit I had with the girls was torture. They seemed to be doing okay, but I still saw the pain in their eyes and I sensed their confusion. The official trial was going to start after the next weekend. This was when the Social Workers would attempt to gather as much harmful evidence against me as they possibly could. They would run around town and interview every person that had ever come into contact with me. These Social Workers were doing some serious fishing. They spoke with everyone - from my high school teachers to all of my friends and even to my boss at the college bookstore. It was complete public humiliation. Now every single person knew what had taken place. Not only did I feel like my privacy was violated and my positive reputation was shot, but I also felt like the privacy of my daughters was completely thrown out the window. I got a copy of the report a few days before Court and after one of the visits with Chloe and Zoe.

I was absolutely stunned and disgusted with what I was reading. To make it worse, at the end of the report there were several pictures of the injury that my daughter had sustained. I thought that would be illegal! A group of at least twenty Social Workers, Attorneys, and Court Advocates had access to these reports that were supposed to be confidential. Clearly they were not. I had a hard time believing that some of these statements were true. The Social Worker claimed that one of my favorite high school teachers that worked with me at the Young Parents Program had made statements regarding my oldest daughter. She had implied that she thought my oldest daughter was "slow" and had symptoms of fetal alcohol syndrome. That was the first that I had ever heard of that.

On top of it all, I even read a report about what Lilah said. She told the Social Workers that I was "just young and I didn't know what I was doing, and although I had good intentions, the girls were probably better off without me." I was absolutely baffled. Either the Social Workers were not being honest with their statements or these people who I thought were my friends and close family members had completely turned against me. I thought that if they truly felt those things about me, they would have confronted me a long time ago. All of these people would be subpoenaed to go to Court and get up on the stand to say these things to my face. I dreaded it.

On the day of Court, my stomach hurt and I felt like I couldn't function. My mom came to my house and helped me pick out something to wear. I wore long black slacks with a red quarter-

234

sleeve shirt that was more on the conservative side. It was obvious that I had lost a ton of weight. I used to have a butt, and it was definitely gone. It was only because I was so sad and lonely and stressed out that I just couldn't eat. I showed up at the Court House and waited in the lobby for everything to get started. Lilah's step mom, Trudy, was nice enough to bring a pizza and tried to get me to eat. Small things like that made a big difference for me.

That day I learned who truly loved and cared about me no matter what. Sadly, it was only a small handful of people. One of those people was definitely not Megan. Megan and her dad ended up giving Donnie and Derrick a ride to the Court House. I was disgusted and in complete disbelief. I thought she knew me better than anyone, and for her to actually help the enemy, in any way, was just a complete slap in the face. Donnie and Derrick walked in with Megan. They all had a presence about them like they thought it was a big joke. They were quick to talk about irrelevant topics, and make lighthearted statements about random crap. As I was called into the Courtroom, Donnie made a remark that caused me to turn around and flip him off. "Wow, someone is sucked up. Looks like that lady just couldn't get off the pipe." Of course, I was the target. For them, Zoe and what happened to her was never the concern. It was all about the drama. It was one, big, shit-talking contest.

I took my seat at the Defendant's table alongside my Public Defender. She mentioned to me that she had not decided if she was going to put me on the stand or not. She wanted to question other people on the stand first. I honestly did not have a clue what was happening. I knew that I was in a Courtroom, and I knew we were there because of what had happened to Zoe, but I didn't really comprehend that this was an actual trial to determine who was at fault for the injury and to determine if I would ever get the girls back in my custody.

Although this was a trial, it had no significance when it came to criminal charges or proceedings. The Judge made it clear that any statements made in the Courtroom would not incriminate me or anyone else and that they were simply gathering the information to determine the placement of my daughters. I wished it could have had criminal consequences, because I knew the truth would come out, as exhausted and confused as I was. I trusted in God to get me through this. Everyone I had ever come in contact with as a teen mom was subpoenaed. My Attorney and I quickly read through the new report that CPS had made for the Court. They did a thorough investigation. They were looking for any indications of abuse inflicted upon both of the girls. The girls even had full-body x-rays, which I know must have scared them horribly.

The report stated that Zoe's left foot had a fracture that appeared to be old. "The fracture is one appearing to be purposely inflicted by another person, such as a hammer slamming down to shatter the bones." This was crap, and it made no sense. If a hammer was taken to her foot, why was it only a fracture? And how is it that her foot was never swollen bruised or even red? She never had a limp either. Zoe had been in daycare since she was three months old. One of the teachers would have noticed. I WOULD HAVE NOTICED. At this point, it was clear that the Social Workers were adding in tidbits of crap to paint a picture of me as a psychopathic mother. They could not provide a copy of the x-ray (not surprising) so the Judge removed this charge. The Social Workers had the girls do a hair-follicle-drug-test as well to track exposure to any drugs that they may have had in the last three to six months. The results for Chloe were fine, thank God. But the results for Zoe were confusing. The test showed that she had traces of cocaine in her system, not methamphetamine. The hospital originally said that they discovered meth in her system, not cocaine. Why didn't the meth show up on the hair test? There is no question that it would have if there had been traces in her system. At this point, I didn't know what to believe, and I started to feel like I was being set up. The report was loaded with lie after lie, but I could do nothing about it. I hoped that, in time, the truth would reveal itself.

As I sat in my seat, with a blank stare on my face, the Judge began to explain what was about to unfold. I knew that he was speaking about the trial, but I did not absorb any of the information that he announced. I don't know if I was in a state of shock that this was happening or whether I was just in denial. The first person that was called to the stand was, of course, Derrick.

My Attorney questioned Derrick first, followed by the Attorneys for the CPS, and then the Attorney representing the girls. They all asked him a number of diverse questions. I thought some of the questions were irrelevant to what had happened. He answered all of the questions with confidence and even cracked a few jokes. What sickened me the most was that the Attorneys even laughed at his sick sense of humor – this wasn't funny. He raised his hand during one of the questions about drug abuse and asked, "Can I plead the fifth?" The Courtroom roared with laughter. I thought this was appalling.

The next person to be called was Lilah. She took the stand and I couldn't tell if she was on my side or not. First, she told the Court that when I had brought Zoe over to her house she felt like I was a mother bear trying to protect my cub. Then she turned around and explained the graphics of her injury, and I really didn't think that was necessary. It was already horrible enough, and I didn't know why she had to add that.

The next person to be called was my mother. She just looked lost and confused. She answered the questions to the best of her ability, but I think the whole thing was just way too stressful for her. I was worried that it was going to cause her Multiple Sclerosis to flare up. Stress is one of those things that can cause MS to get worse. I was worried for her.

The next few people called to the stand were teachers from my high school and the public health nurse, Valerie, whom I had known and almost began to trust. The teachers played dumb, not really answering the questions. I don't know if it was because they were confused, or if it was because I was in the room and they didn't want to hurt my feelings. Valerie especially played dumb. She was questioned about her statement in the CPS report about me telling her that I "drank as a teenager and I drank when I was pregnant." I never drank while I was pregnant. She didn't confirm or deny the statements. Then Megan was called to the stand. As she walked down the aisle of the seating area that led to the stand, she looked over at me with a strange look on her face. She sat down, looked at me again and smiled, like she thought this was a game. She had that smile on her face that I knew all too well. The one that came just before she was going to burst out laughing. She answered the questions and said nothing to help or harm me. I'll never understand or forget that smile at such an inappropriate time.

The last person called to testify was Allie. The reason I asked my Lawyer to call her to the stand was because she was a character witness. She saw me as a mother quite frequently, and she knew how I interacted with my daughters. She saw past the drug use and understood that I always loved and cherished my little girls. Whatever was going on with me, she probably thought I was just lost and with the wrong crowd. Allie was probably the person who testified the most and completely on my behalf, and I'll never forget that. She was the only person that made me feel worthy and like I was a good mother. Allie was through making her last statement, and as she stood up to leave the stand, she made a hilarious remark about a local real estate agent who was buying cocaine from Megan. I thought it was absolutely hilarious. It was definitely irrelevant, but it was hilarious, especially when one of the Lawyers stood up and said "Hey! That's my friend who owns that business!"

The entire trial lasted for three days, from 8:00 a.m. to 5:00 p.m. It was long and brutal. In the end, the Judge made the determination that it was Derrick who was responsible for what had happened to Zoe. The Judge ordered CPS to give me visitation and offer me services so we could eventually be reunited. This was a good thing, but I was still so confused. If the Court believed me, and they believed that Derrick was guilty, why were the detectives treating me so badly and seriously convinced that I was either responsible or knew what had happened?

Chapter 35

This is the chapter of my life that is unforgivable. They say that in order to completely heal, you need to forgive yourself. That will never happen. I have come to realize that it is just something that I will have to live and cope with for the rest of my life. I hate myself for letting bad people back into my life. There is no excuse, and I will never try to make one. I will always regret it, and I will always desperately wish that I could go back in time and make different choices. I know I can't go back. It is what it is, and I'm about to tell you about the biggest regret and most horrible mistake I ever made. It's one of those mistakes that can make you hate someone. It's one of those mistakes that can make you have zero compassion for someone and what they might be going through. This could explain why I lost everyone in my life at that time. I can't honestly say that I blame people for walking out of my life, but I do wish that I could have better understood my situation from an outsider's point of view. After reading this chapter you may no longer view me the same. That's okay. I'm writing this because I have to release it from my system. My mistake will never go away, but I am coping and living with it by using one of my outlets - writing.

After Court, I resumed the routine that I had come to know but would never get used to. I went to work a few times a week and tried to stay busy, but there was really nothing to stay busy with. I eventually stopped talking to Jesse. I don't know why, because he treated me like a total princess. One night after picking up some macaroni and cheese, I went back home and sat on my couch. I had been alone that whole day and was just miserable. I decided to turn on the TV. There was a video of a country song playing that reminded me of Derrick. The song started to make me sad. I didn't know exactly why, but I was sad that I was so in love Derrick and had been betrayed in the worst possible way. I was angry with myself for being sad over him being gone because that wasn't right. I didn't understand my feelings, and I didn't know why I was feeling this way. I didn't acknowledge my feelings - instead I shoved them away because I thought that only a sick person would be feeling the way that I was. I should have just let myself grieve and be. I had lost my daughters and someone whom I was in love with. I was not okay with this kind of grief for him. I wanted to stay angry with this guy. I did not want to feel sad about him. I wanted to be so mad that I wanted him dead.

The next day the detective called me on my cell phone as I was aimlessly driving around, trying to stay distracted. He told me that Derrick passed his voice analysis stress test with "flying colors." "Okay..." I said, "What is that supposed to mean?" "I don't know, you tell me. I'm convinced that you have more answers than he does," he blatantly replied. I hung up on him. I was too upset and irritated with the mixed messages that I was getting. I didn't think that it was fair that one side of the law could determine that he was guilty, while the other side of the law was convinced that he was not. A part of me still wanted to believe that he was not guilty. When I got home later that day I began to think. The only people who actually thought that he was guilty was the Judge in the Family Law Court and maybe a few other random bystanders. Everyone else from the detectives to Megan,

242

to our circle of friends, and to what seemed like the entire community, thought Derrick was innocent. I knew that I didn't have any information, and if he didn't have any information and truly was innocent, then that meant that one of the other two men who were in my home was responsible. There were three other men, but from what I was told, one of them was only around for breakfast that morning. I didn't know when the others had arrived or how long they had been hanging around. I was truly angry that the detectives didn't question every single person who was in my home. I was angry that the detectives didn't come to my house and gather as much evidence as they possibly could.

I didn't understand why they wouldn't do these things, and no one could give me an answer. I thought that might have been something that would have solved the entire case.

Chapter 36

I pulled into the dark parking lot of McDonald's. It was pretty empty, and I was hoping that I wasn't about to be murdered. I sat there for five minutes until I got a call on my cell phone. Derrick was on the pay phone behind the building. I told him where I was, and about five seconds later I saw him walking toward my car. My adrenaline was pumping and my hands were shaking so bad I could hardly find the button to unlock the doors. He opened the passenger door and got in. We sat there for a moment just staring ahead, blankly. "I'm surprised I'm not in jail right now. Ha ha. I thought, for sure, that this was a setup," he jokingly said. "Yeah, I'm pretty sure that we are probably being watched, but I don't really care." I turned my car on and put it in reverse. "Where are we going?" he asked. "I don't know." I said. "I just want to go on a drive." I was secretly hoping that he was getting afraid that I was going to be the one doing the murdering.

After driving down the dark, empty highway and out into the forest where hardly anyone lived, I pulled over on the side of the road and put the car in park. I don't know what possessed me to drive to such an empty place that was unsafe for a girl alone with a possible psychopath, but I wanted to talk to him, and I wanted to be able to yell if I had to you. I, once again, stared ahead into the dark. He did the same. Finally, I couldn't handle the pressure of the anticipation. "So what happened Derrick? I need you to tell me the truth. I need you to be honest, because I cannot handle this and I just need an answer. Do you not understand the seriousness and the severity of what happened to my daughter? It's a big deal and I want to know who is responsible. If you are responsible, you need to just tell me and give me closure. If you know who is responsible, you also need to tell me." He looked at me calmly and said, "Look Elizabeth, I don't know what happened. I went over every possible scenario in my mind, and I really just don't know what happened. I mean it could have been anything. What if it was one of her toys in the bath the other night? Could be the time she fell with that plastic castle in the tub. I don't know - kids are weird. What if she did it to herself?"

I snapped my head up at him. "You're kidding me, right? Do you not remember what I showed you? That was an injury that was inflicted by somebody else, and she could have died! You have no idea how horrible it was the whole time that I was at the hospital. You have no idea of the hell that she went through when she was put under anesthesia because she had to have surgery. I cannot believe that you have the nerve to say that it is her fault!" Tears were streaming down my face. I was so upset I couldn't handle it. I was clearly not going to get any answers from him. He started crying. "Elizabeth, I am telling you the truth. I don't know what happened! I'm sad too. I lost my family. You and the girls were my world!" He reached over and tried to hug me. I sat there stiff and resistant. Finally, he pretty much yanked me towards him. He was hugging me and I was still sitting there - not touching him or hugging him back. I was just crying. "You know what," I said, "I can't handle this. I'm going to get a bottle right now."

I started the car and drove to the store. I got a bottle of vodka. I was hoping that maybe if I got him drunk I could get him to talk. I also wanted to be drunk because I was so confused and miserable. We ended up going back to my house and getting

246

wasted. The more I talked to him, the more I actually believed that he might not know what happened. I tried every type of psychology and reverse psychology that I could think of. I even got to the point where I told him it was okay if he did it, and I wouldn't tell, which was a huge, desperate lie. I was desperate for an answer. I didn't get one. Somehow, we ended up playing Yahtzee for the next two hours – wasted and playing Yahtzee.

Derrick was a very personable guy. He always had a way of making people laugh even if they did not want to. He had a great way of creeping into your mind and convincing you of whatever it was he wanted you to believe. I'm positive that he did the same thing with the detectives. Needless to say, it worked on me. On top of that, I was extremely vulnerable. I was vulnerable and alone and scared. I had no one except him. Derrick convinced me that if we were going to get through this, we had to stick together. He pretty much moved back in that night. From this point forward, I was brainwashed. It was so much easier to just believe him.

I went through the stages of grief, denial and bargaining for any small reason. How he could simply have nothing to do with the injury consumed my entire thought process around the clock for the next four years.

The first few days were pretty uncomfortable. I didn't want to be seen with him. No one would understand. He had me to the point where I was starting to feel bad for him. I don't know why, but I just did. He had me believing that he was also a victim. We stayed locked in my house getting drunk, making food, and playing Yahtzee for probably a week. I surrendered. I was like one of those abused dogs. I had been treated terribly by Derrick My daughter was tortured by who knows what or whom, but I still loved and obeyed my owner. It was all a blur - a drunken blur. The alcohol didn't help my emotions either; I cried and cried and cried.

Then, one day, I just stopped crying. I had no tears left. I had cried enough for five lifetimes. Something about getting back together with Derrick hardened my soul. I was numb and emotionless. I was in total denial. I let myself believe Derrick and the detectives. Finally, I agreed with the detective when he called me once more for the last time. Anyone who made excuses for Derrick or sided with him and his claim to be totally innocent further supported my state of denial. It was okay now. I had Derrick back, and soon enough the detectives would crack the case and arrest the real abuser. I was now safe to go out in public with Derrick if I wanted to.

A week after Derrick returned, I had several missed calls from Jesse. I avoided them hoping that he would just give up. Of course, Jesse came looking for me. He wanted to make sure I was alive, and he wanted to show me his brand new baby boy. I was in the kitchen making fondue for dinner, and I heard a knock on my glass patio door. I ignored it, hoping whoever it was would go away. I was pretty sure it was Jesse. I was afraid that if I answered the door, there would be a fight between Derrick and Jesse. I ignored the knocks for almost five minutes. I was surprised by his persistence. "Elizabeth! I know you're in there. I see you right now. Open the door, I brought my son over to meet you!" I felt so bad when he said this. "Derrick, he is just a friend; don't start any drama okay," I quietly and firmly demanded as I went to open the door. He was with Jake and his baby was in the tiny car seat and looped over his arm. "Come in," I hesitantly said. There was no hiding anything now, and there was no point in attempting to make excuses for my choice. I was surprised when Jesse swallowed his pride and probably also his rage, and extended his hand to Derrick to introduce himself. Derrick mumbled a few words and, of course, was annoyed and grinding his teeth. "Hey man," Jessie looked over at Derrick. "Would you mind if I talked to Elizabeth upstairs for a minute? I just want to make sure everything is okay, and I came to show her my son too," he confidently yet respectfully asked. "Sure dude, whatever works," Derrick surrendered.

Jesse followed me up the stairs to my room. I didn't want Derrick to hear anything that we might say. Derrick did not know that I had slept with Jesse. As soon as the door was closed, Jesse lifted his arms up in confusion, "Are you so in love with him, Elizabeth that you can look past what he did? I am so confused. I don't mean to come here and stress you out, but look what he put you through! He is dangerous! I had serious feelings for you, too. I backed off because I knew that you were already going through so much, but I didn't think that my leaving you alone would lead to him coming back!" The look of confusion and sadness in his bright, beautiful eyes was extremely hard to take. I hugged him and said I was sorry. He brought the last few tears that I had left out of my eyes. "Elizabeth, I am not joking, and you can even ask Jake, but I seriously would have married you. That's how much I love and care about you." he said. "I love you too, Jesse. I really do. I just don't know what is going on anymore. I don't know if he even had anything to do with it now. The detectives are convinced he's innocent," I said, looking at the floor. Jesse continued, "I hope this is just a weird phase. Will you promise to call me if you ever need anything? I care about you, crazy girl." I agreed, and quietly soaked up my tears of regret and guilt with my sweater sleeve. "Do you want to hold my son before I take off?" "Of course! He is so tiny and adorable," I replied.

He took the tiny blond baby out of his seat and handed him to me as I was sitting on the floor, cross-legged in defeat. He ran downstairs to tell Derrick and Jake that I was just holding the baby for a minute before they left. I heard Derrick mutter something that sounded strange, but I wasn't sure what it was. After completely doting on this sweet, innocent little blond baby, Jesse came back up to get him ready to go. He had a look of shock and anger on his face. "Elizabeth!" he whispered. "Did you hear what that dude just said to me?" I shook my head no. "What did he say?" I asked. "When I told him you were holding the baby before I left, he was like, "You might want to go check on her and not leave your kid alone with her. She's crazy!" I felt my face turn red with rage.

As Jesse was buckling his baby back into his seat, I stormed down the stairs, past Jake, and into the kitchen where Derrick was. "What the hell did you say about me? I am pretty sure you are in my house right now, and if you are going to act like a detective, I'll treat you like one and ask you to leave!" I firmly and loudly said. I was happy to say this in front of the guys. I felt extremely disrespected, and I was furious about what he had said. I wondered if he truly thought that.

"Okay, I'm sorry. I didn't mean it like that. It's just that we have a lot of bad shit going on right now and people probably don't want to be involved unless they want their kids taken away too. Remember? The whole town thinks we are child abusers." he said, almost laughing. I was too exhausted to fight any longer. I looked at Jesse and shrugged my shoulders.

Jesse saw the look in my eyes, and he knew I had given up on myself. That night was the last time I saw him. I've thought about him frequently over the years and have tried to find a way to contact him to apologize. I haven't tracked you down yet, so Jesse, I hope this gets to you. I am truly sorry, and I regret that I didn't listen to you because you really did care about me. I hated myself and I gave up. But you didn't give up on me and were there for me on multiple occasions. Thank you, and I hope God is giving you all the happiness that life can offer. You always made me feel worthy, and I can never repay you for your kindness. I'll never forget those few people who still cared when I was at my worst - and you were definitely one of them.

Chapter 37

I visited my daughters once a week and each time it was less emotionally difficult. I hated the fact that I was being watched so instead of always interacting with them like I should have, I sometimes just sat there and watched the girls play. A recent CPS report that was submitted to the Court said, "The mother seems very detached and not interested in communicating with her children during the visits." Basically, I couldn't be sad and show emotion in front of the girls. The forced "no-crying" contract was still in effect. I was still being picked apart as a result of that contract. I had a fear of doing something wrong during the visits. I always told the girls that I loved them "so very much" before I left. Chloe was starting to potty train. During one of the visits she had to go to the restroom, but the CASA worker said she wasn't "good with small kids" so she asked me to take her. Go figure. We had recently celebrated her third birthday at a pizza restaurant. My mom, grandparents, and older sister were there. The CASA worker supervised. We brought them lots of gifts. My little girl was three, and I had already missed out on so much. Her vocabulary was great. There was a light in her that faded on that day that I couldn't take her home with me as she hurriedly put on her jacket. That was the day that her heart was broken. She wasn't temporarily with a babysitter or at daycare - she was being forced to be away from me. They eventually stopped crying. There was a brick wall between us – forced by many different entities: Social Services, the Court, Derrick and even my own numb soul.

I still had this idea that I would get them back. The Detectives just needed to hurry up and solve the case. On one of the visits, about two months after everything happened, the CASA worker looked at me and asked "Elizabeth, I hear your pregnant again?" "What? No, I am not!" I sternly said. What a bitch. Where did that even come from? I was pretty positive that I was not pregnant. Were they analyzing the urine samples I gave when I had drug tests?

I started to think a little more about her statement as the day went on. I finally admitted to myself that it was possible. I had turned into this drunken idiot that gave Derrick what he wanted when he wanted it. I no longer cared about myself. I didn't deserve to care about myself. I didn't deserve self-esteem. I was a pathetic mother. What my daughter had lost was far greater than self-esteem. I wanted to feel her pain and what she had suffered times a million because I deserved it. I was destined to fail in everything else I would do from that point on. I was worthless. The only thing I was good for was being Derrick's bitch. He would remind me of this in subliminal ways. He would jokingly say demands like "Bitch, make me food," or "Bitch, you know you can't live without me." My new name was Bitch. I was the worthless kind.

I got home after my visit to Derrick lounging on the couch as usual. He had started smoking in the house. He reached up and handed me a thick pile of papers. It was a notice from the landlord to pay or move out. I couldn't pay rent; I didn't have any money and honestly I didn't care. Derrick wasn't helping either. I wasn't surprised. I was expecting my life to take a downward dive forever anyway. I sighed. "When it rains, it pours." Derrick said. "I'm sorry. Don't stress - we'll figure it out.

I'll always have your back, Elizabeth." At least I wasn't in this alone.

When you are going through hell, having a person walking through the fire with you makes all the difference in the world. I didn't know how to walk through hell. Bad things had never been a part of my life growing up until I hooked up with Derrick. It's not only his fault, though. I let the bad things into my life. I did not see them when they were roaring in my face, but I didn't look hard enough either, so it's my fault too.

At this point, some people knew that I was back with Derrick, but I didn't know exactly who knew. I did not tell my family. It would upset them too much and they would wonder what the hell was wrong with me. They were already totally confused. It was never in my personality to hang around destructive people - definitely not drug addicts. To become one myself was completely out of character. My family was already worried about losing me to drugs, drinking, self-destruction, and maybe even death. The first person in my family that I told was my mom. She was already at a loss. She didn't encourage it, and she didn't make me feel bad. She knew that at this point, the only thing anyone could do to help me was to just be nice and treat me with dignity and let me know they were there for me. My mom knew all of this, so she just listened to me talk about things. I don't even remember what I said. It was probably all nonsense.

Early one morning Derrick had to get up and go to his first day of work at a job he previously had. The owner liked him and even though he quit, he let him return. That meant I had to drop him off on my way to school. I was starting a summer course for phlebotomy. I was excited at the thought of learning how to draw blood. I wanted to be a nurse anyway so it would be good to have that under my belt.

As we walked out the back door and headed towards my car, I could not believe who was practically running at me. Angry as hell at 7:00 in the morning, my dad had driven an hour to get there just to spy on me. I had stopped talking to him and I'm guessing he became suspicious. It was not like me to suddenly stop contacting him after he paid my rent for me. He was good about doing nice things like that when I really needed help. He visited me more than anyone in my family when I was all alone and miserable, but that was because he lived the closest. Sometimes, I thought he had ESP. He always seemed to call or show up when I was doing something I shouldn't have been doing. He called once when I was fourteen and messing around with a boyfriend in my bedroom. Sure enough, Lilah answered the call and ran the phone up to me before I could even get dressed. I was so busted. My mom was really upset. He also called at times when I was about to use cocaine or meth - out of the blue and always right before.

"Elizabeth! What the hell is going on here? Why didn't you call me? I need to talk to you now!" he yelled. I rushed to my car. I didn't want to face him. I was too ashamed of myself. Derrick raced to the car, too. We locked the doors and I turned on the engine. My dad had blocked me in so I couldn't leave. He came up to the passenger window where Derrick was sitting. "What the hell are you doing with my daughter? You know you need to just stay away from her. If she is going to get her girls back she can't be with you!" he yelled while trying to reason and intimidate at the same time. "Look old man, it ain't your business. Now I gotta go to work so move your truck or we're gonna have problems!" Derrick yelled. "Is that a threat? Are you saying you want to fight? I don't think it'll solve anything, but I'll be glad to take you on," my dad said. Derrick was tall, about 5'11" to 6 feet. My dad was taller at about 6'1". I was not sure who would win in a fight and I didn't want to find out. Derrick was very stocky, and his fists were huge. My dad had been running his own furniture moving business for over twenty years. He was in good shape. This was bad.

254

I felt really bad for my dad, but I was really upset that he had just showed up. I was totally caught off guard, and I was not a little kid! He had no right to be here, I thought. "Dad! Just move your truck! I have to go to school and he is going to be late for work!" I screamed out of frustration. He walked away, shaking his head in disappointment. I really wasn't as angry as I was sad. My dad did a lot to show he cared. I went behind his back and let Derrick come back into my life. I just completely avoided his calls after that, mainly because I was ashamed of myself and I knew he was disappointed. I drove off as fast as I could, and I noticed that my dad was trying to keep up with me. I floored it and took some quick turns and he lost me.

After dropping off Derrick, I drove to school with a lump in my throat and trying not to cry. I couldn't do anything right or make anyone happy. I stopped caring about hurting other people after that. If I cared, it would hurt me even more. I would hide away in my twisted little world and just wait for the mess to resolve itself.

The mess became a little bit messier a few weeks later. I thought that because I was so skinny and under so much stress, there was no way I could get pregnant. I wasn't having periods and thought my entire system was just off balance. I started to feel cramps one night after work. I expected to get my period at any minute. The next day came and nothing. The day after that I was still cramping but nothing. I knew what was going on. I knew exactly what was going on. I was numb to this too. I refused to let anything else screw with my emotions. "Derrick," I said. "What?" he yelled from the bottom of the stairs in that obnoxious, loud whine he frequently vocalized. "We need to run to the store really fast - like tonight. I can't handle this shit anymore." I demanded. "What the hell are you talking about?" he asked, truly confused. "I need to get a pregnancy test. Okay?" I was done explaining myself to the world.

I couldn't hide everything...

Chapter 38

"Women are just weird. Why do they always think they're pregnant?" Derrick asked. "You're a moron. Maybe because women usually end up pregnant at some point! Trust me, I am not doing this for fun. It's the last thing I want to do, but the CASA worker said some weird thing to me at the last visit I had, and I haven't had my period in a while. It's probably just because I'm so stressed." Everything just has to be a nightmare. "I don't know how this curse will ever end!" Derrick laughed. That was very typical of him. If he didn't know how to react to something, he would laugh, even if it were something that was not a laughing matter. I still hear his laugh to this day. It has been over four years since I've seen or heard from him and that laugh rings in my head clear as day. Sometimes I hear it in the voices of other people and it scares the crap out of me. Good ole' post-traumatic stress disorder.

I made Derrick go into the store and buy the test. I was not in the mood to be out in public, and the odds of me running into someone that I knew were about fifty percent in a small-town grocery store. I remember having to cut the corner of an aisle in a hurry a few times when I would see someone that I didn't want to get stuck talking to for five thousand years. I was not in the mood to see anyone. I couldn't answer any more of the "How are you?" or

"Where are Chloe and Zoe?" questions. Derrick was back in the passenger seat within minutes with the small bag concealing the bringer of good or bad news. I didn't feel pregnant - I was just had more cramps than usual. I certainly didn't look pregnant. I was probably at my lowest weight ever, about 108 pounds. Derrick constantly complained, "Your ass is gone! Start eating, bitch!" He had this set idea of how I was supposed to look - right down to the size of my butt.

We pulled in the parking lot of the complex, scanned for any new and unexpected spies, like my dad or maybe a detective. It was clear. I walked through the door and up the stairs to sit and stare at the pregnancy test and determine if I wanted to even take it. Why the hell am I so freaking fertile, I was thinking to myself. I sprawled out on my bed after changing into my pajamas and opened the box to read the directions. It was common sense, but I wanted to put if off for a little while longer. I didn't know what difference it would even make if I found out I was pregnant, but I would probably have to stop taking my anti-depressant.

Being with Derrick didn't make me any happier. It just made me feel less alone. He was actually pretty miserable to be around at that point. He was his same lazy self. He bossed me around and only offered comfort when I was having a major meltdown. "What the hell are you doing up there?" he yelled from below. I sighed and walked into the bathroom with the pregnancy test. Here I was with another pregnancy test. This could be some serious Jerry Springer stuff. I was still only eighteen.

I took the test and set it on the bathroom counter. I fixed my hair and washed my face. My adrenaline was pumping. I didn't want to look at it. I took a deep breath and glanced down. The second line was as blue as it could possibly be. It was even darker than the confirmation line. Yep, I was knocked up…again! I opened the bathroom door and yelled down the stairs. "Derrick! Come to the bottom of the stairs." He walked over. I threw the test down to him and walked back into my bedroom. He came up the stairs and into the bedroom. "Oh, thank God it's negative!" he said. What a complete moron. "Uh, no Derrick, it's not negative." I bluntly replied. "But the line is a negative line. Isn't it supposed to be a plus sign?" he dumbly asked. I explained to him how the test worked. "Oh shit, really?" he said, with a tone of excitement. "I've always wanted a kid. I didn't think I would end up having any. Cool." I didn't get where his excitement was coming from. This wasn't a good thing at all. It was actually the worst thing that could be happening because the Family Court determined he was responsible for the injury to Zoe. If the Detectives didn't solve the case, and I didn't get the girls back, they would take this baby too. I couldn't fathom the thought - it was just too much.

"Derrick, they will take this baby if the case doesn't get solved. What are we going to do?" I asked, completely stressed out. "We'll just get the hell outta here," he replied. "Yeah, how is that going to work? I have to stay here to fight for Chloe and Zoe. If I leave there is no way I would ever have a chance!" I angrily replied. "Look, just calm down. We will figure it out. We always do. If you just do everything that the Court tells you to do, they have to give the girls back," he said. I just sighed and shook my head. He didn't get it. Life was not going to be easy as long as we were together. He hugged me and tried to convince me that it would all work out. Eventually, I believed him. He would have made a great Attorney. He convinced me of the most ridiculous and unrealistic ideas every time. We decided that I would deny and hide my pregnancy for as long as possible. No one could know about this - not even my family.

I was speaking to my mom on the phone a little more as time went on. Sometimes I got annoyed with her. "Liz, you need to be prepared for someone to pay for what happened to Zoe. If they can't figure it out, they are going to put all of it on you. They have to hold someone responsible, and it doesn't look like they know what happened or who's to blame. I know that you would never hurt the girls, but they don't know that. If they did, they wouldn't care anyway. I am not trying to scare you, but I want you to be prepared if they try to take you to jail." She would say things like this frequently. I think that she wanted me to expect the worst because she knew how badly I was already hurting. She didn't want me to be driven mad if I did go to jail. "I understand what you're saying, but they can't arrest me because I am not the one who did it! They will never find evidence to say I did because it's not there," I would often respond. The only thing that they could get me for was using drugs when I was caring for my girls, and if they were going to do that, it would have happened already. As far as I was concerned, they weren't going to arrest me because they were focusing on arresting the real perpetrator. I prayed she wasn't right.

When I got home from work a few days later and there was an eviction notice on my door with the Sheriff's stamp on it. This was a real eviction order. We had to be out in thirty days. I was pretty worried about this but honestly wanted to get out of that place anyway. It was too sad and the girl's room was just empty. It had all of their toys and clothes, but the empty feeling made me sad every time I passed the door. I was miserable and quitting smoking sucked. I knew that it was not worth the risk to my unborn baby. Drugs and alcohol were out of the picture, for both Derrick and I, when we found out that I was pregnant. As far as I could tell, Derrick really was clean. I was a little surprised, but thankful.

As time went on, I started feeling like the Court was distancing me from them as much as they could. My visits were only once every two weeks and the Social Workers never talked about or implied anything in regards to reuniting me with my daughters. The Court and Social Workers all had their own plans; they just had to legally wait to go through the time period required before they could do anything permanent. I held on to the idea that the girls would eventually come home. Deep down, I felt our world was fading and we were getting further and further apart. I resumed my life as best as I could because if I let myself stay heartbroken, I wouldn't live through it. I could not survive the pain if I didn't block it out, just as a person could not survive half of their heart being sliced out and stitched back in just once in a while.

We had to come up with the cash to move, so I started working. I got a full time job with a maid service. I had fun working with them. I drove around town with my co-workers cleaning some of the most beautiful homes that Tahoe had to offer. I didn't tell anyone about my pregnancy because I knew it was just temporary. Luckily, my phlebotomy course was at night, so I was able to manage both for the time being. I loved the class, and I was almost ready to start my internship. Derrick worked at a car maintenance place, and we traded in my car for a white jeep. We didn't trade it in for the typical reasons. Every single time I drove down the highway, if Derrick was with me I was pulled over. The cops gave me all sorts of reasons, but I knew that they wanted to catch one of us doing something illegal. They wanted a reason to arrest us. Despite the cops searching my car and never finding anything, I was still being pulled over for "not signaling" or "not coming to a full stop." I knew that this was bullshit. I was sick of it.

When we finally had enough money to move, we found a tiny studio about ten minutes down the highway. It was in a small complex of about eight units. We called the number on the "for rent" sign, and the lady managing the place, Betsy, met us about thirty minutes later. I didn't know what I would do with all of my furniture, or the girl's stuff, but it would have to work. Of course, we did not tell Betsy about our situation because no person in their right mind would rent to us if they knew. She was really nice and she let us sign the lease agreement right there. We paid the deposit and scheduled the move to be a few days ahead. We decided that the only place to store all of the furniture would be in an abandoned house

261

that was on the same property as Donnie's house. I had seen Donnie only a few times since the incident. I avoided him as much as I could - partially because he could have been the one who assaulted my daughter and partially because he was still with Megan. I was still angry with her. I still felt incredibly betrayed and hurt, and I knew that nothing would ever be the same between us. I had depended on her for a lot more than she understood or even I understood at that time. I needed her to grab me and shake me. I needed her help understanding the severity and importance of standing my ground and entirely eliminating the losers from my life and not going back to them.

She couldn't help me. She was doing the same exact thing. Somehow, I was the bad person. Every person involved was innocent but me according to the community. I had anger building up every day. The night that we put the furniture in our "storage," I had a voice message on my cell phone. It was a young, female voice that I thought sounded familiar, but I couldn't pinpoint who it was. "I think it's pretty hilarious that your daughter was assaulted!" she yelled. That was all that the message said. I didn't understand what the statement was meant to do to me. Why would someone think that something so terrible would be hilarious, especially to a child? I was sickened, but I knew that there was nothing I could do. It came from a private number, and I couldn't put a name to the voice. It's probably a good thing that I did not know who it was because I would have ended up going to jail over a serious attack.

It was one thing to say horrible things about me. People needed something to talk about and because they didn't have answers, they made them up. I didn't like it, but I could handle it. What I could not handle was when my baby girl was brought into the rumors. She needed to be left out because nothing was ever her fault. It was like adding to her trauma. I hated these people.

On a weekend when Derrick was off work, we moved into our tiny studio. We were able to bring our bed, big couch, television set, and the basic necessities. We didn't have enough money to get the gas turned on right away, so we were stuck with freezing cold water and using a microwave for every meal.

Derrick went to work every morning, and my phlebotomy internship was starting. I was really excited and hoping that it would be a good way to support myself financially and show the Court that I wasn't the loser that they assumed I was. I had a few friends taking the course with me, and I don't think that they had heard any of the rumors about me because they didn't bring anything up. This was a relief because I just wanted to be treated for who I was and not what I went through. My first day at the hospital was nerve wracking. They pretty much made it clear that the only way to really learn how to draw blood was to just do it. I didn't want to hurt anyone so our group decided to practice on each other first. I was really afraid to let a rookie stab me for the first time but luckily my veins were prominent so they didn't have to search too far. The girl did a good job and I could finally relax. I did a good job on her too, and the nurse supervising us gave me frequent compliments.

Over the next few days I started to get the hang of it. I was the most nervous in the newborn unit because I really did not want to make a baby cry. When the procedure was done, I was glad. I hoped that I wouldn't be called back to that part of the hospital again. It was too sad but, at the same time, going into the newborn area started to get me a little more excited about my baby. Everything flashed back, and I remembered how precious it was when Chloe and Zoe were born. My feelings were quickly squelched; I was in training and I had to be professional.

After my internship that day Derrick came home. I was starting to become irritated that the detectives hadn't returned my computer to me, which was withheld as evidence when Derrick stole it. They had it for a couple of months now, and I needed it back to do homework and to kill time when I was stuck in the tiny studio on my days off. I called the police department and asked them what I needed to do. They said that they needed both Derrick and I to come in and sign for it because the Judge never determined whose it was. Derrick tried to say that he paid for half of it, but he failed to mention that I paid him back the next day. I wanted it to be officially mine because I don't like sharing. The hours for releasing evidence were almost over for the day so I didn't have time to change out of my scrubs. They were good at hiding my pregnancy anyway. I was three months and probably going to really start showing any day.

We walked into the lobby and waited for the computer. As we were waiting, the detective that I hated the most poked his head out of the door. He was short and fat and the most obnoxious person I had ever come into contact with. "Hey Ms. Jeter! Can I talk to you for a minute?" There was no way in hell that I was going to be put through another interrogation. Over my dead body! "Only if Derrick can come with me," I firmly replied. "I'm sorry, but I know how you guys work, and I don't feel that you have good or helpful intentions." He shook his head and closed the door. I didn't know what that was all about, but it worried me. What did they want now? I had nothing new to tell them. I told them everything that I could think of, plus more. I noticed that before he closed the door he was staring at my name badge - he was for sure trying to read it.

The next week was the same routine, and I was getting close to finishing my internship. The lady in charge of the entire lab gave me amazing compliments on my work and interactions with the patients, and I was excited. The hospital environment felt natural for me, and I could easily picture myself working in it forever.

The chance of this happening was about to be shot down, along with everything else that I would never have.

Chapter 39

It was only a few days before I would get my credits for my internship at the hospital. I loved training for this career, and I was excited at the possibility of working at the hospital. After finishing my hours for the day, I went home and waited for Derrick to get off work. I was hungry, but it was hard to make anything decent because we still had not gotten the gas turned on. There's only so much you can make in a microwave. I was complaining about this to Derrick as soon as he walked in. I used the pregnancy as an excuse. I knew he would cave in and find a way to make me a healthy dinner. He went to the store and came back with a miniature grill with a small propane attachment. He also had a pack of steaks and some sides. "Yes! I haven't had steak in so long! I am starving! Hurry, hurry!" I excitedly pressured him. I changed out of my scrubs and into a cute nightgown that I had. It was a little short and risqué, but I wasn't going anywhere so I didn't care. I had nothing else clean to wear. I plopped down on the couch and put my aching feet up. I turned on the TV and got an unexpected kiss from Derrick as he was walking out the front door to cook. "What was that for?" I asked, wondering why he was being so nice. "What? I can't give my girlfriend and baby-mama a kiss?" he replied. "I love you, that's all." "Love you too," I said. At the moment, I loved the smell of the steak more.

As I was relaxing and watching my show, I heard Derrick begin to say something outside. I ignored it and figured he was talking to a neighbor. I was shocked when I heard a female voice. "Elizabeth? It's Becky from the Lake Tahoe Police Department. I need you to step outside," she said. What the hell? I thought. "Um okay, let me put my pants on because I am in a short nightgown," I said. "That isn't necessary. Just step on out here," she said, with a more stern voice. That's when I knew what was about to happen. I walked outside, barefoot, praying silently in my head. Please God - just don't let them arrest me. I'm doing the best I can - please don't let me go to jail.

"Hello," I said, probably appearing hesitant. Right away, a male officer came up behind me and asked me to put my hands behind my back. "You have the right to remain silent," he recited from memory - the words that I feared and hated. I wasn't sure why I was being arrested. I knew it didn't have anything to do with Zoe because I didn't do anything wrong. "Can you tell me why I am being arrested?" I begged, as tears were rolling down my cheeks and off my chin. "I can't give you much information, except for that you are being charged with willful cruelty to a child," he replied.

I felt a blast of shock and dread hit me so hard I thought I might lose my balance. Derrick sat there, helpless. They walked me down the street where their vehicle was parked around the corner. They must have hid their car thinking I would try to run if I saw them. I was put in the back of the car, and they headed toward the police station. As I was sitting in the back trying to control my tears, the officers were having a casual conversation and listening to a catchy new pop song. It was playing sort of loud. The female spoke of how hungry she was and the male said something about pizza. I looked out the window as they drove me down the highway. I knew that I wouldn't get to see the outside for a long time. I worried that I was going to have my baby in jail.

The officer pulled into the parking garage, opened the door, and directed me to exit the vehicle. I was embarrassed because I was literally wearing lingerie, and there were more male officers than female officers. I walked into the booking area with the officers behind me. I was directed to stand in front of that same blue wall and listen to that same recording that I heard a year earlier. I was un-cuffed and patted down. I was directed to sit on the concrete bench where the booking officer was sitting at a desk in front of a computer. They went over the charges with me and told me what my bail would be. I was stunned, and I knew that this amount was not a good amount because it meant that they did not want me to bail out. "Your bail is $50,000. Do you think you're going to get out tonight?" he asked. "No, there's no way that I'm going to be able to make that bail." "Okay then, I'll call one of the other officers and let them know to get you set up to go over to H pod." I was then brought into that same, cold holding cell. This time I knew that I was probably not getting out any time soon. I didn't know what to expect, and I didn't fully understand my charges. I knew that I wasn't being charged with the actual assault because that would be under the assault category. After doing research later on, I discovered that it was a child endangerment charge.

I was only in the holding cell for a short time, but I had enough time to make my free one-minute call to Derrick. Of course, I was crying and upset and scared. He was on the other end of the phone crying too. Between sniffles I asked him, "What are we going to do if they don't let me out before the baby is born? I don't want to have my baby in jail. Derrick, I'm scared." "Elizabeth, we're going to do everything we can to make sure that doesn't happen. For now just don't talk to any detectives if they try to talk to you, and I'll call your Public Defender tomorrow to let her know that they arrested you." The phone suddenly cut off, and I wasn't able to finish the conversation. A few minutes later a female officer opened the door and instructed me to follow the blue line down the hallway, once again, to go to the dressing room.

This female officer was close to my age, and she wasn't very nice. Unlike the first time I was arrested, I wasn't spared having to get naked in front of someone and bend over so they could make sure that I didn't have something smuggled up my butt. It was completely humiliating and, at that point, I looked more bloated than pregnant so I was very self-conscious of my body. After the humiliation was over and I was dressed in my horrible orange pumpkin outfit, I was again directed to follow the line down the hallway. I walked into that all-too-familiar day room. It looked like everyone had just finished with dinner. I was hoping to God that I would have my own cell again, but I wasn't that lucky. I was put in a cell downstairs with bunk beds. The women's pod appeared to be booked to its maximum. I walked into my cell and put my green container with my hygiene kit and blanket on the floor. The bottom bunk was empty, so I assumed it was mine. It looked like there were blankets on the top one but I didn't see anyone. I had to pee really bad and flushed the toilet connected to the sink forgetting how loud and startling it was. Suddenly, the blankets on the top bunk began to move and flail around. There was someone sleeping there. She was an older woman, but she wasn't missing any teeth or anything, so I was relieved. She seemed relatively normal. I later found out that she was in jail for attempting to run a pedestrian over in the grocery store parking lot. She wasn't a bad cellmate. She kept to herself and was quiet and clean. The only thing that sucked about it was that there was no privacy. If the food in the jail didn't sit so well with my digestive system, I would have to either warn her that I was about to blow up the toilet or, if she was asleep, I would just have to do it as quickly as possible.

My first day in jail wasn't as bad as the first time I was arrested because I knew what to expect. Another thing that made it easier was that I knew a couple of the girls that were in there and they were around my age. One of them, Crystal, was a cute bubbly girl, and she had always been really nice. I remembered her from when I was five years old, and she lived in the same apartment complex as we did. One year on our birthday (I think Merri and I were turning six) she brought us a present. It was a fish bowl with a few goldfish and guppies. We were so excited. I had no idea she would be in jail, and later I found out that she was there because she was in a rollover car accident with her son in the backseat. They later determined that she was intoxicated from drinking alcohol and shooting up meth. It was really sad, and I never thought that she would have ended up using drugs. By this time, I hadn't used drugs in three or four months.

I had no intentions of informing anyone of my pregnancy until I knew what was going on. I didn't know if it would or wouldn't have a negative or positive impact on the Judge. The next day I had my arraignment. My Public Defender was there for a quick minute to explain the charge on the form that the Bailiff handed me. There were a few other inmates being arraigned as well. I pleaded not guilty and was scheduled to go back to Court for my bail review on Monday. This meant that I would worry through the entire weekend not knowing my fate. It was hard not to have hopes that I would be released. Jail was such a degrading and boring place, and I was stripped of anything and everything personal. They even washed the underwear and gave them to different women on laundry day. I wondered how many gross criminals had worn the underwear I had on.

On Saturday, my Lawyer came to visit me. She looked like she felt bad for me. I tried to keep myself from crying. "So, what are they saying I did? Why am I being charged with this?" I asked. She shook her head and lifted her hands in defeat. "I don't know. I mean, they aren't saying that you are the person who did it, but they want to hold someone responsible. They are at least trying to blame the foot fracture on you," she explained. I shook my head. "I know you hear this all the time, but I really don't even believe that she had a foot fracture! I would have known and her daycare would have known!" I affirmed. My Lawyer continued, "I'm not sure how much time they are going to give you, but I'll see if we can get you released on your own recognizance on Monday. Don't get your hopes up though. And you have Court for the custody case on Monday as well, remember?" I had totally forgotten about that. Not good. I would have to go to Court to try to get my daughters back while sitting in jail. I didn't even know how I would have a chance to get them back now. I walked back into the women's pod and headed to my cell to lie down and try to sleep. I wanted to stay asleep until Monday and I practically did.

Criminal Court was humiliating that day. The room was packed with free people, and I was forced to try to walk to the Defendant's table with both my wrists and ankles shackled. The Court really had their way of making you feel like trash. The District Attorney, a short and mean man, made sure he was there when my case was called. He did not want me getting out of jail.

He was quick to publicly explain why. "This woman is a danger! This woman inflicted an injury on her daughter's foot so bad that it fractured the bones! Your Honor, to even consider releasing her is a very dangerous idea," he practically yelled. My Public Defender was in the mood to fight for me that day. "Your Honor, Elizabeth is a victim in this as much as her children. No one knows exactly what happened, and there is no evidence to prove that Elizabeth is responsible! She is only nineteen years old. Despite her mistakes and lack of judgment, she is a good mother and needs to be out of jail to work on getting her daughters back home with her!" she exclaimed. The Judge was scratching her head between flipping through paperwork. "Ms. Jeter, I want to release you on your own recognizance, but I

270

simply do not have enough information about this case to be confident with that decision. For now, I will reduce your bail to thirty thousand, and we will schedule you to return for your next Hearing where you can plead guilty, innocent, or no contest. Your Public Defender will go over the details with you." I stood up and walked back to the chair I was sitting in before. They couldn't schedule me in for another three weeks. I wanted to die. I did not know how I could manage another three weeks without knowing what was going to happen. I was completely miserable.

I went to the Family Court hearing embarrassed and miserable as usual. The Judge noted that I was incarcerated and asked me if I wanted to schedule visitation with the girls while I was in jail. "No, Your Honor. No, thank you. I just don't want the girls to ever have memories of seeing me in jail," I politely said. "I understand and I don't blame you Ms. Jeter." The Hearing was quick. It was just to check up on the status of my reunification plan, which, so far, was okay on my end, or so I thought. I could tell that the Social Workers were gleaming with joy. They loved the fact that I was in jail. After that Hearing, I called my mom in a panic. "Mom, if you don't take them, we'll never see them again. I am so serious! They are going to stop the reunification plan because I'm in jail. If they do that, the next thing that will happen is my rights will be terminated. We will never see Chloe and Zoe again!" I begged and sobbed. I figured that since I was already unloading a bunch of bad news, I might as well tell her that I was pregnant. "You are?" she asked calmly. She didn't get mad or throw blame or judgment at me. I was relieved that I had gotten it out of the way.

My mom came to visit me at least once a week. I anxiously waited for Court so I could find out what my fate would be. She tried to help calm my anxiety. On one of the visits, she told me that she and my stepdad hired a Lawyer, and they were going to try to get the girls out of the Foster Care System. She initially couldn't take them because her husband was building their home, which was still

271

basically a frame. CPS would not approve it as safe enough if she tried to keep the girls there. They ended up renting a home and having it inspected and approved for custody. The Court did an ignorant job at deciding where to put the girls. The Social Workers always had some pathetic excuse as to why they couldn't go with my mom.

When the day my Criminal Court case finally came, I was called to the door that would lead me to get ready to be shackled up. I was four months pregnant and starting to look it. When I sat down on the side of the Courtroom, my Public Defender sat next to me and handed me some paperwork. "Okay, Elizabeth, I sat down and spoke with the Judge about your case. I explained the situation to her, and I told her that you would be willing to go to rehab if she released you. This is your plea bargain."

The Defendant will plead guilty to felony charge 273(a), child endangerment.

The Defendant will serve six months of incarceration, with thirty days served.

The Defendant will serve three years formal Probation, not break any law, and avoid all drugs and alcohol, including marijuana.

The Defendant will be permitted to serve the remainder of her sentence at a Substance Abuse Treatment Facility, and she will have to be escorted to the facility by an employee of the Police Department.

I read the agreement. I could safely serve six months and be out in time to have my baby. With good behavior, my six-month sentence would really only be four months. For this reason, I took the deal. I pleaded no-contest. Before the bailiff escorted me back to the H pod, my Lawyer handed me another piece of paperwork. This was for the custody case. Josh's Aunt Mary wanted to take the girls out of foster care and home with her. I remembered how nice she was when she came to the hospital and how Chloe appeared to feel secure with her. The Court wanted to know if I agreed with the decision because Mary lived four hours away. It would be more difficult for me to visit so I ended up saying 'not decided' on the form. I really wasn't sure if this was a good thing. I just didn't trust anyone. I went back to tell Crystal what had happened in Court. I was happy that I was at least not going to prison, but I was still sad to be there. I knew that I would have to tell them I was pregnant because I needed prenatal care.

The days slowly crept by, and I got into somewhat of a routine. Crystal made it a lot easier for me to be in jail. I always had someone to talk to and she was always positive about things. She was really funny too. A lot of times when we were bored we would just sit there and make fun of the other inmates who were really disgusting. They tried to put Crystal in a cell with a woman who was missing a leg. She was afraid of the woman's prosthetic leg and it was hilarious. The woman had some sort of mental disability as well, and it took the jail about two months to realize this. I guess the lady was always trying to steal Crystal's snacks which we had to pay for through the commissary. Crystal got to the point to where she refused to go in her cell.

My situation wasn't a piece of cake either. I think I went through about nine different cellmates because I just could not stand them. After I was moved from my first cellmate, I was put into a room of my own. I was really excited but it only lasted a day. After dinner one night, I was laying down reading, which is mostly what I did in jail, and a girl walked into my cell with her green tub. I rolled over and pretended to sleep. I wasn't in the mood for the drama of a new cellmate. She was close to my age with blond hair and a curvy build. She was crying and it was annoying. She climbed to the top bunk and lay there crying. Two minutes later she had stopped crying and I heard a rhythmic sound coming from up top. It was going on and on. After five minutes of wondering if she had a really bad itch, it sank in. She was masturbating! Two feet away from me! I flagged down the passing guard doing his walk-through. "Mister, my new cellmate is masturbating in here!" I frantically exclaimed. He looked at me and laughed and rolled his eyes. "Okay, Jeter. I'll have her move to her own cell, and I'll tell her that she's not supposed to do that." I wanted my own cell but they were all upstairs. I was pregnant and they didn't let pregnant people go upstairs. I was miserable. My next cellmate was no better, but at least she didn't masturbate! I had to eventually complain about her too. She never shut up, and her squeaky voice just about killed me. She hung all these colored pictures from coloring books on the wall. I did not want to stare at that every day. I felt like I was in a mental hospital when I was locked up with her.

My next cellmate also had some serious problems. She reeked like a dead fish. After she showered, she reeked like a wet dead fish. When I realized that it had to be coming from her privates, I panicked and ran out to flag another guard down. He could have gotten me beat up with what he did next. "All right, ladies!" the guard yelled as he quickly opened and closed the heavy cell doors. "I hear someone smells like a dead fish!" he roared in his manly, military-toned voice. I told Crystal about my dilemma and we were both sitting in the corner of the day room hysterically laughing. I was relieved that he was nice enough to not make it obvious that it was my cell that stunk. He finished his sniffing of all sixteen cells, and he went back to mine after to ask what smelled so bad. She must have been used to her own stench because she was dumbfounded. I felt kind of bad, but I couldn't handle it anymore!

Chapter 40

I had been in jail for about six weeks, was around five months pregnant, and had my first doctor appointment the next day. I didn't want to go because of the complete humiliation I knew I would face, but I had to make sure my baby was growing and healthy.

The Sheriff, who sometimes escorted me to Court, was the one who was transporting me to the doctor. This was the same office that I went to for my first two pregnancies. I was really hoping that I wouldn't have to see the same doctor that knew me. It was so sad that things had fallen apart the way they did. I was shackled but at least only on my wrists this time. My bright orange outfit was beyond noticeable; I would surely stand out in the waiting room. The doctor's office was right next to Donnie's house. I had a fantasy of sneaking out of the office window and running away. I knew it wouldn't really be possible, but it was fun to imagine. It must have been lunch hour because there wasn't a single person in the waiting room. I was called back to the examination room and the Sheriff followed me. A female doctor greeted me. I hadn't seen her before. She was very nice and treated me like a person, not a criminal. After the exam, she told me that she was going to have a nurse draw my blood and do an ultra-sound. "There is a new test that we do to screen for spinal cord defects. It is optional, but if you want to do it just let the nurse know, okay?" I thanked her and waited for the nurse to come for me.

The nurse and the Sheriff were chatting up a storm and laughing. She opened the door and had me follow her around the corner. I sat in a chair and she began to draw four tubes of blood from my arm. The Sheriff was hovering over me, and the flirting between the two "professionals" was getting on my nerves. When she was drawing the last tube, I mentioned the other test that the doctor told me about. "Oh, yes, that one. You would have to go over to the hospital to get it done and make sure that the state would approve it since they're paying for it," she said, in a loud and sarcastic tone. The Sheriff decided that he wanted to add to the conversation as well. He looked at the nurse and said, "I don't know about you, but I pay taxes, and I don't think I want to pay for that test." The nurse sarcastically laughed and agreed, "Um, nope. Me neither!" I felt my face turn red with fury. My medical care was not their business, and they went out of their way to make me feel worse than I already did. I felt as low as I could. Once again, my self-worth rolled over and died.

I was very grateful that the doctor had been so nice. After my blood test, she walked me into the ultrasound room so we could try to see if she could determine the sex of the baby. The Sheriff closely followed behind me. I thought he was being extremely nosy. I thought it was totally unnecessary, and I think my doctor thought so too. We walked into the sonogram room, and the doctor asked the Sheriff if it was necessary for her to leave the office door open. He said no, and she shut the door immediately. My ultrasound was definitely not a moment that I wanted to share with him - a total jerk making it completely clear that he hated his job.

Before my downhill spiral, I was quick to judge people who were in bad situations because I assumed that it was entirely their fault and they could have prevented it. Because of my experiences, I no longer judge anyone. You never know why someone may be in the situation they are in. You can't know what they're feeling inside, and you'll never know who they could one day become. Never, in a million, years did I think that I would be a teenage mother shackled and pregnant for the third time, degraded by law enforcement and shunned by people whom I had once respected and looked up to. I was mad that this was becoming my new identity. That was never supposed to be me.

The doctor put the jelly on my stomach and apologized for it being cold. She then put the machine's sensor on the cold jelly so she could get a clear picture. I didn't know what I was having, but I assumed it would be another girl. I saw for the first time a sweet and tiny little picture of the miniature body. The baby's legs were crossed so she could not give me a definite answer, but she said that if she had to guess, she would say that it was a girl. I was really excited. After seeing my baby I began to feel like I really was pregnant, and not just in a state of denial. Before the ultra-sound, I hadn't connected with my baby. I was terrified that I would end up having her in jail or lose her to Social Services when she was born. After the ultrasound, the doctor gave me about ten pictures to take with me along with a folder full of prenatal information. I was really happy that I had so much literature to take back to the jail because there wasn't a whole lot to read there, especially about pregnancy. The jail staff only let me take two of my ultrasound pictures with me. I had to leave the rest of them with my confiscated personal property. It was pretty stupid because the pictures weren't even on photo paper. They were on thin paper, and I knew that they could have made an exception. But the woman felt like being a bitch as usual. This was the same person that had 'credit-carded' me the previous year.

I showed my jail buddies the pictures of my baby, and everyone was excited to have something new to talk about. That night I laid down to read one of the books that saved me from getting too deep into my fear and grief. For the first time, I felt my baby move. I knew

277

what to expect, and I knew that it would initially feel like a very light thump. The baby's movements became very strong and very frequent. I thought it was kind of cool that I had a little friend with me through this horrible nightmare. It was so bizarre to think that there was a living baby inside of my body again. That gave me an unexpected comfort. It just goes to show that I ended up pregnant for a reason. If it had been just me sitting there in jail for those sixty-two days with nothing to love or anyone to talk to, I might have just called it quits. I did wonder about how people committed suicide while in jail. One way would be to take the sheet and strangle yourself, but you would have to do it carefully and be creative. There weren't very many places to hang the other end of it. If you didn't do it the right way, you would just fall to the ground taking the ceiling light fixture with you, and the jail population would be surrounding you as you woke up wondering what the hell your deal was. I never thought about killing myself while I was in jail, because it would be too much work and I had someone else now that needed me alive. Her survival depended on me.

I didn't want to be dead, but I had moments where I felt so empty and alone that I thought it would at least relieve my pain. It was like a chronic illness except it wasn't physical pain. It was deep and cold. It was lonely and tragic. My heart was struggling to beat. It had to beat extra hard because a big part of it had been taken away. I didn't know if I would ever be able to really get through it. How am I ever going to be happy if I don't get to watch my babies grow up, I asked myself. How could I ever possibly return to the ambitious, motivated, and happy girl that I once was? It really didn't seem possible. The only thing offering me just enough hope to hold on was the new little gift that God wanted me to have.

There were two other pregnant women in jail when I arrived. One of them was close to my age or maybe a little older, and she was much further along than I was. She was about seven months pregnant. She had been arrested for fraud. She and some others managed to make fake checks. The Judge sentenced her to a year in jail. That meant that she would have her baby while she was incarcerated. I was sure that she was numb to her situation just as I was to mine. Her Public Defender was trying to get the Judge to consider releasing her in time to have her baby, so she was still not sure what would happen. I felt so bad for her, and her situation scared me. I was so worried about being in the same situation. It was a terrifying thought. The other lady who was pregnant was about four months along, and she had four other children that she and her husband had permanently lost custody of. I didn't ask why, but she appeared to be pretty levelheaded and normal. I assumed that it was probably a drug addiction that she couldn't kick. Drugs will change people and alter their ideas of reality. I was happy that I was clean and away from that.

The next night after dinner, Derrick showed up for his visit. He was really good about consistently showing up for as many visits as he was allowed, which was only two per week. I showed him the sonogram picture. He told me to stand up and show him my belly. It was definitely looking pregnant, but I could still hide it if I had to because the shirts were so baggy. My medical information was going to be kept completely confidential, and the nurse reassured me that legally they could not tell anyone. Derrick always put money in the books he brought me, and every week I had $50 to get what I needed from the commissary. He also somehow paid the outrageous collect call fees so I could talk to him for fifteen minutes every night before I went to bed. I'll admit that he did make the torture I was going through as comfortable as it could possibly be. He also wrote me letters on a daily basis so I had something to read every night before I went to sleep.

In one of the letters I wrote to him, I told him I wanted to have my pregnancy book that I had read when I was pregnant with the girls. I wanted to be able to refer to it every week to see how my baby was growing and developing. He could not send me the book because it was a hardback copy. Instead, he scanned and made copies of every single page. Every week of my pregnancy he would send me the relevant information. I began to believe that he really did have good intentions and he really did love me. As far as I could tell, he was not using drugs while I was in jail. He was his regular weight, and he never came to a visit with the pale and tense face he had when he was high.

I was proud of him, and I started to gain respect for him again. He stepped up and took care of me in the best way that he could - even more so since I was stuck behind bars. Over time, we became more emotionally connected. He was the only person that knew what I was going through. He went through it with me. The struggles that we endured would cause other relationships to weaken or fail. The opposite was happening for us. We thought that if we could make it through this, we could make it through anything. I don't know if it was the Court battle we were fighting together or the pregnancy, but I became more attached to Derrick than I had ever been to any other person. I felt like I knew him even better than before and that he just wanted to take care of me as well as our new baby. Throughout letters and rare visits, we fell in love all over again.

My dad tried to visit me towards the end of my jail stay. When the correctional officer announced it over the loudspeaker, I knew that it was someone unexpected because I already had my visits for the week. "Can you tell me who it is that's requesting to see me, please?" I yelled into the speaker. "It is a man by the name of Ron," he replied. "Okay, I am not going to accept this visit. Can you please tell him not to visit me in the future?" I asked. He said that he would relay the message. I knew that my dad was only there to give me a guilt trip and that was the last thing I needed. Plus, he didn't know that I was pregnant. It was becoming more difficult to hide the pregnancy and I had to move up a size in my orange pants to make room. I called my mom later that night just to talk because I felt most lonely at night when I was supposed to be at home and in bed."

Have you heard from your dad lately?" she asked. "Actually, he tried to visit me today," I replied. "Oh no, Liz, you didn't see him?" she asked sounding worried. I knew that something was up because rarely did my mother have sympathy for my father and vise-versa. "Merri told me that your Grandpa passed away a few days ago. He was probably there to tell you that Liz!" Damn it! I thought. "Now I feel horrible! I didn't want him to see that I was pregnant, and I figured he was just going to yell at me!" I felt so bad. If I had known, I would have just dealt with the possible conflict and accepted the visit. I didn't know my Grandpa too well because they lived five hours north, but my Grandparents were both so nice to Merri and me as we were growing up. Our Grandma always had pies in the oven and our Grandpa always kissed us on the forehead and pretended to rub it in so it would stay there forever when we left. I had hurt another person I loved when he was already hurting. It seemed as if the only thing I could accomplish was to hurt people in spite of my good intentions. Life was no longer in my control in any way, shape, or form. The only thing I could do was pray for God to take the wheel and help me get through my mistakes and the pain they caused.

Chapter 41

Another three weeks went by, and I still had not heard anything from my Public Defender about getting me out of jail and into a rehab facility. At that point I had no desire to use drugs and, as dumb as I could be at times, there was no way that I would ever use them while pregnant. I never understood how a woman could even have the desire to use drugs knowing that she was pregnant. When I quit smoking, it sucked, but I wanted to because I was afraid of harming my baby. I wanted to be anywhere but in jail, but from other women's stories of going to this particular facility, it honestly sounded like heaven. Having to wake up at 6:00 in the morning to do a meditation session for thirty days sounded totally miserable. A pillow and a regular bed, regular food, and something to drink besides a carton of milk, sounded like heaven. I was desperate to get out of jail. I began calling and nagging my Public Defender every day. She was usually busy, so I had to leave a message with her assistant.

Once a week on Thursday nights the jail offered an outreach meeting for inmates who had been sentenced to jail more than once. At first I thought it would be nothing but a bunch of nagging women talking about their problems. I already had enough of my own to deal with. However, I noticed that if I stayed busy the time went by a lot faster. While I was waiting for news from my Lawyer, I tried to stay as busy as possible. The restlessness and anxiety was just about killing me. I liked Janet, the leader of the group. She was older and an ex-addict with time spent in prison. At one point she had been in the very jail we were sitting in. She was able to recover and told us that part of her recovery was to help other people who were in similar situations. She was really laid back and let everyone have a chance to talk.

I told her about how I was trying to get out of the jail and into the rehab facility. I didn't know what the holdup was and I told her I was getting nervous because I was almost six months pregnant. "Elizabeth, I'll call SRR for you. I work for them part-time so I might be able to help you get over there." I was so happy that I had someone who would actually help me. I was not used to other adults, especially community role models, giving me any kind of civilized treatment. I had a feeling that Janet would be back in the next day or so to help get me to the recovery center. I was wrong. She showed up about an hour later, ready to get me "the hell out of there." She even said it in exactly those words.

An officer came to do a quick inspection of my cell and make sure that I had cleaned my area for the next inmate. I was completely surprised, and so was he, when the entire pod of at least thirty women began to clap loudly to display their excitement for me and that I was finally on the path to going home. The officer was thoroughly baffled. "Wow, Ms. Jeter, you're a celebrity in here!" I just laughed. I didn't know what else to do. I thanked all of them and hugged as many of them as I could on my way out and wished them good luck. I gave each person whom I had become close to a personal item because I knew that they would appreciate it more than I would. I had a stack of romance novels sent to me by Derrick and my mother and an entire laundry-sized bin full of snacks, soap, and pretty much everything on the commissary list. I could care less about taking any souvenirs with me from my 62 days in jail. I was ready to get out of that sad place, start over, become a better person and hopefully get back to being myself again - if that were possible.

For the last time, I walked down the blue taped line and waited in that same cold holding cell that I had been in two months earlier. It felt like I had been there for years. It was by far the longest two months of my life. A female officer opened the heavy, clanking door and asked me to walk across the walkway so I could change into my regular clothes and get my personal items back. I was so excited...until I opened the green mesh bag to discover a tiny, slutty nightgown. There was no way in hell I was putting this on and going to the recovery center to introduce myself! I told the officer about my dilemma and she laughed and told me not to worry about it. She went into the laundry area and returned with a white t-shirt and sweat pants. I could do this. So much better than what I had, I thought.

When I was finally dressed and ready to go, I went to the desk next to the exit area and signed for my small bag of jewelry and thirteen dollars. It must have been leftover money from my commissary fund. Gina was waiting for me just behind the door. The receptionist lady wished me luck and said I was free to leave. For the last time, I heard the door buzz to unlock, and I stepped out into the beautiful sunshine and let the rays soak into my face. The air smelled amazing. I felt as if I had just landed in some beautiful vacation destination.

One of the most valuable lessons that I have learned in life was one that I learned on that trip to jail. It was from a female inmate I had met and had initially disliked. The more I got to know her, the more I realized that she was just a quirky person with a funny sense of humor. I actually became friends with her. I was talking to her about halfway through my stay and telling her about how miserable and anxious I felt every day. "Humans were made to adapt to their environment. You'll be okay, just tough it out. It's only temporary.

Time is the worst thing that can be taken from you, but it is also the one thing that will eventually reach its destination." Her words helped me get through the time I spent in jail. Any time I was feeling sad or depressed, I heard her voice in my head. I was made to adapt to my environment, I would think to myself. Eventually my time would be served, and I knew I would get out of there. Time is one of the worst things that someone can take from you because our time to live is limited.

I was so excited to be outside, and I was so excited to know that I did not have to go back into that lonely jail. I even jumped up and down for a minute practically attacking Gina with a hug as I thanked her. She looked at me like I was crazy, but she knew where I was coming from. We walked toward the bus stop and sat down on the bench while waiting for our ride down the highway. I knew of the place we were going, but I had never actually been there. I had no idea what to expect except for the tidbits of information I had gotten from some of the other inmates who had previously been there. They were supposedly very strict and would kick a person out for breaking the smallest rule. If I got kicked out, I would have to go back to jail and start the entire sentence over again. I had every intention of listening to the counselors and cooperating to the best of my ability, but I was still afraid. I had developed the strong belief that everyone was out to get me, and no matter what I did, it would never be good enough. The system had made me feel like I was invalid. Nothing I would say mattered anymore because I was officially a felon. I was now entering into society as a convict. My dreams of becoming a nurse were entirely over.

I thought about all of this during the bus ride. When the bus pulled up to our stop, we got off and headed into a small convenience store that was on the way to the recovery center. My eyes grew wide with excitement when I came face to face with soda and candy bars. Gina paid for my candy despite my protests.

"Hurry up and drink your soda, hon, we are right around the corner from the building." "Okay! Watch this!" I said as I began chugging my favorite bubbly pleasure. I was a champ at chugging drinks from my beer drinking party days. I almost finished the entire bottle and belched as we walked down the residential street. Gina again looked at me like I was crazy. I was feeling a bit crazy in my own little way. We approached a white house, and I was totally confused. "Where are we?" I asked. "This is the Recovery Center silly," she replied. I hadn't realized that it was in an actual house. I thought it might be more like a medical center. I knew the neighborhood that we were in because my mom had a friend who lived nearby. I hoped that she wouldn't see me at any point during my stay. How embarrassing that would be.

I checked in and answered a hundred questions for the staff member behind the desk. "So, let me ask you, Elizabeth, have you ever used drugs before?" He wanted to know when and exactly how much I had used. "I didn't use drugs until I was eighteen so that was last year. It started with cocaine, and after that I did meth pretty hard for a few months until I lost everything," I answered. "Do you think that you have a problem with drugs now?" he asked. "Yes, because in my opinion, even using drugs on a single occasion is a problem. It should have never happened but it did." I was ready to be honest and face the stupid choices I had made. Plus, I knew that if I lied it would just take even longer for me to get home. They would know and keep me past the thirty days to get me out of denial. I was sure they saw that on a regular basis. When I was in jail, there were plenty of women who would admit to using drugs but would never admit to being an addict or that it was a problem. I thought it was sad. The only way they could ever get better was if they first admitted to themselves the reality of substance abuse and their addiction.

The counselor allowed me to call Derrick because I didn't have any clothes to wear. I told Derrick that I had made it to the rehab, and I asked him to bring over anything that he thought might still fit me. I only had a pair of yoga pants and maybe some sweats in my wardrobe at home that would actually fit. Derrick showed up about twenty minutes later but the counselors did not let me see him. I was bummed and being out of jail made it all the more difficult. The counselor walked back into the office dragging my huge duffel bag. They searched through it to make sure there wasn't any contraband. The female counselor, who didn't speak English very well, held up my pink nightgown and shook her head. She thinks I brought that slutty thing on purpose, I was thinking to myself. I tried to explain to her how it was with me, but I gave up when she wouldn't stop interrupting me. I wouldn't care if she confiscated it as contraband; I didn't want to ever see that thing again anyway. As the search continued, the counselor pulled out two outfits that I didn't recognize. They had tags on them. I realized that they were cute maternity sweat outfits. I thought it was so sweet that Derrick cared so much that he actually thought of something like that for me. Derrick began to change when he discovered that I was pregnant and even more so when I was arrested. He was a totally different person. I couldn't wait to get home to him, start over, and hopefully repair our lives.

The female counselor walked me over to the women's house on the property. There were three houses that were part of the Recovery Center. The house for the females was the big white one. Millie introduced me to two girls who were about my age and looking bored on the living room couch. She then showed me to my room. The room was big, with four twin-sized beds, one in each corner. It was also right next to a bathroom, which was perfect for my midnight pee attacks. She said that I had a few minutes to put my things away and get settled before lunch would be ready.

It looked like only one other person was occupying my new room, and they must have been somewhere else in the building.

After putting my clothes into the built-in dresser drawer that was attached to my bed, I fell back onto the mattress. I enjoyed every second that my head rested on that pillow. It was so amazing, and my pregnant body and hurting back were instantly feeling better. I could finally relax and breathe. I would rather have been home, of course, but I was not about to make one complaint. I had a pillow and a real mattress! The toilet wasn't attached to the same sink that I used to brush my teeth! I was elated. The girl I had met on the couch poked her head into my room and announced that it was time for lunch. I followed her into the building next to the house and, once again, was in heaven as the smell of grilled cheese sandwiches danced up my nostrils.

I sat down to eat with a huge cup of apple juice. I had missed juice and other drinks. Cartons of milk and soap-scented water had gotten old very fast. I couldn't fully grasp the fact that I was really out of jail. I was afraid that I was going to wake up to the grumpy officer announcing breakfast on the loudspeaker. That would have ruined me. The first night that I slept in my new bed I was surprised that I actually didn't sleep very well. I must have gotten used to the flat hospital bed mattress that the jail had.

The Recovery Center was very big on routine. Every morning they would wake us up at 6:00, and before we got dressed for the day, we would meditate for thirty minutes. One of us would have to read out of the official book of Alcoholics Anonymous and discuss whatever else the counselor on duty decided we should talk about. After getting dressed in a hurry, we would go back to the kitchen to eat breakfast. Immediately after breakfast we had our first class. The class lasted until it was time for lunch. After lunch, they would give us an hour of free time to do whatever we wanted. In my case, it was just sitting there and being lazy because the pregnancy had me so exhausted. After our hour of free time, the counselors decided on an activity for all of us to participate in. I think the point of this was to show the importance of teamwork and how important it was to pull your own weight. It taught us about accountability, and the activities were used as an example to show us how the actions of one person can have a big impact on the rest of the team. They didn't have to teach it to me, though, because I already knew it, understood it, and completely agreed with it. I wasn't dumb. I was a smart person, and I had really great grades when I was in college.

Then I started wondering how I, an intelligent person, could have made such stupid and reckless mistakes. I explained this to my counselor during our private sessions, twice a week. She continued to stress the importance of self-forgiveness. For someone who didn't understand what I actually went through on a personal level, it's a lot easier said than done. I didn't want to forgive myself. I felt like forgiving myself would make what had happened to my daughter okay. That would never be something that was okay with me. I had no plans of forgiving myself.

After our daily activity was over, we went to the kitchen for dinner, and by 7:00 we had to be in the living room of the women's quarters for our nightly meeting. Rehab wanted to introduce us to the routine of regularly attending meetings in place of using drugs or alcohol. All of the meetings had outsiders attending. It took me a minute to understand who these people were and why they were there. I had never been to a meeting before, so I didn't know how they worked. Different organizations participated: Cocaine Anonymous, Alcoholics Anonymous, and Narcotics Anonymous.

I quickly determined that I liked the Narcotics Anonymous meetings the best because I felt like the people who attended were super non-judgmental and down to earth. They weren't afraid to crack a joke, and they were totally honest with themselves and the group - not worrying about their image so much as their recovery. By the time the nightly meetings were over, I was extremely exhausted from the day. I brushed my teeth

290

and jumped in bed as fast as I could. My time in treatment went by much quicker than jail, and it was way more productive.

I was still able to keep in touch with Derrick through mail, and he was able to come and see me on Sundays for four hours. My first visit with him was amazing. We hugged and couldn't stay away from each other. I missed him so much, and I just wanted to go home so he could participate in the rest of the pregnancy with me. I wanted him to be able to feel our baby move, and I missed sleeping next to him despite his obnoxious snoring. It was like how we were at the beginning of our relationship. He found a better job that was paying a much higher wage than his last one. Our landlord owned a construction business and hired him when she learned that he had experience in the field. He was making almost twenty dollars an hour. He was paying the bills and even spoiling me as much as he could while I was away. Everyone else who had family visiting seemed happy and excited. The on-call counselor announced that if we wanted to, since it was such a nice day, we could walk to the beach and have our visit outside of the house. It was about a 20-minute walk, and Derrick and I held hands the whole way.

We stopped at a convenience store on the way, and he let me get a 2-pound bag of buttered popcorn flavored jellybeans. The lake was sparkling and beautiful, and the temperature at the beach was perfect. Everything was so beautiful and perfect. Being in jail for so long put a damper on my senses, and now they were all in overdrive. I just wanted to lie on the sand and stare at the clouds. Derrick was lying next to me and put his hand on my belly. For the first time he felt our baby kick. He was really excited and stayed intently focused on my stomach for the remainder of the visit. I thought it was funny that such a tough-looking guy was suddenly emotionally in-tune with our relationship. He must have missed me pretty badly. The visit came to an end when we returned from the beach. I was sad that he was leaving, but I was excited that I only had a few weeks left before I could go home.

On the last week of my stay in rehab, my appetite went insane as my baby was growing more and more. We weren't supposed to eat during the classes in the morning, but I felt my blood sugar getting low so I had no choice. I pulled out a bear-claw from my sweatshirt pocket and as quietly as I could, I unwrapped the snack. The instructor's name was Michael. He was in his late forties, and he seemed very cocky and set in his ways. I always paid attention but avoided asking too many questions because of his reputation for putting people on the spot and embarrassing them. "Ms. Jeter! What are you sneaking over there?" he loudly asked. I thought I would make light of the situation, because surely he would understand since I was in my last trimester. "Sorry! My baby got hungry, so I had to eat something!" Everyone in the class laughed, even the guys. "You can't blame your actions on your child! Maybe if you kept your legs closed you wouldn't be having to interrupt my class by breaking the rules!" he yelled. I raised my eyebrows in shock. Most of the other women had a look of disbelief on their faces. I could not believe what I was hearing. I didn't argue any further, because I was going to go above him and do everything possible to get him fired. I was so sick of these "professional" people thinking it was okay to humiliate and degrade me. My situation was none of their business. I started writing a letter to give to the director of the facility as soon as the class was over. As soon as I was done, I asked my roommate what I needed to do to get it sent to the right person. I found out that the director was dating Michael. Damn it! I thought. I gave up on my quest to get the idiot fired and tried to let go of what he had said.

On the second to the last day of my treatment, our afternoon class was a women's-only session. The lady leading the group was someone I hadn't seen before. She was really nice, and she made the group fun and interesting. Before the class ended, she had us complete an exercise. We were to write a one-page "goodbye" letter to our drug of choice. She said the exercise would help us put why being sober is a positive thing into perspective, and it would help us let go of the drugs. She said that many people went through a grieving process as they became clean and drug-free. We were going to share our letters with the class when we were done, then burn them in a fire pit as a symbolic method of letting go. "Okay ladies! You will have twenty minutes to write your letter, starting now." The clock was ticking and I was getting nervous. I honestly could not find it in me to write a goodbye letter to meth. It didn't even deserve that much from me. I was mad at the drug - not missing the damn drug! I was missing my babies. So instead, I wrote a poem to my girls. Subconsciously, my mind needed to say goodbye because it never had that chance. At this point, I had not seen them in three months. It was hard controlling my tears as I was writing, but I managed to hide my pain. I wasn't sure how I would read it out loud and still hide it.

When I finished sharing my letter, I looked up to see every woman including the counselor, quietly sniffling with tears rolling down their faces.

Chloe and Zoe,
I am writing to you from a place far away
Your hearts are with mine, no matter where you stay
I hurt for your pain, the mistakes that were made
I was lost in my world, too young and afraid
Never in this world did I want to see you cry
Never in my life will I ever say goodbye
My babies, my gifts, my heart and soul
No breath I breathe in, can ever be whole
Until you were gone, I was so very blessed
Your hugs, your laughs, your cuddles on my chest

I miss you, I ache, every minute, every day
I never imagined you would be sent away
All in God's time, you'll come back to me
Like the butterflies who fly, setting our hearts free
My prayers he hears, unanswered I will wait
No matter the time, it will never be too late
To hug, to laugh, to smile and to hold
I will trust in our God for our lives to unfold

Chapter 42

I got through the poem with only crying a little bit. I had to release that pain and fear. I was still unsure of what my fate as their mother was going to be. I was stunned that every single female in the group was touched enough to cry. Maybe they were relating to their own losses. I knew that when I got out of treatment I wanted to find a way to help other people through similar painful situations.

The day for me to return home arrived before I knew it. I woke up that morning extra early so I would have time to make myself extra pretty. I was not allowed to have makeup there, but I did get to have my curling iron. I wore the cutest outfit that I had and eagerly waited for eight o'clock to arrive so my counselor could complete my treatment plan and release me. I cleaned up my area, gave all of the women a hug and wished them luck, and hauled my duffel bag over to the same building I checked into thirty days earlier. If it weren't for Gina, I would still be stuck in jail. She was the only staff member in the entire jail who had cared enough to see that I got out of there. I hoped that I would see her again so I could thank her.

My counselor asked a few questions for the end-of-treatment questionnaire. It was only ten minutes before she handed me the phone to call Derrick to pick me up. He was there within minutes, and I was so excited to be going home. Derrick helped me survive one of the most miserable experiences of my life and we were connected even more from the circumstances. I was convinced that he definitely was not the person who hurt my daughter.

He walked in and grabbed my duffel bag for me. I followed him out to the car, and he kissed me in a way that said he needed me. I needed to be needed. My girls were gone and probably didn't need me anymore. At least someone did. I excitedly hopped into the Jeep and we took off. It was so cool to be driving down the road and know that I was actually going home.

I walked into our tiny studio, and I was very pleased that Derrick had taken the time to clean it up for me. He was usually sort of a slob. I walked in and I noticed that it smelled like my Grandparent's home had smelled when I was little. It was a combination of laundry detergent, second hand smoke, and cat litter.

Derrick announced that he had a surprise planned for me. We woke up early the next day and drove to the Bay Area where he grew up. That was where we first fell in love and officially said the L word. It was awesome to get out of town and be surrounded by people who didn't know what was going on and could not judge us. We spent the weekend catching up with his friends, shopping and driving around San Francisco. One thing that we had in common was that we both loved to spend money and shop like we were rich. We were both spontaneous and loved to randomly get out of town, even if it was just for a day. After the weekend trip was over, it was time to get down to business. I had three months to prove to the Court that I was worthy of being reunited with my girls, and they would not need to take custody of the new baby because everything would be safe. I had the constant fear that they would take my baby away when she was born, and I was prepared to do everything possible to make sure that didn't happen.

I continued my treatment at the Outpatient Facility, and my first six weeks were intense. It was Monday through Friday from 10:00 a.m. to 2:00 p.m. I wondered how the other people in the group were able to hold jobs with that kind of schedule. Part of my outpatient treatment was to attend three meetings a week on my own time. I went to the Narcotics Anonymous meetings and occasionally Derrick went with me to show his support. I thought it was pretty bad that he was such a good liar and that the Court thought I needed drug treatment even more so than Derrick. He wouldn't even admit that he was ever addicted to drugs! At least I could set my ego aside to admit the truth.

Derrick and I both decided to sign up for a parenting class at the Women's Center. We wanted to make the Court happy for the Hearings on Chloe and Zoe's living status, and we wanted to avoid another case with our new baby. We consistently attended every week for the duration of the ten weeks required and were issued our certificates as proof. I had a Court Hearing coming up, and the Judge wanted to know what progress I had made since being released from jail. My Public Defender sat down next to me when the case was called. I tried desperately to hide my pregnancy. Derrick had bought me a big winter-weather jacket and it did a good job. I was eight months pregnant, though, and if anyone noticed, no one said anything.

"Hi Elizabeth." Laura said. She looked like she was going to say something bad. She had a look of sympathy on her face, and that was not a good sign. She was a tough bulldog and wasn't the type to have sympathy for many people, but she knew how hard I was trying. "The Social Services knows that you're with Derrick, so they want to put in for a motion to terminate your parental rights," she quietly said. "I don't understand how they can do that when no one has been arrested for what happened. We still don't know what happened, and I just completed rehab and everything. Derrick and I are going to submit a hair follicle drug test to the Court to prove our stability and recovery," I pleaded with her. I would do anything to prevent this and she knew that. "The fact is, Elizabeth, that you are with Derrick after you accused him. They don't know what to make of it and still think the girls would be at risk," Laura said in a sympathetic yet factual manner.

The Judge looked at the paperwork with my proof of completion of classes and programs. He made a note to the Court to have the transcriber get it on the record. "Ms. Jeter has made considerable progress, and I want to recognize that. I am going to set the motion for two weeks from now, and I will submit her documents to the Court for evidence." It was a quick hearing, and the bailiff handed me a card with my next Court date. I was hoping that since the Judge noted my progress they would extend the next hearing date and give me extra time to finish up whatever it was that they wanted. I was extra busy after this hearing. I checked in with Probation and asked for a document saying that I had been compliant. I did several voluntary urine analysis drug tests, and Derrick and I began to log my three times a week meetings. I was trying to complete every request that I thought CPS could possibly request of me. That way, it would not be possible for them to deny me my girls.

As the Court date neared, I was getting anxious and scared. I was almost nine months pregnant and my hormones were getting the best of me. Derrick had moved us down the street into a house that his friend used to occupy. It was a two-bedroom house, and it had a fenced back yard. It wasn't huge, but it was much better than what we had been living in. Now our baby would at least have its own room. When Chloe and Zoe came home, there would be more room for all the girls. Everything, at that point, was just an intense and miserable wait.

The Judge ordered the Social Services to schedule a visit with the girls the last time I was in Court. My mom picked me up on a Saturday, and we made the long five-hour drive to see them at

298

a park in the town they were living in. I was very nervous and afraid that they would not remember me. It had been four months since I had last seen them, and when kids are that young, four months can feel like a lifetime. I hoped that it hadn't been so long that they had forgotten me. My mom's car was making me carsick, and I was glad when we arrived. We had brought presents for them. The CASA worker was supervising the visit, and I really hated her. She didn't even have kids, and I wondered why anyone thought she was so qualified to be an advocate for a child who could hardly even talk! Chloe was only three and she did talk, but it was that cute three-year-old babble that usually only parents can translate. Right when my mom approached the swing set, the girls dropped everything they were doing and ran her way. They had grown. They had grown a lot, and Zoe didn't even look like a baby anymore. She had a lot more hair and was talking very well. Chloe was gorgeous and tall and skinny. She had her dad's physique, but her face was all mine. The girls were hugging my mom's legs as she was digging into her bag for their presents.

I got down on the ground because I read that kids communicate better if you get down to their level. As tears were accumulating in my eyes, I put a smile on my face. "Hi beautiful girls!" I softly said. "I miss you so much! Are you having fun today?" I asked. I didn't know if I should expect a response or what would happen. They continued to hug my mom's leg, and as I spoke to them they had confused smiles on their faces. I could see it in their eyes that they were hurting and hesitant to reattach themselves to me. It was really sad, but as the visit progressed they warmed up to me a little bit.

Zoe was calling Mary mommy at this point. I wanted to cry the first time she said it but I didn't. I tried to appear as level headed as I could because the CASA worker would report any little incident to the Court in a flash. Chloe called Mary by her name. Part of me didn't blame Zoe. She had to have someone to call mommy, I thought. It just hurt that it wasn't me. Towards the end of the visit, I walked

299

with Chloe over to the swing set and pushed her. "Chloe, mommy is very sorry, okay? I love you so much, and I will always love you! Are you happy?" I asked. She knew exactly what I was saying to her, and she said a quiet "Yes." Zoe was all over the park, reminding me of her ADHD father, but Chloe was more shy and reserved. I hoped that Chloe understood what I meant and would remember me saying those things to her even after the visit.

Everything in my life was so unpredictable at that point, and I did not know if I would ever see them again. It was all so sad and strange. The close bond that we had shared was lost, and I prayed that I would have the chance to repair it. When the visit was over I gave both my girls hugs and told them how much I loved them and how sorry I was. I kept my statements as simple as possible, hoping that they could understand what I was saying. I didn't handle the goodbyes well, and they cut deeper and deeper as time went on. As my mom was saying goodbye to them, I walked back to her car, not wanting to give the CASA worker the satisfaction of seeing me cry. So many people were making decisions for me. Why did they have the right to decide the fate of my children after all I went through to make it right? I was about to discover exactly what that fate would be.

Chapter 43

I returned home and told Derrick all about the visit. I couldn't help but cry and worry about what would happen. I was so sad that I wasn't as connected as I had always been with my girls and mad that, in spite of my poor judgment and mistakes, any one would have the right to take that away! I lay on my bed and cried for two hours. The first hour I cried for Chloe and Zoe, knowing that I hurt them and knowing that they must be so incredibly confused. I know that kids always blame themselves, but I hoped that they didn't ever think that any of this was their fault. The second hour, I cried for our new baby. I cried because I was preparing for the worst, and the reality that CPS might take my baby away from me was a real one. Everything was sinking in and I would be forced to face the pain of it at some point.

Before the Court Hearing for Chloe and Zoe, I wanted answers from the CPS, and I wanted them in person. I was sick of hiding my pregnancy. I wanted to find out if they could tell me what could be done about Chloe and Zoe and what I had to do to get them back with me. I was getting scared and desperate. I wanted it to be clear that I would do whatever it took. The day before the Court Hearing, I walked down the street and crossed the highway. Derrick was working, and he didn't know what I was doing. I walked into the lobby and asked the receptionist to see if a caseworker could speak with me for a moment. Five minutes later, a short man with dark hair in his fifties called me to the back where his office was. We sat down, and I was shocked at the first thing he said to me.

"When is your due date?" he asked. I made up a date that was a few months off, trying to confuse them and make it difficult for them to plot to hurt me even more. "Look," I said. "I just need to know what I need to do to keep my parental rights. I will do anything that you ask of me. I would even leave Derrick if I had to. I lost time to do these things when I was arrested, and I need to show to you and the Court that I'm serious about taking care of my daughters and fixing the situation." "I can't say with confidence that there is anything I can do for you, Elizabeth. I'll speak with my supervisor and look into it, but most people who make those decisions already have their minds made up." He was useless. He didn't even try to give me the information I needed. He didn't even act like he cared about anything except trying to be nosey and scribble down notes about my pregnancy. I left after he said he would give me a call later in the week. I knew that he would not. It was all a waste of time, and I was even more worried. I prayed and prayed for God to help me get through this and to allow the Judge to see my progress and desire to fix my life and the lives of my girls. I told God that with me being so pregnant, I didn't think I could handle losing my babies forever. The night before I had Court, I fell asleep with a bad feeling, and I cried until I started dreaming.

My alarm went off at eight in the morning. Derrick had taken time off work to take me, because he knew that I would need him if everything went bad that day. He was convinced that it would be okay. The few other people that I discussed it with were also sure that it would turn out in my favor - simply because I had completed every possible self-improvement class on the

302

planet! I wanted to believe that it would be okay, but I wasn't able to get my hopes up.

We drove down the icy highway and managed to find a parking spot only five minutes before the hearing began. We waited in the lobby along with ten other couples that were probably suffering through the same thing that I was. I was surprised when my name was called first. I wanted Derrick to go in with me, but it was a confidential hearing because it involved minors.

The seats were maxed out with what looked like Social Workers, Police employees, and other people wearing badges around their necks. If it's so private, why the hell does it look like the media is here, I was thinking. I had no clue who they were and wanted them the hell out of the Courtroom. I told my Lawyer this, and she managed to get the Judge to kick half of them out. That was when I noticed that I had never seen the Judge that was currently before me.

I asked my Lawyer where the other Judge was. He had handled my case since the beginning and was actually qualified and knowledgeable enough to make such a huge, not to mention final, decision in my life. "He is sick today so this is a temporary Judge," she said. She saw the look of frustration and anxiety on my face. "I can't tell you what is going to happen, but I'll fight to get this postponed, okay? It's not a promise that I can even do that," she said. She had that same look of sympathy on her face. She looked like she didn't even want to be there. The Judge called the case number and had the Recorder document everyone in attendance. Mary was there. When I heard the Attorney for CPS mention this, my heart shattered because I knew what was going to happen.

My Lawyer was fighting as hard as she could even though the circumstances were entirely against me. She mentioned every single accomplishment that I had made since I left jail. This included twelve weeks of parenting classes, thirty days at a rehab facility, six months at an Intensive Daily Outpatient Center, nightly Narcotics Anonymous meetings, counseling sessions, and weekly drug testing.

The Probation Department had written a letter stating my compliances, and it seemed that the pile of certificates I quickly obtained would have shown my desperation to be with my children. My Attorney had the Bailiff give the Judge the documented proof.

During the time my Attorney was fighting our case and saying everything possible to delay the hearing, I heard the whispers of the employees of Social Services, the Court, and the CASA workers behind me. To them, I was nothing more than a drug-addicted liar who never was, and never would be, a good or capable mother. Now, it was I who was one of those pathetic women that I used to shake my head at in shame. It was all business to them and the closing of another case that they would be free to shake out of their hair.

When the Judge began to speak, the people behind me became silent and still. The Judge said a few sympathetic words of praise acknowledging the completion of my recovery classes. Not once, though, did his eyes directly meet with mine. I was silently begging him to just look at me, as I held my head up with a determined desperation. I wanted him to look at me, and I wanted God to let him see through me and just give me a fighting chance. When I realized that he was not going to look at me, I dropped my head in defeat. Please, God, please just give me a chance. I'm so sorry for making so many mistakes and I'm begging for your mercy. Please God - just don't let this happen. I silently prayed.

As he was speaking his final ruling, I flashed back to the best days of my life - the days that my girls were born. I endured pain that I was never really prepared for. Their lives depended on this pain. The pain was just as real as they were, which made it painfully beautiful. The moment that I saw their faces and heard their first cry singing into my heart, I knew that I could go through the pain a hundred times over again. Nature pumped

304

endorphins and serotonin through my body, and I was elated with joy. To hold in my arms the most perfect and pure gift that anyone can ever receive is what makes life and all of the pain it can cause, completely meaningful and perfect.

My gifts were about to be taken away forever. I managed to hold onto my dignity as I was hearing the most feared statement of my life, which was being ordered by the Judge, as permanently and painfully as anything could possibly be.

"The State of California and the county of El Dorado are granting the motion to terminate all parental rights of the biological mother, Elizabeth Jeter. The minors, Chloe and Zoe, ages three and four, will remain in the custody of the state until final orders for placement have been determined."

The Judge was slamming his stamp down to certify the orders as if it were a signal to the Clerk to hurry through the paperwork and get on to the next, I felt it slamming intensely into my chest. It burned, ached and scarred. I was branded - branded as nothing more than a "birth-mother." When the stamp from my punishment rose, it stole the flesh of my heart with it. I felt as if they died. They were gone. I would not see them again. I wouldn't have any more visits, and I wouldn't know where they were at all times.

Their first cries, smiles, laughs, words, teeth, steps and sweet pieces of artwork brought home to hang on the fridge were gone. I would have to hold on to these memories as tightly as I could because when I would inevitably become broken with pain in the long years ahead, I would no longer have the privilege of holding my daughters for any comfort or to uphold my responsibility of comforting them. Though Zoe was so young that she may not remember me down the road, I held on to the hope, and prayed to God as hard as one can pray, that Chloe would have just one first memory of me holding her, laughing with her, and loving her.

Please God, just let her remember how much I love her. Please don't let her forget. She can tell Zoe the truth when no other will. Please...

Just don't let her forget...

It was done. I sat with my head in my hands and my face soaked with the consequences of my punishment. I didn't want to get out of my chair. I just knew that the crowd of big shot Social Workers was gleaming with pleasure. They took joy in my pain. I wondered if Mary did too. I didn't want to believe that it was over and there was nothing else that I could do. My Lawyer reached over to lightly rub my back in sympathy. I looked up at her and thanked her for the fight. As I hesitantly turned toward the isle leading to the exit, I kept my head down, not wanting to give my audience any more gratification from seeing my tears. I slightly glanced up to the left, and for a split second, I made eye contact with the woman who was taking my babies home with her to be their new mother. The only thing I hoped to accomplish through this brief exchange of eye contact was to etch into her mind for the rest of her life the broken soul that I became from losing my daughters on that sad day in 2007. I wanted her to always be hesitant to say any negative words to my Chloe and Zoe as they grew older. I wanted her to see my true tie to them, induced by instinct and nature, which we would always share - in spite of all the orders, separation and words. According to me, and even more importantly God, Chloe and Zoe were my children. Not hers.

A woman I had never been introduced to that was in charge of the Family Drug Court followed me out of the Courtroom and stopped me to offer a hug.

"Sometimes, the hardest thing in life is allowing one's self to let go. I'm so sorry for your pain."

Out of an entire community made up of Counselors, Social Workers, Probation Officers, Attorneys, Law Enforcement, teachers and every citizen who had a role with the objective to help those in need, Olga was the only one who showed me true compassion. She thought I was worthy of comfort, and her hug may have been the tiny spark that kept my flame of hope and faith ignited - as it would soon be blown away…. again.

As I sit here in reflection and ending this chapter with tears in my eyes, I am grateful to see the beauty in this pain that now has purpose. I do not have tears from reliving the devastating experience. Today I have tears from feeling the tremendous joy in knowing that humanity is capable of empathy, compassion, and forgiveness. If only we could all be more like Olga.

I will always love and miss my little girls, and I still hold onto the hope that one day we will be united again.

Chapter 44

"My name is Elizabeth...and I am an addict." I was sitting on an old run down couch in a musty room at a local church. I knew that if I were to have any chance at all to keep my new baby, I had to surrender and succumb to this new identity. I was a self-proclaimed drug addict. Deep down, I knew that wasn't the real me.

I hadn't used any substance for about ten months. I stopped the self-destruction about two weeks before I found out that I was pregnant for the third time. Whenever I put anything into my body, whether it was alcohol or drugs, I knew that I was allowing myself to be the bad mother that they all had named me to be. I knew that I was disrespecting my daughters. Getting back together with Derrick, not to mention becoming pregnant with his child, was the ultimate disrespect. It was the ultimate disrespect towards my family, my daughters and to myself. I was surprised to discover that I was pregnant. My mind and body had been through such shock and tragedy that you would think Mother Nature surely would have known better - even if I didn't.

A few weeks away from my due date, I spent my days obsessively researching the law and what I could do to beat it. I spent my nights lying in bed crying because I was afraid for my unborn baby. My future was completely uncertain. My life didn't have any direction or stability. I told this to the small group of women at the Narcotics Anonymous meeting. I saw the look of compassion in their eyes. At least they took me for who I was regardless of my circumstances. I was sure that they'd probably heard it all.

I woke up one morning and just couldn't handle any more uncertainty or anxiety. Derrick was working so I didn't have our only car. If I could get just one answer it would be worth it. I put on my extra-large light brown fuzzy coat and started walking toward the highway. It was about a fifteen-minute walk from where I lived. It was cold and snowy, and I had to take extra care not to slip on the black ice. When I walked into the waiting area, I became sad as I was reminded of the heartbreaking visits I had with Chloe and Zoe. The vision of Chloe racing to put her jacket on so she could leave with me will never leave my mind. "Mommy! I want to go in YOUR CAR!" she cried. She had pure fear and desperation written on her face and a deep sadness in her watering eyes. I had no way to soothe or comfort her. The Social Worker was rushing me to leave and claiming that I was "just making it worse." "Do you have no soul?" I asked the merciless, red headed woman. "You're making them cry. It's time to go now," she coldly replied.

All of this flashed back to me as if it were happening in the moment. Most of these Social Workers behaved as if they had no feelings and didn't have any children of their own. Their lack of understanding and compassion, along with their deliberate lies and fabricated reports, ripped my family apart. As I spoke with more and more parents through my classes and meetings, I came to realize that there was a serious problem within the CPS organization. A woman who was only a few years older than me had permanently lost her 5 and 6-year-old daughters to the system. Ironically, they allowed her to keep custody of her newborn baby boy. I did not understand how or why this selective separation was taking place. If a mother is deemed fit to care for one child, then it seems she certainly should be fit to care for all her children. I do realize, however, that I did not know all the facts. I hoped that they would allow me to keep my baby.

I walked down to the Social Services office for two reasons. I wanted to see if there was anything else that I could do to have one more chance to get my girls back - even if it meant leaving Derrick. The other reason, which I deliberately would not bring to the surface, was to find out if they knew that I was pregnant and if so, what their plans were. I wanted to find out if they would offer me services again. If they mentioned my pregnancy, I fully intended to beg them to give me the Court-ordered list of improvements I would need to make. I wanted to get this done before my baby was born to prevent them from taking my baby.

"Can I help you?" the receptionist kindly asked. For the most part the women at the front desk were always nice to me. "Yes, I just want to find out if I can talk to one of the caseworkers who was in charge of my recently closed case." The woman dialed an extension behind the glass window and had me take a seat. I was out of breath and trying to carry myself in a confident manner. It was just impossible. I couldn't even pretend. Finally, a short man opened the door and called my name. He didn't smile as I approached, and he stayed quiet and cold. He led me down the hallway and into his office. I thought it was strange that a man in his late 50's had an office overflowing with toys and stuffed animals and cartoons all over the walls - yet he was such an ass at the same time. Maybe he needed the extra distraction in his office to avoid scaring little kids to tears. I was almost scared to tears.

"How are you Elizabeth?" he nonchalantly asked. He really could care less. "Your caseworker is on vacation for two weeks, and I'm taking on her responsibilities until she returns." Great, I thought. As soon as he mentioned this, I knew there wasn't any hope. There was a very small chance to appeal my case, and I knew that there was nothing else I could do. This man would have no mercy. "I just wanted to see if there is any way at all to appeal the decision of the Court. I'll do anything for a chance to prove myself. I'll leave Derrick if that's what it takes. I've completed my 6-week intensive outpatient treatment, parenting classes, voluntary drug testing, and anger management, everything I've been able to think of. I can't stand the thought of never seeing my daughters again, and it's taken a while for the seriousness of everything to sink in. I think I've just been in shock." Before I could say another word he interrupted me. "Like I said, your caseworker is on vacation. I have no say in any of this, and all I can do is leave her a message." My heart sank to my stomach. This man wasn't about to answer any of my questions or offer any kind of hope. Before I could respond to him he quickly added, "So when is your due date?"

The familiar adrenaline rush of fear pumped through my body and I became weak. I had to think fast. This was a clear indication that he was going to take note of my due date and file for state custody. I lied. "It's in March," I simply replied. Maybe it would buy me enough time to have my baby before the hospital got the memo. Just maybe they'll forget about me and let me move on with my life, I silently wished. "Are you planning on taking this baby too? Can you offer me services so that doesn't happen?" I pleaded. "Well we can't offer services for something that doesn't even exist yet," he sarcastically replied. Does he really think my baby doesn't exist yet, I thought. His response confirmed his lack of compassion for human life – especially babies. There couldn't be a worse person than him to do this job. After getting nowhere and ultimately making things more difficult and possibly even setting myself up, I left and started the walk back home.

"Well, he didn't say they were taking the baby, right?" Derrick asked. "Of course not. They're not going to tell me something like that!" I fired back. "Don't they have to tell you if there is an open case or a pending case?" he asked. "I don't know, but I don't have a good feeling." I curled up in bed and tried to be strong and stop the tears. I was so sad. I was sad because I hadn't even met my baby yet, and I just knew there was going to be trouble. "Don't worry Elizabeth. They won't take her. I won't let them. If we have to, we'll get my parents involved. They'll get a Lawyer if it comes down to it. We're not going to let them take our baby away." He had that believable and convincing tone that I always believed and trusted. It was much easier to just believe him and focus on getting through the rest of the pregnancy. I knew that this baby was a fighter. This baby went through grief and jail and rehab with me and then lost Chloe and Zoe with me. I knew that my baby had to have felt my pain. My new goal was to bring this baby into the world and offer him or her a life that was safe, quiet, happy and peaceful. I was going to offer this baby all that I had failed to offer Chloe and Zoe. I wanted so much to do this right.

Even though I failed so miserably, I still held on to hope. If I didn't at least have hope, I would have nothing. Hope gave me a reason to live. The dreams I had of coming out on top of everything helped me trudge through the mud every day - and it sure as hell was muddy. I remember how attached I became to country music and the lyrics. The songs were always about real people with real problems and heartache.

Chapter 45

It was Super Bowl 2007, and I was just about as big as I could get. Everything hurt. It hurt to walk, breathe, roll over, and to try and put up with Derrick. He would come home from work with that familiar, gut-wrenching tightness on his face. After nailing him and guilt-tripping him as best as I could, he still denied using any sort of drugs. It was easier to just believe him and drop it. My intuition knew better but I ignored it. I couldn't deal with his crap at that point in time.

I was excited that it was Super Bowl time. It was a good way to take my mind off of everything. I made tons of food that day. It was freezing cold outside, and I welcomed the idea of lounging on the couch with an enormous plate of hot food, which sat perfectly on my pregnant tummy. Just as I was about through with the cooking, Derrick announced that he invited his brother to come over and watch the game with us, and his brother was bringing three other friends and a baby. Part of me hated the idea, but part of me wanted to be able to hang out with other people and just be normal. I wanted to be a part of the world again and do things that everyone else did. More than anything, I wanted to prove to myself that I was normal and the people whom I was around were normal. Everything that had happened to me was all some freak accident, I recited in my head. Derrick's words invaded my mind and found their own way to my hippocampus and became stuck in my frontal lobes for years. Sometimes I wondered how a person could have such control. At different times over the years I thought he was some sort of supernatural demon.

Everyone showed up with alcohol, cigarettes and marijuana. My dinner wasn't so exciting anymore. This included a younger couple with a newborn baby. I became angry because I saw myself from an outsiders standpoint. I allowed my babies to be around these people and the substances. It was pathetic. It was bullshit. There was no excuse that could make this scenario okay. I simply couldn't handle it. I went into my bedroom and locked myself away for the night. I was hoping that Derrick would at least come in to see what was wrong, but he could care less. I didn't see him again until about 2:00 a.m. The next morning when I woke up and rolled out of bed, he had already left for work.

As I walked into the living room to make something to eat, rage came over me. The house was absolutely trashed. I saw empty beer bottles everywhere, old rotted food left out, and dishes left all over the place. I called Derrick. "You call those people your friends? If they can't even respect your home, what makes you think they respect you? I cleaned house and made dinner all day yesterday! Am I just your bitch now or what?" I screamed. "You know what hoe? Shut the hell up! It's my house and I'll have any one I want over, and I'll tear it up if I feel like it. If you hate it so bad then clean the mess up!" he hung up. He had an excellent way of making me feel worthless. I picked up the tall glass cups off of the hutch and threw them as hard as I could onto the front door. As they shattered, the purple mixed drink stained the walls. It reminded me of blood. Then I wished it were my blood. I wanted to just die and get it over with. I didn't even care if Derrick killed me. When he returned later that day he had his bipolar mood shifted back to normal. He was decent and he cleaned the house.

There was nothing left to do besides wait. Wait for the unknown. Wait for the next set of daggers to cut mercilessly into what was left of my heart. When the daggers were finished with my heart, they would stab holes of grief into my brain. The holes would take a very long time to heal. They would be there until I took my last breath on earth.

I remembered when the Social Worker asked me for my due date, and I gave him a date that was actually past my due date. I came to the conclusion that it would actually be better for me to have this baby as soon as possible. I knew the nurses were already informed of my high-risk status. Derrick and his entire family behaved as if everything would be perfectly okay. His mother and I exchanged emails on a daily basis, and she actually became a very good friend. She was really the only person I had to talk to that wouldn't swear at me or attempt to throw random objects my way. She sent a new crib, baby clothes for a boy and a girl, toys, and pretty much everything that we would need. The baby's room was all set up with everything in place.

When I was in my 37th week of pregnancy, I went to the health food store and purchased a small bottle of castor oil. I was tired of being pregnant and sick of living with the suspense and fear that I wasn't going to be able to take my baby home. Whatever was going to happen, I just wanted to get it over with. Derrick was mostly enthusiastic and optimistic about the entire situation. He did make good points. He pointed out that technically CPS would have no reason to take our baby away from us. I could easily pass any drug test, and I had done everything that the Court ordered me to do. CPS would not be able to prove that the baby would be in immediate danger. He told me over and over again that he would not let anything happen. I thought maybe nature was trying to hide the possible outcome so I could get through childbirth - and maybe my own denial.

I opened the bottle of castor oil around 9:00 p.m. It took me a couple of hours to drink the entire bottle because it was so disgusting and oily, but I was determined. I wanted to have his baby on time. The contractions finally came and they came frequently. At one point they were about 2 minutes apart and lasted for 30 seconds. Eventually they slowed down and completely went away. Luckily, I'm quite experienced when it comes to meditating my way out of throwing up. I went to bed miserable and sick and even more frustrated. I was hoping that my next doctor appointment would confirm some sort of sign of impending labor.

As the technician scanned my very pregnant belly, she was focusing on the monitor to determine if there was a recent loss of amniotic fluid. She pointed to the red area and the blue area. The red indicated my uterus and the blue area indicated the water that was supposed to be in it. There was hardly any water. My doctor informed me that if the ultrasound detected a loss of fluid, they would induce me that same night. "If that's what your doctor says, then it looks like you're definitely going to be heading to labor and delivery tonight." I was excited, and seeing my baby on the screen erased any fear and doubt I had been struggling with. I was going to live in the moment and focus only on a having a safe delivery. Something came over me that completely allowed me to relax and let go of all of my fears.

My doctor poked her head into the ultrasound room to ask the technician about the status of the scan. She informed her that I had little to no water left. That was all she needed to hear. "Are you ready to meet your baby?" she asked. I smiled and nodded, and she knew she was asking me the question I'd been waiting for. After wiping the gel off of my stomach, the doctor led Derrick and I down the hallway to the labor and delivery room.

I was so excited to meet this life that was hiding in me for so long.

After I was strapped in, and practically stuck to the bed, the nurse informed me that they would begin my induction around midnight. There wasn't anything to do except wait. After watching the clock relentlessly, midnight finally came and the nurse started the induction. About 2 hours later, I was in full-blown labor. I made it clear from the start that I wanted an epidural. I really didn't want to go through the same pain that I struggled with previously. Since Derrick fell asleep before my induction, he wasn't any company to me. I was becoming upset and annoyed. He didn't try to help or reassure me when he knew I was going through the pain of the contractions. I was sure he would probably stay asleep during the birth of our child. At that point, I didn't even care. If he was going to behave like an arrogant jerk, then he didn't deserve to see our new life arrive.

Around 2:00 a.m., the contractions were as strong as they could get, and I began to feel that horrible pressure. The nurse came in and I requested an epidural. After waiting in pain for another half hour, I was relieved to see the anesthesiologist walk into my room. This was when one of the nurses woke Derrick. They had him assist with the process by holding me as I slouched over his shoulder. I didn't even feel the pain of the needle tapping into my spinal column. I was worried that the epidural wasn't going to kick in soon enough for the delivery. The anesthesiologist was taping the catheter in place, and I knew that this baby was literally right there. I didn't tell them this because I was worried that they would stop the process. Thankfully, I was completely numb just in time for the Ring of Fire.

My baby girl was born less than an hour later. Her cry was so sweet, and I rubbed her head and spoke to her hoping she would recognize my voice as they put her on my stomach. The doctor then said, "What's her name?" "I don't know yet," I calmly said. Derrick immediately said, "Her name is Danielle." I had gone over this with him on a daily basis for the last nine months. He wanted her to have a name beginning with the letter D. He was trying to get as close as he could to naming her after himself.

"It's a girl? Oh my gosh!" Derrick's mother, Wanda, was screaming over the phone with excitement. My baby was quietly sleeping in my arms. We were full of complete joy. My fear was replaced with elation. I felt completely euphoric, and I loved this little girl so much. Derrick was surprisingly good with her. He remained calm when she cried and fell asleep cuddled up to her so I could rest.

The sun had risen and the nurse woke me up to check on my vitals. Derrick and the baby were still sleeping, and I was trying to figure out what I would name her. It's not that I didn't like the name Danielle. I actually thought it was kind of cute. What annoyed me was that Derrick only wanted that name because it would complement his own. It was irritating that I was the one who carried this baby for so long, and he wouldn't even consider other possible names. I was excited his parents were coming to meet their first grandchild. They began driving from Texas when they got the news that I was going to be induced. The drive would probably take two or three days. The nurse brought my breakfast into my room and raised the head of my bed so I could sit while I ate. My left leg was still slightly numb from the epidural, so I wasn't quite mobile. The nurse came back into my room a few minutes later. It was time for my baby to have her first bath.

Chapter 46

The nurse needed to wake Derrick so she could take the baby over to the nursery to clean her up. He yawned and stretched across the cot-sized hide-a-bed. "Well, it looks like we're in the clear," he said. "If they were going to take her they would have done so already." I glanced at the clock and it was nearing eleven. It was a weekday and his conclusion made sense. We definitely would have heard something by now. I was so happy that things were happening as they should and without incident. I was eager to take our baby home and settle into my new routine. I heard some chatter coming from the hallway. Shortly after, I heard one of the nurses laughing loudly. "Whew, that scared me for a minute," I said. Derrick started snoring. I was still exhausted and thought it would be good to get some rest myself while the nurses were giving the baby her bath. I immediately began to drift off.

Suddenly I heard the door to my room open. I assumed that the nurses were just returning my little girl. I wanted to see if she was hungry enough to nurse. I wanted to establish breastfeeding right away, and so far she hadn't had any problems. When I opened my eyes and looked toward the door, two police officers in their black uniforms slowly walked in. Adrenaline and shock slammed my entire body. A man with shoulder-length hair wearing a badge followed behind them. "Derrick!" I yelled in a panic. He didn't budge. "DERRICK!" I yelled even louder. He sat up as if he were ready to fight. "What?" he asked, still in a daze. "There are cops coming in here!" I cried. His face went from confused, to concerned, and to pissed off all in an instant. He stood up and walked toward the end of my bed where the officers and Social Worker met him. The Social Worker looked down as his clipboard. "Are you Elizabeth?" he demanded. "Yes. Why are you in my hospital room?" I replied, making an attempt to get myself together. "Is this…uh…Derrick?" he asked, again glancing down at his clipboard. "Yes I am Derrick," he replied. "The State has ordered us to assume custody of your child, and I'm here to enforce the Court Order." Tears ran down my face. Derrick stepped toward the Social Worker. "You're not going anywhere with my baby. If I have to go to jail, I will. Trust that," he sternly replied. One of the officers stepped closer to Derrick to guard the Social Worker. "Hey man, just sit down for a minute. You don't want to go to jail. I don't know your situation, but I would be upset too. I do know that if we have to take you out of this room in handcuffs, it's just going to make your situation a hell of a lot worse." Derrick sat down. I was surprised at the empathy that the officer was showing.

"What reason do you have to take my baby?" I demanded. "I've done everything that I could possibly do to prevent this from happening. I've completed rehab, parenting classes, drug testing, and I am on good terms with my Probation Officer. The State is pretty much telling me that I can't have any more kids. Is that what it is?" I furiously asked. "The State isn't telling you that you can't have any more kids. We have case reports saying that you accused Derrick of hurting your other child, Zoe," he said, looking at his clipboard again. "I didn't know who to blame when that happened! There were multiple people in my house, and I don't know what happened! The detectives never even figured it out. If you think that he is responsible, then WHY isn't he sitting in jail right now?" I challenged. "I can't answer that question, but Social Services has determined that leaving the child in your care will put her at a substantial safety and health risk."

I buried my face in my hands and cried so hard that I couldn't breathe. The pain was all coming back – the painful reminder of all I had already lost. This was the pain of having no control over the whereabouts and well-being of my babies. This was the painful reminder that no matter what sort of improvement I made, I was still a bad mother. The Social Worker left the Court ordered document on the counter and they began to leave my room. "So I can't even see my baby while I'm here?" I yelled after them. The Social Worker slowly turned around. "Yes, you can see her in the nursery." He walked out.

The pain all came back to me - the pain from being in the hospital with Chloe and Zoe, and the pain from a loss that can't possibly be understood unless personally endured. Once again, this system was defying nature. My maternal instincts were naturally fierce, and there was nothing I could do to protect my baby and keep her with me. I was wrong when I thought that my tears were gone. When I thought I couldn't possibly cry any more, I cried even more. After losing Chloe and Zoe, this little girl was the only thing that gave me a reason to stay strong. This little girl kept me going when I was locked inside a cold jail cell for sixty-two days. I felt her kick for the first time as I was lying on my hard concrete bunk about four months pregnant. From that moment forward, I didn't feel so alone anymore. I had someone else to keep me company, and I had someone else to love. As she grew, I held on more and more. At around six months pregnant, I was released from jail to spend thirty days in a rehab facility. I felt safe and secure and happy that my unborn baby and I could at least sleep on a regular bed. I never in my life thought I would be so excited to see and squeeze a pillow. She moved around more and more every day. She was my little angel. If I felt like crying, she moved around even more. She reminded me that I had a reason to smile. I had a reason to love, hope and live. Her life saved my life. If I hadn't become pregnant with this perfect little girl, I could very well be on the streets today, or even worse, dead.

I was hurting deep, deep down yet so excited to meet this baby and learn who she would become. I was looking forward to raising this baby with everything that I learned from the mistakes I made and everything that I knew I was now capable of. My actions as a mother to Chloe and Zoe were unforgivable. My love, however, was always strong and genuine. I grew up in a safe and secluded little town. I had never witnessed anything dangerous. I had never seen a dead body. I had never suffered through trauma. I didn't know that I was one of the few lucky ones.

Until you've been quickly drawn down into the world of drugs and crime, you'll never know what it feels like to live in that world. Why? It often feels like nothing is different. It quietly creeps into your life, and your perception of reality stays the same. I didn't even see it coming. When you're using a substance, you lose sight of what normal is. I never, ever predicted such a tragedy could happen and such a loss could result. It happened to me and it happened to my children. My new baby was my only hope. Admitting to my faults and trying with my entire being to redeem myself would never be enough. It proved to be true that I would never, ever be forgiven. There would not be a second chance.

I cried because I was furious with the world and furious with myself. I was angry that I so tightly held on to so much hope that turned out to be nothing but a lie. Everything was a lie. I couldn't trust anyone. I couldn't believe anything. I also couldn't count on the community police officers and Social Workers to help guide me in a safe direction. As a child, we're taught that these are the people we should trust if there is an emergency or a crisis. These people are supposed to be the ones who want to help you. Then when you're not a child anymore - you're the bad person.

Sometimes I just wanted to scream - WHY DIDN'T YOU TELL ME! WHY DIDN'T YOU FORBID ME TO SEE HIM! WHY DIDN'T YOU ISSUE A PERMANENT RESTRICTION ORDER! Isn't it the job of the community to help create a better quality of life? Couldn't just one person - my Therapist, my Probation Officer, the Judge, or ANYONE, just tell me to run!

The truth is they did. They tried anyway. Never directly, but the hints were there. For being so academically smart, I was actually quite stupid! I was ignorant, blind, and selfish. I was still a kid. I missed out on hanging out with friends, going to school functions, and following my dream of becoming a nurse. I spent my high school years pregnant and taking care of a family. I never thought that I would someday want those years back. I wanted to make up for those years, but no matter how much I tried it never felt like enough. I didn't stop to think that those years would be gone, and they would never be there again. Trying to make up for the lost time ruined my life - and it hurt others in the process.

Derrick sat next to me on the hospital bed and held me as I hysterically cried for over six hours. His aunt came to visit after she heard the news. His parents were on their way from Texas and driving as fast as they possibly could. Worst case, at least maybe they could take her. That way she would not be in a foster home, and I could try to get off Probation early so we could just move there to be with her. That had been our Plan B for a while. We didn't talk about it too much because the thought of this happening was one that was too much to bear.

Derrick's aunt immediately hugged me as I sat helpless and heartbroken. "I'm so sorry," she said. What else could she say? I didn't even know what to say. It was sad, embarrassing, shameful, hopeless and heart wrenching. I was sick of sitting in that hospital room. I just wanted to leave. I heard my baby crying from across the

325

hall, and I couldn't take it. I wanted to run to her and pick her up to be with me. I couldn't do that. I couldn't hold my own baby in the room that I was in. I couldn't hold her and love her in privacy and peace. It had to be under the supervision of the hospital staff. "I'm ready to go. Just take me home," I sniffled. "There is no point in being here if I can't have my baby. I'm just going to get attached to her and everything is going to be that much more difficult when they take her to some foster home." I was giving up. I wanted to badly self-destruct. I wanted something to numb the pain. "I want a damn cigarette. I just want to get out of this hospital. Everything was for nothing!" I screamed. "I lost two babies, and I guess I just have to deal with losing another one," I cried. The easiest thing to do was give up. It hurt too bad to hold on to any more hope. I was done.

"I would probably want to do the same if I were in your position," Derrick's aunt offered. "But try to think about everything that you do first. The nurses are watching you and if you just walk out, they will report it to the CPS. Then it will really look like you don't care about your baby!" she said, trying to rationalize with me. I was unstable, but she did have a point. I would have to just deal with the pain and stay. "Derrick, can you go to the nursery and hold her? I don't want her to feel neglected. She might recognize your voice," I cried. He kissed me on the forehead and did as I asked. His aunt followed behind. I was so overwhelmed that the only thing I could do to cope was sleep. I rolled over onto my soaked pillow and cried. I cried myself to sleep hoping that I would wake up to my baby in my arms and everything would be okay. It's all a nightmare. I'm going to wake up.

Less than two hours later, I heard my mom's voice in the hallway. I vaguely remember talking to her on the phone in a hysterical panic. I knew that she said she was coming to visit, but I didn't know when she would show up. She walked into my hospital room and I woke up just as miserable as before, if not more miserable. It wasn't another nightmare. It was reality. I became angry. "Are you ok sweet pea?" She asked as she sat on the edge of my bed. "No! I'm not okay. I'm so sick of everything and I'm done trying. I just want to get out of here because there is no point in sitting here and getting attached to her! They're just going to take her away forever, and I can't handle any more pain!" I yelled and cried all in the same sentence. "But Liz, you can't think like that! There is always hope, and while you can, you need to go be with her and hold her! She's in there screaming her little head off - probably because she wants to nurse. She's a newborn and she needs you Liz," she tried to rationalize with me. Eventually I got up with her and went to the nursery to see my baby. Derrick and his aunt were taking turns holding her. I told my mom to go ahead and hold her first. She was getting prettier and prettier every passing hour. I could tell that she was hungry. A while later, my mom said her goodbyes and left the hospital. It was probably too sad for her too. Before she left, she told me that she and her husband would try to take her if the Social Workers would allow it. I didn't ever see how that would work. My mom was civil with Derrick because of the circumstances, but she and my step-dad saw him for who he was, and they did not like him at all. He would never be allowed to go near their home. It just wouldn't work.

I held my baby girl and rubbed her head as she nursed. She latched on immediately, as if she sensed that she would soon be deprived. I cried as I held her and thought about what was going to happen. She would soon be taken from all she had known. She would not get to have my warmth while I cuddled her, and she wouldn't have my scent to calm her down. She wouldn't have the food which nature provided for her - she would have a stranger and a plastic bottle. I held her in the rocking chair and cried and got up only when I had to use the bathroom. I didn't want to sleep because I was afraid she would wake up crying. I wanted to give her as many

327

antibodies as I could while I had the chance. I asked the nurse to please wake me up if she cried, and I asked her to not give her a bottle. Mother Nature took over and I held and loved my baby until I physically couldn't stay awake. After hesitantly retreating back to my hospital room for the night, Derrick reassured me that he would wake me up if he heard her cry. As I was beginning to doze off and Derrick was ending a conversation with his parents who were now twelve hours away, my hospital door opened. One of the nicer nurses came in rolling the bassinette holding my baby. She wheeled the bassinette up to the side of my bed. "Here is your baby," she said quietly, as she handed me my swaddled little girl. "I can't make any promises, and you'll have to go with it if I suddenly have to take her back to the nursery, okay?" "Of course," I replied. I didn't know exactly what was happening, but I did know that my baby was in my arms again, and it made me feel better to hold her in my own room. Derrick walked toward the bed to say hello to his baby as I began to feed her.

"I don't know the exact situation, but I've seen lots of mothers abandon their babies. I know a good mother when I see one. I am documenting in the report that you've been holding her for hours on end and quietly crying. This isn't the first time I've seen this happen to decent parents. It's happening all the time now," the nurse confided. "We wanted to ask you, is there an official document or order saying that they can legally do this?" Derrick asked. "Actually, I was going to let you know that I haven't received anything yet. For all I know, the order could come through the fax machine in a few hours, but I did ask them to send something over and they haven't done it yet. I began thinking about Plan B. Part of me wanted to take our baby and just go. We could start driving to Texas. They couldn't touch our baby if we could get to another state that was so far away. The only thing that held me back from this was that my Probation had not ended. I still had two years to go. I knew that being a fugitive on the run wouldn't solve anything, and it would just make everything worse in the long run. I still considered it for a moment. Derrick and I talked it out and decided to deal with the crappy hand we got. I got to hold and feed my baby for four hours in peace that night. The nurse somehow saw and believed in my love for my baby, and she'll never know how much those four hours meant to me. She put her job on the line just so I could have a few precious hours holding my new baby and cherishing the short moments that would be abruptly taken away. When the nurse on the new shift walked in, she quickly took my baby out of my arms and returned her to the nursery.

Chapter 47

It was around 6:00 a.m. when the nurse took my little girl back to the nursery. I was so exhausted, and although I had only gotten around five hours of sleep in the last 48 hours, I still couldn't sleep knowing that she was in the other room. We took shifts to spend time with her, and as every hour passed, I became more and more anxious. As delusional as the idea was, I still had a desperate hope that it was all a big mistake, and they were going to soon realize this. The compassion that I received from the nurses allowed me to hang on to that last tiny little shred of hope. If a nurse who had been working in the hospital for over 20 years could see my intentions, then surely I could get the Court to see them as well. On day three, the same Social Worker showed up in my hospital room. He was delivering the Court order and informed us that the Court date would be on Tuesday. It was only Saturday. I was trying to think of ways that I could prolong my hospital stay just so I could spend more time with my baby and avoid her being placed in a foster home. If I could stay with her until Tuesday, then I could go to Court with all of my documents as proof that I had rehabilitated myself. The Court would have to give her back to me. I still held on to hope because I had no other choice, and, of course, I was very attached to her.

Around midnight that night, Derrick's parents finally arrived from Texas. They walked into the labor and delivery unit, and they looked completely exhausted. They had been driving for 29 hours straight. We all stayed up with our baby until about 4:00 a.m. His mother cried most of the time. I finally went to sleep dreading what was going to happen in the morning. I had a feeling that the hospital was going to discharge me. My feeling was right. I slept until about 8:00 a.m. and woke up to one of the nurses taking my vitals while explaining to me that the doctor said it was safe for me to be released and spend the rest of my recovery time at home. Luckily, the same nurse who let me have my baby for four hours in privacy was working that day. She went out of her way to extend my stay for as long as possible. I was able to spend the remainder of the day in the nursery with my baby until later in the evening.

Derrick's aunt and parents returned to the hospital to visit. I was still sad and miserable but having the extra support around made it a little bit more bearable. I forced myself to take a shower and put on my clothes. It was nice to get out of the hospital gown. I was afraid to go back to my room to pack my things. If I took too long, they might take her sooner. Then I wouldn't get to see her again. We all passed her around for the remainder of my stay and talked about what we could do to fight the system. Around 8:00 p.m., one of the Social Workers arrived holding a car seat. I felt sick to my stomach. My baby was supposed to be going home with me in the car seat that we had for her - not some old and used Social Welfare System car seat. I said goodbye to her before Derrick. I knew I wouldn't be able to handle staying in the room as the Social Worker prepared my baby for a 2-hour drive down the hill to stay in some foster home that I knew nothing about. I cried, and then kissed her, and I told her that I loved her and I would see her soon. I really had no idea when that would be. I handed her to Derrick and picked up my bags. I stood there for a minute and watched him cry while he held her. That's when I walked out. Between him and his mother crying, it was just too much.

I paced outside the nursery room and then walked through the halls and out the entrance door. As I walked down the long hospital corridor, I held my head down. I didn't want anyone to see my tears. I would save the hysterics until I at least got into the car. When I went through these same doors only four days ago, I was so excited to meet my new baby and start a new life with her. I had erased any fears that I had, and I was absolutely certain that she would be going home with me. When I walked outside, I noticed that the weather was perfectly fitting for this misery I was feeling. It was dark, cloudy and raining. It looked like hell and it felt like hell. I was now living in another hell.

I finally found the Jeep in the parking lot, opened the door and sat in the passenger seat. It stunk like stale cigarettes. For the first time in nine months, I lit a cigarette. I knew that it wasn't going to help anything, and I knew that it was flat out ridiculous to start smoking again, but I didn't know what else to do. I wanted to rip my hair out, bash my head into the windshield, or even down a bottle of booze. I knew that I was just thinking on impulse, and I would not normally do any of that again, but I was so depressed. I saw Derrick walking to the Jeep. He opened the door and got into the driver's seat. We just sat there for a few minutes waiting for his parents to come. I saw the same nurse who had treated me so decently running towards our car. I rolled down my window to see what she wanted. I thought I might have forgotten something in my hospital room. She had tears in her eyes, and she reached through the passenger window to give me a hug. "You take care of yourself okay? And you bring that baby here to see me when you get her back okay?" I had tears in my eyes as I hugged her back and thanked her. "I promise I will. Thank you so much for everything." She had to go back in to finish her shift. As she walked back towards the hospital, we backed out of the parking lot and drove away. It was the saddest drive of my life.

Derrick's parents and his aunt followed us back to the house. His parents were going to be staying with us, and his aunt lived right down the street. By the time we pulled into the driveway, it was almost dark. As much as I appreciated his parents coming all the way from Texas, I definitely was not in the mood for any sort of company. It's not that I didn't want them to be with us; I just didn't know how to grieve in front of so many people. As I got out of the car, I grabbed the bag that was next to the diaper bag that we had packed for our baby. Seeing the diaper bag made me sick to my stomach so I just left it in the car. I didn't want to bring it in the house because I would be even more upset than I already was. I really wasn't prepared for how hard it was going to be to go home without my baby. I went straight to our bedroom to lie down. I told Derrick that I was just tired. He went back to the living room to visit with his family. The house was extra cold that night, and I had never felt such emptiness in my life since I lost Chloe and Zoe. My baby was not in my belly anymore, and she wasn't in my arms either. I felt cold and alone and empty. I wondered if she was okay and who was taking care of her. I wondered if she could sense that I was not with her. I just wanted to hold her and make her feel secure and safe in my arms - in the arms of the only person that she had known from the beginning of her existence. I pulled my blanket over my head and cried myself to sleep.

Derrick let me sleep for a couple of hours. He came into the bedroom to tell me that his parents were hungry, and they wanted to know if I wanted to go with them to grab something to eat. The only place open at that hour was Denny's, and it actually sounded really good. I hadn't eaten hardly anything while I was at the hospital because I was so distraught. My appetite was definitely catching up with me, and it would only get worse as my

334

milk started to come in. I didn't know what I was supposed to do about that either. I didn't have my baby to feed, but I wanted to be able to nurse her every chance that I could. Everything was so frustrating, and I just didn't know how I should handle the basics anymore. We all drove together in one vehicle down the highway to grab a late dinner. I ordered strawberry crepes, and I slammed down a Pepsi. I hadn't had a Pepsi in a long time because it gave me really bad acid reflux when I was pregnant. I felt a little bit better after I put something into my stomach. After we ate, Derrick's mom asked me if there was anything that I needed from the store. I didn't want to spend her money, but I desperately needed to get a few things including a breast pump and pads. Dealing with the symptoms from post-pregnancy is not the most exciting thing. When you have a brand new baby, you hardly even notice these inconveniences.

I almost felt like I could understand what it was like for the women who had to suffer going through the loss of a child. My situation was very different from an actual death, because I knew that my baby was alive and okay. However, emptiness and then loss immediately after pregnancy and delivery is one thing that I'll never forget for as long as I live. If Derrick's parents hadn't come all the way from Texas to show their support and do what they could to help, the entire situation would have been much more difficult. Derrick and I probably would have been fighting, and we wouldn't have been able to tolerate each other's emotions very well. At least we had a set of parents there to help us. They made us dinner every night and took us shopping to get things that we needed. The day after I was sent home, a very heavy snowstorm kicked in. It lasted for a couple of days. When the snowstorm eased up, there was only one day left until we had go to Court and try with everything in our power to get our baby back. I was still in my recovery phase, but it wasn't going to stop me.

I spent every waking hour researching the law and printed out documents from all of the self-improvement classes that I had taken over the last six months. I was going to go to Court prepared, and I was willing to do anything that it took to get my daughter back. I really didn't know what to expect from the Attorneys and Social Workers, but I imagined it probably wasn't going to be anything nice. The night before Court, I came to the conclusion that the only way that I would ever be able to get my daughter back would be to get the CPS on my side. If I couldn't get them on my side, I would never see my baby again. The Judge automatically did what they wanted. I hadn't heard of one case where the Judge ruled in favor of the parents if the CPS objected. I didn't know exactly how I was going to do this, but if it meant leaving Derrick, I wouldn't think twice. I was sure that my mom would let me stay with her if it came down to that - as long as I wasn't bringing Derrick along with me.

Our first Court Hearing was on Tuesday morning. We made sure we brought along Derrick's parents as well as his aunt. We wanted to look into any and all options to keep our baby as close as possible to us. I hated this place. I hated this Courtroom and I hated the people in it. I never wanted to go back to this place again, and I had done everything that I could think of to avoid that happening. Here we go again, I thought to myself as we were nearing the entrance to go through the metal detector. My stomach was in knots and I was worried that I was going to get a full-blown panic attack. Our case was the first to be called. It was the same scenario as it always was. The Attorneys were laughing and joking with each other, and to them, it was just another typical Tuesday morning. To me, it was a hearing that was extremely important, and I was so desperate to see that it would go as well as possible. I took it upon myself to hand every single Attorney in the room a packet that I put together with copies of my progress. My Attorney arrived at the very last minute. She advised me that I probably should have gone over the paperwork with her before I freely gave it out. She made a good point, but I wasn't thinking about that. Each folder for the individual Attorneys also had a cover letter. I did my best to explain the current situation I was in, as well as how the events in the past led to my progress today. I made it clear that I took full responsibility for my actions, and that I had every intention to do whatever necessary to better myself as a mother. It was my desperate plea; it was the only way for me to get the point across.

Luckily the Judge that was in charge of the case was the same Judge that I had with Chloe and Zoe. If it had been this Judge instead of that temporary Judge who terminated my rights at my last hearing for the girls, things just might be completely different. Everyone updated his or her arguments, and we went through the same routine that I was unfortunately all too familiar with. The Judge had compassion for me. Despite the snow and the inconvenient traveling that the Social Workers would have to do, he ordered that Derrick and I would be allowed to have five visits per week with our baby. I was completely surprised, and although I was very disappointed that we clearly were not going to be able to take our baby home, I felt as if this was a very good sign. I didn't see why the Judge would allow me to have so many visits with my baby if his long-term plan was to terminate my rights. This was another little glimmer of hope that I was given, and it certainly helped me carry on with what was left of my motivation. The Attorney for the Social Workers argued against this and attempted to get the visitation schedule reduced to two days a week. The Judge was firm with his order, and I was so relieved and happy. A small amount of my pain and fear was lifted that day.

Chapter 48

Derrick's parents ended up staying with us for about three weeks after the baby was born. They came with us to all of our baby visits and cooked dinner for us every night. It was a very sad time for everyone, but it was also one of those defining moments. Everything that a family is supposed to do for each other was reaffirmed. The first visit that we had was in the lobby of the new Social Services office. It was probably about a mile down the highway and in a nicer part of town. I was happy to learn this because I didn't want to go back to that same room that held the vivid memory of Chloe putting on her jacket and wanting to go home with me. I didn't want to have to associate that with my current situation because it would only be a hard reminder of what I had lost and what I could potentially lose again.

After taking a seat in the waiting room, the four of us twiddled our phones until a man walked through the front door carrying the car seat that securely held my little girl. I was so happy to see her but at the same time so heartbroken that it had to be under these circumstances. I had been pumping breast milk every day and freezing it in sterile bags - hoping that the Social Worker and Foster Parent would be willing to give her my milk instead of formula. Under different circumstances, I probably could have been a millionaire if I found a medical facility willing to pay for it. I can't even count how many times I heard nurses in the past call this strange booby milk "liquid gold." I knew that even a small amount would help with her immune system. It was just unnatural for a newborn baby to immediately begin drinking formula. Before leaving for the two-hour visit, I grabbed the cooler bag that came with my breast pump and packed it full of icy milk. I hoped that the Social Workers wouldn't think that I was totally weird. It was an instinct on my part, and I just couldn't help it. When the Social Worker arrived I asked her about this, and she said that she would take it to the Foster mother. She couldn't guarantee anything, but I was very happy that she was at least willing to try for me.

She took my baby out of the car seat, and I eagerly reached for my sleeping little bundle. She was wearing a really cute pink outfit with cozy socks and a cozy hat. She was very clean, and she looked totally content. I immediately felt that the foster mother was taking very good care of her. Just being able to hold her and see her was extremely reassuring for me. It felt like a pound of bricks was lifted off my shoulders. After 20 minutes, I knew that Derrick's mother was probably dying to hold her too. I handed her over and everybody passed her around. When she woke up and cried I wanted to see if she would nurse. I didn't have my hopes up because I knew that she had been drinking out of a bottle and that was probably what she was used to. I awkwardly sat in the chair and prepared to nurse her as discreetly as I could with a blanket over my shoulder and covering most of her little body. She began to nurse immediately. I was in complete awe that it was so easy and natural for her to do this after being away from me for five days. The hormones that are released when you breast feed are like a natural antidepressant. When she was nursing, and even when I would use the pump, I became extremely relaxed and tired. It was a good tired. It was just enough to calm my worried thoughts and let my mind rest. When she was through nursing, I burped her and passed her around again. This was the point that I no longer felt constant fear for my baby and our future. Instead, I felt a strong sense of hope and determination. These visits were just enough to keep me going because I knew that the reward at the end of this dark tunnel would be so incredibly worth it.

My next visit was the very next day. It started well but didn't end well. The entire family came for the first hour, and then they went to the store for the second hour to let me spend time alone with her. I wanted to nurse her again. Only a few seconds after they walked out the front door, the same male Social Worker poked his head through the door and called me back to his office. I felt like a little kid who was in trouble. He wanted to go over the report that he had prepared which he would be presenting to the Court at the next hearing. I was surprised that the report wasn't completely horrible. It wasn't glowing, but it wasn't as bad as I expected. He was facing his computer, and I was holding my baby and sitting in a chair behind him. She began to cry, and I knew it was a hunger cry. She was not at all content. Out of common courtesy, I asked if it would be okay if I nursed her. I told him I would be discreet and not show anything. I'm still angry with myself over this because it was not a question that I should have had to ask anyone. It was my right, and it was my daughter's right. "I wouldn't," he said in a tone that was somewhat sarcastic and somewhat firm. I concluded that he thought I was completely stupid, or crazy, or both. Maybe he was just uncomfortable with the idea altogether because he was a man and he just didn't get it. "Can I ask you why?" I said, unable to keep my tears back. "Because we have events, and we don't have a drug sample from you yet. We have to confirm that you're not using drugs because it passes through the milk."

Tears were rolling down my face and I felt extremely humiliated and degraded. How any mother could give birth and resort to using drugs one week later, even if their child was taken from them, is beyond me. I was so upset that they actually believed that I was that kind of person. Even though I had been given so many mixed messages about the perceptions of what others thought, I knew for a fact that this was not the kind of person that I was. I would never be that kind of person. My baby continued to cry as I tried to offer her the plastic bottle with disgusting formula that smelled like a sewer. She would not take the bottle. She knew that I was with her and she knew that I could provide her nutrition. Holding her in my arms and not being able to at least offer to her what was definitely available only built up my frustration and anger. The only way that I could express this was by crying. If I said anything or reacted in any kind of hostile manner, they would certainly document it, record it, and give it to the Court. I was being watched constantly and I had to prove that I was stable and could remain stable under stressful circumstances.

When the female Social Worker walked into the office to transport my daughter back to the foster home, I was sad to part with her. At the same time, I was relieved to get the hell out of there. I knew that the car ride would probably put her to sleep, and I definitely had to vent to Derrick and his parents about what had just occurred. Before leaving the office, I turned to the Social Worker as I was approaching the door. "Can you please schedule a drug test as soon as possible?" "Yes, I'd be happy to do that." He actually looked surprised that I was the one requesting to do this. I'm sure that the majority of the parents he worked with didn't insist on taking a drug test. After he spoke with the local Recovery Center, he told me that I could go in at noon before my visit the following day to give a urine sample. I was happy that they scheduled me in quickly, but I also knew that the results would not be in for three days. The next day, we all left early so I could go to the Outpatient Recovery Center for my test. All of the drug tests I had previously taken were in an environment where I had a decent amount of privacy. Even the female Probation Officers let me do my business behind a closed door. There was just one time when an officer went into the bathroom with me, but she completely faced the corner of the room. I walked into the lobby and signed my name on the clipboard to wait in line for my turn to pee in a cup.

The lady at the front desk was very nice and she called me back within a few minutes. I was a little bit taken aback when she walked into the restroom with me so casually. "You know, I swear I've seen you before. Have you been here for classes?" "Yes, I went through 30 days of inpatient and several months of outpatient. But I was pregnant so I was probably really fat when you saw me." She thought that was pretty funny and laughed. As I very awkwardly dropped my drawers, it was extra humiliating because I was still dealing with the three-week period that women go through after having a baby. My granny panties were pink with flowers. I felt like I was back in my potty-training days. I really, really hoped that nothing unexpected would happen and completely gross her out. She must have seen me struggling, both awkwardly and mentally, because she went out of her way to reassure me that this was nothing new. "Don't worry about it - you are totally fine, and I know you just had a baby. Trust me I've seen a lot worse." She started laughing. "I can only imagine," I said as I laughed with her. After the ice was broken and the weirdness was confronted, I felt like I could trust her. She seemed to be really down to earth and super open-minded.

She asked me about my current situation. "So what's going on? Now that I'm remembering you better, I thought that you were doing really well." "Well, I have been doing really well. I've done everything that I've been asked to do - and more. I was afraid that this was going to happen, so I did whatever I could to prevent it. Of course, it still happened," I sighed. "What happened?" She looked at me with serious concern in her eyes. "They took my baby away about eight hours after she was born," I replied, still feeling grief and

343

embarrassment. "Are you serious? I can't believe that! Why would they do that when you've been working so hard, and it is documented that you've been clean?" "I keep asking myself that same question," I replied. "I did everything that I could, and I guess it wasn't good enough. They won't even let me nurse my baby until this drug test comes back clean. I have a visit with her in about 20 minutes."

She glanced to the side and thought for a minute. "Usually they can take 2 to 3 days to come back. But wait a minute!" Her eyes lit up and she rushed over to a cabinet that was in the hallway next to the bathroom. She pulled out a dipstick test kit and walked over to the counter holding my bottle of pee. It was kind of funny to see someone so excited and rushing around while holding my pee. I knew I liked this lady for a reason. She wasn't afraid to be herself, and she didn't judge or hold any past mistakes against anyone. She followed the directions using the test that would provide instant results. She put the negative drug test on the fax machine to scan a copy of the results panel for me to take with me so I could nurse my baby. I was so excited. I thought that it was so nice of her to go out of her way to show me she really cared and that I was worth it. She was also one of the few people who kept me going. Just that one, simple act of kindness and compassion made me feel human again, and it made me feel like I could still find myself and be okay... at least maybe someday.

Chapter 49

About a week after I got out of the hospital, Derrick's mother was on the phone with Derrick's brother, Donnie, planning a time that he could come over for dinner and visit while they were still with us. After she hung up the phone, she rolled her eyes and informed me that Donnie asked about bringing Megan over for dinner as well. "Hon, I told him I had to ask you first. I'm not sure what kind of terms you're on, but last time we talked about her it didn't sound good."

I had a feeling that she was playing dumb. Even from what Derrick had told her, she knew very well that Megan and I were definitely not on good terms. I could understand her position though, and I could understand how she wanted to stay neutral. Both of her sons had girlfriends who were once best friends and now were complete enemies. I knew that the only reason that Megan wanted to come with Donnie was because she wanted in on the gossip and she wanted to be a part of the drama. She wanted to involve herself in everything, and she was so two-faced that it made me sick. I knew for a fact that she was a huge contributor to the horrible and disgusting rumors I had heard. "Yeah, I don't think that it would be such a good idea. I'm still pretty hormonal, and I can't honestly tell you how I would react if she walked into my house." I tried to stay as calm as I could when I said this, but I was really furious, and I already had adrenaline pumping through my veins.

They must have gotten the message because the next night when Derrick came over for dinner he handed me a sealed card. I faked a smile and told him thanks, but I'm sure that he saw the irritability behind my grinding teeth. I really didn't even know how to react. After all, she told the world that I was a horrible person for being with Derrick. If she really believed that, then why the hell was she sending me a sympathy card? It seemed that CPS taking my baby from me would have been more of a victory to her. I opened the card after going into my bedroom. I didn't want Donnie to be present for my possible reaction - whether it would be my hysterical laughter or shredding the card to pieces in pure rage.

Elizabeth,
Even though you probably hate me, I just wanted to let you know that I am sorry about your baby. When I found out, I cried. Let me know if there is anything that you need or anything that I can do for you.
-Megan

Once again, I was confused as all hell. Every person that I had once trusted with my life had sent me completely mixed messages pertaining to the kind of person I was. I didn't know what to think about it...but I did know that it definitely wasn't love. It was her insecurity and reaction to the trauma that occurred. They all wanted an answer - even if it meant making up some delusional lie that made sense to them. It angered me. I was the one that wanted an answer. I was the one that lived every day not knowing for certain if I would be safe. There was always a constant uncertainty in my future. There was no one that wanted answers more than me. Outwardly I may have concealed this desperate desire for the truth out of fear of further judgment, but on the inside I was dying more and more with each passing day. My identity became what others assumed me to be. I was a little bit of everything - a drug addict, a loving mother, a psychopath, a great college student, a liar, and a role model teen mom. That was who I was.

To go from living with a definitive purpose and a clear direction, to hardly surviving the loss of everything, is an emotional trauma on many different levels and to many different people. As I lost my self-identity, every person around me lost my identity as well. I no longer knew who I was, and neither did they. The only thing that I ever needed to hear that would have helped me and the situation I was in was a simple I'm here for you.

To run around town and openly disclose information related to the trauma, whether it was a fact or a lie, was the ultimate disrespect. It was just as bad as stomping my skull into the cement when I was already down and bleeding. Not only did it push me further down into the hole of hell that I was already frying in, it also showed a lack of character and ill-intentions by exposing and exploiting an innocent child - only to cause them further harm. There was nothing that anyone could do or say to apologize. The damage was done.

We had another Court date during the second week I returned home from the hospital. This particular hearing would tell us which direction the case was going to go. It could only be one of two ways - services or no services. It was going to be a chance to get my baby back or not a chance at all. I woke up feeling nauseated because I was so worried and nervous about what the recommendation would be. The Hearing was at eleven in the morning, and I couldn't seem to sit still as we watched the clock. I put on the best outfit that I could squeeze into and prayed that the Judge would at least see my willingness to follow any direction that pointed to my baby girl coming home.

In the beginning, our relationship with the male Social Worker started off badly for obvious reasons. As we began to see him on a regular basis and allow him to get to know who we were, he also opened up to us in return. He presented himself as more of a person, versus a judgmental Social Worker. Maybe that was my mistake with Chloe and Zoe. Maybe I should have just let the Social Workers get to know me... I would frequently ponder this idea. Surely, if they really understood who I was, they never would have taken my babies away from me. I think this was a factor.

The Bailiff called our case number as we nervously sat in the lobby. The four of us eagerly stood up and walked in to the Courtroom as the Bailiff held the double doors open. Luckily, there wasn't much of an audience. The only people present were those who absolutely needed to be there which included all of the Lawyers and the Court staff. I approached the Defendant's table that I hated with a passion. I took my seat next to my Attorney as she was scribbling notes into her agenda. She looked up at me with a smile, and I immediately knew that it was probably good news. "I can't say for sure what the Judge is going to do, but I think that they're actually going to offer you services." I was so relieved that I felt like crying. They were actually going to give me a chance to be the mother to my newborn daughter when just a few months back they took my other two girls away from me forever.

The Judge walked in from his break and we all stood up as the Bailiff announced his presence. He instructed everyone to take a seat and reached over to retrieve the file that the Clerk was handing him. He opened the case with the same speech stating names, case number, and what the ruling was about. As usual every party had their argument but because I had taken so many steps to improve myself the best that I could, the Child Protective Services recommended that we get a chance to be unified with her daughter. The Judge didn't seem to argue with this recommendation or even question it. He ruled in the favor of the

Child Protective Services and ordered that the visitation stay the same. Four visits a week for two hours per visit. Of course, I would have loved to be able to take my baby home with me, but I was trying to look on the bright side. I realized that I was very lucky to have the opportunity to be able to be with her on a limited basis for the time being. The also ordered everything else that the Child Protective Services recommended including continued outpatient drug treatment courses, random drug testing for both of us, parenting classes, and regular attendance of narcotics anonymous meetings. I was fine with all of this. I just wanted to hurry up and start so I could once again provide documents of completion and move forward with everything. Before the Hearing ended, we learned that they found a foster home in our local town that was able to take our baby. Ironically, this was going to be the same foster home that Chloe and Zoe were in. I was happy that she was at least going to be in the same town, but I was also a little bit nervous because I knew that the person who had taken her was taking excellent care of her. I hoped that changing homes wouldn't affect her.

When the hearing was over we walked out into the lobby. Derrick's mother was so relieved that she actually walked up to the Social Worker and gave him a hug as she cried. She thanked him over and over again, and he patted her shoulder and replied with "You're welcome." The sense of loss and sadness that we all had was immediately transformed into hope and promise.

Derrick's parents stayed for another week after the hearing so they could visit with the baby before they had to go back to Texas. As much as I appreciated their help and support, I was eager to get back into a normal routine and begin everything that the Judge ordered me to do. When Derrick's parents started to pack up their things and load them into their car, his mother began sniffling. "It's just been so bittersweet. I really hate to leave, but at least we can leave knowing that you'll be able to see your baby and eventually have her back home." As she hugged me goodbye she whispered to me that she left something under my pillow in the bedroom. I was surprised and couldn't figure out what it could be. Derrick hugged both of his parents, and I could tell that the two men were fighting back tears. They walked out the front door and got in their car to drive 29 hours back to their home.

I walked into my bedroom to see what Derrick's mother left and I found a card. I opened the envelope and a check for $1000 fell out of the card. She knew that we were struggling financially, but I didn't expect her to help us out this much. It was definitely a relief to have this kind of help because we had so many things going on. When I went into the living room to show Derrick what she had left, he was sitting in a chair in front of the stereo system. He had a Tim McGraw song playing, and there were tears streaming down his face. The only other time that he had cried was in the hospital when we had to say goodbye to our baby. I can only imagine that he had a lot of emotion built up that he felt he needed to conceal because there were so many other people around us. I decided to tell him about the check later on, and I didn't ask him what was wrong because I already knew. Now that his parents had left, reality was going to set in and the hard part was about to begin.

Chapter 50

Derrick returned to work rather quickly because he really had no choice. He went to attend as many visits as he could, but there were times that he had to leave the car with me or drop me off because the visits were so frequent. His boss didn't yet know about our situation. Every time they dropped her off for a visit, she had a bottle and I could tell it was formula. It was getting more difficult to pump when I needed to because of all the things that I had to do on a daily basis.

I continued Intensive Outpatient treatment per the Judge's order. These classes were held three times a week for four hours per class. Since I had already been through this, I wasn't really learning any new information. Sometimes the classes would be interesting, but mostly it was just a long annoying ramble from another drug addict with serious legal problems. I couldn't help but wonder who was really sober. Of course they all claimed to be, but I had my doubts. I did, however, find the most comfort from this group on a sad day in May. I woke up in the morning still groggy and made my way to the coffee machine. When the coffee was made, I sat down to my computer as usual to check my email and try to get my day started. I had an email from my mom. The moment I read it my heart sank and I began bawling my eyes out.

Chloe is four today. I'm so sad and heartbroken. Take care of yourself Sweet-pea. Love, Mom

This would be the first of many birthdays that I would be away from her. I had been so busy and focused on getting my baby back home that I didn't even know what day it was, but I knew my mind tried to block it out. I sat at the computer desk and just cried. I was so sad. It felt as if my heart were breaking all over again. I went to our visit that day with puffy eyes. I tried to present myself as best as I could, and I hoped that they wouldn't think anything bad about me. She mostly slept for the visit, which was for the better since I wasn't mentally there anyway. I was with Chloe - wondering if she was okay and wondering if she still thought about me. Nothing was her fault, or Zoe's fault, and I was so very sad at the thought of them maybe thinking that it was. I wanted desperately for this pain to go away and to wake up from this horrible nightmare. I wanted my babies to be back with me. I really couldn't accept that they were just gone. I was dropped off at my scheduled class at the Outpatient Center and didn't know how I would get through it. The counselor started the group off with everyone going in a circle giving a quick rundown of how their progress had been and how they were doing in general. I knew that I wasn't going to be able to hold my tears in. I was typically pretty stable in the group sessions and didn't show too much emotion. Everyone looked surprised when I couldn't explain what was wrong because I was crying so hard. They knew that there was really nothing that could be said to make it better. They were just there for me. They gave me hugs and pats on the back and zero judgment. It was probably the best help that I could have gotten from anyone at the time.

I started Drug Court shortly after our last Court Hearing. It was extremely nerve-racking. The Judge, along with Social Workers and my Attorney, would go over all of the progress that

I had made for the last two weeks and make any revisions if they felt it would benefit me. One of the first things that I did was explain that going to Alcoholics Anonymous groups were not helpful because the members made it clear that it was only for a group for alcohol abusers. They kind of seemed like they believed that alcohol abusers were better than drug abusers. God forbid if I were to accidently say, "My name is Elizabeth, I am a drug addict." I had to be sure to say, "My name is Elizabeth; I'm an alcoholic." It felt stranger to call myself an alcoholic than it did a drug addict - whether that makes me a bad person or not. The Court understood my position and they allowed me to replace the Alcoholics Anonymous meetings with Narcotics Anonymous meetings or Cocaine Anonymous meetings. Either way, I had to go to a lot of meetings. They wanted me to go to five meetings a week. I was extremely busy with my schedule every day, and it was more difficult to sit through the night meetings. This was the time that I just wanted to put on my pajamas and watch TV. But after attending each meeting, I was always glad that I went. I always felt better about my situation because it was clear that I was not alone.

I began to wonder why the Court didn't order Derrick to do anything except drug testing, and he refused to go to the meetings with me for support. Deep down I knew that he really needed these classes - probably more so than I did. I started to resent the fact that I had to do more work than he did to get our daughter back. He definitely helped put me in all of the horrible situations and allowed some really low-life people into my home and life. He was the one that put drugs in my coffee and exposed me to substances that I never wanted to even be around. It was hard for me not to become irritable over this, and I was quick to snap at him. I understood that I made my own choices and I was responsible for them, but at the same time he had issues just as much as I did, and he should have been doing just as much work to better himself for our daughter.

He started to come home with that look on his face again. It was the same look that he had when I was pregnant, and it was the same look on his face that I vividly recall when we used drugs together a year ago. I carefully questioned him - only for him to lash out at me and twist the conversation around to where it somehow ended up being my fault. He never confessed to using any substance, and once again it was easier for me to accept his lies than deal with the truth. Deep down, a part of me knew that if the Social Services were to order a hair follicle test, he would surely fail. The better half of my brain desperately wanted this to happen. Then the Court would see that it wasn't just my fault, and I wasn't the only bad person who made mistakes. This would give me an excuse to take my daughter and leave.

Occasionally, I would daydream about taking my daughter and going to my mom's house. I knew she would take care of us while I got on my feet, and I would be away from this person who gave me so many conflicting messages. We were speaking more now, and she was always supportive when I would tell her about my new accomplishment or the last visit with my baby. I tried to avoid talking about Derrick because I already knew how she felt, and I knew that it wouldn't be a productive conversation. I made sure that I was on time for every visit, and every time I saw my little girl she got bigger and bigger. It was adorable when she started smiling, and I always remembered to bring my camera with me to the visits. Eventually, the visitation was transferred to the Foster Care office. The staff agreed to supervise the visits because they were so frequent, and the Social Services had other visits to supervise as well. I liked the visits better here. The women that supervised them were always really nice, and they never made me feel uncomfortable or bad about my situation. The next Court Hearing wouldn't be until my baby was 6 months old. It was horrible to have to think about waiting so long to get her home, but at least being able to see her grow and visit her almost on a daily basis gave me the opportunity to bond with her and let her know that I was her mom.

Besides the typical issues that I had with Derrick and my thoughts of him never changing, everything was going as good as it could for the situation. His boss called me one day after my outpatient classes and asked me if I was interested in picking up some part-time work. She needed an assistant for all of the administrative tasks that she was too busy to handle. I gladly accepted. We needed the extra money, and it was nice to begin living a life outside of Court orders. She first had me pick up some cleaning jobs to fix up post-construction projects. It was fun and it kept me busy. Eventually I was working in her office and running errands for her. I hated getting up early, but I knew that it was good for me and it would help to rebuild my self-esteem.

On June 24th, 2007, Derrick and I took a trip down the mountain to do some shopping. Our Court date was coming up next month, and we were hoping we'd get unsupervised visits so we could at least see our daughter at our home. Her room was all set up but because I knew that I was going to nurse her when we brought her home from the hospital, we weren't in a hurry to get a crib. I had planned for her to sleep in the bassinette next to me. We definitely needed to get a crib so we'd be ready for the Social Workers to come over and do their home inspection. We got our baby the nicest crib that the store had. It was a cherry-oak color, and we really didn't care about the price tag. We were both happy and excited as we packed up the Jeep and headed back home to set up the crib. As we were making the drive back home, we noticed a huge cloud of smoke. The cloud was definitely not there when we left just a few hours earlier. "What the heck is that?" I panicked. "Is that smoke?" I asked, totally confused. "Whaaaa...what the hell?" Derrick was just as confused as I was. "Is Tahoe on fire?" I wondered out loud. As we drove closer and closer to home, it became more evident that it was indeed our town that was on fire. By the time we drove through the state-line, it was so smoky that it was difficult to see very far ahead. As we drove around the bend of the lake, we were actually seeing flames on the top of one of the mountains. This was definitely not good. We didn't know the exact neighborhood, but we knew that the foster home that our daughter was in was in that area. Luckily, she was with a temporary foster mom while the foster parents were on a week-long vacation. We closely watched the news as we set up her crib, and we were eager to see her the next day.

We walked into the office and she was sleeping in her car seat. We talked with the foster care workers about the fire and heard stories of them having to assist an elderly couple who had been evacuated from their home that later burned to the ground. "Your baby is with the temporary foster mom we told you about, and her house actually caught fire and burned to the ground. She told me that she literally had just enough time to grab the baby and the diaper bag and that was it. I asked her if we needed to find a new place for her to go, but she offered to keep our baby with her while she stayed with her close friends. We had to inspect their house for safety and everything was just fine. We were so surprised that she was so insistent on continuing to watch her considering the circumstances. "I am so glad I didn't know this information yesterday!" I laughed, thinking about how freaked out I would have been. "That was awesome of her, and please make sure you thank her for me," I said, thinking about how selfless this woman must be. I felt very grateful that our little girl seemed to be in good hands as hard as it all was.

Our next Court Hearing arrived before we knew it. Of course, I was nervous because the Court System and Social Workers were unpredictable. But I knew that I was doing the very best that I could, and I had a feeling that they would see that. The Judge quickly looked over the report and granted us unsupervised visits three times a week. They would take place at our home, and we

356

would get to have her for four hours at a time. I was so excited I could hardly contain myself. Finally I could be a mommy in my own environment without having to sit in an uncomfortable chair the entire time. I was looking forward to the little things, like cuddling with her on the couch, showing her the flowers in the front yard, and feeding her lunch. Derrick had to work the day the foster care worker dropped her off. A part of me was kind of happy that I didn't have to share the first visit at home with him. She did extremely well and hardly cried. She had never been to our home so she wasn't used to the environment, but she at least knew who I was. Everything felt the way it was supposed to, and I was bummed that it had to end. I knew, however, that she would come home sooner than later. The fact that we were making progress was a very good sign.

After about four weeks of unsupervised visits, we were granted overnight visits. My Attorney was able to get this accomplished at my Drug Court Hearing. We would get to keep our daughter for the weekends and resume the same daytime visitation during the weekdays. She was practically home for good - except some back-and-forth inconveniences. To make things easier for everyone involved, Derrick decided to buy a truck from his brother. That way, I could pick up the baby at the Foster Care office once in a while to make things easier on them.

When we went to pay Donnie for the truck, Derrick left the Jeep idling, and I got in the driver's seat. He had just received his tax return so he had extra money. He was taking longer than usual, and I was getting suspicious. He came up to the driver's window and I rolled it down. "Hey…" "What?" I demanded while getting inpatient. I was having another bad day. It was Zoe's third birthday, and I was exhausted and wanted to go to sleep. At times, I noticed it was becoming more and more difficult to focus on the present moment. I was stuck in the past and refused to accept that my girls were gone. I didn't speak of it nearly as much as I felt it. I frequently would get vivid flashbacks of some of the precious moments that I shared with them. I would tuck them into bed as they dozed off to Charlotte's Web, and I would see them run to me when I picked them up from a long day at daycare. It couldn't be over. There was no way it could end like this. I'll get them back too. This isn't real.

Derrick had that look on his face. He was high. He had money, and he was in there forever. He had gotten high with his brother. "Do you wanna smoke some shit tonight?"

"What the hell, Derrick? Are you stupid? We could lose everything we've worked for, and they'll drug test us!" I said in a panic. I knew that it was over for me. I immediately began feeling physical symptoms of wanting the drug. For the short amount of time that I used it, this drug was still hiding inside of me. It was waiting to be reactivated. I became jittery and anxious. I could almost smell the smoke. I was taught that the best way to stay clean was to simply avoid tempting situations. I actually doubted I could even if I tried. As long as I was with Derrick, I would be introduced to the temptation of the life-sucking drug, methamphetamine. I didn't think I would have control. It had all the control. It had me rationalizing and making excuses as to why one time would be ok. I was being blinded by desire. I was mad as hell, because I knew that I probably could not say no. After losing everything I loved to this drug, I was becoming powerless to the situation.

"Whatever. Just hurry up so we can go home," I said. "Look if you don't want to, I'm fine with that. I'll go in and tell him never mind. You should see how much shit he has though! It's gotta be over a pound!" he said excitedly. He knew that this mental vision would only secure his urge. He knew that I might give in. "I don't care!" I yelled. "Just hurry up!" He returned to the house and came out a few minutes later. He started the truck, and I followed him home. I didn't even use the meth yet, but I was already feeling like I had. I felt like an idiot for even considering it. Once again, my physical and mental desire for this drug was becoming strong.

The next day I felt completely horrible and stupid. I wanted to confide in someone, but I knew that if I did, it would surely ruin my chances of getting my baby back. I had to keep this under lock and key, and never do it again. Everyone has a relapse; it's normal - I would repeat to myself. The damage was done, and the only thing I could do was to try to move forward and do the best that I could. After this big screw up, I realized how quickly and easily I would lose my chance of getting my baby back if I didn't stay 100% on top of everything, including my sobriety.

Chapter 51

I was always excited to tell my mom about any recent news that was good. I desperately wanted her forgiveness, and maybe even one day her approval. When I spoke with her over the last year, the conversations were mostly good ones, but she always had a tone of doubt and fear in her voice. I would definitely never get her approval for as long as I was with Derrick. No matter how hard I tried, or how great of progress had been made, her granddaughters were gone, and she blamed him. As with everyone else who knew about the situation, there had to be someone to blame. If no one took the blame, there would be no closure, and nothing would make sense. It was her way of making sense of it all. I however, was left hanging. I couldn't face reality - whatever it may have been. It was too mean, ugly and cruel. It wasn't something I could allow to exist in my world. I became quiet and irritable every time she would bring it all up. There was nothing I could say. Nothing would make it okay, and nothing would bring them back to our family. The damage was done. I so badly just wanted my life to have a sense of normalcy. I wanted to be happy like other families. I wanted to have a man to show off to my family. I wanted a guy who loved and adored me and doted on my every move. After all, my twin sister had recently become engaged while stationed in Germany. I only spoke with her maybe once a month because the calls were so expensive, but she loved and accepted me and never brought anything up that she knew I didn't want to think about. She just wanted to talk to me and joke around like we always had, remembering funny things we did as kids, or stupid things in high school. She is my twin and she always made sure that nothing ever changed that. After my mother asked me if I wanted steak or salmon as the main course for my sister's upcoming wedding, I immediately knew that Derrick would not be invited. Derrick would never be that guy that I wanted him to be. Whether or not he had a say in it, it would never happen.

"Salmon," I replied in a dry tone. I was on the verge of tears, forcing myself to hide the fact that no matter how badly it upset me, he would never be invited to any family affairs. Getting upset would only reinforce to myself that a huge part of me hated myself for being with him. And the other small and barely-there part loved Derrick and had an emotional need to always stay by his side. He stuck by mine. He frequently reminded me of this. He came back to me under investigation and risking his image as the innocent one. The least I could do was just stay with him. He ignored the warnings of his friends and family to be with me, so I would do the same. It was only fair.

My twin sister wanted me to be her maid of honor. I almost thought, for a split second, about just not going to the wedding at all. But then I remembered that Merri never said anything bad to me about Derrick or Donnie. She didn't do anything wrong. She never hurt me. The family drama wasn't her fault. She was simply getting married, and of course, expected me to be there. I spoke with Derrick and his mother about my mixed feelings of going to the wedding without him. They both understood and urged me to go and support my twin sister. With their approval, I felt better about going and finally gave my mother the green light. The wedding was on a weekend in August. I was excited to

362

see my sister. I hadn't seen her in a year and a half. She was so far away from me this entire time. I went to bed early on a Wednesday night. Merri and her friend from the Air Force were going to pick me up the next morning. I was scared and nervous, but so excited to hug my twin.

The last time my entire family had gotten together was at my own wedding when I was only sixteen. With a brand new baby whom I cherished beyond words, working hard to finish school, and doing what I thought was the right thing to do, I had a beautiful and promising life ahead of me. With a beautiful little baby girl of only two months who looked just like me, Josh and I were washed from our mistakes and teenage sins as our ceremony closed with a family baptism. The guests at my wedding may have not have fully understood; they were witnessing one of the most symbolic, innocent and treasured moments of my life, memory and being. If there were ever to be such a heavenly and perfect transition into womanhood from childhood, this is what it would be. As the drops of pure and holy water ran down the soft, fuzzy head of my little girl, she offered the church and the guests her first real smile. God and his angels were standing with us on that bright, beautiful day, and it was even known to an infant.

That was just a memory. I no longer had my baby and my adoring husband in this life. Those I lost were never going to come back. The three of us, which quickly became four, were one unit. We struggled in the end, but we always loved each other, and we were supposed to always have each other. The young woman, wife and mother that I had become, which had formed my identity who I loved and accepted, began to slowly and deceptively die that summer night, when I chose to run to Derrick.

I'd fallen from a celestial, euphoric existence into a deep-rooted, deceptively suicidal burning pit. I didn't have my new little family to come to the wedding with me. I was suffering, sad, ashamed and confused. I was horrified to be in the same room as just one family member from the day of my first wedding. I would soon be sitting in the same room alongside all of them - all of them and more. I'd have to be strong and remember that Merri's wedding was a happy day for her to remember. I didn't know how on earth I was going to hold myself together. As I drifted off to sleep just a few hours before dawn, the only thing I knew to do was pray.

God, grant me the serenity to accept the things I cannot change, the courage to change the things I can, and the wisdom to know the difference. Amen.

Beep! Beep! Beep!

What felt like only five minutes later, my alarm clock was screaming at me to get up and get in gear. Merri would be at my house in an hour, and I had to get dressed and pack my bag. We were going to be driving for about five hours to the Pacific Coast where the wedding would be. My stepdad rented the clubhouse at an upscale golf course and it was sounding like it was going to be a fancy affair. When I was all dressed and ready to go, I said goodbye to Derrick while he was halfway asleep in bed and grabbed my bag as I walked out the front door. I didn't think it was necessary for Merri and her friend to actually come inside of my house. I wanted to avoid any conflict at all costs. Right as I nervously lit my cigarette, a small black car pulled into my driveway. The second I saw my twin step out of the passenger side door, I instantly forgot about the drama and excitedly ran to hug her. I forgot how short she was. It had been so long, but it was as if we had never been apart which I knew would be the case. We did share the same uterus together. I couldn't ever expect anything less!

My twin sister's friend, Valerie, was really nice and friendly right away. That was a relief - so far so good. Merri handed me a small gift bag with shiny tissue paper sticking out from the top. "What's this for?" I asked slightly confused. "Oh, it's a gift! The bride is supposed to give all of the bridesmaids a gift," she announced. I could instantly tell that my mom and Merri had gone completely all-out for this wedding. They must have done a number on my step-dad's wallet! I smiled to myself.

After opening my gift, which was a notepad with the sweetest letter a twin could ever write, I safely put my gift away inside the house before closing the door behind me. Before we officially got on the road, we had one quick last-minute detail to tend to. None of the bridesmaids had their shoes yet. As we were heading towards the "Y" shopping outlets to find matching shoes, Merri pulled her cell phone out of her purse and started talking to someone. It sounded like she was getting annoyed with whomever she was talking to. When she hung up the phone I put the pieces together and realized that she had been on the phone with Lilah. I guessed that Lilah didn't want to be around me. I hadn't heard from her since the last time I saw her in Court when she took the stand to testify all that she knew about the case and me as a mother. "Merri, I can just wait in the car if it makes it easier. It's totally fine with me, I understand," I offered, secretly hoping that I could get out of an awkward situation. "Liz, she's being really immature right now and I'm not going to let her make you feel unwelcome. Plus, she's with Jessica right now anyway, so it's probably just making it worse." Jessica was one of the girls that we had grown up with. We met her when we were only eight years old, and she almost became like a sister to us. Lilah always favored Jessica, and I started to believe that Jessica was the little sister Lilah always wanted to have. Their relationship never bothered me, up until this very day. I had accepted the fact that Lilah would probably never talk to me again. I was dealing with it, and I wasn't going to let it get to me. However, when I found out that she was openly talking about not wanting to be around her disgusting little sister (me) in front of Jessica, I broke down. I felt like I was being ganged up on, and in that moment, I truly felt like scum. As a teenager I always looked up to Lilah and tried to impress her in any way that I could think of. She was the type of person who held herself above most everyone else and any person was lucky to be her friend.

Lilah and Jessica met us in the shoe store after Merri told our mom how rotten she was being. I assumed that my mom called Lilah and chewed her out. Just as I expected, she walked into the store with her fake smile and gave me the fakest hug I've ever felt. I would have rather she just ignored me. It was insulting that she thought I was so stupid that I couldn't see what was behind her two-faced behavior. I walked around the store pretending to be occupied with dresses and jewelry to avoid being stuck in a tiny aisle as they shuffled through boxes of shoes trying to find five matching pairs. When we were finally on the road for good, I couldn't help but wonder if the rest of my family felt the same way about me. Was I that bad to be around? Was I really the scum of the earth that I felt like?

When we arrived at our destination, I instantly recognized the hotel. We were staying in the same hotel that our grandparents took us to when we were little kids. It had an outdoor patio with a beautiful fishpond and giant Koi fish. I immediately had a flashback in time, about sixteen years ago, where I was standing in the same exact place feeding these fish. My grandparents were sitting at the table to my left, and I ran to them and gave them both long hugs. It was all so familiar, and my grandparents made it feel that much better. For a short while, I forgot about everything that was worrying me and making me anxious. I was just happy to be in this temporary time warp. My grandparents still saw me as the little girl that I was desperately searching for, and because they still saw her, I knew that she was still in me - somewhere…hiding…but still there. I hadn't realized how much I truly missed my grandma and grandpa.

After getting settled in our hotel room, I met my sister's soon-to-be husband for the first time. The groomsmen were all in another hotel room living it up with jack and coke. I was watching everyone as they poured themselves drinks to celebrate. I wasn't supposed to be drinking at all, but I asked for my own anyway. With my mother's close (and almost glued to me) eye, and my twin sister with me, I knew that nothing could get out of control. I was too anxious to not have a drink. We had a fun night and I was excited for tomorrow to come. We were going to be having the rehearsal dinner. Merri bought me a cute polka-dot dress and I wanted to wear it. It had been a long time since I had a reason to dress up.

The night of the rehearsal dinner, we all piled into a few vehicles and designated some sober adult drivers for the wild groomsmen. The restaurant was amazing. It was like walking down to an underground jungle. We even had to take an elevator to get to the very bottom. It was like nothing I had seen before. So far, besides Lilah, everything was going just fine. That was until I saw my dad and stepmom sitting at a table talking with some of the groom's relatives. They didn't see me notice them. I quickly turned away and stepped outside. I was panicking at first and then broke down crying again. This time I couldn't figure out why. Seeing my dad sparked probably every emotion I had ever felt, all in one moment. I was overwhelmed. I puffed on a cigarette and tried to tell my mom what was wrong. I was sad, mad, confused and let down. I didn't know if I was feeling let down by him or let down from myself. The last time I saw him was when he confronted me after seeing Derrick and I walk out of my apartment that April morning. After that incident, he tried to visit me in jail to tell me that my grandfather had passed away, but I refused his visit. I thought he was coming to lecture me or make me feel even worse. When I found out what the real reason was after speaking to my mom on the payphone the next day, I felt like a total jerk. I was sniffling for the rest of the night. If I saw him smile, it would cause me to miss him and despise him all at the same time. After the rehearsal, everyone packed into the vehicles and retired for the night. Tomorrow was going to be a big day and there was not going to be room for anyone to be hung over. Merri's friend and I drank until the alcohol was gone. She listened to my problems, and she made it clear that she had my back and didn't like Lilah because of the way she treated me. I thought it was so nice that she immediately gave me support after just meeting me and possibly hearing who-knows-what from who-knows-who at the rehearsal. This girl was awesome.

The next morning we woke up around 9:00 am. We all had to go to the salon to get our hair done and get ready for the ceremony. I was slightly hung over, but after eating I felt much better. Of course I hid this from most of my family. My rationing was that it was probably better to be an alcoholic than a drug addict, right?

The music started, and suddenly we were walking down the aisle to take our places for the ceremony. It was a beautiful ceremony, and my sister looked like a princess. The next hour was spent in the church taking post-nuptial photographs with the wedding party and guests, and then we were off to the reception. I was the most excited about this. When I left my house, I told Derrick that I wanted him to pick me up a few hours into the ceremony. I figured that I was going to be really miserable the entire time and that I would be wanting to get out of there as soon as possible. He called me around noon to say he was on his way, and Danielle was with him. We had an overnight visit with her scheduled for that day. Since the drive was five hours, I figured that I would have plenty of time to hang out with my sister and have dinner at the reception. He would have to make stops to feed and change Danielle, and if he came too early, he would surely give me time to at least finish eating. My grandparents and uncles had been asking about Danielle from the time I arrived. I had to explain that I only had her a few days out of the week at that point. I knew that they all wanted to see her, so I had planned to bring her to the reception for a few minutes before I had to leave. Derrick knew the situation, and I didn't think he'd mind.

After the newly married couple danced, dinner was served to the more than two hundred guests. As the appetizers came out, the D.J. approached the wedding party's table and asked us who wanted to make the first toast. Shit. I thought, avoiding his eyes. Not it! I mentally exclaimed as I casually turned away. The real problem was that I was scared as all hell. I knew that a good portion of the people in the room, from close family to friends of family I'd known my entire life, to an entirely new extended family, had probably heard at least something terrible about me at some point in the last year. Everyone from the bride's guest list knew that I had babies. About half of them were at my own wedding four years earlier. Although probably unintentional, their blank smiles and unsure eyes said it all. They knew my babies were gone, and they knew they weren't coming back to the family. I knew that they all knew this because not one person ever asked me where the girls were. I surrendered to the fact that it would be best for me to just stay silent and make sure that Merri knew that I loved her and that I was happy for her before I left.

The guys gave their speeches. One of them was already hilariously trashed. Valerie was next. She recalled the days that she and Merri spent in basic training and some other cute stories. Lilah was nowhere to be found (go figure) and Jessica was last. Her speech was nice, short and sweet.

I'VE GOT A MILLION MORE THINGS TO SAY THAN THAT! THESE PEOPLE DON'T KNOW MY TWIN!! I affirmed to myself as I eagerly hopped out of my chair after kicking my shoes off. I grabbed the mic from the D.J. as he was bringing it back to his station. Not thinking twice, I walked onto the dance floor where the others had given their toasts.

The room grew silent.

As I stood in front of my twin sister, my best friend, and my right hand from my first breath of life, I saw the same bright-eyed, blond little pipsqueak three-year-old that shared some of the most precious childhood memories with me that any two kids could share. Running on green grass, building forts in the woods, plotting to terrorize our mom, beating each other up in school, and loving each other so much we couldn't stand it, all flashed before my eyes. Tears welled up in my eyes as I recalled my twin sister patting me on the back when we were only ten, and telling me it was okay to cry after being worried sick over our young mother's recent diagnosis of illness. It was okay to cry. She saw everything I was seeing. Words weren't even necessary, but I somehow managed to tell the story of Lizzie and Merri...for everyone to hear. When I was done with giving my toast and everyone cheered, I walked back to my seat to her right. We were so eager to hug that we almost missed a few times. Regardless of my personal battles, I would have never missed an opportunity to publicly tell my best friend how much she means to me.

I'll never forget how sad I became when my phone rang that day. We were in the middle of eating a delicious dinner and the party was barely getting started. It was Derrick. He had arrived to pick me up much earlier than I expected. My heart sank. "Well since I'm in the middle of eating dinner, can I have a little more time?" I begged. "You got to be fuckin' kidding me. I just made a five-hour drive and you want me to just sit here in the parking lot with our kid in the back? Not happening." He was practically yelling at me. I hung up the phone and Merri knew what was happening. "You have to go, huh?" she asked. My chin started to quiver as I was trying very hard to fight my tears. "It's ok Liz, I understand," she said. Her friend Valerie offered to walk me out since Merri was busy being the new happy bride. Before we left the building, I stopped at the table where my entire family was seated to say goodbye. I gave everyone hugs, and my grandparents and Uncle Tony asked me where Danielle was. "She is out in the car," I told them. "Well bring her in! I want to see my great niece," my uncle said in a playful demanding way. I pulled my phone out of my purse to call Derrick to see if he would mind if I brought her in for a few minutes. "Hell no! If they can't even be around me, what makes you think I am going to let them be around my daughter? Nope. Not happening." I hung the phone up again and started crying even more this time around. I couldn't handle the conflict mixed with so many emotions of anger, confusion and loss. My family members had a look of disappointment on their faces, and I walked out of the building sobbing. Valerie walked me to the car that was parked toward the back of the parking lot. I dried my tears and doted on Danielle as I stepped to the side for Valerie to say hello to her. She gave me a hug and I got into the passenger seat, not knowing when the next time would be that I would have the chance to be in the same room as my entire family again. The reunions were becoming more few and far between, and I had a feeling that I wouldn't get to see everyone again for a long time.

Derrick was in a better mood once we started to drive. He was asking me questions about how my time was, and I answered them in a monotone manner. I was angry with him. It suddenly became clear to me that he was the exact reason why I was not an active part of my family as I always had been. He was the reason why I couldn't even introduce them to my daughter. I felt empty and sad the further away we drove. I couldn't handle any more, and I broke down crying. "I…I'm just sad because I didn't realize how much I missed my family until I saw them again…I don't want to live like this!" I cried. "You have got to be kidding me!" he yelled. He abruptly pulled to the side of the road into an empty lot with nothing but dirt and trees. My adrenaline was pumping and I couldn't understand why he had become so violently mad. "GET OUT! GET THE FUCK OUT!" He yelled. "Dude! What the hell? I'm not allowed to be upset that I never get to see my family anymore?" "GET OUT OF THIS CAR.

NOW!" I could tell that he was serious. I grabbed my purse off of the car floor and opened the passenger door stepping out into the mud. It was lightly raining. I thought that if he really did leave, I could probably call my mom and she'd find someone to come pick me up - although I didn't even know where I was. In defeat, I sat on a log and waited. Derrick was sitting in the idling Jeep and Danielle was getting fussy. I said nothing to him. I wouldn't even look in his direction. If he wanted me to get back into the car with him, he was going to have to do a ton of sweet talk and apologize. After about ten minutes, he did just that. The rest of the ride home was quiet and I resented him irreversibly.

Chapter 52

I worked extra hard in all of my classes and went to every meeting that I could get to. As far as I could tell, Derrick also was staying clean. The visits with our daughter, Danielle, were going as scheduled, and I loved taking her to the front yard with me to look at all the pretty flowers I had planted. It was like a temporary retreat and always put me into a hypnotic meditative state. She was getting to that adorable age where her personality was coming out and it was effortless to get her to smile. During our next hearing, we would find out if the Judge would approve for her to permanently come home. This would not mean that we'd be out of the system, but at least until the case was closed, she could be with us.

I took her with me to my next Drug Court Hearing just a few weeks before the official hearing for custody was scheduled. Halloween was coming up, so the Judge and Supervisors of the program decided to have a Halloween-style Drug Court meeting. I wasn't going to look like an idiot and dress up, but Derrick's mom ordered Danielle an adorable costume that I wanted for her. It was a baby lamb outfit. She looked so pathetically cute it was ridiculous. When the Judge called my name, I walked up to the desk holding my little lamb. He shuffled through the paperwork as usual. "So I heard that you taught Danielle how to clap?" He curiously asked with a slight grin on his face. The Judge was a kind, older man who sincerely cared about the families who were going through this hell. He was evenly spoken and had a mixed look of compassion yet accountability in his eyes. "Danielle, clap!" I said to her in my annoying squeaky voice. She excitedly clapped as she made some baby-babble noise, and the whole room made those "aaawhh" and "so precious" comments. If only clapping my hands together could get them to adore me just as much…I thought.

The two weeks came and went, and it was time for Court again. Derrick's mother flew into town again to show her support. She knew how nervous we were and how hard we were working. Obviously, we didn't tell her about our slip-up. A few days before Court arrived, our Social Worker randomly arrived at our house. We had Danielle with us, as we did more often than not lately. "Here, Derrick, I'm sorry it's last minute, but if you can go and get this taken care of before Court, it will help with the Judge's decision," he said as he handed him a piece of paper. "Ok, no problem," Derrick confidently responded. When the Social Worker left, I asked Derrick what the form was. "Oh it's just a drug test," he said. "No big deal." I was relieved to see his reaction, because it confirmed to me that Derrick had indeed been clean.

The next day we pulled into the parking lot for the office where the test was scheduled. Derrick's mother was at our house with Danielle, and I decided to wait in the car. I mainly went along for the ride because I wanted to stop and get food on the way back. About five minutes after Derrick entered the building, which was surrounded by other offices, I saw him walking slowly back to the Jeep with the form in his hand. By the way he was walking and the look on his face, I could tell he was mad. He got back into the driver's seat and turned on the car. "What is wrong?" I nervously asked. "They're trying to take a hair sample, that's what's wrong!" he practically yelled. "Derrick, it's probably

374

been over four months since we messed up. Why are you so freaked out?" I demanded. "Because, it's not going to be clean alright?" he shot back. "What the hell? When was the last time you did it? I thought you were clean this whole time!" I yelled. I could feel my face heating up every passing second. "I did some shit with Jeff like two weeks ago. We had a ton of shit to do and I didn't know they were going to test my hair!" he yelled back. "Derrick, you have to take it," I sternly said. "If you don't take it, they're going to count it as a dirty test anyway and we'll have no chance." I reasoned with him and he finally went back in to take the test. He did shave his head about a week ago. I should have known. He was trying to cover his worst-case scenario. I was so sick of his lies and his deceit. I wanted him to fail the test. I already had it planned out if he did.

The next morning, we met the foster care lady at the office and we all headed to Court together. She had a box of Danielle's things that the foster mom packed for her. They were already assuming that Danielle was coming home. I wasn't sure if anyone had the test results yet, but I assumed that the test was either negative or they were still waiting for the overnight results to come in. Derrick, his mother and Danielle headed out for the car, and I made it a point to pull the Foster Worker aside before exiting the building. I quietly whispered, "Can you relay a message for me if something unexpected happens?" I asked. I definitely had her attention. She looked concerned and confused. "Sure Elizabeth, what is it?" "Derrick acted a little strange yesterday when he found out that his drug test was going to be a hair follicle test. I'm not saying that I think he's been using drugs, but if that test comes back positive, I need the entire Court to know that I WILL leave him to get my baby back." I tried to hide the stress from my eyes, but I'm sure it was obvious. "Of course I'll tell them. I'll just give your Social Worker a call on the way to Court to give him a heads up, is that okay?" "Yes, I would appreciate that, thank you," I said as I rushed out to meet the rest of the family in the car. I didn't want them to know what I had just said.

As we pulled into the parking lot, I was nervous and worried, but I did feel better that I at least said something to someone about it. There was no way in hell I was going to be away from my daughter again because I was with a low-life drug addict. I felt somewhat liberated.

Our case was the first to be called. My stomach was in knots, and I was happy that Derrick's mother was holding Danielle at the moment. I needed to be able to compose myself in case the worst was about to be announced. The Judge started doing the usual with going over paperwork, and he didn't point out any sort of negative drug test. Once he was done with the overview of our progress, I immediately knew that Derrick had somehow passed that test. I was confused and relieved. The Social Workers all talked highly about our progress and recommended that Danielle come home permanently. Once they made that verbal recommendation, I knew that she would get to come home for good. "The Court grants both parents permanent custody of the minor child, and will put another six months of services in place." The Clerk handed me a card with the next Court date, which was six months away, and we were done. We got our baby back. It had been the most difficult, heartbreaking last eight months, but I somehow got through it. My baby was coming home for good and I could rest easy knowing that I wouldn't have to give her back. Everyone was very happy for us and excitement filled the air as we packed up and drove home. I called my mom and told her the good news right away, and I truly felt like I was a stronger person for getting through the hoops of fire.

We got settled and into our routine as a family, and Derrick's mother went back home about a week later. Danielle made a great transition and hardly even cried. I knew that she knew that I was her mom. She always took to me more than she did Derrick, and

I loved every second of it. I continued all of my classes and meetings, and as they came closer to completion, Derrick's boss asked me if I wanted to work for her part-time. I loved the idea of working, and I knew that it would be a good change from all of the classes I was trying to complete. I enrolled Danielle in daycare part-time, and began working about a month after she permanently came home. I felt like I was accomplishing so much more than I had been able to in the last year and a half. I was proud of myself and I felt like a responsible adult again. It was still difficult for me to go out in public much for fear of seeing someone who had heard terrible rumors about us. At least our boss didn't know the full details. She treated me like a person right off the bat and didn't have anything to doubt about me.

Christmas was coming up soon, and we were able to get permission from the Court to fly to Texas for a week to spend the holiday with Derrick's parents. The only thing that was going to be a serious task was trying to put up with Donnie. Derrick's mother was somehow able to convince Donnie to go to Texas with us. It annoyed me and made me feel ill, but she didn't know anything about the kind of guys her sons were - typical motherly denial. It was pretty pathetic how quickly she would believe some untrue story one of them might tell her. Regardless, I was still curious to see how they would all interact under the same roof for over a week.

After Derrick and I had worked a long day, we were finally released with our Christmas bonus checks in hand. Our flight to Texas was a redeye, so we had to hurry up and pick up Danielle from daycare and go home to pack our things. Once we were all packed and had Danielle all cleaned up, we loaded everything into the car and headed to Donnie's house. I hated even driving toward that neighborhood because I knew that he always had large amounts of drugs. By the time we got to Donnie's house it was around 8 o'clock at night. Our flight was going to take off in around three hours, and the drive was almost 2 hours, so we had to hurry. I stayed in the car with Danielle while Derrick went inside to get his brother. At least this time around I was pretty sure that he wasn't going to end up coming back to the car high. He was always really concerned about what his parents thought, and I could not picture him doing anything like that right before a visit. Donnie, on the other hand was a totally different ordeal. Not five minutes had gone by and they both were walking toward the car. I was going to give Donnie the front seat, but before I could even offer, he opened the back door and got in. It kind of made me a little bit uneasy because my daughter was back there, but at least I could see her and know about everything that was going on. About an hour into the drive we had to stop for gas. Donnie went inside saying that he needed road soda. After Derrick filled up the car and Donnie got back in, we started to drive. Immediately I heard a can crack open. Derrick must have known what was going on. "Donnie what in the hell are you drinking?" he asked. "Oh, nothing brother. I told you I was going to get road soda. I thought you'd be cool with that since I mentioned it." "Dude, I didn't think you were really going to get three 24-ounce beers to drink in the back seat. We have a baby in here and if we got pulled over that would be really bad." "I'm sorry man. I'll hurry up and get rid of these," Donnie replied as he began chugging his 24-ounce beer. He probably drank all three of those beers within a matter of minutes. Each time he finished one he threw the can out the window. We could only hope that a cop car wasn't hiding behind the dark corner.

I could tell that he was catching a buzz. As each minute passed, he became goofy and he wouldn't shut up. I wondered if he was even going to be able to pass through security with as drunk as he was acting. When we finally got through security, we went to our terminal and they soon began to call ticket numbers. At the last minute, Donnie said he forgot about the letter that he meant to mail. We told him there wasn't time to go get it, but he was acting like it was an emergency, and he wouldn't take no for an answer. Derrick and I gave up on him and figured that he was probably going to miss the flight and be stuck in Reno. When we were already seated on the plane, he somehow got through security a second time and was heading towards us. There were three seats in a tiny row and this was definitely going to be a super uncomfortable and annoying flight if you couldn't fall asleep. Donnie definitely had no plans of falling asleep even though it was the middle of the night. I knew that Derrick was trying to tame his temper when he ordered a couple shots of Jack Daniels from the stewardess. Derrick hardly ever drank, and he was usually always against it. That's when I knew that he was having a really hard time dealing with his brother. Being uncomfortable and frustrated, I begged Derrick to give me half of one of Donnie's drinks. He finally did, and I chugged it as fast as I could trying not to gag on the aftertaste. I fell asleep for the duration of the plane ride and about three hours later was awaken by the pilot announcing, "Good morning passengers. It looks like it's going to be a beautiful day and a mild 75° with clear skies. Welcome to Houston and prepare for landing."

`I woke up pretty groggy and a little bit disorientated, but I was super excited that we were about to land. I had never traveled so far away from home before. Donnie and Derrick slowly woke up and put their seatbelts on after the stewardess nudged them. The landing was a bit rough but I survived. After twenty minutes of impatiently waiting for the plane to park and set us free, we crammed ourselves between the other passengers and could not wait to get off the plane. The airport was huge and I was in awe. After walking for what felt like a mile, we finally saw Derrick's parents in the distance. It was still dark outside and they looked just as tired as we were. As soon as we approached, there were the usual hugs, and their mother was crying. She did that a lot. I was so confused as to why someone would cry over being so happy. Maybe she was so happy it made her sad. I put on my cheese smile and wanted to get to the parking garage to light a cigarette. I was having a bad craving, but I changed my mind pretty fast. It was humid as all hell and it was dark outside! This climate was totally foreign to me. I was just a crisp, fresh air mountain girl. I knew nothing about the humid South.

As we drove through the city I practically had my face pressed against the glass of the window. The buildings were so big and bright and there was just so much stuff to look at! I was accustomed to seeing trees and maybe a bright casino or two, but nothing like this. This was amazing. I felt as if I hadn't even been living in the real world my entire life. Tahoe was just a big illusion. A mountain with a hole in it that kept you in your own little comfy bubble and not even wanting to consider leaving. Before we pulled into their driveway, I had already decided that I wanted to move there. Derrick's mother and I had exchanged emails, and I had entertained the idea half-seriously, but now I was damn serious. And I was going to let everyone know.

Their house was huge, and the ceilings were incredibly high. Derrick led me up the huge staircase to the bedroom we would be staying in, which was once his for a few months when the family originally relocated. His bedroom looked like a time vault from about ten years earlier. He had a few pictures of old cars hung on the walls, and he had some pictures of him with his high school friends. It made me kind of sad for him when I saw these. He looked like a fun, innocent kid. The look on his face expressed true happiness and love for life. He definitely didn't have that any more. He once had told me that his life didn't really start to go downhill until he moved to Tahoe and had to live with his brother. Derrick tried to stay with his parents in Texas when they made the move. He was eighteen, and didn't really have anywhere else to go. After a few months in Texas, he became homesick and missed all of his friends. He couldn't take it anymore so in the middle of the night he snuck out of the house and got on a bus back to California. After realizing that he couldn't couch-hop from friend to friend, he decided to move in with Donnie. Bad move.

Our week in Texas went by way too quick. We went out to eat a few nights, and we did lots of Christmas shopping. I was not looking forward to returning home. The thought of it made me sad and I just wanted a normal life away from Social Workers. Derrick's mother was so excited when she heard that we wanted to move there, she started crying. We didn't know how long it would take but we did know that I still had a year and a half of Probation left. I had heard of people getting off of Probation early from complying with the terms and conditions of it. When I got back I was going to do some research and see what I needed to do to make this happen. We said our goodbyes, and had a miserable flight home. The turbulence was terrible and people were getting sick. Donnie was getting some sort of turbulence psychosis and cursing at the stewardess and pilot. For the next few months, the only thing I could think about was starting my new life as a cowgirl in Texas where nobody knew my name, my drama or my heartache. If they didn't know about it, they couldn't bring it up to remind me. I wanted to forget that anything bad ever happened and live the rest of my life normal. It was the only way I'd survive.

Chapter 53

When we got back into our regular routine, I began to do some research and think of ways that I could quickly prove to my Probation Officer and the Social Workers that I was ready to be set free. I had a feeling that the Social Workers were going to recommend that the case be closed in a few months, but Probation was a different story. Although I had never violated any terms of Probation, it was apparently still pretty hard to get off of early. I immediately put in a request for an interstate compact transfer. Basically that would transfer my Probation over to Texas from California. My Probation Officer helped me set it up, but it wasn't up to him - it was up to the state of Texas. That was a big fat denial pretty much right away. I was really bummed and I felt a little bit defeated, but I knew there still had to be another way. I then asked my Probation Officer about getting off of Probation early. He told me that I would need to finish at least half of my term, which was coming up in a few months. That made me excited, and he almost made me feel as if he would help me.

With this little glimmer of hope of getting out of this town that gave me nothing but flashbacks and anxiety, I began to do everything that I could to go above and beyond. I became super involved with my NA meetings, and I even volunteered to lead the Thursday night meeting when the other members announced that they were shorthanded. This was the women's meeting that was held at the church. At first I was ridiculously nervous, but I quickly realized it was no big deal. I pretty much read out of a binder and led things like the Serenity Prayer and group discussions. I always left that meeting feeling good about myself and feeling like I was possibly making a difference in the lives of others. My sponsor, Jenny, was so touched by my story and my willingness to share it, that she asked me to go with her to the Saturday morning meeting that was at the Inpatient Rehab facility where I once resided. I thought it would be kind of cool to tell my story to the group of people there, especially because I knew exactly how they were feeling and how hard it was to live somewhere that was completely different from their normal environment.

I even told them about my other girls and how the case was never solved. I tried as much as I could to point out the positive aspects so my story could be one that offered hope and encouragement instead of depressing sadness. Midway through my story, I paused to take a breath and think about what I would talk about next. Every person in the room was intensely staring at me, and some even had their mouths dropped open. I was pretty sure that I had their attention. My story had the same elements as some of the other stories, but it was definitely its own, and it was definitely intense. I continued. "I often received comments about how shocked people were that I was actually doing so well after everything that had happened. Sometimes you just have no choice but to keep going. Even if you have the smallest amount of hope lingering in the distance, hold on to it like you'll never see it again. Everything happens for a reason, a greater purpose. You may not be able to see what that purpose is right away or even for a very long time. But in the long run, there is a purpose. Losing my daughters has taught me so much about myself. It has taught me about the kind of person and mother I want to be. I see the joy in small things today, and I try to focus on what I do have and keep faith that what I don't have will one day come back to me. I have to be a good role model for my daughters. When the day comes that they want to know who I am, I want them to be proud that I'm their mom. The last thing I want to do is disappoint them even more. These meetings are better than a $300 therapy session. The Steps are all you'll ever need to heal every single aspect of your life. They force you to understand yourself, learn about yourself and eventually forgive and love yourself. I'm only on my fourth Step, but I've already felt the weight of so many burdens and regrets begin to ease up a little. I'm learning that it's okay for me to be sad, and I also have a group of people I can call if I feel like I just can't handle it any more. The best advice that I can give is to stay open-minded. Fake it 'till ya make it. There is nothing more awesome than living a clean and sober life and actually enjoying it. And I can promise you that if you continue to go to meetings on a regular basis, get a sponsor, and work all the Steps, you'll be able to say the same for your own life. You'll get your life back, and you'll really begin to live it. My name is Elizabeth and I'm an addict."

The group of twenty or so patients in the meeting room applauded so loudly that I almost couldn't hear. That was a good sign. It meant that I got through to them. I wanted to show them that I'm a real person who made real mistakes, and staying strong is the only way to go. I affirmed to myself as I was leaving the rehab that helping others was by far the best way that I could ever help myself. I felt like I had a place in the world.

Not too long after I spoke at this meeting, I was asked by a couple NA members to go with them to the jail to speak to the inmates. The thought made me nervous, but my heart was nagging at me to go. I wasn't sure if I could get through because I had just been in jail a little over a year earlier. I thought that the jail had rules when it came to whom they would allow to speak to the inmates. A group of four of us went to meet with the sheriff who was in charge of coordinating meetings within the jail. He was very passionate about making sure that the inmates were able to attend these meetings. "I don't care if you were in jail six months ago. If you've turned your life around, and other NA members can attest to that, I want you to come in and speak to the inmates. You will give them a good example that it is possible to quickly turn your life around." I was in. I was going to go with the group of ladies next Thursday night meeting.

From what I could tell Derrick was still sober, but then again I never really knew anything about him. I assumed that he had enough common sense to avoid making bad choices since we had our daughter back full-time. He wasn't typically very supportive when I went to my meetings or volunteered to do extra stuff either. He tried to make me feel guilty by saying that I should have been spending time with Danielle instead of attending meetings with drug addicts. He was so backwards at times it just repulsed me. Regardless of what he said, I still went to the jail to do the meeting I offered to do. He put up the biggest fight over that. It was almost like he was weirdly jealous in a way, and he didn't want me to do well. I always spoke about this when I went to the meetings because I didn't know what I was supposed to do about it. I was truly in an abusive relationship. But Derrick was all I knew. I didn't remember what it was like to live a decent life. My decent life left me when I lost my rights to the girls.

It was a cold, icy night. The three other ladies who were also going to speak at the meeting came and picked me up. We rode to the jail together, and I was surprised that they were just as nervous as I was. In that sense, at least I knew what to expect. We walked into the visitor area to check in and put our stuff in the lockers. The sheriff in charge led us back to that room that I vividly recalled sitting in not too long ago - pregnant and not sure when I would ever get out. I'll never forget the smell of that place either. The best I can describe it is like the smell of your elementary school cafeteria, in that it's one of those smells that never leaves your memory. We took our seats at the square table and waited for the inmates to come in. It was strange that I was there, but in civilian clothes and having the option to walk out at any time. It made me feel so thankful that I had my freedom and things were turning out to be okay. One of the other women began the meeting, reading from the binder and saying the prayer. They all shared their stories, and I was the last to share mine. When I was through speaking, I had that dropped jaw look again. The inmates were all polite, and I recognized the look of defeat and shame in their eyes. Just like myself a while back, they just wanted to go home. The meeting was finished, and I went home to spend the next few days in a depressed and somber state. The jail experience was miserable. What was even more painful was the realization that I had really been there. The experience forced me to reflect back on all of the sadness and pain I had been through in the last few years. What was so depressing, with or without me even knowing it, was that all of the sad things happened not just to me but to my daughters as well, could have been prevented. They didn't have to happen. My lack of judgment and extremely poor choices were the ultimate reason that I would not see my babies again for a very long time. As I would lay in bed at night unable to sleep for this very reason, a part of my heart was trying to reach its way into my mind. It was screaming at me to run. It was begging me to open my eyes and see the true life that I was choosing to live. Being with Derrick, whether he was responsible for Zoe's injury or not, was not the real question to be asking myself. The fact that I did not know who hurt her was reason enough to never, ever return to him. I didn't acknowledge that fact. It was too much to face. I had burnt most bridges and didn't really have anywhere else to go. I was forced to stay in Tahoe and the county with my Probation and the CPS case. Suddenly leaving Derrick would only raise suspicion of the Court and prolong everything that I was trying to get out of. I was sure that my best bet would be to move to Texas. Getting out of town and starting over, maybe, just maybe, Derrick would become that happy kid that I saw in the pictures in his Texas bedroom.

I had a more than typical attachment to Derrick. I read somewhere and at some point, that when a couple goes through a trauma together, it either rips them apart, or brings them closer together. Derrick always told me that he went through everything right there with me. He may have been a part of the investigation, but he didn't go through what I did. When Zoe was in the hospital, he didn't suffer through a four-day hospital stay helplessly watching his own child being treated like a guinea pig to intern doctors. He didn't have to see his child being put under anesthesia as she collapsed in his arms. He didn't have to hear that his child had been given highly toxic chemicals that could have killed her. He didn't go through shit.

I would think about the same things night after night, yet never allow it to click in my head that it was time to leave. My ration was that I had already lost the girls. I stuck with Derrick for this long, and it would have all been for nothing if I left. I had to stick to what I believed. It couldn't be anything in the middle. I was going to stay with Derrick because that's what I chose to do after the trauma. I made my bed, and I was laying in it.

A week before the six month review for the custody case, I had my last Drug Court meeting. I didn't know it was going to be my last though. When I walked in, my Attorney excitedly told me that they were going to graduate me. I was really happy about this, but I was also shocked and unprepared. My case was called along with the others so the Judge could determine if he would agree or disagree on each recommendation, which in my case was graduation.

"I...I just don't think I'm ready to set her free yet," he said out loud as he was scuffling through my thick folder of progress reports. "Your Honor," my Attorney spoke up, "Ms. Jeter has completed everything and more that the Court and Social Services has asked of her. Unless there is an objection that I'm unaware of, I think it's time to let Elizabeth move forward with her life." "The Department agrees, Your Honor," the Attorney for the Social Services Department added. After Danielle's State Attorney spoke up on my behalf, as well as Olga, the Judge finally gave in. He agreed to graduate me from Drug Court. Drug Court was probably the most intense hearing I had to attend. Its primary focus was accountability. The spotlight was on me - and every single move I did or didn't make. I knew in my gut that I really wasn't ready to move forward, but I wasn't about to make an objection. It would confuse everyone and prolong being stuck in the system.

After all of the cases were called, Olga called the names out of those who were moving on from Drug Court and asked us to stand up and follow her to the back room. I was totally confused and almost died of embarrassment when I saw what was hanging on the wall - about ten burgundy colored caps and gowns. Oh…my…God… I thought to myself as I felt my face turning bright red. This is not happening. I feel like I'm graduating from kindergarten again! I was at least holding Danielle in my arms, so she was giving me something to do besides awkwardly stand there, swimming in a burgundy gown. Then it got worse. From the back room of the Court, I heard the song start playing - the graduation big-deal-symphony thing. I made sure to get behind everyone else. I wanted to hide so badly. As we walked out to the floor of the Courtroom, the other Drug Court families and the Court Staff started loudly applauding. Oh…my…God…I thought to myself, again. Olga walked up to each of us and put a sash around our shoulders and handed us flowers and gift baskets. When I saw that there was candy in my gift basket, I became a little more excited. The Judge gave his "congratulations" speech, my Lawyer gave me a genuine look of approval and kissed me on the cheek, and I was all done. I'll never forget my Lawyer offering such a sincere gesture of love and concern for me on that day. She had been the only person, in a long while, whom I had gotten that from.

Chapter 54

I had finished Drug Court. I was no longer ordered to attend a specific number of meetings every week. I had completed my outpatient treatment, and besides Probation, I was almost finished with everything. I was still subject to random drug testing, but they didn't call me in one time during those last few weeks. I was in the final stretch.

Up until the big Court date that would determine if the case with the CPS was going to close, I still attended meetings and made sure to walk a straight line. I knew that they could pull any sort of random stunt at the last minute so they could be sure that we were really clean. Derrick had claimed to be clean, but ever since the drug test incident, I knew that his word was as good as gone. I always called him out whenever he appeared to have that look on his face, but it never did any good. If anything it would cause an argument. I continued to work up until a few days before the Court date. I had been late one too many times, and the boss lady was fed up. So was I. Danielle attended daycare in the mornings and Derrick refused to drop her off. In addition, it took me longer to get ready to leave for work because I'm a female. It was the same place that Chloe and Zoe once went to. Of course, the staff had a general idea of the situation. They were, after all, subpoenaed to the custody hearing, where I had to go back and recall every vivid, painstaking moment. When I was already fifteen minutes late and had not even left the house yet, I sat on the couch in defeat after changing a last minute dirty diaper. My boss had warned me yesterday, that if I were late again she would have to let me go. I couldn't argue with her, because I was indeed ten minutes late minimum, every day. Plus I was kind of ready for a break anyway. I called my boss ready to face the situation. "I'm sorry, the baby…" "Honey I love you, you have done great working for me, but I need someone who can promise to be on time every day. It's just not going to work out," she interrupted. I could hear the frustration in her voice, but she was still as nice as she could be about it. "Okay, I understand, and thank you for everything," I sincerely responded. "You're welcome baby, I'll let you know if I have any smaller jobs you can help with." We hung up and that was that. I was bummed and kind of embarrassed, but also kind of happy that I could kick off my shoes and do nothing for a while.

Doing nothing was a bad idea. When I had nothing to do, my thoughts raced through my mind constantly. These were mostly my thoughts of my girls, whom I missed and just wanted to hold so desperately. Then I would think about what happened - and who caused it. Then I wondered if I were safe and if Danielle was safe. After the cycle of flashbacks and anxiety, I'd shut it down. I'm fine. Obviously he didn't do that. He'd be in jail. It was just some freak accident.

My days were slow and boring. I took care of Danielle during the days, watched her watch Sesame Street, and fed her peaches or carrots, and so on. I was eager to get to the meetings by the time night rolled around and Derrick came home. He came with me a few times, to show his support. During the last meeting I recalled him attending, he actually said he was an addict before he began to speak. I was floored. I glanced over to my sponsor with a sly smirk on my face. She knew exactly what I was

392

thinking. Accomplishment! It may be a baby step, but it's progress! This gave me a bit of hope and comfort. Derrick displayed some sort of character showing humanistic qualities versus his normal overly superior, egotistical one. I was still running the Thursday night meetings and met the group of women at the beach for my last lead. The summer had come, and it was staying light out longer. We bumped the time back an hour so we could meet at the beach. It was a perfect place to take an inventory of our thoughts and actions and just allow ourselves to be human and in recovery. The sunshine brought a natural high, and we had some pretty deep discussions. We were sitting in our circle that day and talking about the beauty of enjoying life sober. I had just begun to speak my turn. "Elizabeth, addi..." when BOOM!

"What the hell was that?" I said in a panic. It sounded like a car crashed in the parking lot. All of the women quickly turned their heads toward the loud noise of impact. "Whaaaaaa-aaaaaah!" Oh no. Oh my God! My mind raced as adrenaline pumped through my veins. One of the little kids was screaming. The group of kids were all playing together close to the mothers in the vacant parking lot about twenty feet from where we were sitting. It was Emily's daughter, Aleah. Aleah was barely three at the time. Everyone raced over to the scene in a panic, screaming. I didn't think I'd be able to handle it if she was seriously hurt. Ever since I woke up that morning and witnessed what I witnessed with Zoe, I was extremely sensitive to any sort of pain or fear that a child may be facing. Derrick and I had some battles over this because I was constantly so worried that something bad could happen to Danielle. I was over-protective to the point of it causing anxiety for the entire family. I tried to contain it, but I even feared leaving Danielle alone with him for just an hour.

As I approached the scene, I saw the little girl kicking and screaming as she was lying on the pavement of the dented car next to her. There was a heavy woman about thirty feet away from the damaged vehicles, belligerent and flailing around drunk. Her shirt was too small, and her rolls were freely flailing along with her arms. The mother of the little girl was in a panic trying to keep her still in case she had a spinal injury. The paramedics along with the police arrived in about five minutes. The beautiful and serene afternoon had quickly transformed into uncertain chaos. The paramedics quickly strapped the little girl to a backboard and reassured her mom that it was a good sign that she was aware enough to be so upset and screaming and crying like she was. After mom and daughter left in the ambulance, the police determined that the little girl didn't take a direct hit, thankfully. She was playing on the other side of the vehicle (which belonged to my sponsor) that was hit. The impact from that vehicle was what caused her to fall to the cement. It took the police officers a full hour to get the woman into the back of the patrol car. They had to call for extra backup because the woman was dead weight at that point. A few hundred pounds of dead body-weight apparently takes some strong manpower to transport. When all was said and done, those of us who were still at the scene ended the day by closing out with saying a prayer for the little girl who was hurt, and also for the woman responsible. It was ironic what happened that day. It was proof that while one person's reality can be full of hope and content, there could be another person just a few feet away on the brink of death, or even worse, causing a death. It's the only certain guarantee in life. Everything in life has a polar opposite. I was thankful that I had been able to attach to the positive side. I was also feeling stupid for the many mistakes I had allowed myself to make over the years. Most importantly, I realized that life was constantly going to be full of pain and uncertainty. I was hurting and aching over the absence of Chloe and Zoe, but I was so incredibly happy that they were alive and well. One day, I just might have a chance to hold them again. I told myself I would never, ever go back to living like that again.

394

Besides the occasional emotional distress I was in, everything at home seemed to be going in a good direction. Our custody hearing had arrived before I knew it. I was nervous in the lobby as usual, but I wasn't nearly as nervous as I had been on prior occasions. We were called in by the Bailiff and walked to the Defendant's table to sit next to our Public Defenders. It was pretty pathetic that this had become routine for us, but I was hopeful that it was all about to come to a close.

"Your Honor," the Social Services Attorney began, "I can't begin to express how thoroughly impressed the department is with the mother and father of Danielle. I'm sure I speak with most of us when I say that we all saw little to zero hope for this family back when the case first began. They've gone above and beyond what we've asked of them not giving us any reason to doubt their ability as parents in the process. We're proud to recommend that the department should close this case." I was stunned to tears. I had extreme feelings of guilt for screwing up, and I felt like I had been deceiving. On the other hand, I was still proud of myself for trying as hard as I could. My efforts were not going unnoticed, and that was showing to be true in this very moment.

Every official in the Court had something nice to say about us that day. I expected that the hearing would be the typical, emotionless ruling. Even the Judge said very sincere words of praise and kindness. He ruled in favor of all involved and closed the case. We were free from this nightmare - the nightmare that ripped my newborn baby away from me just a year before. I proved to myself that despite the circumstances, I could achieve anything that I put my mind to. When all odds were entirely against me, and the likelihood of getting Danielle back home was slim to none, I still did it. Leaving the Court felt as if a thousand pounds had been lifted off of my shoulders. It was exciting and I was looking forward to really beginning my life.

My Probation Officer had agreed to help me get off of Probation early, or at least try, by scheduling a Court Hearing and offering his recommendation. The whole reason for this was so we could pack up and move to Texas. With everything going so well in the past few months, I was no longer 100% sure that I wanted to leave my hometown. We began to socialize more and had friends over for barbeques and weekend camping trips. It was easing into summer and the weather was perfect. I wasn't ashamed to go out in public as I had once been. I felt normal again, and I felt as if I were better understood and maybe even forgiven for my mistakes. Being with Derrick and having our baby together wasn't something that felt like a shameful thing at this point. I had confessed and owned up to my mistakes to myself and to the Court, and they all knew this. Derrick was another story and was great at putting up a front. He was so great at this that even a Judge, who had probably seen it all, couldn't see beyond his lies and false claims. He hadn't been 100% honest to me or to the Court about his sobriety, and I wondered how often he had been using drugs on the side. All of these thoughts were brewing in my subconscious, but it was easier to brush them to the side. Things were looking promising and I had to accept that.

My Court Hearing was two months away, and I knew that passing months were probably my last in my hometown. We were already looking into the cost of moving, and Derrick's mother already had offered to pay for the expenses that we couldn't take on. Derrick continued working, and I stayed at home with Danielle. I had some friends who also had young babies come over once in a while during the day just to have something to do. One of these friends was someone I had met years ago who had a short fling with Donnie back when Derrick and I first started dating. She then met someone new and ended up having a baby. She claimed to be clean, but I wondered if she really was. Any person that was associated with Donnie and Derrick was a drug user. Most of them were still using drugs. We would occasionally look back and remember the days of getting high and fixing things that weren't broken. She saw it as more of a humorous thing, because she hadn't suffered the dire consequences that I had. It was hard for me to ever smile in response to her memoires.

One afternoon after Derrick had gotten off of work, I knew something fishy was going on when he called me into the kitchen. He never called me into his proximity for something unimportant. He was smoking a cigarette under the kitchen fan, and Danielle was in her high chair finishing her dinner. I had no idea what was going on, but I knew that it couldn't be bad because he was in a good mood. He looked over at Danielle. "All right Danielle, are you ready for this?" She smiled and clapped. Oh God. This is awkward - really awkward. I think I know what he's about to do. As I was sitting on the kitchen counter near the stove, nervously puffing on my cigarette, he turned in my direction and pulled something out of his pocket. He opened a box that had a shiny gold ring with hearts cut from diamonds. "Will you marry me?" he asked.

Chapter 55

Once I saw the ring, I became more excited than nervous. I definitely was shocked at this proposal. It was completely unexpected. I had periodically been nagging him about our future and how I thought he needed to make up his mind. I thought that if I was going to be living a life that my family did not approve of, among many others, I might as well do it the best way that I could. Or at least live in a way that I thought was morally the best way possible. For Danielle's sake as well, I wanted us, as her parents, to be a good example. She needed to grow up with us being married as a committed family unit.

"Of course I'll marry you!" I shyly said as I put the ring on my finger. I felt my face turning red and Derrick was kind enough to point it out. I told him to shut up as I buried my face in my hands. He kissed me and I told him that I loved him. "Yay. I'm excited. Look at mommy's ring Danielle!" I said as I walked over to her and kissed her head. Without considering the fact that my family disliked Derrick with a passion, I went to my computer to send them an email along with a picture of my ring. I figured it would be best to break the news through an email than over the phone. I didn't want to call and let the excitement I was feeling become destroyed and ruined with guilt. Derrick called his parents to tell them the news, and of course, they were excited. I felt a sense of relief, and thought that just maybe all of the troubles we had encountered over the last few years had made us closer and taught Derrick a lesson on the value of life. He was still coming home every day appearing to be clean, and good events were continuing to unfold. Perhaps this has caused us to become somewhat complacent.

After the case for the CPS was closed, I eventually stopped attending meetings altogether. I went to a few meetings for the first couple of weeks, but after that Derrick convinced me that I didn't need the meetings, and that they were only four lowlife people who couldn't manage their problems on their own. Whenever I mentioned that I wanted to go to a meeting, Derrick would always have a good reason for me to not go. We would go out to dinner, invite friends over, or pretty much anything that didn't include a meeting. It became more difficult for me to try to go than not, so I just gave up on it. I couldn't see going to meetings on a regular basis anyway. It wasn't something that I wanted to do long-term. I definitely believed in the program, and I knew that it worked, but a part of me wasn't convinced that it was the only way to live a healthy life, as they had claimed it to be.

I only had to check into Probation once a month at this point, and before I knew it our way of life had become very similar to what it was when I still had Chloe and Zoe. We began hanging around with people that we both knew were not good influences. This included Donnie and his new girlfriend. Donnie always had a way of making you feel like it was perfectly okay and normal to be around him. Ultimately, that's all we were seeking. We just wanted to feel like we were normal people, living a normal life. I could not ever go over to Donnie's house without feeling the physical effects of addiction. The simple fact that I knew there were drugs in the house caused my body to feel placebo related rushes. It was like a feeling of being high without actually using anything. Derrick was always extremely influenced by his brother. It was like a chain reaction. Derrick influenced me and Donnie influenced Derrick. It only took a few times of us socializing with Donnie to begin entertaining the idea of using drugs again. We had it all planned out to move to Texas as soon as I got off of Probation, which was only going to be in less than a month. We knew that once we got to Texas, we would not be using any sort of illegal substances. We didn't want to live that lifestyle, and his parents would never permit it any way. We somehow were living with a mentality that we might as well get our partying out of the way while still could. This gave us plenty of excuses and reasons for it to be okay to use it one last time. This is where the insanity of addiction comes in. For a person to actually make the conscious decision to ingest a harmful substance into their body while still being sober is pure insanity. Insanity is repeating the same behavior and expecting different results. I was insane. After all I had been through, and all of the heartache and pain, I still had an excuse to make it okay to use drugs. Even though I had accomplished more than I ever thought possible, and even though I had impressed higher authority who I never thought could take me seriously, I was still punishing myself. I was never really happy, and the deep clean that lived in my spirit would never go away. The fact is, I didn't know it at the time, but I hated myself. I hated myself because I chose to be with Derrick over choosing to fight to get my girls back. I was unwilling to face the truth. I was unwilling to accept the fact that I had chosen to be with someone who was dangerous and brought danger into my home. I would never accept the fact that I was one of those women who was too stupid to see what was really going on. As much as I loved Danielle, I never felt like I deserved to have her.

At one point, one of my friends asked me if I had Danielle to try to replace Chloe and Zoe. I became defensive and almost angry that she even asked me that question. I explained to her that I knew that Danielle would never replace Chloe and Zoe or any child for that matter. Was I feeding myself my own lies? Why in the world had I not acknowledged the fact that I was not taking birth control around the time I became pregnant with Danielle? Maybe I subconsciously needed a reason to live. Maybe another baby was the only reason I would have to keep myself alive. Maybe I had to prove to myself and everyone else around me that Derrick was a good person, and by becoming pregnant and choosing to be with him, my good judgment would only show this. I never acknowledged my pain, and I never wanted to. I just wanted to live and be happy one day. Maybe if we started having fun again, and periodically using drugs just for recreational purposes, Derrick wouldn't want to leave Tahoe because we'd be having so much fun! I would wonder. I didn't want to leave Tahoe, but after the big fuss I made over moving to Texas, I felt like an idiot for changing my mind, and I didn't know how to express this. The only way I could express this was through self-sabotage. It gave me an outlet to express my pain, guilt, grief, confusion and uncertainty. We used drugs one time. There is never just one time.

The only difference from my life with Chloe and Zoe to my life with Derrick was that when Derrick and I used substance, we used it at our house and wouldn't let others into it as long as we had Danielle. I had become paranoid about this, and Derrick went along with it. A few times he made remarks about how he'd never, ever allow his brother to be around Danielle unsupervised. I wondered if he was saying this because he truly meant it, or if he was saying it to cover up for his own guilt. I would never know. I paid close attention to every move of his, by instinct, and never became suspicious of his interactions with Danielle. I also did this when Donnie would interact with her. I never had any suspicions with his behavior either. It still didn't make me feel any better. I knew that it had to be one of them. I was hoping that one day I could find some little bit of proof to resolve this in my own mind. I never got what I was looking for. I never expressed to any other person what I was looking for either. It would make me look like a careless person socializing with people like them while knowing that one of them was a sick, horrible person. And to top it off, I was allowing them to be near my baby. When the CPS case closed, my anxiety went through the roof. At least when it was open, Derrick knew that we were being closely watched, and he knew that socializing with his brother would badly influence his choices. The pressure had been lifted, and my fear of another tragedy had increased beyond measure. It started when we started to use substance again.

Danielle was put to bed on a Friday night, and Derrick was at his brother's house picking up $400 worth of crystal meth. I was anxious and restless and nervous, aimlessly pacing my living room as the placebo high was rushing through my body. We decided that since I had Court on Monday, we would go all out on this last weekend we had in Tahoe. As soon as I was off Probation, we were packing up and getting on the road. Probation hadn't given me a drug test in probably about six months, because they knew that I was testing through the Social Services, and they always got a copy of my clean results. I didn't even have another meeting scheduled with Probation anyway, so I was already practically off. Derrick came home with four bags of crystal-clear meth. His brother had been selling mass quantities and was happy to give some of it to Derrick. Before he would let me take a hit off of the pipe, which had been purchased at a local gas station and disguised as an incense holder, he weighed and divided the drug into smaller quantities. I wasn't sure why he did this, because he didn't have anyone to sell it to. He took the bags and hid them in our attic. He only kept a small quantity on him for our own use. The last time we relapsed, about five months earlier, we snorted the drug. This time we were going to smoke it, which caused almost an instant euphoric high. When I took the first hit, I immediately felt the drug rushing through my bloodstream. It was relaxing but I had that alert and aware feeling that I always wanted to permanently have. I could accomplish anything. If only I was allowed to use just a small amount for the rest of my life, I could always feel happy and motivated to conquer life.

The first night we used it, I did my usual routine and probably spent twelve hours straight sitting on the couch doing crossword puzzles. I thought it was harmless, and the only thing coming out of it was that I was learning! I would not move on to the next puzzle until I finished the one I was working on. I wanted to prove that I was smart enough to finish them myself without cheating. I eventually had to switch from using a pen to a pencil, because I had to go back and make corrections several times. I had these puzzles down to a science. When Danielle woke up, I would get her dressed, feed her breakfast, and let her run around and play. When I went to stand up after sitting in the same position for such a long time, I became incredibly dizzy, almost to the point of blacking out. I sipped water to stay hydrated, but I definitely didn't eat anything. My mouth was too dry, and if I even tried to eat I would instantly gag. Chain smoking, crossword puzzles and drinking water was what I did. Derrick played video games with the same diligence as I worked on crossword puzzles.

On the night of day two of our binge, the paranoia crept in. We hadn't slept at all for forty-eight hours, and we didn't plan to sleep. Sleep was not something that happened when we were on a binge. Trying to fall asleep was horrible, and the darkness only increased the paranoia. Around three in the morning, Derrick became convinced that there were Secret Service Agents surrounding our house. I knew it wasn't true, but any slight sound of the house settling would cause me to wonder. I was more concerned that our house was about to be raided. With us being in the last stretch, it wouldn't surprise me if they wanted to set us up to fail once again. What everyone did not know was that I was already doing this.

After quietly lying in bed watching Derrick point a pellet gun at the entrance of our bedroom door for what felt like hours, he finally fell asleep. When he fell asleep I got up to check on Danielle, and I decided to bring her in bed with me. I didn't trust Derrick at this moment, and I wouldn't want him to mistake her for a secret service agent or something. I put her next to me and next to the wall, and nodded on and off until the next morning.

Sunday morning came along. I felt disoriented and sick from the drug leaving my body. We had gone through all four bags of the meth in only two days. There was only a small amount left. I knew that the only way to feel better was to use what we had left. Derrick broke it up into lines, and I continued using it every hour or so because I felt like it wasn't working. My tolerance had become strong, and no amount was going to give me what I wanted at this point. Around three in the afternoon that day, the phone rang. It was a 573 number, which was usually either the Social Services office or Probation. It was Probation. My Probation Officer left a message on our machine saying that he wanted to see if I was available to stop in the next day for just a few minutes. He had some questions to ask me about my Court date, which was on Wednesday. "Wheew. I thought he was going to suddenly drug test me!" I said in response to his message. "You better start pounding water. He probably is going to drug test you," Derrick replied casually. "No way. He trusts me and a drug test takes a few days to come back with the results. There isn't enough time to do that with my hearing being on Wednesday," I confidently replied. I had the entire system mastered. I needed to give them what they wanted and I would be fine. He probably just needed to verify where I would be living when they set me free. I was sure it was something simple. But to be safe, I drank as much water as I could, ate cloves of raw garlic, and took handfuls of vitamin C. I obsessively researched online ways to get the drug out of my system, and that is what I came up with. Plus it gave me something to do to stay distracted.

405

My mom called that same afternoon asking me when my Court Hearing was. She wanted to come and visit me before we left for Texas. She hadn't seen Danielle since she was born, and wanted to get some pictures as well. I told her about my meeting that afternoon, and she said she would come pick me up for lunch beforehand.

Monday was bright and sunny. I had gotten about ten hours of sleep the night before, and I thought I would be feeling rested enough to get through the day. My body was still trying to recover from the weekend binge. I was short of breath and I felt like my chest was going to cave in. I put Danielle in the cutest outfit I could find for her, and I showered and got dressed. I was glad that Derrick had to work that day, and knew it would help avoid conflict. My mom had become a little more supportive of my situation, probably only because she saw that I made enough progress to get away from the CPS and the entire system. We still didn't talk about Derrick and knew that it wouldn't give either one of us any closure to do so. She picked me up and I strapped Danielle into her car seat in the back of her car. We went over to a local clinic area that was connected to a dental office that Lilah was working in. My mom surprised me and said that Lilah was going to come to lunch with us. I hadn't seen Lilah since that terrible day in Court. I hadn't even spoken to her since that day. We had about thirty minutes to wait for Lilah to clock out for her lunch break. As we were sitting in the car waiting, my guilt and panic began to hit me all at once. When I spoke to my mom over the phone, it always showed its ugly face. Actually being in the same area as her intensified it beyond measure. My subconscious became confused when I was around my family. My family forced me to recall my life before Derrick, which was happy and content. I had made my choices and lifestyle that I was living become my new 'happy and content,' which was everything but happy and content. This confusion put me into panic. Coming down from the drug did the same. Since I was familiar with the clinic that was attached to the dentist office, I told my mom that I had to run in and see one of the nurse practitioners. I needed something to take this anxiety off of my shoulders. If I presented myself in this anxious manner when I went to see my Probation Officer, he would surely drug test me.

I went into the clinic and begged them to see me on the spot. I was in luck. They called me back within about fifteen minutes. The young doctor walked in and she was really nice. I explained to her that I was about to move to Texas, and I was having extreme anxiety. "Is everything going okay at home with your husband?" she asked, knowing all too well what my problem really was. "Yes! It's actually better than ever. I don't know what my problem is but I keep getting panic attacks. My heart is racing and I feel like I can't breathe." She put the meter on my pointer and measured my heart rate. It was extremely fast and she looked concerned. She wrote me a prescription for a drug similar to Valium, and gave me enough for my trip so I wouldn't be shorthanded while traveling.

We all went to lunch at a Thai restaurant, and I tried to eat as much as I could. Lilah put on her fake smile again, and I was surprised when she actually kissed Danielle on the forehead before we parted ways. My mom took me to the pharmacy to drop off my prescription. After pulling in my driveway, we said our goodbyes. Something was telling me that it wasn't going to be the last time I would see her before I left. I wasn't as worried about it as she seemed to be.

Lunch helped me to feel a little better, and after Danielle woke up from her nap, it was time to head over to Probation. I thought about just not going, or calling to reschedule, but I didn't want the stress of that hanging over my head when I knew that it would all be fine if I just went in. I packed up the baby and started driving down to the Probation Office. When I was called back, my officer started our meeting out with the usual hello, and how are you. Then he

407

began. "I spoke with the District Attorney about getting you off early, and at first they were completely against it. I had to do a lot of convincing, but finally got them to agree to let you go." "Awesome, thank you so much," I smiled, bouncing Danielle on my knee to keep her busy. "The only thing that they want to seal the deal is for you to submit a clean drug test."

Chapter 56

Panic struck me. It struck me hard. It was as if I was hit full force with defeat all over again. My body was rushing with adrenaline, my heart was pounding, and my face felt hot. I somehow hid my panic because he didn't have any look of concern on his face. He knew that my test would come back clean and it would all be just fine. As I was trying not to shake, I reached into my purse and pulled out the prescription I picked up before arriving. "Well, I was prescribed this and I don't know if it will have an impact, but maybe you might want to document it?" I asked, hoping that this detail could miraculously cancel out this unexpected test. He wrote down the prescription strength and said that it would not have an impact. A female officer, the same officer that took me into the jail last year, approached the office doorway and asked me if I was ready. She was stern, and not very friendly. She looked suspicious of me the entire time. My officer offered to watch Danielle while I did my test, but the second I set her down in the hopes that she would want to run and explore the hallways, she screamed her little head off. "Just bring her in and I'll hold her while you test," the female officer said. We went into the bathroom, I signed the label that would go over the urine sample, and handed Danielle to the unfamiliar woman. Danielle was hysterical. It wasn't difficult for me to pee because I had been drinking so much water. I knew that the sample was extremely diluted, but I still had a horrifying feeling that everything was about to plummet. Before walking through the exit door, my Probation Officer wished me luck and we said our goodbyes. It wasn't goodbye. I would be seeing him again very soon.

Once I was back on the road heading home, I was free to melt down. I was crying so hard I almost couldn't breathe. "I'm sorry baby. I'm so, so sorry," I cried as Danielle was innocently playing in her seat. I had failed her again, and after already being placed in three different homes in her short life, she was about to be placed somewhere else. I selfishly allowed myself to screw up in the worst way possible not even considering what kind of impact this could have on her. I was devastated. I felt so much pain, not for myself but for my baby. I was a loser. I would never know how to function as a productive person, and three children were suffering because of it. I chose drugs over my own flesh and blood. I chose to live selfishly over living as a responsible and loving mother. I chose to cave to my addiction and over making their safety a priority. I was a bad mom. I was ruining lives. I destroyed their childhood, ripping away any sense of belonging and security that they temporarily had. I deserved to sit in jail and suffer. They didn't deserve any pain.

Once I got home, Derrick was still working and had no idea what was going on. His phone battery must have died because I could not get a hold of him. I set Danielle down to play with her toys. I walked into my bedroom and shut the door. I screamed at the top of my lungs. I had to get it out and I didn't want to scare my baby in the process. I wanted to rip my hair out. I wanted to die. There was nothing left to do except wait for Derrick to come home. I sat on the couch and watched Danielle play with her toys on the living room floor. We only had one option to keep her out of the system. They would take her away from me forever this time. I couldn't handle the thought of that happening. That was

410

not an option. Derrick walked in from work that night. It was getting late. I had tears rolling down my face and he instantly knew what was going on.

"We have to go," I cried. "Fuck!" he yelled. "You gotta be kidding me," he said, on the verge of tears. That was that. We had to start driving. The only vehicle we had that could make the long drive was the truck he got from his brother. It was a two-seater, and I originally wasn't going to go because there was no room. But, if I didn't go, I would have to sit here alone, and wait for Probation to come and arrest me. I decided that I would sit on the center console. I wanted to say goodbye to my baby too.

It was late at night and we were on the road. We packed all of Danielle's important things, and the toys that we knew she liked the most. As we were driving Derrick called his parents. "I have bad news, and we're on our way right now. Elizabeth was sick last week and loaded up on Vicks and some other cough medicine. They gave her a drug test, and now we're worried that it will show a false positive," he said. After a short pause, he replied to his mother, "Ok, I'll keep you updated. We'll probably be in El Paso tomorrow around noon. We're not going to stop; we're driving straight through." He hung up the phone. "My parents are leaving right now and they're meeting us in El Paso, so we don't have to drive all the way through Texas." "That's really nice of them. If we went to their house I wouldn't want to go back to hell at all," I said.

Becoming a fugitive on the run was tempting. It made sense. But I just knew that I would prolong everything even more, and probably end up with a prison sentence if I did this. I felt as if I were living another nightmare, and couldn't understand why I was so stupid. I cried on and off for the entire drive. The anti-anxiety medication didn't seem to help at all. It took away my panic attacks, but it didn't take away the reality of my life, which is what I really wanted. We were in Los Angeles around three in the morning. My butt was sore from sitting on the center console in an awkward, curled up position, but I dealt with it. Danielle was sleeping for most of the time, but when she woke, she was happy and in a good mood. It was almost as if she knew that we were protecting her and making sure that she wasn't going to be stuck in a foster home. By the time we rolled into Phoenix, it was dawn. Derrick was close to nodding off, and we had to roll the windows down and turn up the music. I remember thinking about how beautiful this place was, and how I would love to escape here forever. We pulled into a rest area to clean up and change the baby. We tried to sleep, but we were just too overwhelmed and feeling like we needed to get to El Paso as soon as possible. Probation had probably not gotten my test back yet, but it was only a matter of hours. If we were going to be pulled over, it needed to happen after we dropped Danielle off. Around noon, we were speeding into El Paso, Texas. Ironically, Derrick's parents had arrived almost exactly when we did. We met them at a Denny's that was right off of the Interstate.

"Hi, hon," his mother said as she gave me a hug. "You look so skinny, Elizabeth," she noticed. "I know, it's because I was sick and couldn't really eat much, and now I am too stressed to eat," I replied. They never brought it up, but I wondered if they really knew what was going on. We had lunch, and I practically had to choke it down. When we finished eating, we walked out of the restaurant like zombies, and I approached our car to change Danielle and make sure she was comfortable. She was happy and smiling, and I didn't know how to hand her over. I picked her up off of the driver's seat she was laying on, and I hugged and kissed her smiling face, trying not to cry. Tears rolled down my cheeks as I fought to hide my pain. "I'll see you soon, sweet girl," I whispered as I hugged her tightly, not wanting to let go but having no choice. We held it together until we were on the road, this time without our baby. When we got on the freeway, we both silently cried and blankly stared ahead. There was nothing left to say or do, except return to our hell. Our hell that we had caused and could blame nothing for except our own selfish behavior.

414

Chapter 57

After stopping in Phoenix to rest in a motel room for about six hours and then hours and hours more of driving through the mountains in California, we finally made it home. It was the day after dropping Danielle off and nearing noon. We were both on the brink of delirium. The only thing we wanted to do once we walked inside was sleep. I had a feeling that the luxury would be short-lived. Derrick went straight to the bedroom and passed out. I got on my computer, which was facing the living room window in the front of the house. It couldn't have been more than five minutes after getting home when I saw a Probation Officer walking up the front yard. I rushed back to the bedroom to tell Derrick. "Wake up! Wake up!" I shook him as hard as I could. He wouldn't wake up. I was going to jail. I nervously approached my front door and opened it. A group of probably ten Probation Officers stormed into my home. My Probation Officer told me to sit down on my couch. The others asked if anyone else was in the house and I told them that Derrick was sleeping in the bedroom. They managed to wake him up and had him sit next to me on the couch.

"Where's Danielle?" A young, snooty Social Worker charged in with what looked like an intern. She was holding a clipboard and demanding to know where Danielle was. I let Derrick do the talking.

"She's on vacation with her grandparents. Sorry, but that's all you're gonna get outta me," he firmly said. "Elizabeth, your last drug test came back positive for methamphetamine. I need you to stand up and face the other way," my Probation Officer said. I did as he asked, and my rights were read to me. I wasn't surprised, and I had been expecting this to happen. I was hauled off to jail for the third time, and I was forced to sit there not knowing what was going on with the CPS. I was horrified that they were going to get Danielle. If they did, I would never see her again. At least with Derrick's parents, I could go to Texas to be with her once my Probation ended. And as of now, that wasn't going to be any time soon. I would have to finish out my remaining year and a half.

As I walked into the booking area of the jail with two Probation Officers escorting me, I sat down and began to cry out of guilt and embarrassment. The officers were asking me tons of questions and truly trying to figure out why I messed up so badly at the last minute. "I don't know...I...I just don't feel like I deserve anything good. With what happened with my other daughters, I just feel like the damage is done and I'll never be okay," I cried. I was borderline ugly crying. I could hardly talk. I looked at the Correctional Officer and begged her, "Can I please have my own cell. I don't want to be put in the same room as everyone." "Why honey?" she asked, surprisingly concerned. "Because I was here doing a meeting probably a month ago, and they're all going to think I am so pathetic," I sobbed. I was humiliated. I could already hear them laughing. Not to mention, I was PMSing extra bad, and I was totally sleep deprived. "Sweetie, they'll all be nice to you, and out of everyone, they'll understand your situation the best," she said, trying to make me feel better about it. It didn't, but it was nice of her to show that she cared. I sat in the holding cell and was called back to strip down and put my oranges on. I hated this place, but I did it to myself. Luckily, the female officer didn't make me bend over and cough. Ugh.

I went straight back to my cell, and luckily I was put in a single cell. I slept all the way until they called us out for dinner. At least this time I remembered to put my shoes on. I was used to this place. I knew what to expect. Once you spend even a night in jail, you never forget any small detail. A crowd of women gathered around me wanting to hear all of the gritty details. At first I was annoyed, but then one of them made a remark and I started cracking up. The way she said it just brought good humor to the ordeal. "When you first walked in, I turned over to Tory and was like, holy shit! The lady that did that meeting is here!" There was nothing funny about my situation, but imagining what they must have thought when seeing me walk in was pretty hilarious. I was a horrible example. But they were the first to forgive me.

My stay in jail was very difficult despite knowing what to expect from already having been here two times over. I knew that I would probably only have to serve thirty days, which would really only be three weeks with time docked off for good behavior. The part that was the most difficult was being unsure if the Social Workers were actually going to go all the way out to Texas to take my baby. I was only able to get updates once a day when I had my phone call. Derrick told me that they were trying to get Danielle, but as of current they had not. When I went to my bail review hearing, the District Attorney was there and I could tell that she was pissed. "Your Honor, Ms. Jeter is a clear danger to society, and more worrisome, her daughter conveniently ended up in Texas immediately after she gave us a dirty drug test. The Child Protective Services has exhausted every measure to get custody of the minor child. I made a call to the Center for Missing and Exploited Children, and there is nothing that they can do because we don't know where the child's physical location is," she ranted. I couldn't figure out why they were making my Probation violation more of a case involving

417

my daughter. I thought that criminal and custody were two separate cases. I'm pretty sure that they were all incredibly upset over this because they felt played. They probably thought that I was deceiving and using drugs the entire time, which really was not the case, but there was no point in trying to bring this up because they wouldn't believe me anyway.

I went back to the pumpkin patch only to wait for more news. A few days later, my Lawyer came to talk to me. "Now we all sat down and had a meeting over this. Everyone is dying to know why you did this when you were about to be let go. Were you using the entire time?" she sympathetically asked. "Now tell me the truth Elizabeth. I've always fought hard for you, and I'm asking that you really be honest with me." I told her the truth. I told her that it was a last minute mistake, and I didn't know why I did it. "Some of us think that it could have been a form of self-sabotage," she said. I started crying, again. "It probably was. After losing Chloe and Zoe, I just don't know how I'll ever recover," I sobbed. "I don't know what happened to this day, and it's so hard and confusing and it bothers me on a daily basis. A part of me feels like I'll never deserve anything good because I lost them." She nodded in compassion. "Well, I spoke with the Judge. She agreed to let you out of jail if you will be willing to sign over temporary custody of Danielle to the grandparents. Is that something you think you can do?" "Yes. I think it would be for the best. I'll do anything at all at this point, as long as it keeps her out of the system. I know that they'll take care of her and she'll be safe and happy, and I can just try to focus on getting off of Probation." We ended the visit and I felt better that I at least had a plan.

A few days went by and I still hadn't heard anything from my Lawyer. I felt like I was rotting in jail. I called Derrick that night after dinner. "Can you see if you can get your Public Defender to put the custody paperwork together and bring it in with a Notary?

418

I want to get these orders signed and put into place because I am terrified that they will find a way to take Danielle," I asked him. The very next day, he had the paperwork completed and I was called back to the visiting area to sign it for the Notary. The woman was nice and urged me to take my time reading through all of it before signing. I skimmed through it and couldn't sign it fast enough. The night before, I had received a letter from Derrick's mom. She had included some pictures of Danielle, who was sitting on her grandpa's lap and flinging ice chips at him. She looked really happy and very content.

Dear Elizabeth,

I hope you are hanging in there, hon. I am so sorry that you are having to deal with all of this especially after you worked so hard for the opposite to happen. I just want you to know that Danielle is safe and happy, and we are here to take care of her for as long as you kids' need us to. Remember, that if you decide to sign over custody, we know that YOU are her mother. Even if something ever happened between you and Derrick and you went separate ways (God forbid), we would never, ever keep her from you. This is all temporary, and we'll do whatever it takes to get you all here one day. We love you.

Love,
Mom

It was a weight off of my soldiers knowing that they weren't upset with me. At least we still had their support and knew that our daughter was in the best place she could be for the given situation we were in. I went to Court, and after spending exactly twenty-one days in jail, the Judge let me out. I had to report to Probation twice a week until my next hearing. The Judge made it clear that if I took off running, she would send me to prison. I was glad that I hadn't seriously considered doing that when we were driving Danielle to El Paso. Derrick picked me up, and I was so happy to see him. I practically jumped on him as I walked out of the exit door. He was on his lunch break from work, so he only had time to drop me off at home. As I was getting out of the truck, he gave me some unexpected news. "Oh, by the way, a guy that I work with, Mike has been crashing at our place during the week. He lives in Nevada City and he's just doing a temporary job for the company so I told him he could stay here since you were gone and all." "Uh…okay." I replied, not knowing who the hell this guy was or what I was about to walk in to. I leaned over to give Derrick a kiss and he drove off. When I walked in the house, it was a complete disaster. There were beer cans all over the place. There was a smelly dog I had never seen before. This was definitely not my home. A few seconds later, Mike popped out of the spare bedroom. "Elizabeth! I'm Mike! How are ya?" he asked as he headed my way, giving me a hug and patting me on the back. He reminded me of my Uncle Tony, and for this reason, I instantly liked him. "I'm actually packing my stuff up right now to give you your space back. I'm sure you both have a lot going on and I don't want to be in your way," he said. "You are welcome to stay if you need to, I don't mind!" I sincerely replied. He had already booked his motel room, so there was no convincing him. He left about twenty minutes later.

I didn't have much to do except clean my house. Derrick came home early and immediately started to help me clean. I thought it was really nice of him, and I was wondering if just maybe, after losing his own child, he would begin to understand how important it was to stay clean and appreciate things more. I'm not saying that I fully understood everything, but I did have an appreciation for the smaller things in life. I did know what I did not want for my life. I also knew that my addiction had control over me, and if any person used drugs around me, I would instantly relapse because I couldn't say no. I didn't think that Derrick fully understood that. How could he? He would never admit that something else had control over him.

After getting out of jail for the third time and experiencing a huge loss for the third time, my life had no direction and I definitely had no sense of purpose. Derrick and I were getting along probably better than we ever had. I thought about the fact that he was free to go to Texas whenever he wanted. He didn't have Probation forcing him to stay in the state. Despite all of the drama, he still stayed by my side. No other person stuck with me like he did. This caused me to attach to him significantly more than I had before, and I became extremely dependent. He was the only person that really understood me, and would never leave my side.

We resumed hanging out with the same group of people as we were before Danielle went to Texas. We didn't see a reason not to. We didn't have a reason to behave or think about our choices and actions. My meetings with Probation spread out to once every two weeks, and I could easily predict when I would have my next drug test. We spent a good amount of time over at Donnie's house. He was renting a room from another guy, but the guy was rarely there. Donnie probably chased him off. Eventually, the guy gave Donnie notice that he was moving out. Before I knew it, Donnie and his girlfriend, Casie, were hauling their things into our house. Derrick didn't even ask me if they could move in. He announced it. "Well, they can stay for maybe a week but that's it. I'm too OCD and they'll probably end up getting us in trouble," I firmly replied. "Check it out, I told my brother that he could stay. I'm not going to put a time limit on it. He has nowhere else to go." I was surprised that he was being so insistent on this. He normally couldn't stand to be around his brother for more than a few hours, and now he suddenly wanted him to live with us. I was not okay with this. As far as I knew, Donnie could be the one responsible for what happened to my daughter. I was sickened and could not bear the idea of being under the same roof as him. The only times I would tolerate it was when he had drugs. I used him for his drugs and pretended to like being in his company, and I thought it was the same for Derrick. He had an unhealthy sympathy for Donnie and I couldn't figure out why. Everything went even further downhill, and this was the point that my addiction took off full force.

Chapter 58

It was a Friday afternoon and Derrick had come home from work and fallen asleep. I was bored and feeling depressed more than ever. These days, our refrigerator was always stocked with beer, thanks to Donnie. Donnie and Casie were gone and probably selling a sack, so I decided to start drinking some beer. I popped open the top with my lighter and chugged about half of it. Within ten minutes, I was on to the next. Since I got out of jail this last time around, I had a constant feeling of depression. It wouldn't ever let up, and I was always feeling sad and worried. I thought that I knew what it meant to be depressed before, but I was wrong. This last mistake I made relapsing and losing my third child over it was enough to put me over the edge. I was young and resilient, but there is only so much emotional damage that a person can handle. I was broken, and this time, I had no hope to hold on to. I had nothing to look forward to, and my only purpose was to simply survive. I came to the conclusion that it was never going to end, and my life would forever consist of a bad series of events until I eventually died of a broken heart.

I was sipping on my third beer while sitting on the concrete stairs of my front porch and smoking a cigarette. I was waiting for Donnie and Casie to get back to see if we were going to get high for the weekend. Derrick was starting to become a little worn out from all the partying, but he wanted it. I tried to talk him out of letting Derrick and Casie move in, but he insisted. I made the best of the situation and eased my depression with meth as much as I could. After finishing my third beer, I sat on the couch. I noticed how oddly silent it was. Out of nowhere, the silence started to scare me. I began to feel extremely dizzy and disoriented. I couldn't figure out what was going on, and my heart started to pound. I couldn't breathe. I thought I was going to die. Gasping for air, I barely made it into the bedroom where Derrick was sleeping. "Derrick!" I managed to scream as I was shaking him and trying to wake him up. "Derrick! I can't breathe!" I cried as he lay still, snoring. I accepted the fact that he was not going to wake up, and I accepted the fact that I was going to die. I was dying. My life was about to end. I laid flat on my back on the foot of the bed. I closed my eyes and said a prayer. Our Father, in Heaven, hallow be thy name. Thy Kingdom come, thy will be done, on earth...

I opened my eyes, shaking and still feeling the rush of adrenaline. I was still alive. With tears rolling down my cheeks, I was thankful for that fact. But I was mostly sad. I was sad that I was convinced that I was dying, and Derrick did nothing to bring me comfort. This was when I needed it the most, and he offered me nothing. I thought back to the time when Danielle, Derrick and I were at the grocery store. I became dizzy, not knowing at that time that I was having a panic attack, and crouched down in the middle of the aisle. "Derrick, I feel like I'm about to faint. Don't leave. I just need a minute..." I begged him. He became furious. Gritting his teeth, he walked over to me pushing the cart with Danielle and the groceries. "Get the hell up," he quietly growled. "You look like a crazy idiot!" he condemned as he walked away. He left me in the middle of the grocery store to fend for myself. When we got to the parking lot, he told me that I was an embarrassment and needed to get my head together.

424

When the effects of the panic attack went away, I lifted myself off of the bed and walked into the living room. I was scared and feeling extremely helpless. I didn't know what to do, so I called my mom. I went outside and sat in the car so Derrick would not hear me. "Hi Lizzie" she answered. "I just had the worst panic attack of my life!" I broke down. I told her everything, including the part about me using drugs. I told her how Donnie and Casie had moved in, and it had been nothing but chaos. "I'm sorry Liz. I know you're suffering, but this is the life that you are letting yourself live. The only way that you're ever going to feel better is if you just leave, and you know that I am always here for you if you ever decide to do that. But you have to be sure," she said. She was right. There were many times that I called her wanting to leave only to change my mind in a matter of hours. When I did decide to leave, it had to be for good. My mom and step-dad taking me in wasn't something to take lightly. I'd probably only have one shot at that, and if I messed it up, I would really have no place to go. She told me that she loved to me and to call her back if the situation got worse.

When I went back inside, Derrick was awake and in the kitchen making dinner. He was in a good mood, and I was the complete opposite. I told him what happened, and he seemed more irritated than concerned. "You are such an ass hole!" I screamed at him, unable to hide my anger. "Whatever," he mumbled. I locked myself in the bedroom and got into bed. I cried again. I just wanted to fall asleep and forget about the last three years of my life. If they could be erased from my memory, I would maybe have a chance. A few minutes later, Derrick was tapping on the door. "Unlock the fucking door. Quit being dumb. Dinner is done." He said as he walked away. I wasn't in the mood to eat, and I certainly wasn't in the mood to be anywhere near him. He always claimed that he had my back, but where it counted the most, he failed miserably. Ten minutes later he was furiously banging on the door. "What the hell! I made us dinner and you're just going to sit in here all night!" he yelled. "I'm sorry if

I don't feel good! I am not in the mood to sit out there and pretend like things are okay. "They're not!" I screamed. I set him off into a serious rage. He kicked the door open, breaking it to the point of wood chips snapping to the floor. "You are such an ungrateful bitch!" he wailed. "After everything I do for you, this is what I get? FUCK YOU!" he yelled. I was scared at this point. He was mad to no return. I didn't yell back because I didn't want to make it worse. He was acting furiously unpredictable. He quickly paced into the kitchen and in just a few seconds returned with a hot frying pan that had a sizzling steak in it. "Here's your fucking dinner!" he loudly yelled. He grabbed the hot steak out of the frying pan with his bare hands. Before I could even comprehend what was happening, the steak flew past my face so closely that grease splattered on me. It hit the wall so hard that it made a loud bang. In shock, I sat in bed quietly, hoping that there wasn't more to come. When he left the bedroom and began eating his dinner, I quietly grabbed my purse and quickly bolted out the front door. I didn't know where I was going, but I knew that it was dangerous to be in the same house as him. I sat away from the front door, on the side of the front porch. I was shaking and scared as all hell. It was late, and really, I had nowhere to go. After sitting outside in the dark for almost an hour, Derrick came out to apologize. I knew that I would never forgive him for what he had done, but at least for the time being I could go back inside and think about what I was going to do. When I left for good, I was going to have to carefully plan my escape. If I wasn't discreet enough, I could end up leaving in a body bag instead.

The next day, I went to the local clinic. I knew that my depression had control over me, and I wasn't going to be able to tame it without help. I explained my symptoms to the male doctor who I had seen before. He wasn't very nice and he was very quick to Judge. "Look," he began. "Just because you come in here and tell me that you are not feeling well, doesn't mean

426

that I can automatically hand you prescription drugs." He was indirectly accusing me of trying to get drugs out of him for reasons other than what I really needed them for. I was desperate to feel better and I wasn't about to take his crap. "You don't understand what I am telling you. I've tried everything that I can think of to feel better without medication, and it's not working. No matter what I do, I am constantly sad and thinking about negative things and I have zero motivation to accomplish anything." I began crying and he could see the frustration in my face. He started to ask personal questions about my living situation, trying to figure out what the root cause was. I was forced to beat around the bush because I could not tell him the full situation. I was too humiliated and I just didn't want to talk about it. I only wanted to feel better. He prescribed me an antidepressant and an anti-anxiety medication. I began taking them right away because I knew that it could take up to two weeks for them to kick in.

When the medication did finally kick in, it definitely took away my depression, but it also acted as a numbing agent. Things didn't bother me as much as they did before, and I lived my day-to-day life on autopilot. I noticed a significant difference, mainly because the little things that would normally upset me had no impact on my mental stability. The first few days when I started taking the medication, I had another meltdown. Everyone living in my house was a complete slob, and they never cleaned up after themselves. After nicely asking Derrick to help me do the dishes and him blatantly refusing, I was at my wits end. I took every single dish in the house and smashed it on the kitchen floor. If there were no dishes to eat on, there couldn't be any messes. I ended up slicing my foot on one of the shards of glass, and I was gushing blood and didn't even notice it. When Donnie and Casie walked in from one of their drug deal missions, their mouths gaped open in shock. Derrick didn't react in his angry rage like he normally would have, probably because I even shocked him. I was going crazy. He even cleaned up the broken glass with his shop vacuum when my rage settled. I must have gotten my point across, because from that point forward, people went out of their way to clean up after themselves.

As the weeks moved on, I began to notice something strange about Casie. She was eating a lot for someone who was high on meth, and she was actually gaining weight. But she was only gaining weight in her abdomen. I wasn't sure if she even noticed it, because she wore shirts exposing her stomach on a daily basis. When one of my friends was over, I asked her to pay attention to my suspicion and tell me what she thought when Casie wasn't around. After bringing a bowl of soup to her bedroom, my thoughts were confirmed. "Oh my God! She is definitely pregnant!" Crystal said. I was baffled. How could she not know and us know, that she was pregnant. I had been pregnant enough times to know that she was about four or five months along.

Chapter 59

After pointing out my thoughts about Casie to Derrick, he started to become more aware of the environment that we were living in. He began paying attention to the horrible details. She was still getting high every day. We were high every chance that we had, but we didn't have a baby growing inside of us. Derrick asked Donnie if Casie was pregnant. He completely denied it. We concluded that because they had nowhere to go, we might as well start looking for another place to live. We were in a bad situation and mutually decided that we wanted to try to get our lives together. Casie had gotten a bad cold the following week and had her mom take her to the emergency room. When they came back home from the hospital, Casie was holding an ultra sound picture in her hand. "Apparently I'm pregnant," she announced with a look of curious hesitation on her face. I tried to act as if I was truly shocked, but it was pretty difficult to be surprised over the obvious. The following week, on a day that we knew they would both be out of the house, we packed our things and moved. We moved without telling them because they had made up their minds that we were going to support them and pay all of the bills. We found a small trailer across the highway. The only reason that I was okay with moving there was because it was brand new. No person had lived in this place before and it even had vaulted ceilings.

The place looked cozy and would definitely work out until we were able to leave. At this point we had exactly a year left. I was scared to get my hopes up, because I knew that a lot could happen in a year.

When Donnie got back to an empty house, he called Derrick and flipped out. We were pissed. Derrick held his ground, and before hanging up on him, pretty much told him to grow up. I was so happy in our new place. It was clean, and people-free - for the most part. A couple of months went by, and Donnie and Derrick started talking again. Donnie and Casie managed to get into their own house, which was just down the street from where our old house was. We went over to visit not knowing what to expect. The house was bigger than I expected, and it was definitely an older house. Casie was definitely looking pregnant. She seemed to be clean as well. Donnie was definitely not. All I had to do was look at him and it became obvious. I felt bad for Casie. I didn't know how she was able to deal with that.

We went over to their place to hang out on a regular basis. The group of junkies grew, too. It was pathetic seeing everyone, including myself, sitting in the living room for hours on end, just in case Donnie might return with a sack. Usually he did, but sometimes he didn't. Using crystal meth had become a way of life. It became normal to us again. Nothing positive or productive ever resulted from using it. The guys would spend hours, and sometimes days on end, working on a vehicle that wasn't even broken in the first place. Both Casie and I did crossword puzzles. Although she was sober, I could tell that she was struggling.

This time in my life that I had more than one encounter where I thought I would die. The three of us, Donnie, myself and Derrick, were all coming down after days of no sleep. Marney had been our supplier lately. She was Donnie's ex. She eventually moved in with them. I thought it was kind of odd, but her and Casie got along like best friends would. Marney was working,

Casie was extremely pregnant and sleeping a lot, and Donnie and Derrick were working on the same vehicle that they began to work on over two weeks ago. I was really tired and wanted to go home. I asked Derrick about five times to take me home and he was completely ignoring me. Finally I grabbed my purse, walked passed him, and said, "I'm going to be waiting in the car, I'm ready to go home." "Alright. It's gonna be a while though," he replied. After patiently waiting for ten minutes, I got frustrated and honked the horn. It pissed both of the brothers off. They were on the verge of paranoia, because they were coming down and it was a side effect. "Control your bitch," Donnie said to Derrick. "Excuse me!" I retaliated. "Hey! Sit there like the bitch you are, and I'll take you home when I'm ready, dammit!" I was so infuriated that Derrick had not stuck up for me, but he was siding with his brother!

Without thinking about my safety and the probable precautions, I decided that I was going to honk the horn until Derrick got into the truck and took me home. I was extremely upset and I felt like they were ganging up on me, and calling me derogatory names did not help anything. It was only adding fuel to my fire. When Derrick realized that I wasn't going to stop honking the horn, he turned to his brother and said, "I'll be right back bro," as he angrily paced to the truck. He started yelling and screaming at me the second that he got in. "Bitch, you want to go for a ride?" he laughed in an eerie way, and I knew that he had some sort of idea. As he backed out of the driveway, he was burning rubber. He was driving psychotically and I was definitely scared. The moment that I knew I was in danger was when he turned the opposite way on the highway from where we lived. "Where do you think we're going?" he laughed. "I don't know Derrick, but I just wanted to go home and you were ignoring me. I don't feel good and I didn't think that it was unreasonable to ask you to take me home when I have been waiting for hours." "Too late now, bitch. I'm gonna take you on a fucking ride, bury you in the dirt, and maybe I'll even dismember you after I kill you." He laughed.

His laugh was pure evil. I knew that there was something seriously wrong happening, because his laughter seemed genuine. No sane person would laugh after threatening to murder someone. No sane person would threaten to murder someone in the first place. As we began to drive through a suburban neighborhood, which was leading to a four-wheeling trail that I was familiar with, I knew that I needed to somehow bring attention to myself, in case I didn't come back. If I suddenly went missing, at least I could maybe have a witness to get this psychopath locked away. I saw a woman standing in front of her house, watering her yard. I rolled down the window and screamed "CALL NINE-ONE-ONE!" Derrick laughed even more. "You are so fucking pathetic," he cackled. He was getting joy from my fear. The woman looked up and smiled at me. You have got to be kidding! I'm probably going to die in a few minutes, and all I get from a bystander is a damn smile? It was just my luck.

Derrick sped through the bumpy trial, catching air a few times. I made sure that my seatbelt was tight around my waist, and I firmly gripped onto the overhead bar. I hadn't seen Derrick laugh so much...ever. When we got to the peak of the mountain, overlooking the airport and the huge green forest, He stopped the truck. He turned it off and looked at me. "You know, if I wanted to, I could kill you right now, and no one would ever know. No one would even report it was you because no one likes you. YOU'RE A FUCKING LOW-LIFE!" he yelled. I sat in my seat silently, looking straight ahead, with tears rolling down my face. I did not respond to Derrick because I wanted to decrease my odds of being slaughtered. He stopped talking and just sat there for about ten minutes. We sat in silence. He started the truck and began down the mountain. The ride home was silent, and he dropped me off at home. Luckily, he went back to his brother's house.

432

I called my mom crying again. She had to be getting tired and stressed out from all of these horrific stories. She said what she could to comfort me, but I knew that as long as I was with Derrick, I would never really be safe. That night, Derrick came home acting as if nothing even happened in the first place. I still didn't know how I should react to him, because he had been becoming more and more unpredictable. He sat in the office while I laid on the couch blankly staring at the TV. "Elizabeth, come here," he demanded. I went into the office to see what he wanted. "You wanna smoke some shit?" he asked. I had heard that phrase come out of his mouth more times than I could count. It was his way of saying I know you don't really want to get high, and I know you don't want to live the life of a drug addict, but I know that if I ask you, you can't say no. It was almost as if it was his way of justifying his own use. As long as he had the green light from me, it was my fault that we were addicted to meth. And of course, I couldn't say no. My body and my mind were trained to instantly accept this evil substance. It lied to me when it always told me that it would make me feel better.

The next morning, I read the newspaper online with my coffee as I always had when I woke up. On the front page was a picture of a young man who went to the same school as I did. His name looked familiar, so I clicked on the article. This brave man was killed in Iraq. He was a native to Tahoe, and he was also the brother of a girl whom I had become acquainted with over the years. She was on the same cheerleading team as Merri and I, and she also worked at the daycare that Chloe, Zoe and Danielle attended. My heart was breaking for her and her family.

Derrick and I took a drive into town to get breakfast and then continue our binge at Donnie and Casie's house after. The radio was on one of our favorite country stations, and a song started to play that instantly reminded me of the soldier that was killed, and what his family must be going through. This is just a dream... the song went on. I got dizzy and started feeling sick. I reached into my purse to swallow what was left of my last anti-anxiety pill. Derrick knew that when I reached for those pills, I was in distress. He was surprisingly compassionate, but he didn't ask me why I was having a panic attack. I didn't tell him either. I was feeling incredibly guilty and selfish. Soldiers were fighting in a war overseas in a totally foreign and dangerous place while I was wallowing in self-pity and getting high every minute that I had the chance. Soldiers like the one in the paper were losing their young lives to keep a low life like myself safe and free. My morals, values and everything I once held a firm grip on were gone. They had faded away and I hadn't even stopped to notice it. I thought about the grieving family and prayed for them every day for the next month. I wanted God to know that I still cared, and a part of my true self was still in me, begging to come out. I prayed and asked God for his help to just get me out of the situation, no matter what it would take. Although my prayers weren't immediately answered, God gave me plenty of warnings and chances to run away. I had them all along.

Chapter 60

The days went by, the pain lingered, and nothing changed for the better. Moving out of our home to get away from Donnie was only a temporary fix. In a sense, it probably heightened our drug use simply because we were able to go home at the end of the day and leave when he started getting crazy. Excitement was building around Casie's pregnancy though. I put together a baby shower for her, and I got to meet her family. They were all nice, and definitely seemed like they were clean. Casie had two younger sisters. I started to see them more regularly as everyone was stopping by their house to see how Casie was doing. Eventually, it felt like they were a second family. Casie's mom always seemed to stay positive and have a good attitude about things. It was refreshing to be around her. She was unaware of the drug use that was going on, and we were all pretty good at hiding it. On a cold October night, a few hours after Derrick and I had returned home, the phone rang. It was Marney. "Hey, what's up?" I asked. "Oh nothing much. Just watching preggers here stand over the toilet and wondering why she can't stop peeing on herself." I laughed, "Really? I'm so excited! Is she getting contractions yet?" I asked. "Yeah, she's getting a few. But she wanted me to call you to tell you what was going on. We're waiting for her mom to get here to take her to the hospital." I told Marney that I would be there first thing in the morning, but to call me if she started progressing super-fast.

Casie and I spent a lot of time together over the last months. It was her first pregnancy, and she always had questions to ask me, knowing that I would probably have some helpful advice. My respect for her grew over this simple fact. She was paying attention to her pregnancy, and I thought that it was a good sign. Her maternal instincts were kicking in, and with the chaos that was always happening in that house, I thought that they should probably be in overdrive. Derrick and I had discussions about how Donnie would be as a father. There were rumors of him abusing Marney's children, and we knew that he had a violent temper when he was coming down from meth. His violent temper mixed with his delusions, which were happening more and more, was a very dangerous combination. I did some research on mood disorders to see if I could find out what was wrong with him. He was progressing into insanity more and more each day. I came to the conclusion that he was either bipolar, which became worse with the use of drugs, or he had meth-induced psychosis. Whatever it was, it was scary.

The next morning I woke up hours before usual eager to get to the hospital to see how Casie was doing and if she had the baby yet. Derrick had to work, so he had to drop me off early at the hospital. I tried to tame my excitement when I walked into the hospital room. Casie wasn't happy, which was a good sign! It meant that she would hopefully have this baby sooner than later. Her entire family was there, and we all quietly kept each other occupied. I was surprised to see that Donnie seemed to be calm and collected. He stayed that way for most of the time. I thought that perhaps he might have been sober. The baby wasn't born until later that night. When it was time for her to push, Casie's cries from the pain gave me flashbacks, and I had some anxiety over it. I thought I could handle it just fine, but because I remembered exactly what she was feeling, it freaked me out. Her mom and Donnie were the only ones allowed in the delivery room. I was glad, because I was on the verge of fainting. Her sisters and I were curious to know what was happening. We came up with a sneaky idea to go outside and around the hospital to the window of the room she was in. "Holy crap!" I whispered. "I can't believe the window is open and the curtains aren't shut!" I exclaimed. We sat on the grass, leaning against the wall of the hospital building. We were too scared to look, plus it just made us feel like creepers. So we listened. In only about thirty minutes, we heard a few cries of pain and suddenly, a squeaky cry. The baby had made it safely into this world and it was a boy! Casie's sister had a tear streaming down her cheek and of course it caused a chain reaction. There was nothing more beautiful than the birth of a new life. The sound of this baby crying was so sweet and innocent, and I prayed that he would be safe and taken care of. I vowed to myself that I was going to be there for Casie as much as she needed me, and maybe I could, in some way, give back support and help protect him.

Derrick arrived at the hospital when the nurses were cleaning the baby up in the nursery. We were standing in the entrance doting and snapping hundreds of pictures. I stepped in a little further after the nurse told us it was okay to go in. I saw the same rocking chair that I sat in not too long ago, holding my own newborn baby, and grieving over her being torn from me. It all came back, abruptly and vividly. I was having a flashback. The nurse looked at me, and I think she could sense that something wasn't right. My eyes were watery, but I held my tears in. "You can come in further to see him, if you want," she softly offered. "Oh it's okay, I don't want to be in the way," I smiled in response. "Are you sure?" she asked again, concerned. "Yes, I'll get to see him plenty when he goes home, and I think my fiancé is here to take me home anyway," I said, as I backed out of the room. I was flooded with emotions.

I was sad and missing Danielle, and I was angry and jealous that Donnie and Casie were getting to take their baby home. At least Derrick and I had both been sober and truly wanted to stay that way. Why is the system so backwards? I asked myself, trying to find some sort of answer. I went back to the hospital room to say goodbye to Casie, but she was still being taken care of by the doctor. Derrick approached me, after he took a quick glance at the new baby. "So why the hell have you been talking to other dudes?" he quietly growled under his breath. I honestly had no idea what he was talking about. I tried to blow it off, but he kept pushing me and pushing me. "Can I just have a ride home, please?" I asked, trying to avoid a repeat life-threatening situation. "You can fuckin' walk!" he casually said. It was probably less than twenty degrees outside. I was wearing close-toed heels, which would probably cause me to slip and fall. I did not want to have to walk home. He wasn't letting up with this accusation though, and he was beginning to get loud about it in the attempt to humiliate me. It was getting late, and I was tired and emotionally exhausted. I gave in and started walking home. I was freezing, but I walked as fast as I could to heat my body temperature up. I heard screeching tires behind me, and I quickly veered to the side of the road. It was sounding like I was about to be run over. Derrick pulled up next to me "Hey! Get in," he yelled. "I'm not going anywhere with you!" I cried, wiping the tears from my face before they froze to it. I wanted him to actually act like he wanted to take care of me. I wanted him to at least pretend that he was sorry. He did none of that.

"Have fun walking then," he said as he sped off. I couldn't figure out what was going on. I knew for a fact that I had not been talking to any other man at all. I couldn't figure out where this idea came from and I didn't even know what I did to deserve the torture. It wasn't until later that I realized that he was probably acting this way because he was also grieving over the loss of our own daughter, and wondering why his brother was able to keep his child. Either way, the baby was adorable and we loved him regardless. We may have had some jealousy issues, but they were no one else's fault but our own. When I finally got home, I was surprised that Derrick hadn't even arrived yet. He's probably out getting high with his brother as a way to celebrate the new baby, I thought. I took off my jacket and I turned up the heater. I put my pajamas on and began to get ready for bed. Derrick came home, and he still had his cocky attitude. I was sick of it and I didn't deserve it. "What the hell is your problem?" I screamed at the top of my lungs. "I haven't done anything wrong to you at all, and on a day when you know that I'm sad and emotional, you go out of your way to talk a bunch of shit that doesn't even make sense." I yelled even louder. He was already amped up for some reason, and raising my voice was the worst mistake that I could have made at the moment. I was standing in the kitchen with my arms in the air staring him in the eyes. I saw red, burning fury. My intuition told me to run.

I bolted down the hallway as he was gripping the orange clay pot that held up an indoor tree; the tree had become all I had left to love and nurture. When I witnessed him angrily tear it out of the pot, the strong bamboo roots not standing a chance, I felt the fear of death pumping through my veins. Knowing my life depended on it, I leaped into the bathroom as I heard the whoosh of the heavy pot racing past my head. The loud shatter and storm of soil brought a gasp to my soul. Locking the door behind me, I knew that if he wanted me dead, this frail trailer door would not save me. I opened the blinds to the tiny window above the toilet, hoping that my older neighbor might be home to hear my screams. Silence overcame the weak trailer walls. The only sound I could recognize was the fast beat of my broken and empty heart. An overwhelming desire to surrender my life exhausted me, as I opened the door and fearlessly walked into the hallway. Pale, with clenched fists, he was eerily silent. The gaze of Satan on his face pierced my conscious awareness of where I was and who I had become.

I avoided his eyes all together, hoping it wouldn't encourage any more violence. I was shaking as my hands reached for my purse. It was only a few feet away from him. I needed my anti-anxiety pills. I felt panic raging through my body, and I wanted to nip it before it got out of control, and pissed Derrick off even more. As I pulled the medication bottle out of my purse, he suddenly and fiercely slapped the bottle straight out of my hand. It fell to the floor. I couldn't bend down to get it, because it would put me in a vulnerable position and he could easily knock me out. He snatched the bottle up, opened the lid, and walked into the hallway where the pile of dirt and broken clay was resting. He dumped all of the contents of the bottle into the dirt. "Derrick! Stop! I need those and you know that!" I screamed, in tears and begging him to have some sort of compassion. "Fuck you, and your pills!" he roared, as he began smashing them into the dirt and grinding them with his shoe. I couldn't believe that he had gone to this extent when I hadn't done anything wrong in the first place. When he was finished crushing up the only thing that took away my anxiety, which was mostly caused by him, he left the house. I sat on the floor in the pile of dirt, with it splattered all over my pajamas and face from his attempt to kill me with the pot, sobbing and trying to recover any pieces of my relief that I could. I felt just as filthy on the inside as I was on the outside. He showed me first-hand that I was nothing but dirt.

Chapter 61

The very next day after this fight, we sat down and had a talk. It was calm, and it was civil. He was the one that initiated the conversation. He must have woke up and felt bad about the night before. I slept on the couch, and being my stubborn self, I was not going to be the one to do any ass kissing. He opened up to me and told me that last night was extremely hard for him as well. He said that he was pissed off because his brother is such a screw-up, and did nothing to deserve the baby, but still got to take him home. Although I was still sickened by him, I shook my head in agreement and I was glad that he was at least talking about it. I told him that I felt the same way, and the way he treated me last night hurt my feelings even more and caused me to lose trust for him. "I want to be able to trust you Derrick. You are all that I have right now, and if I can't trust you, then I can't trust anyone. You make it hard when you suddenly accuse me of things when I do nothing to deserve that. Of course I'm gonna get mad and start yelling, you would do the same thing." "Listen. I feel really bad about what I did, and I know that there is no excuse for it. All I can do is apologize and try to work on my temper." I thought that it was a half ass apology, but I didn't really have anywhere to go, so I sort of had to accept it.

We got dressed and went to Donnie and Casie's house to visit the baby. Everything seemed like it was pretty stable over there for the first time ever. It just seemed like they were two happy parents, and the baby was content and sleeping. We passed him around, and left to go get dinner. On the way to one of our favorite restaurants at the casino on the very top floor, Derrick unexpectedly brought something up. "So, when are we getting married? Is that still even happening?" He laughed, only halfway serious. "I don't know. Do you still want to marry me?" "I don't know, you're pretty," he said, raising one eyebrow and giving me a grin." I sighed, "Okay, so that means yes." I gave him my snotty look that I knew he secretly loved. "Why don't we stop at that chapel that's on the highway that they just put in place of that old tax office?" I asked him. For future reference, I am curious to see how much it would cost to get married. I also thought it would be something fun to do before we went to eat. We pulled into the parking lot of the tiny chapel and rang the doorbell. A short, chubby woman opened the door and she was extremely bubbly and chipper. She invited us in and asked us if we were ready to get married. "Well, I don't know about right now, but we did want to find out what the fees are," Derrick said. I sarcastically made a comment in response to Derrick's comment. "Now, we're just friends, but we thought it would be interesting to come to a chapel and find out all there is to know about getting married." The woman laughed, and I think I kind of confused her. She showed us where the ceremony takes place, and she went over the fees with us, which weren't as high as we expected. Derrick had just gotten paid, so we were actually entertaining the idea. We thanked the woman for the tour and went to our dinner.

While we were eating, we talked about it further. "So, do you just want to go get married tomorrow?" he asked me. He was getting more serious about it, and I had been bugging him about it pretty much since we got together. I wasn't jumping for joy, but I thought that maybe it would help our relationship, and it would be good for our daughter to know that we loved each other. "Let's just go for the marriage license tonight, and then we can think about it." We went back to the chapel that was open 24 hours, and the woman became really excited thinking that we had returned to get married. "Not just yet, but we did want to go ahead and get the marriage license. That way when we do decide to tie the knot, we will at least have some of the paperwork out-of-the-way." As we were filling out the paperwork and providing our driver's licenses to the woman, we both became a little impulsive and just decided to pay for our wedding, which would be the next day. As we were sitting at her office desk, I shamelessly looked at Derrick. "We might as well just prepay for it now, because if we don't do that, we are never going to end up getting married." He shrugged his shoulders, with a look on his face that indicated he knew I was probably right. We paid almost $300 and knew that because it was such a good chunk of money, we were going to have to go back the next day and actually follow through. I had nothing to wear, so we figured that we would go to one of the department stores down the highway before we left for the chapel in the morning. I didn't want to get super fancy, but I at least wanted to look nice for pictures.

I had a very difficult time falling asleep that night. My mind was racing and I didn't know if it was from excitement or total, complete fear. We woke up early the next day because our wedding was scheduled for noon. We needed enough time to find something to wear and break the news to Donnie and Casie. While I was taking a shower and getting ready, Derrick said he was going to go down to the store to find something to wear. "Since we are running short on time, can you look and see if there are any cute white dresses for me? It doesn't have to be fancy, but I definitely want it to be nice." "Yeah, I'll look and call you when I find something." Derrick came back after what felt like only about 15 minutes. I thought that he probably didn't have any luck finding me a dress because he had been so quick to return. He had two bags in his hands, and with a look of curiosity on my face, I asked him if he found what we needed. He pulled out a white dress for me, and I was completely surprised because it looked exactly how I had envisioned it to be and it ended up fitting me perfect.

When we were all dressed and ready to go, Derrick called Donnie to see if he wanted to go along. Donnie was still sleeping but Casie was awake and said that she wanted to be there. We decided to just show up in our wedding attire, and woke Donnie up. He walked into the living room all groggy and confused. It was kind of funny. "Whoa, what are you guys doing? Are we getting married today, or something?" "Yep, do I look adorable?" Casie, laughed. "You look beautiful!" I did feel pretty that day. I had my hair down, and it was long and the ends were curled. I hadn't been dressed up for anything in a very long time. Casie's mom and sister showed up just a few minutes after we got to their house. They were just as excited as the rest of us, and I gladly invited them to come along as well. I wanted to get a lot of pictures, and on top of it, I thought it would be a blessing if we at least had some people there. The closer it got to noon, the more nervous I got. I pulled one of my dirt infested anti-anxiety pills out of my purse and chewed it up. I couldn't tell if it was a normal case of nervousness, which most brides had before their wedding, or if it was because my subconscious was yelling and screaming and kicking and trying to tell me something. It didn't matter, it was going to happen, and I ignored my fears.

After the baby was dressed and ready to go our wedding guests followed us less than a mile down the street to the chapel. We walked in and I was worried that I was going to faint. The lady that was going to do the ceremony kind of made a big deal out of it - bigger than I really wanted. She actually made me walk down the tiny little three-foot aisle. She played really cheesy classical music on a tiny little radio, and I honestly just wanted to

444

die because I was so mortified. I hated that everyone was staring at me, and I was rethinking my excitement over inviting everyone. I would've been thrilled to have a brown paper bag placed over my head. When my long and enduring walk down the aisle was finished, I stood in front of the efficient and Derrick was right next to me. She had us grab each other's hands. I don't remember exactly what she said, but it felt like she went on forever, and I just wanted her to shut up. I was shaking, and it was not going away. In fact, it was actually getting worse the closer I got to saying I do. After what felt like an eternity of awkward torture, we both finally got it over with. We kissed and we were done. We stayed in the chapel for a few minutes to get pictures, and I made sure that we got pictures with the new baby. I was sad that it wasn't our daughter that we were holding in those pictures, but I still was happy that the baby was there. That was it - we finally got it over with and were married. I never asked him, but I'm pretty sure that Derrick was feeling the same way. We just weren't very publicly affectionate people, and it was more of a pain than anything, but we felt like it was the right thing to do.

After it was official, we went home to change into more comfortable clothes and packed an overnight bag. We were going to get a suite in the casino and spend our honeymoon having fun at the poker table. Derrick hardly ever drank alcohol, and any time I did, he got extremely annoyed. He made an exception for tonight. Before we got to the casino and checked into our room, we stopped at the liquor store and got a couple of bottles of Jack Daniels. When we walked up to the concierge desk, we told the receptionist that we had just gotten married and it was our honeymoon. We had a suspicion that if we told them that we were there for a special occasion, we might get a discount on our room. The man behind the desk began to check us in, and with a grin on his face, he handed us a special card and said, "You can thank me when you check out. I'll want to hear how your stay was." I didn't know what we were going to be walking into, but I knew it was going to be awesome. It was even better than I imagined it to be when we opened the door. We walked into the bright room with Roman style couches and vaulted ceilings. We had a huge Jacuzzi, the bed was awesome, and the view was probably the best view that the entire casino could offer. We were on the very top floor, and looking out the window was truly breathtaking. Our room was overlooking the entire Lake surrounded by green forest. We invited Donnie and Casie along with her mom and sister to come say hi if they wanted to. It was still early in the day, and we probably wouldn't head down to gamble for a few hours. They stopped by and instantly understood why we were so eager to show off our room. They stayed for probably an hour, and I held the baby most of the time. He was so tiny and sweet, and he was so content when he was sleeping. From what I could tell he didn't really cry very much. The time that I noticed he cried was only when he wasn't being held. He was a little cuddle bug and I felt like I could hold him forever. It made me miss my own baby, and it made me sad that I had to miss out on those precious times with her. I snapped probably one hundred pictures of him in that hour and kissed him goodbye when they left.

After grabbing something to eat at one of the restaurants in the casino, we headed back up the stairs to get ready for some black jack. Because Derrick hadn't had anything to drink in such a long time, he didn't remember that his tolerance level was low. He got drunk pretty quick, and I had to convince him to take me down to gamble. He didn't put up much of a fight like he usually would, because he knew that it was something I really wanted to do. And after all, it was our wedding night. We stayed downstairs until about three or four in the morning. We had a blast at the blackjack table and our luck was high. We walked away with over $400. Our entire wedding had already been paid for in our winnings. We sat with some really nice people, and I think one of them might have been a man I should have recognized, but I was just too much of an 88 to know who he was. The other people at the table were looking at me like I was a total moron for not knowing who this guy was, but it wasn't my fault that I was too young! When we left the casino the next day, we both agreed that we had an amazing time. We knew that it was one of those nights that we would never forget.

Chapter 62

When I got the courage to tell my family that I had married Derrick, I was surprised and also relieved that they went out of their way to congratulate me. They were showing their support for me the best way that they could, even if they didn't want to.

The binges quickly resumed, and it wasn't long before Casie fell back into it as well. At this point, it took a lot to get me high, and it almost seemed like I needed it just to feel normal. We mostly hung out over at Donnie's and Casie's house because it was easier for them since they had the new baby. Donnie was beginning to lose his temper even though the baby was only a couple weeks old. When the baby would cry, he would yell at him. Derrick tried to step in and say something to Donnie, but it didn't have any impact. Donnie was high and back to his meth-induced psychosis type behavior. When Casie was at the store with her mom, and she had left the baby in Donnie's care, and there were a few times that I almost couldn't handle the circumstances that he would put his baby in. He was revving up a remote control car inside the house, and it actually had fumes blowing out of it. The baby was only 2 feet away. Right away, I went and picked the baby up hoping that I wouldn't upset Donnie. Luckily I didn't, and he seemed like he was more relieved that I was tending to his baby. Another time, the baby had a dirty diaper. I told

Derrick, and I offered to change him, but Derrick insisted that his brother change him. "It's his son, he needs to learn how to do things like this." Donnie was very rough with his baby. There was nothing calm, or gentle about the way that he handled him. It upset me and gave me pretty bad anxiety.

When Casie got back from the store, we sat on the couch and talked for hours while the guys were working on electrical stuff. The little baby was fussy and he seemed like he had a tummy ache. I could tell Casie was tired, and she was overwhelmed and didn't know what to do. I offered to hold the baby, and she gladly handed him over. I put him on his tummy, on my knees, and rocked him back and forth. He fell asleep within just a few minutes. Casie asked me questions about what to do if this happens, or what not to do if that happens. I gave her the best advice that I could, and I knew that she was paying attention. My main fear was that she trusted Donnie, naturally, because he was the baby's father. I didn't know how to tell her that he was scaring me without it offending her.

Later that night after the guys had come inside, the baby woke up again and was crying. The second that Casie handed the baby to Donnie he baby started screaming even louder and more intensely. It was almost as if the baby was afraid of his own father, even though he was only a newborn and most would think that a newborn wouldn't know the difference. Donnie began throwing the baby in the air as if he were a father playfully tossing his toddler in the air. The baby's head was bouncing back and forth because he had no control over his muscles in his neck yet. "Bro, you don't do that with a newborn baby. You're gonna end up breaking his neck. He just wants to be held still and in a calm environment." Derrick tried his best to intervene, but Donnie wasn't trying to hear any of it. "No, he's just fine. I don't know how else to make him shut up." I saw the look of fear and rage come over Derrick's face and he looked my way. "Let's get out of here." We left right then, without even saying goodbye.

When we got home, as I was folding laundry I was trying to think of a way that I could anonymously make a report. I always thought that I would never wish the CPS on my worst enemy, but this was a case that would be warranted. I wondered if Lilah would be willing to make a report for me. Lilah hates me, what am I thinking. Derrick and I talked about what we had witnessed. "I can tell you this right now, we are not going over there anymore. I'm sick of getting high all the time, and that baby is going to end up dead. I want nothing to do with it." "Neither do I, that's the last thing that we need right now. But imagine how you would feel if something actually did happen to the baby and we could have prevented it." He nodded his head in agreement, but he still didn't know what to do. I had decided in my mind that the next time I spoke with one of my friends, I would see if I could get them to make an anonymous report for me. That way I wouldn't feel like I was in the middle of it.

Derrick stayed true to his word, and we did not return to their house. I could tell that he was getting tired of the self-destruction, and he had an overwhelming sense of fear for his nephew but simply didn't know how to go about it. We were starting to get along again, and it was probably because we had been sober for a few days. We talked about our daughter, and our plans to move to Texas, and how nice it was going to be to finally get away from the chaos. This time around, every single inch of me wanted to leave this town. It had become dark and unpredictable. It felt lonely, and every time I left the house to go out in public, I had a severe panic attack. It turned into agoraphobia. Besides the times that we went over to Derrick and Casie's house and the occasional dinner outing, I did not leave the house. I thought it was better to just avoid the panic situation altogether.

On our third day after we left Donnie and Casie's house, Derrick got up early to go to work, and I decided to sleep in. A few hours

451

after he left, I was woken up from the blaring sound of sirens that were speeding down the highway directly in front of our house. I tried to fall back asleep thinking that they would fade away, but they kept going on and on and on. It was a solid five minutes of sirens, and they were loudly screaming in my ear. When they finally faded, I rolled back to my side and tried to go back to sleep. It was probably around 10:00 in the morning. Normally sirens don't really grab my attention as much as these did. I just thought it was strange that they had lasted for so long. About five minutes after the sirens faded, I was almost back to sleep when the phone rang. I had caller ID, and I didn't know who was calling, so I let it go to the message machine. I was sleeping upstairs, and I heard the muffled sound of the machine below me. It was a woman's voice, but I wasn't sure exactly who it was. It sounded like it might be important, so I picked up the phone while the person was leaving their message. "Hello?" I tried to sound more alert than I really was. "Elizabeth! It's Casie's mom!" She sounded frantic. I could barely make out what she was saying. "I'm on the way to the hospital…he…he's not breathing!"

Chapter 63

"Wait, try to breathe," I said, trying to make sense of what I was hearing. "Who isn't breathing?" I asked, praying that I had heard her wrong. "The baby! He's not breathing!" she screamed in terror. "WHAT? Is he okay? Where is he?" I panicked. "He's in the ambulance on the way to the hospital right now. I'm following the ambulance. I don't know what's going on! When Casie called me and said he wasn't breathing, I rushed over to her house, and the ambulance was putting him in the back!" "Oh my God. I'll be at the hospital in a few minutes, okay?" "Okay, HURRY!"

I hung up the phone, unsure of how I was going to get to the hospital. Derrick was at work, and I knew that if he knew what was going on, he would have been driving back here like a maniac. I called one of my friends to see if she would give me a ride to the hospital. She arrived about five minutes later. I paced back and forth wondering what I was supposed to say to Derrick. Just as she was approaching my front sliding door, the phone rang again. It had been about fifteen minutes since I spoke with Casie's mom. I recognized the number. I hesitantly answered the call. "Hello?" "Elizabeth, it's Casie's sister." The sixteen-year-old girl was sniffling. "Is the baby okay?" I begged. "My…m…mom says to tell you that baby Donnie is no longer with us." She broke down in hysterics. "Oh my God.

I'm...so sorry. I am on my way okay? Tell your mom that I will be there as soon as I can." I hung up the phone. A part of me knew that this was coming. From the moment I was able to understand what Casie's mom was saying, my gut was telling me that the baby was not going to be with us anymore. "

What's wrong babe?" Crystal asked as she saw the look of despair on my face. I walked outside on the deck where she was standing, holding her keychain. "He's dead. The baby died." I said in an emotionless tone. She was speechless for the first few moments. Not knowing what to do, I kicked the glass sliding door as hard as I could, hoping that it would shatter. It didn't. I cried and Crystal gave me a hug. Derrick needed to hurry up and get home. I couldn't get a hold of him, and I thought that maybe his cell phone had died. The only other thing that I knew to do was call his boss. I told her what was going on, and she said that she was going to send him home, but she'd tell him that I wasn't feeling good and I needed a ride to the doctor. That way, he wouldn't end up driving like a maniac and end up hurting himself or someone else on the way. When he pulled into the driveway, he was in a perfectly happy mood. There was no nice way to break the news, so I just said it as calmly and straightforward as I could. "I have really, really horrible news." "What?" He looked totally confused, and probably thought that I was sick. "It's the baby."

That was all that I had to say. He knew that the baby was gone. He calmly turned around, facing the bed of his truck. I was happy that Crystal was with me because I didn't know what to expect. A few seconds later he violently punched the tailgate, slicing his knuckles open. He moved away from us trying to process the information. "I'm going to fucking kill him," he said, with a look of complete seriousness on his face. To calm him down, I went against my personal beliefs and tried to help him keep an open mind. "You need to just calm down and not jump

454

to conclusions. It could have been anything, we don't know yet. Babies die of SIDS. And if they had nothing to do with what happened, you definitely don't want to start pointing fingers, because imagine how they would feel if it's something that they had no control over.

Crystal had to leave to pick up her son, and we decided that we should start heading towards the hospital. We didn't know if they were still there, but we didn't really know what else to do. When we pulled into the side of the hospital where the emergency room entrance was, we saw the entire family walking out of the front doors. They were all walking slowly with their heads down, and the hospital's Reverend was with them holding a Bible. We parked and got out of the truck, hesitantly walking toward them. We didn't know how we would comfort anyone, and I had personally never encountered a situation where a family had lost a loved one. As soon as Casie saw me, she walked over to me bawling her eyes out, and I put my arms around her. I held her while she cried for probably 10 minutes. I felt the pain radiating off of her soul. It was deep and it was brutal. I had not experienced a loss quite like she had, but I knew what it felt like to permanently lose a child. There was nothing that anyone could say or do to make the painful fact change. Donnie was in tears with his arms in the air as he approached his brother. "My kid is dead, man!" he bawled as his brother tried to comfort him. The hospital had scheduled the baby to be transported to the morgue, where his little body would wait until the coroner picked him up for an autopsy.

When it was determined that there was nothing left to do at the hospital, we all headed toward their home. It was tragic walking into the living room, seeing all of the baby's items as if he were still alive. We all thought that we were still hearing him cry, but it was more of a desperate yearning wish. Derrick called his parents to break the news. He made sure that his mother was sitting down knowing that she was going to be absolutely devastated. The Reverend stopped by to offer more support, and it was then that I realized how beautiful and meaningful words could be. "You just have to know, in your heart, that something as innocent and beautiful as your baby, is safe in heaven with God. There is no other place that he could be except for with our Lord." The day had gone by very slowly, and it was almost as if everything were in slow motion. It began to get dark outside, and shortly thereafter, a pair of police officers arrived to carry out their standard investigation. They asked for simple items, like the can of the baby's last formula that he ate, a diaper and the wipes that were used, and they asked to be led to the place where the baby was found unresponsive. They were only in the house for a few minutes, and they were very kind and compassionate to both Donnie and Casie. Derrick and I went home that night. We were both feeling sad and upset that we hadn't acted quicker. If we would have just listened to our intuition, he just may still be alive. He would be almost six years old today.

Chapter 64

The loss of the baby was so incredibly sad that it could never be put into words. In a way, it helped Derrick and I realize how lucky we were. We had gone through a horrible series of events, but at least we knew that we would see our baby again. Death is permanent. Donnie and Casie would have to live without ever seeing their son again. There were no second chance, tinge of hope, or ways around it. He was gone.

We wanted to pitch in to plan his funeral, but the autopsy was taking so long that we couldn't even set a date. Donnie started to become angry that the detectives wouldn't allow him to see his son's body. Their reasoning for this was because the autopsy was so extensive that it would probably be a traumatic site. My suspicion proved to be true when the detectives were suddenly asking Donnie, Casie, and her entire family to come in for individual interviews. That is when I immediately knew that there was more to the story. The detectives even contacted Derrick and I, asking if we would go for interviews. I blatantly refused, recalling the horrible days back in 2006. I was not about to offer information that I had no knowledge of, and from my experience, that is always what they wanted. They wanted an easy answer. They wanted to just close the case. We agreed to an interview, under specific circumstances. The only way that we would speak with them was if they came to our home and they agreed to leave if we asked them to.

They respected our request and came to our house the next night. We told them all that we knew, all that we saw, and even all that we suspected. Derrick was in tears because he didn't want to believe that his brother could be responsible, but deep down inside, he knew that it was probably the truth. The detectives clearly saw how vulnerable he was. They used this as their opportunity to share some information about their findings. "Now, we understand that you are hurting. The last thing that we want to do is make it worse. However, there is some information that we feel is necessary that you know. We need you to think of anything and everything that you can remember about the days leading up to his death." We sat on the couch, giving the detective our full attention. "This baby did not die of SIDS. This was not an accidental death. We have proof, in pictures and reports, that this baby was murdered. He probably suffered for about eight hours before he died of asphyxiation. In our opinion, it is one of two people who are responsible. We do not believe that Casie is responsible." "I'm just trying to really process what you are saying right now. Can you prove this with photographs?" Derrick asked. "Yes, but I strongly advise you to not look at them. They are extremely disturbing, and it is one of those things that will most likely never leave your mind." "So exactly what kind of evidence do you guys have?" "Well, I'm not going to offer every single detail, but there were four bruises found on the back of the baby's head. They were about the size of a fingerprint. The baby had a bruise around his mouth in a circular shape, determined to be the shape of his pacifier. When you put that evidence together, it appears that his head was pushed down into his mattress until he was no longer breathing." I started to feel sick and dizzy. Derrick's face turned pale. I had a hard time figuring out when the detectives were actually telling the truth, or if they were lying and trying to find some sort of evidence. But, in God's name, I couldn't find any reason why any person would fictitiously make such claims. They left, and Derrick went back and forth trying to decide if he believed them or not. I could tell that he did believe them, but he was fighting it because he didn't want to believe them.

Because we had been supporting Donnie and Casie since the day that the baby died, it was hard to just suddenly, 100% cut them off without being obvious that we were suspicious. A few days later, Casie, Donnie, and Casie's mom and her sister showed up unannounced. I was upstairs sleeping as usual, and Derrick was down stairs watching TV. I didn't mind that they were there, but I started to become annoyed and upset at the sound of Donnie's voice. The way that he was laughing and joking almost convinced me that he could have been responsible for what happened to my daughter. I got dressed and walked outside without saying a word to anyone. I got on my phone and I called my mom crying because I was so frustrated and disgusted. My mom called Lilah, and Lilah actually offered to pick me up for lunch. While I was waiting for her to pull up, Casie's mom came outside to talk to me. She could see that I was upset. She didn't have extensive knowledge over what happened to my daughters because I rarely spoke of it. I was trying to give her the information and somehow I hoped that she saw the connection between what happened to her grandson and the irony of what happened to my daughter, two years earlier. She didn't understand, and I can't blame her. I was mostly vague when I tried to explain. I thought it was nice of her, though, that she at least tried to talk to me. Lilah picked me up and she was really nice to me. I was surprised that she even came in the first place. She was on a positive affirmations kick, and she gave me some ideas of things I could say to myself every day to try and get through my living hell.

When I got home later that day, everyone had left, and I explained to Derrick why I had to get away. I even explained to him my conflicting feelings over what happened to Zoe. He was understanding and compassionate. He then started to bring up things that were discussed when I was gone. Long story short, they were all blaming Marney. I didn't know Marney well enough to feel like I could form an opinion. It was easier for Derrick to go along with this belief, though. As the days went on, he allowed himself to completely believe this idea to be true. After all of the horrible fate, events and chaos, he allowed Donnie back into our lives on a regular basis. I was hurting for Casie, and I wanted to be there for her. It was extremely hard for me to stay neutral. Any time I thought about my daughter, a wave of fear would crash through me. The fact that I was probably in the same room as the person responsible gave me complete terror. I had to consistently make sure that I was stocked up on my anti-anxiety medication because I truly could not handle reality. I knew that Casie was struggling quietly in her own mind. I knew that she was confused and was unsure about what to think when it came to the death of her son. I had been struggling with a similar feeling for a few years at that point. Whenever we had time alone, I always brought it up to her, and I told her that I didn't know exactly how she felt, but I had a good idea. I wished that somehow she and I could just run away from these men. I found it odd that Donnie constantly wanted to stay in the home where the baby died, and Casie could not bear the thought of it. Casie frequently came over to our house to stay the night because it was just too hard for her. Donnie claimed that he did not want to leave the house because he felt like he was leaving his baby. The circumstances, and the relationships within the circumstances, were incredibly confusing and dynamic. The detectives eventually let up on interrogating Donnie and Casie, but we all knew that they were being watched. If they were being watched, that meant that Derrick and I were also being watched.

Chapter 65

The temperature began to drop as the holidays arrived. I got used to Derrick deciding to be around his brother, and once again, these people became normal. We all quickly gave up on life ever being happy and hopeful. Our best escape came in a small shiny rock. Crystal meth always came in to save the day. We were all empty and numb, and we didn't even care that we were most likely under a microscope. I was still on Probation, and I honestly didn't care. Going back to jail could have just been better than living as I was. I found myself praying a lot on a daily basis. Even when I was under the influence, I still prayed. A part of me felt guilty because I was high, but the other part of me wanted desperately to be saved. I told God that I trusted him, and I trusted that he would point me in the right direction if I allowed him too. I wanted to surrender, but I didn't know how.

I knew that my addiction was worse than it had ever been before because I found myself frequently hallucinating and seeing things that weren't really there. They were extremely vivid and it terrified me. My only comfort was that I knew that what I was seeing was not really physically in the same location. It was just a hallucination. They frequently happened when I didn't expect them to. One of the worst hallucinations that I had was after I had been up for a few days. I approached the extra bedroom downstairs, because that's where I kept all of my clothes. It was late and I was exhausted, and I just wanted to put my pajamas on. The office was dark, and most of the lights were off. Derrick was sitting in the living room watching TV. I saw a very tall creature that resembled something which would be half man and half demon. It was about 7 feet tall, and it was wearing my pajama pants. He was standing in the entrance of the spare room. The reason that I thought it was so real was because I could see every single pattern in my plaid pants clearly. I panicked and would not go back into that room. I made Derrick do it, and I made him turn on the light. Other hallucinations were when my houseplants morphed into monsters with tiny little claws and when I thought a helicopter was circling our house, and I was definitely going to jail.

After using such large quantities of meth and being awake for so long, the comedown was horrible. When we ran out of meth, the best thing to do was fall asleep. But it was nearly impossible to fall asleep with remnants of the drug left in my body. I became sick to my stomach, my mouth wouldn't stop watering, and I couldn't get comfortable, no matter how hard I tried. This was always the time when Derrick wanted to have sex. It was the worst time possible, but he wouldn't take no for an answer. I was afraid to refuse him because I knew that when he came down, he became extra angry and he had the potential to get violent. He always begged for a blow job, even though he knew that it wasn't going to happen. "It will gag me. If your wife puking on your dick is something that turns you on, then let's get started." He would finally drop it after whining like a baby. He always tried to bend me into a weird position that I just couldn't handle. I wasn't a damn yoga junkie, and it was almost as if he thought I was freaking Gumby. I would complain and roll my eyes, and be thankful that I got it over with. I wondered if I was the only woman who saw this as a chore. With all of the stress that I carried on a daily basis, combined with my medication and flat out exhaustion, I never had any desire for sex. He never failed to remind me that any other girl would be, "begging." I rolled my eyes.

I didn't even realize that Halloween had come until the day it arrived. I had nothing special planned and neither did Derrick. I had him go to the store to get a bag of candy just in case some of the neighborhood kids came by. I decided that I would celebrate the holiday with two 24-ounce beers. I found myself drinking more often these days. That is, only when I could get away with it. Derrick got really mad at me every time. There may be a few reasons behind this. It could be from the time that we were driving home from a dinner with friends at the casino, and I wanted to go to their house afterwards and he didn't. I was pretty wasted. When the turn came up on the highway that led to our friend's house, I turned the steering wheel in the direction that I wanted to go. I underestimated the power of a slight turn, and we flew off the side of the road and smashed into a stop sign. Derrick was in total shock and almost on the verge of tears. I immediately began apologizing and told him that I didn't think that would happen. I was super freaked out, and then I was afraid that we were going to get pulled over. Derrick had been drinking, too. We would both go to jail if we were caught. "I'm sorry, I promise I'll do whatever I can to make sure that your truck gets fixed. But right now you need to hurry up and back out and start driving!" He cranked the wheel and backed out of the dirt ditch we were in. The stop sign was completely demolished and lying flat on the ground like a pancake. When he got on the highway, he was still shaking in shock. I had to coach him, and my drunk, confident self was happy to take the lead. "You better step on it! Hurry up and get up to speed with the rest of the traffic. We are going to get caught if you don't!" As he sped up and got to the normal speed limit, we passed the intersection that we were supposed to be turning on. I

463

didn't have my glasses on so I tried to turn us onto the road about fifty feet too soon. As we passed through the green light, I noticed a police car waiting on the right side of us. The car was waiting to turn left, in the direction that we had just crashed. There was still dirt flying up in the air. The rest of the 15-minute drive home completely sucked. I was convinced that the cops were going to catch us. We somehow got lucky.

The other reason than that caused Derrick to hate me consuming alcohol even more is one that I am certainly not proud of. It's one of those tales that you hear and shake your head in disgust. You always know that you'll never be one of those girls. Well, when I got drunk, I wanted excitement. I wanted to break the rules and see what I could get away with it. I don't remember exactly how I ended up at his best friend house but I did. I was wasted and it was probably one in the morning. Derrick's best friend ended up bending me over his truck in the garage of his house. It may have been my subconscious way of retaliating. Derrick had already slept with his best friend's girlfriend, and it upset me more than I realized. Without getting into the dirty details, I was a definite slut for the night. For the record, this was before we were married. For the record today, I no longer consume alcohol.

I was sitting on the couch bored out of my mind on Halloween night. Derrick smoked a bunch of pot that night and he fell asleep early. I was annoyed because I wanted to at least have some sort of excitement. It definitely wasn't going to happen. I chugged my beers as fast as I could, knowing that they would only give me a short buzz. I ate some snacks, and zoned to the TV. I forgot, again, that it was Halloween night, until I got a knock on my glass door. I picked up my bowl of candy and opened the sliding door. The person standing in front of me was definitely not a trick-or-treater. It was a big guy, probably about 6 feet tall. He was wearing a blue windbreaker jacket. It had gold letters painted on it that read PROBATION. My adrenaline kicked in, but it wasn't as bad as it could have been since I was slightly buzzed. The big Probation Officer welcomed himself into my house and waved in everybody else tagging along with him. They all marched in, and they found my can of beer sitting on the floor. Luckily it was sitting on the floor away from the couch that I was sitting on. It had become routine for me to always think of the little things that could possibly get me in trouble. "Whose beer is this?" "Oh, that was my husband. He drank it and fell asleep. He's upstairs." I responded. The Probation Officers were searching the crap out of my house, and they were all completely in awe over how nice the trailer was. It was in the crappiest neighborhood that you could think of, and it didn't look like anything special from the outside, but when you walked in, it was seriously like a mini castle. One of the nicer Probation Officers went upstairs to search. Derrick was asleep, and I became annoyed that he always seemed to be asleep when these people were trying to ruin my life. I was pretty nervous when the officer went upstairs, because I knew that Derrick had a bag of pot with him, but I didn't know exactly where he was hiding it. The officer came down the stairs and didn't announce any illegal findings. Somehow, they didn't even know that I had been drinking. I must have played it off pretty good.

The time started to go by a little more quickly as I got into the routine of doing absolutely nothing, and pretty much wasting away. Derrick eased up on wanting to hang around with his brother. We still saw Donnie and Casie periodically, but it wasn't nearly as much as it had been before. I had come to the conclusion that Donnie was a horrible influence on his brother and horribly influenced every aspect of his brother's life. Derrick had actually become pleasant to be around. He treated me with decency and our fights were very infrequent. Before we knew it, Thanksgiving arrived. I wanted to have Thanksgiving at our house, and Donnie wanted to have Thanksgiving at his house. I didn't like going over to his house. It

465

made me sad and it had negative energy. We couldn't agree, so I decided that I would just make a Thanksgiving dinner on the day before Thanksgiving. That way I could cook and make everything how I like it. I did just that, and it was amazing. On Thanksgiving Day, Derrick and I got dressed and ready to head over to their house. We initially had planned to simply go over there, watch football, eat dinner, and leave. We should have known better. When we arrived, there was a good dog and brandy, and the turkey was cooking in the oven. Donnie was acting like his usual erratic self, but I didn't think that he was actually using drugs this time. He appeared to be more drunk than high. Derrick and I hadn't used nearly as much as we normally did in the last month. This was probably because we stopped going over to his brother's house as often. We both knew that as long as we didn't allow ourselves to go anywhere near it we would be okay.

What started as a somewhat calm football game and dinner, quickly turned into a crazy and chaotic night. I was sipping on egg nog and brandy, but I wasn't going overboard. Derrick and Donnie lost complete control. Within a matter of hours, they were literally chugging the alcohol from the bottle. Donnie hopped on one of his dirt bikes and thought it would be fun to go on the four wheeling trail. This trail was probably about 2 miles away. He pretty much took off without even saying anything. Hours and hours went by, and he still had not returned. It was starting to get dark, and it was definitely cold outside. Dinner had been done for a while, and it was starting to get cold. I told my drunken husband and Casie that we should probably call search and rescue. If he were stranded out there in this weather, he would definitely freeze to death. I got on the phone and made the report, and the woman was super nice and said that she was sending her team out right away. When I hung up the phone, I turned around and Derrick was burning rubber in his truck heading towards the trail. These guys were a bunch of idiots. I assumed that Donnie was probably going to return, but now Derrick would be lost. There was no stopping them. They were drunk and they were not controllable.

About an hour after Derrick left, Donnie came stumbling into the house with three other people at his side. It was two girls, about my age, and a guy that looked a little younger than me. I could tell that these kids were drunk, and they definitely weren't belligerent. Donnie was a horrible sight. He had blood all over his shirt and it looked like he was stabbed in the arm. The brunette girl was holding his arm, which was wrapped in a bandage. She walked him into the kitchen and told him to sit down. She introduced herself and said that she was a nurse in the military. I have never seen these people in my life. Donnie was slurring and he could hardly explain to Casie and I what had happened. The girl claiming to be a nurse was able to translate his drunken slur. "So basically, we found him when he left the McDonald's drive-through. He was bleeding, and at first when we tried to help him he yelled at us. We weren't going to let him just take off in the condition that he was in, because he would probably end up killing himself traffic. He got this cut on his arm because he walked through the drive-through and tried to order a burger. They wouldn't let him order, and told him that he to go inside. A person that was in a car behind him apparently said something to set him off. He walked up to their car and punched their windshield. That is how he got this cut on his arm."

Sadly, I wasn't surprised over the stupidity of his actions. It was almost kind of humorous, but it was just so stupid that it made me feel stupid to think it was funny. This cut was very deep, and it definitely needed stitches. Donnie refused to go to the hospital. The nurse found a first aid kit in the bathroom and cleaned out the wound. She tightly held the gash together, while her friend tightly wrapped the bandage around his arm. I was sitting outside smoking trying to let the weirdness sink in. I heard a clinking truck about a mile down the road. It wasn't driving very fast so I didn't think it was

467

Derrick. The truck turned into the driveway. It was so messed up that I didn't even recognize it. It looked like Derrick had been 14 wheeling. It really looked more like he was on a suicide mission. The radiator with absolutely crushed in, and the headlights were practically hanging from their wires. Derrick stumbled out of the car, extremely drunk, but I didn't think he was as drunk as he was when he left. I wasn't even really all that worried about him when he was gone. He deserved to get a DUI. He knew how stupid it was to get behind the wheel drunk and he chose to do it anyway. I was not having sympathy for him that night. He walked in and he and his brother started talking, but I couldn't understand what they were saying because they were slurring. I made their plates of dinner hoping that they would eat and began to sober up. They scarfed down their food and slowly became a little bit more aware.

The three kids that had escorted Donnie home were in party mode, and they walked down to the liquor store to get more alcohol. I was kind of confused and wondering why they were hanging out over at this drug house on a holiday that most people spent with their families. After Casie told them about the baby, they began to ask me questions every chance that they had. They only asked me when she wasn't around, and I thought it was really weird. They didn't even know who any of us were, but they were asking me detailed questions about who I thought was responsible. I gave them honest answers, and said that I didn't know for sure, but if I had to guess it would be Donnie. I thought that saying this would cause them to want to leave. But they didn't, they just started drinking more and more, and eventually they were dancing like whores in the living room.

All of the guys in the house quietly snuck to the back room and shut the door. When the girls realized that there friend was back in the room with Donnie and Derrick, they freaked out. "Eric! Get out of there, NOW!" The blond girl angrily screamed.

I assumed that he was her boyfriend. This is where everything went bad, and it became officially the worst Thanksgiving of my life. The blond girl was trying to force her way through the closed door. It pissed off Donnie. He shoved her back. The brunette retaliated and pushed Donnie who then punched the brunette. The other guy jumped in the middle and tried to calm both of them down. He ended up getting knocked out in the process. Donnie literally grabbed the two girls by their hair and pushed them off of the cement stairway. They landed on the ground in the front yard.

I was just standing to the side definitely not wanting to get in a fight. I thought for sure that after Donnie did this, the kids would be running for the hills. It only intensified their anger and they retaliated even more. They were trying to physically fight Donnie. He took it as a challenge and pretty much beat the crap out of both of them. The young kid was caught in the middle, and I felt bad for him. He was just trying to keep the peace, and I could tell that he was worried about his girlfriend. He approached Donnie calmly and tried to ask him to calm down, and he promised that he would get the girls off of his property. For no good reason at all, like Peter from the Family Guy, Derrick walked up to the kid and punched him in the face, knocking him hard to the ground. He was knocked unconscious. The girls took off down the street yelling that they were going to call the cops. I thought it was probably a good idea that they did that.

Now there were two drunken idiots on one side and a knocked-out kid on the ground. I wasn't going to just leave him there, so I started dragging him into the house so I could get him on the couch and make sure that he woke up okay. He woke up about five minutes later, and I could tell that when he sat up, he was dizzy. Derrick quickly apologized to him, and he apologized about his girlfriend's behavior. It was bizarre how the guys suddenly became friends. The kid was worried about the cops coming because he was on Probation. Donnie didn't want to deal with the cops either. They both ran out back and hid in the shed. Casie somehow disappeared. She was nowhere to be found. I figured that she probably went over to her mom's house. She was already emotional and heartbroken, and I couldn't blame her for wanting to get out of that situation.

Derrick and I sat on the front porch waiting for the cops to come. They showed up and took a report. We explained that we were just the guests for Thanksgiving dinner, and everyone else who had been fighting had disappeared. The cops seemed like they were having a busy night and told us to call them if the same kids showed back up looking for more. Somehow, the fight started all over again after the police left. The girls showed up again looking for Eric, and when we told them that Eric wasn't at the house, they wouldn't take no for an answer. Eric and Donnie must have heard the chaos, as they came running out on their hiding. Everyone was beat up all over again. It was really bad. After the three kids stumbled away threatening to call the police again, I yelled at Donnie and Derrick and told them to get into the truck as I opened the driver side door. We went straight back to our house, and Donnie was dripping blood everywhere. Casie called me to say she was on her way.

Donnie was definitely not sane. He was standing in the doorway smoking and didn't even noticing his gushing wounds. He wouldn't stop rambling on and on. He began talking about his baby, and that's when he had my attention. "I didn't know that you weren't supposed to do that," he sobbed to himself while looking down at the floor. "My dad beat the shit out of me growing up. I thought that's what you were supposed to do!" he cried. Oh God, I thought. He just confessed to the murder of his son.

Chapter 66

Luckily, the cops didn't show up at my house that night. When I woke up the next day, Donnie and Casie had already left. I had a talk with Derrick who wasn't very happy with himself and his actions from the night before. I told him what I had heard his brother say. He had a look of disappointment. He knew that something was eventually going to come out from someone, or whoever had any information regarding the death of the baby. "There is just too much bad shit that happens when I hang around my brother," he said, more to himself. He looked my way and said, "We are never, ever hanging around them again. I'm over it," wanting to make sure that I agreed. I did. We decided to hang our heads low, and we hoped that the police wouldn't end up showing up at our house to arrest him.

Within a matter of days after Thanksgiving, Donnie had been arrested for assaulting the girls that night, and a detective was trying to get a hold of Derrick and me by phone. We thought that it was probably a good sign that he was calling us because that meant that he did not have enough evidence to arrest Derrick. At this point, we were smart enough to know to never speak with any detectives about any case that could possibly go against us. We avoided his phone call and did not return his messages. By the next week, he was showing up at our front door. The first time he came, we were at the grocery store. We came home to a card on our front door.

Since Donnie was in jail, we knew that they either had enough evidence from the assault to arrest Derrick or they had been waiting to find any little reason to arrest him. If they had evidence against Derrick, they would have arrested him when they arrested Donnie. Derrick obviously was going to flat-out deny any involvement in the physical altercation, and of course, I was not going to testify against him because we were married. We were both uneasy with the idea of this detective continuing to stop by our home unannounced. I convinced Derrick to call the number on the card, and we would just make it clear that we didn't have any involvement and the detective would be on his way.

Just a few minutes after Derrick made the phone call, the detective was back at our house for an interview. He came inside and he was pretty rude. Derrick told him his side of the story and the detectives practically laughed. "We all know what really happened that night, and the young man that you knocked out, Eric, ended up with two concussions to his head. Now I just came here to see if you would take responsibility for your actions like an adult, and we could work with you. But if you make my job more difficult than it has to be, you're probably going to be in jail for a long time." Derrick and I already knew all about the game that he was playing. He was trying to make threats and scare us into confessing. It wasn't going to work. The detective turned to me, "Now Elizabeth, I know that you were there that night. And I know that you saw exactly what went on. Am I going to have the same problem with you as I do with your husband?" "I'm not exactly sure what that is supposed to mean, but when there is a fight between 10 different people at the same time, it's kind of hard to see exactly what happened with one particular person. I wasn't paying attention to Derrick. I was paying attention to the women because I was worried that they were

472

going to try to involve me in the fight." This wasn't a lie. I was almost positive that there was a law protecting me from having to testify against my husband. I wasn't going to lie to the detective, but I also wasn't going to offer information that would be incriminating to Derrick. The detective was extremely rude, and I thought that he had a lot of guts to be so hostile when he was in our own home. Derrick asked him to leave after a few minutes, and as he walked out the door. "We are going to pin you for this, Derrick. You can either make it easy on yourself, or we can do it the hard way."

About two weeks later, I had my routine visit at the Probation Department. I was assigned to a new Probation Officer, and for the most part, she was pretty nice. After she updated my file, she announced to me that someone wanted to talk to me. I thought that I was going to be arrested or something. She got on her phone and dialed an extension. Probably 30 seconds later, a man walked through the doorway. I was pissed. It was that same rude investigator that stopped by our house. He was using the fact that I was on Probation as leverage to get me to talk. "As with the terms and conditions of your Probation, it's mandatory for you to cooperate with law enforcement," my Probation Officer said, almost as if it were scripted. The detective was acting extra nice. He was too nice and seriously phony. Ms. Jeter, let's go for a quick walk. I followed him down the hallway and through the exit door of the Probation Department, and then across the hallway into the Police Department.

When he led me back to his office, he immediately picked up a small black box and pushed a button. Obviously, I was being recorded. I was so incredibly irritated that they were using this as a method to try to get more information with the threat of violating my Probation if I did not offer what they wanted to hear. I went through the details of the night, step-by-step. I told him that I didn't see Derrick knock anyone out. "I don't know, maybe I saw something out of the corner of my eye, but I can't remember." "Why won't you just tell the truth? That's all we need from you. If you just tell me the truth then I can let you go and you won't end up getting in any trouble over this." "See, this is why I don't talk to people like you. I've been there, done that. You guys lie and say anything that you want if you think it will give you what you want to hear so you can close the case and move onto the next investigation. At one point I trusted you. I trusted higher authority, and I never thought that you would do me wrong. I was completely mistaken. My daughter was hurt and you guys had the nerve and ignorance to actually think I knew what happened. Well, I didn't. And there still hasn't been anyone put away for it. Do you have any idea what this did to my family and so many other people?" I was having flashbacks of sitting in that interrogation room a couple years ago, and I was taking my anger out on this guy. I was extremely upset and crying. I think I shocked him a little bit because he laid off trying to get me to talk. "And why would I get in trouble for this? I have not done anything wrong. It is not my fault that this happened to take place in the same area as myself." "Well, because you put Eric back into the house after he was knocked unconscious, it sounds like you were an accessory to the crime." I was furious. "So you are telling me that because I tried to help this kid, I'm going to go to jail over it?" "I'm not saying anything, it's not going to be up to me. It's up to the District Attorney's Office." Luckily, I had to take a drug test before the Probation Office closed for the day. They were closing in about 10 minutes, so he knew that I had to go back. For some reason, he felt compelled to escort me back. "Are you going to pass your drug test?" "Yes. That's not going to be a problem," I dryly said.

From reading a copy of the police report that Casie brought to our house shortly after Donnie was arrested, we all knew that the District Attorney was taking this very seriously. I began wondering if we were both going to be arrested for this. Derrick tried to play it off like there just wasn't a way for us to get into trouble over it, but I had my doubts. It was early in the next year, 2009, and I only had about six months until I'd be released from Probation for good. This worried me even more. I knew that there would be something that ruined it all and kept me from moving. The best way I could cope was to use drugs. We both used. We regularly hung out with our neighbor who was a closet-tweaker and owned his own small business cleaning hot tubs for expensive vacation homes in the local area. He gave Derrick part-time work, and he would pay him with drugs. After the death of the baby, Derrick had a difficult time showing up at his regular job on time. His boss agreed to let him go and not contest when he filed for unemployment. From Derrick taking his truck on a 4-wheeling drunken ride, he had pretty much totaled it. It was useless, but we were at least able to sell it for parts. Pretty much, we were jobless, carless, on drugs and living in a trailer. Everything turned into complete shit.

Chapter 67

Since Donnie was in jail, we were hanging around with an entirely new group of people. These people all worked for our neighbor, Aaron. One of these men was in his 60s. He looked as if he could be a homeless man on the streets and he practically was. Aaron paid for him to stay in a room in a crappy motel. Although he was married, it didn't stop him from sleeping with the woman who managed the place. She gave him a discount. I spent most of my time obsessively researching the law, trying to figure out what to expect. So far, it had been a couple of months, and we hadn't heard anything about the case. A part of me assumed that if something were going to happen, it would have already happened. Another part of me was worried and I had a bad feeling. I was able to find a website that provided a list of all of the local criminal cases. It appeared to be an automated system, so I was hoping that if a warrant were to be put into place it would show up here. I checked this website every day. So far all seemed good. If we could just get through the next few months, we could be out of here and on our way to Texas.

Aaron somehow acquired a car - if you could call it that. He was selling it for $500, and we thought that we would probably be able to get it for $400. The vehicle ran extremely well and had low mileage. It was really ugly, a burgundy color, and made in the 80s, and it was a Lincoln town car. Luckily we were able to get the vehicle before someone else did. After almost four months without a car, we were happy to have anything - as long as it ran. We were smoking crystal meth on a daily basis, and it seemed like the supply just never ran out. We smoked more than we had ever done together and even more than when we were hanging around Donnie. I became paranoid that we were going to be arrested for the Thanksgiving fight, and I didn't want to be left alone at home. The drug-use contributed to my paranoia. I started to go on the jobs with Derrick, and I helped him clean out the hot tubs for the vacation homes. Plus, I thought it was fun to be able to see these homes. They were huge and some of them had more than three stories. I pretty much clung to Derrick wherever he went.

Before we knew it, Danielle was about to be two years old. The thought of missing her second birthday was simply not an option for us. I didn't even bother to ask Probation if it would be okay to drive to Texas to see her. I already knew what their answer was going to be, and I already knew that I was going to go regardless of what they said. The only thing that asking them would really accomplish was telling them that I was going to leave the state for two weeks, which was completely illegal. I didn't care, at that point - I just wanted to see my daughter.

After getting some jobs done, we saved enough money for the gas to get to Texas. We already knew that the vehicle we had would make it. Our main concern, however, was getting pulled over. It was one of those vehicles that just had that look - that typical crack head or kidnapper car look. Honestly, it was embarrassing even riding in this car. It was, however, the best and the cheapest that we could afford. When we realized that we had saved enough money, we just kind of got up and impulsively left. There was nothing more to do except sit around, so we figured that we might as well spend this time with our daughter. We left with just enough meth to make the drive to Texas. It was my first time driving there. I knew it was going to be a long drive, but I didn't know how long it was actually going to be. This was a twenty-nine hour drive not including stops. I was anxious to get there, but I didn't know if my daughter was going to even know me. It had already been almost a year since we dropped her off in El Paso. She was only a little over a year old, so I was convinced that she was probably not going to remember me. The drive seemed to go pretty smooth for the first twenty-four hours. We drove all the way to Flagstaff stopping twice for gas. The sun was coming up, and we had been smoking meth all night. When we stopped for gas, I went to the restroom to change my clothes and wash my face. We spent the entire day driving through Arizona, New Mexico, and finally we got into Texas. Driving through Texas was going to be the longest part of the drive. There had been a couple of close calls with us getting pulled over on the second day of driving, but somehow we were okay. When it began to get dark, we were both getting pretty tired and knew that we should probably find a rest stop. As we pulled in to one, I was surprised at how nice it was. We could tell that Texans were clearly proud of their state. "Don't mess with Texas!" was a phrase that I saw probably twenty times since entering the state. There was a lobby, and it was almost like a museum. The restrooms were huge with a row of showers on the other side of the toilet stalls. It was shiny clean, and I knew that if I were going to get a chance to take a shower in a decent area, it was going to be here. We both got cleaned up, and although exhausted, we figured that our remaining meth would probably get us to our destination that night.

This was when the drive became intense. I was too afraid to fall asleep because I thought that Derrick looked like he was beginning to nod off. We were at the point where the meth was no longer working. We tried to snort it instead, thinking that maybe if we used it differently, it would miraculously wake us up. The most that it did, at best, was keep us awake for another ten minutes. Derrick continued to say that he was fine, but I knew that he probably wasn't. Around midnight, we had just a couple of hours of driving left to do. We got lost in Dallas for probably an hour, and I remember thinking that the city looked so futuristic. The tall buildings were brightly lit up in different neon colors, and the freeways were windy and going in every direction. I remember the city lights the most and what caught my attention immediately were the lights of the police cars. Every few minutes of driving we passed someone who was pulled over with the bright lights of the police officer behind them. The lights looked like fireworks. They flashed red, white and blue, and I had never seen police lights quite like these ones. When we finally got out of Dallas, the police lights must have found a place inside of my mind. I was getting close to the hallucination phase of the binge, and the fears in my subconscious were starting to emerge. We went through a few towns, and more than once we drove on a freeway with air patrol monitoring the speed limit. I thought for sure that these helicopters were after us. I threw my glass pipe out of the window making sure that it shattered. I knew that I wouldn't need the pipe anyway because Derrick and I already decided that we weren't going to need to use meth once we arrived at his parent's house.

My exhausted mind had me thinking that somehow Probation knew that I had left the state. I kept my panic contained for as long as I could. When we finally got away from the helicopters, I thought that just maybe we might make it to our destination. That's until I looked in my side mirror to see blaring police lights directly behind us. They were flashing that same red, white and blue. This was it. We were being pulled over. "Derrick! There's a cop behind us! We're being pulled over!" I said in a panic. He did not slow down - if anything, he sped up.

480

Chapter 68

"Derrick! Why aren't you pulling over! We are about to go to jail. Oh my God," I said, trying hard not to panic. I knew that if I got too loud he would probably reach over and knock me out. I closed my eyes, and when I opened them about five minutes later, we were pulling into a rest stop. "What is going on? I am so confused. Weren't we being pulled over?" I asked, genuinely wondering if he somehow dodged the cops or if I was just crazy. "We're pulling over because I'm nodding off, and you need to go to sleep," He replied. "No, we weren't being pulled over, and there are not any helicopters following us. We've been up for too long." Without questioning his statement, I nodded in agreement. Even though we were literally an hour away from his parents, we just couldn't do it. We had to stop and sleep - even if for only a few hours. It was around two in the morning, and would sleep until it got light out. He got out of the front seat and got into the back seat. I was bummed that he didn't let me take the back seat because I had been hallucinating and was afraid. I was nervous about everything, and because I had been up for so long, I had the constant feeling that I was being watched. I saw another helicopter flying above us, and I was sure it was there to keep tabs on our whereabouts. I don't know if it was really there or not. It probably wasn't.

The physical and psychological consequences of extreme drug abuse are dire. If it doesn't kill you physically, it'll certainly kill you mentally. I got to a point where it was almost impossible to really comprehend what was going on and if what I was seeing was really even there. Derrick had a higher tolerance than I, and if he ever did have the same hallucinations as I, he never made it known. If the grip on us got any tighter, methamphetamine would surely be our demise.

After sleeping for what felt like five minutes, Derrick opened the back car door and walked to the restroom area. It was just beginning to get light out. Derrick called his mother to tell her we'd be there in about an hour. He drove through a fast-food place to grab something to eat. We snorted the last small amount of meth that we had, knowing that we probably had no choice if we were going to stay awake long enough to make it. Normally, if at home, we would've slept for two or three days. Luckily, we'd probably be fine with sleeping for most of the day when we arrived. His parents knew how long we had been driving, as they'd made the long drive more than once themselves. It was exhausting. Derrick was nervous, and I could tell by the way he was acting. I asked him what was wrong and he responded, "I just feel super bad about doing all of this shit right before seeing my parents and Danielle. I'm worried they're going to be able to tell." I couldn't blame him. I felt just as bad, and I definitely wouldn't have done this if I were going to see my own parents. At least he has a conscious I thought.

Finally, we pulled into the community where his parent's house was. He was driving more slowly than usual. He really was nervous. We pulled up to the front of his parent's house and parked on the side of the street. As soon as we got out of the car and grabbed our bags from the back seat, his mother came out of the front door. She hugged us both, and we walked into the house. It was just as it was when we flew out over Christmas

482

almost two years ago, only there were baby toys all over the place. There was a playhouse with a huge slide going down the side. This thing was sitting in their kitchen. I knew right away that my little girl was definitely spoiled. That was a good thing. Danielle was out on the back patio with her grandpa. I put my purse on the counter and followed Derrick outside.

She looked up at him first and had a look of hesitation because she was probably a little bit confused. I called her name calmly, "Danielle! I missed you!" I said, reaching my arms out. She smiled and said, "Mama!" and ran up to me. I picked her up and held her and hugged her, remembering how badly I had missed her. My heart was dancing as I realized that she remembered me. She still knew who I was, and I was revived with hope. My baby girl had grown, and she had more hair. It was curly and pale blond. "I love you so much," I told her as I squeezed her with another hug. I set her down after ten minutes, and she walked over to her daddy. She knew him too, and she just needed time to process everything. He picked her up and she smiled.

We spent ten days with our daughter. For her birthday, I had brought a blanket I was crocheting for probably the last year. We bought her a few more presents earlier in the day, and I wrapped them while Derrick and his dad made her the cake. I thought it was kind of cute - two grown men in the kitchen slaving over a strawberry shortcake for a two-year old. They did a good job, and after we sang to her, I had more than one piece. It was a small family affair, but she was happy and that's all we cared about.

We went swimming, out to dinner, and lived like a normal family. For ten days, we got to sober up and forget about the horrible lifestyle we had built for ourselves. Something about getting away, cleaning up and being with our daughter was magical. I wanted this forever. Derrick was a different person. I'm sure that I was, too. We were happy and content. I tried as hard as I could to block away the imminent reality of this ending. Before we knew it, it was time to go back. We had to go home. I had to get off of Probation and take care of business. We packed our bags and set them next to the staircase before visiting with our daughter before we hit the road again. She heard us

Chapter 69

We had Aaron keep tabs on our house for us while we were gone. He kept an eye out for anything that might indicate we were being sought out. Derrick called him on our drive home, and so far, so good. We pulled into our driveway completely depressed to be home. The town had a dark, heavy air about it. It was cold and snowy and we wanted out. Luckily, there was no evidence of anyone showing up at our house while we were gone. It had been snowing, and there weren't any footprints leading up to our driveway. I had also been checking online for any new cases against us and didn't see anything.

We resumed working for Aaron and tried to save as much money as we could. Not surprisingly, we always ended up spending what we had on meth. It made us feel better about ourselves and our failures and life in general. Derrick started to open up to me more. We would have long, deep conversations about our future, and how if we just stuck together and kept going, we'd get through it all. We would one day have a bright future, and maybe even one day, we could have more kids. We wanted to go to Texas, buy a house, regain custody of our daughter, and just be normal. We wanted to do family stuff, not drugs. We knew that if we could just get away from this trap and the people in it, we would be okay.

On a Friday morning a few weeks after our trip, Derrick had an early job to go to. It was much too early in the morning for me. I slept in on the living room couch after saying goodbye to him. A loud knocking on the front sliding door startled me. My heart was racing, and I was buried under my blanket from sleeping. I stayed as still as I could. The curtains covering the door were translucent enough for me to make out the silhouette of the person standing behind it. I very slowly and quietly peeked out of my blanket. The person was very big and tall, and I knew from their shadow that they had a jacket on. It looked exactly like the shadow of a Probation Officer. I carefully put the blanket back over my head, and lay as still as I could until I heard the steps of the person walking away. I quietly rolled off of the couch and literally crawled to the back bedroom where the phone was. I had to call Derrick to warn him before he got home.

"Derrick! Someone was just banging on our door. I think that it was either Probation or the Police. Before you come home make sure to look around in case they are watching us!" I frantically said. "It could have been anyone. How do you know it was a cop?" he asked. "Trust me, I know that knock!" I confidently replied. "I'll be home in a few minutes," he said before hanging up. Within a few minutes, Derrick had snuck into the house through our back door. We were both sitting in the back room quietly, and I was online looking through the case index. I clicked on the search box and typed in our last name. The same, long wrap-sheet came up. Between Derrick and Donnie, it was almost a full page of criminal and civil offenses. I scrolled to the bottom where I knew that anything new would be listed. I stopped in my tracks in a full panic. My name was on that list. Since I had been married, I hadn't had any criminal charges against me. The ones that I did have were in my other name. Right above my name was Derrick's. I sat on the floor leaning against the wall with my head in my hands crying. "Not again...WHY IS THIS HAPPENING AGAIN!" I screamed. Derrick knew that I had discovered what we had feared. "Calm down, you don't know what it is yet. It could be something minor," he said, not sounding confident in the least bit. There were penal codes next to our names. I copied and pasted them into a search engine. I looked mine up first - ACCESSORY TO A CRIME - (FELONY). "WHAT THE HELL!" I screamed. I didn't even do anything to hurt a damn person that night!" I cried, almost in hysterics. Derrick put his hand on my shoulder, trying to comfort me. I looked up his offense next - ASSAULT WITH A DEADLY WEAPON (X).

"Assault with a deadly weapon?" I thought out loud. "What are they talking about, Derrick? You didn't have any weapon on you!" I said. "They're probably talking about my fists. I think I remember the detective saying something about that, and I just laughed it off thinking that it wouldn't be legal to charge me with that," he said. "But what does that (X) mean in the parenthesis?" he noticed, comparing it to mine which said felony. I scrolled down to the reference guide at the bottom of the page where it said, X-STRIKE.

We were both shocked. This was serious. This was more serious than we ever could have been prepared for. This was worse than the charges that were brought against Donnie, and he was facing three years in prison. "Pack your shit. We're getting out of here," Derrick said in a hurry. "Where are we going?" I nervously asked. "I have to go to Court for a Probation review in three weeks, Derrick. If I don't show up it will make everything worse," I said. "Don't worry about that. We'll talk about it later. Just pack your shit," he said. I started packing. As I was stuffing my clothes into the biggest duffle bag I could find, I heard Derrick on the phone. He was talking to Aaron. He hung up. "I'll be right back," he said, bolting out the back door. I had my things packed and ready to go when he came back. He was holding a keychain with probably at least twenty keys on it. He had a smirk on his face. "Oh gosh. Are we really?" I asked. "Oh...yeah!"

he said in excitement. We quickly put our things in the trunk of the car and took off down the highway.

Before we went to our destination, Derrick got on the phone and started talking to someone speaking Spanish in bits and pieces. We picked up a Mexican man. I hadn't seen him before, but he was really friendly - in a goofy kind of way. We drove to a few different motels, where he would go into one of the rooms and come back out. Finally, on the third stop, he came back with a big smile on his face. When he got into the back seat, he pulled a bag out of his pocket. "Hey man! I got it!" he said, showing off the eight ball rock of crystal meth. "Dammit, Carlos! Put that shit back in your pocket!" Derrick yelled. "I'm sorry man!" he said, putting the bag back into his pocket. Wherever we were going, we were taking Carlos with us. We didn't drop him off like I thought we were going to. We drove about fifteen minutes passed the state-line, and pulled into the driveway of a four-story mansion. The party was just getting started.

Chapter 70

Drugs, sex and filet mignon.

For the next three weeks, we stayed in four different mansions. Aaron had the schedule of upcoming rentals, so we knew that wherever he told us to go, it would have to be vacant. The First mansion had four levels. The first level was the kitchen and the master bedroom, which was huge. The second level, which led down a flight of stairs, was a living area with a huge TV and surround sound, a computer, four bedrooms and a hot-tub out on the back deck. The next flight of stairs led to the third level, which was the floor with the games. There was a Pool Table, an Air-Hockey game, a Ping Pong table, and a Foosball game. The fourth level was what would have been the maid's quarters if the place were occupied. There was a kitchenette, four bedrooms, and a few couches.

The place was not yet cleaned up from the last renters, so I decided to clean. It probably took me two days, but I wanted to have a solid excuse to be there in case anyone came by. The only people who could maybe show up were the actual cleaning people, or the owners. Derrick had the equipment laying out by the hot tub at all times for the same reason. For the most part, we were high the entire time. I have no idea how we had the money for drugs and filet mignon, but we somehow managed. I hate to say it, but this was probably the most exciting, laid-back and nerve-wracking three weeks of my life. We were officially fugitives running from the law, and it brought some sort of exciting element to our lives. We became closer than we ever had during our time on the run. We knew that we wouldn't ever be caught in these mansions, and we were able to just enjoy our time together. We let ourselves pretend that this was our life, and we had nothing to worry about. After getting a call from Derrick's mother about a week into our mansion hopping, we couldn't help but worry. She was crying.

"The cops called me and they are looking for you two! I said you weren't here and he said something about being careful about making sure you didn't come here, because he 'wouldn't want to see anyone get shot!" I told him that if they shot my son, I would hunt him down and end his life!" she screamed. We reassured her that we weren't going to be heading that way until this was all resolved, but we were worried that this had turned into something more serious than we ever thought it could. When the day was getting closer for the cleaning company to show up to prepare for the next set of guests, Derrick called Aaron to find out where our next hideout would be. When he got off the phone he looked nervous. "Aaron said that last night our house was surrounded by the SWAT team. They all had guns and vests on." he said. "What the hell! They're acting as if we have killed someone!" I complained. Derrick was seriously wanted by the Police Department. We had a talk later that night decided he should try to run for as long as he could. If I could just get off of Probation, we could leave the state that would never offer us a good life, or even give us a fighting chance. We knew that when I went to Court in a few weeks, they would arrest me. But they would eventually have to let me go because I was innocent. I would take it to trial and the Jury would have no choice. We

490

would figure out a way for him to hide for a few months until I was free, and then we would leave.

We went to our next location and had even more fun than we did at the first. The mansion had five stories, and I literally got lost the first time I explored. The first floor was a bit outdated with a look from the 70's, but it was still nice with antique furniture. The second floor had six bedrooms including the master with a huge flat-screen television set mounted to the wall. The third floor was where we spent most of our time. We got high, played poker, blasted country music on the speakers, and got high again. The other two floors had more bedrooms and the maid's quarters. We were living the life that we always talked about. Through our despair and self-destruction, we were falling in love all over again. Our connection was deep. The trauma and tragedy, more than most people ever face, had given us no other choice but to cling tightly to all we had left - each other.

When we were lying in bed one night and unable to stay awake any longer, Derrick had his head on my chest. He was listening to my heartbeat. "I will always love you, more than anything, Elizabeth. You're the legs to my table. If you fall, I fall. Don't ever forget that," he passionately said. "I'd like to believe that because we've been through so much and somehow we're still lying together, that it's just what it is supposed to be." I said. "It's been hard, and sad and confusing. And I don't know why, because it would certainly be easier to not love you, but I do. It's like I don't even have a choice in the matter. I love you with everything in me, Derrick." I ran my fingers through his shaved buds of hair. "No matter what ever happens, I love you and I always will. Don't ever forget that." He lovingly replied. We fell asleep hugging each other, which was something that rarely happened. We were confused and scared. We didn't know what would lie ahead. Nothing was certain. The only thing that was certain was that we loved each other. We would fight to be together, no matter what it took.

As each day came closer to my Court date, we became anxious and somber. Derrick hadn't been feeling well for the last few days. On a morning that we had fallen asleep in the living room area on two separate couches, he woke me up because he was breathing heavily. It was about six in the morning and barely getting light outside. "What's wrong?" I asked him in a daze. "I don't know. Can I have one of your anxiety pills?" he asked. This was when I knew that something serious was going on. Derrick would never admit to his defeating feelings or emotions. His manliness got in the way of that. I handed him one of my pills. "Are you breathing okay?" I asked him, concerned. "I don't know. My chest hurts," he said, trying to pace his breathing. I asked him what his other symptoms were, and typed them into the search engine on the computer that was in the corner of the room. "Your symptoms are either consistent with altitude sickness, or a heart attack. I think we need to go to the hospital now," I said, trying to stay calm. "That's not happening. They'll know I've been tweaked out, and they'll probably call the cops. I'm NOT going to jail," he replied. He was flat-out refusing to go to the hospital. I begged him and told him that his life could depend on it, and he wouldn't budge. He started to become disoriented. I wondered if it was altitude sickness. Although our home was in the mountains and we were used to high altitude, this particular vacation rental was way up in the mountains and probably close to a thousand feet higher than we were accustomed to. I started the car that was hiding in the garage and managed to convince him to get into the passenger seat. "We just need to drive you down the hill to see if this subsides, ok?" I begged. If it was altitude sickness, his symptoms should slowly ease up.

I drove Derrick down the hill and parked us in the empty lot of a grocery store. I ran into a gas station to get him some water. We sat in silence for probably an hour. I periodically asked him how he was feeling. When I asked him for the third time, I glanced over to see tears streaming down his face. "Are you still having chest pain?" I asked, concerned that he was getting worse. "No. I'm just overwhelmed with all this and I don't want you to leave me. I feel like shit that you're the one getting in trouble over this and who knows how long they'll lock me up. We should just run. It's the only way shit will ever get better!" he said, completely frustrated and broken. I rubbed his head and looked at him knowing that we couldn't run. I didn't have to say anything for him to know this. Running for good would only make this bad situation even worse. As much as I loved him and wanted to be with him, but I was too close to getting off of Probation to let that be an option.

We drove back up the hill and spent the last few days sobering up and appreciating our time together. After Monday, we didn't know when the next time would be that we could be together. I spent the night before Court with Derrick in the hot tub. I stared up at the stars, thinking about life, the universe, and if it could possibly have anything good planned for me. I still had hope. It was the only thing keeping me alive.

Chapter 71

My relationship with my father had improved in the prior months. When I had the relapse that caused me to land myself back in jail the last time, I gave up on trying to hide anything from him. I came to the conclusion that lying to him didn't do any good. If anything, it only made him more frustrated. I decided to be brutally honest with him. When I told him everything over an email, I expected him to write back and be totally furious. When he responded and thanked me for being honest with him, I was surprised. If I had known that brutal honesty was all that he wanted, I could have done that a long time ago. Most parents have a hard time handling the truth, especially if it involves illegal activity. My dad had his own history of making mistakes in his younger years. He just wanted to know what was going on.

In the few days before my Court Hearing, I called my dad to let him know what was going on. Of course I didn't come out and say that I was still using drugs, but I told him about the rest of the drama. "Well, I don't have any jobs that day. Do you want me to go to Court with you?" I was glad that he was offering to do this because I knew that Derrick couldn't go with me. I knew that I was probably going to be arrested, and I was definitely nervous. "If you don't mind, I would definitely appreciate that." Before getting off the phone, he told me that he would meet me in front of the Court fifteen minutes prior.

I woke up that morning feeling sick to my stomach. I was slow to get dressed, and I honestly didn't care if I was on time or not. Either way I was going to jail. Derrick dropped me off in front of the Court, quickly kissed me goodbye, and told me he loved me. I nervously headed towards the entrance where my dad was standing. "Well, if they do arrest you, I'll head over to the Sheriff's office and put money on your books," he offered. I knew that I would need some money on my books because I was going to have to get shower shoes. We walked into the Court and took our seats next to the crowd of other nervous people waiting for their case to be called. Two hours went by before they called me. I was so nervous that I had to walk out of the Courtroom to pee every fifteen minutes. The female Judge called my case, and I walked up where my Attorney was. I hadn't seen her in a while and I wished that I could have talked to her and explain the situation before they called me. I left the details with her secretary a few days earlier, but I wasn't sure if she had gotten them.

The Judge went through the paperwork and started speaking as if the other cases didn't exist. Clearly, the Court was unorganized. For a moment I thought that I was going to get off without going to jail. Before I knew it, the Bailiff sitting at the desk to my right quickly jumped up and walked up behind me. "I need you to place your hands behind your back," he calmly said as he put those heavy metal cuffs around my wrists. Not only was I miserable, I was also embarrassed. There were probably at least one hundred people in the Courtroom and they all were seeing me be handcuffed. There wasn't much else to do except to go to the booking area. The Judge scheduled an Arraignment Hearing for the next day. I walked over to booking with the Bailiff escorting me and instructing me to stay on that all too familiar long blue line. The reality sunk in. As I was sitting at the same table I had sat at three other times, I realized that this time I really did not do anything wrong. It made me think back to all of the other times I had spent in jail. I had done something wrong at some points to end up there, but every single arrest involved Derrick. Whether it was his powerful influence that he had over me, or actions of my own, he played a role. When I was escorted to my new cell after changing into my oranges, I made my bed and lay down. My depression and grief quickly turned into anger and frustration. I was angry with Derrick. I was angry that I was sitting in jail and he was not. He was supposed to be the one sitting in jail.

When I went to my Arraignment the next day, it was a little bit after 12:00 noon. Before the Judge called my case, my Probation Officer came up and sat in the chair next to me. "Okay, so here is what's going on," she said as she looked at her clipboard. "I know that you don't want to be here, and honestly, I don't know what your involvement was. If you can tell me where we can find Derrick, I can probably get you out of here in a couple of hours." I became eager to give him the information that I had. I was done with jail, and I wanted my life back. This last round of heartache got me to my wits end. When I had time away from Derrick and was sitting in my jail cell, I was able to really think about the situation that I was in. It wasn't good. It was full of empty promises. We couldn't just wish our lives to be better. Something serious had to happen before I could fully understand this. For me, it was happening in this moment as I sat in an orange suit with shackles on my wrists and ankles.

I gave my Probation Officer as much information as I could. I told him what Derrick was driving, and I told him where he might be. I didn't remember what the physical address was, but I had a rough idea of how to get there. My Probation Officer helped me draw a map on a piece of paper from the clipboard, and he said that he would keep me updated. I wasn't let out of jail that day, but the next day I was. Both my Probation Officer and my Lawyer came to see me. My Lawyer explained to me that the Court didn't want to let me go because they thought that I might either run or help Derrick continue to hide. My Probation Officer expressed the same concern. He told me that he wanted to recommend that I be let out, but he didn't know if he could trust my judgment. I reassured him that I was completely done with getting in trouble, and I was thinking about filing for a divorce. I gave him my word that I would not run, and I reminded him that out of all of the other times I was in trouble, I never ran. This worked in my favor, because the next day when I went to Court, the Judge let me go home. She reminded me that if I were to run or even help Derrick hide, she would send me straight to prison.

After putting my own clothes back on and collecting my personal items from the calendar, which was my purse, a pack of cigarettes and thirteen dollars, I walked out of the exit door, and I was on my own. Luckily, my house was only a fifteen-minute walk away. I smoked a cigarette as I made the walk, pondering how important it was to have my freedom. I value my freedom and I knew that it would always be at risk as long as I stayed with Derrick. When I got home, my house was empty and cold. I didn't know what to do, so I called my older sister. She listened to me while I cried on the phone, and a few hours later she brought me a bag of groceries and a book that she thought might help me. I cleaned up my house, got into my pajamas, and made myself cozy on the couch with my book. When I opened it, I saw that she had written something on the inside flap.

Lizzie,
You are the bravest person I know. I'll always love you no matter what.
Lilah

Although unexpected, I thought that it was extremely nice of her to write that. She went out of her way to do something to help me feel better, and it helped me to regain a little bit of my

498

self-worth. I read the first few chapters of the book, and it really did help me feel better. It had a bunch of positive affirmations in it, and it helped me to understand why I had put myself in these situations.

Later that same night, I got a phone call from Derrick. He was calling me from a payphone because he was too paranoid to use his cell phone. "I'm so glad you are out of jail. I really want to see you. I'm so miserable without you," he said, genuinely sounding miserable. "I want to see you too, but I'm so worried about getting caught. They will send me straight back to jail," I said, hoping that he would understand. "I'm running out of clean clothes, and I really need some stuff from the house. If you just walk down here, no one is going to find out. I'm staying in the trailer that's next to the old house that Donnie and I used to live in," I sighed, and agreed to bring in his stuff. I felt bad for him, but I was also really worried that I was going to get caught. I put on my jacket, packed up the bag for him, and started walking. I left through the back door, and cut through the rest of the mobile home park where it would be more difficult to spot me. It was freezing outside, and the walk was longer than I thought it was going to be. It was really dark and making me nervous. I got to the trailer and called out so he would hear me. He opened the door and I walked in. It was abandoned, dark, dingy and cold. Right away he hugged me and told me that he loved me. I gave him his things and sat down on the couch that he was sleeping on. Technically, it was the seats from a two-door pickup truck. He was cold and depressed, and I had mixed feelings about it. I didn't know it at the time, but I had lost complete respect for him. I had a defensive wall that had been formed, and he was partially to blame. I showed him compassion, talked for about an hour, and told him that I had to go.

Before leaving, he pulled me next to him one last time. "Let's just run. We are never going to get out of this. In my mind, the only way to get back to our daughter is to run." I could see where he was coming from, but I had just gotten out of jail. There was no way in hell that I was going to risk going back. I gently responded, "We can't. We just have to hang in there. Maybe you should just get it over with and turn yourself in. The sooner that you take care of it, the sooner that we can leave." Deep in my heart I had no intentions of leaving with him. I was hoping that he would turn himself in so I would be free to really begin my life. I would never be able to live an honest, safe and content life if I were to stay with him.

Only a few days after I was released from jail, I was sitting at home watching TV when I got a phone call. It was the County Jail. They had finally caught Derrick, and he was arrested and being charged with three felonies. I also got a call from Derrick after he was in jail. "I just wanted to let you know that they arrested me, and I don't know how long I'm going to be here. I got tired of hiding, so I guess I'm kind of glad that I'm just getting it over with." He regained a little bit of my respect because he was showing some willingness to take responsibility for this. Tears fell down my cheeks. "I love you, and as soon as I can, I'll put money on your books. Try to hang in there, and when I get the car I'll come and visit you." Somehow, our car ended up with the old man that was friends with our neighbor and his name was Lowell. I didn't know how to say his name right, so I just called him Lolo. I sent Aaron a text message asking if he could have Lolo drop the car off. Within a few days, the ugly burgundy car was back in my driveway. I had decided that I was going to try my very best to stay away from drugs, and see what I could do to support myself.

Less than a week after getting out of jail, I realized that I needed to get a job as soon as possible. Since the whole town thought nothing of me anyway, I went straight to McDonald's. When I walked in, I saw one of the girls that I was in jail with while I was pregnant working behind the counter. She smiled and asked me what I wanted to eat. I told her that I was actually

500

looking for a job, and I needed to start working right away. Her eyes lit up with excitement, and she went back to get the manager. He hired me on the spot, issued my uniform shirts, and I was going to start that same night. I was embarrassed that I was going to be working there, but it was a lot better than sitting in jail or going without food. I called my mom to tell her. I was curious to see what the reaction was going to be. "Aww, good job. Lizzie! Most people wouldn't do what you did today, and I'm very proud of you. A job is a job, and you are doing what you need to do." Her reaction gave me a little bit more confidence, and I went to work that night feeling a little less ashamed. I was lucky that the manager was there full-time. When I got home every night, I was pretty tired, but I felt like I was doing the right thing. Everything was going okay until I agreed to give my jail buddy a ride home after work. Instead of taking her home, we stopped at one of her friend's houses, only to get a sack of meth and start the self-destruction all over again. I just could not say no.

Chapter 72

I went to the jail to visit Derrick as often as they would let me. He seemed to be hanging in there pretty well. The District Attorney's office was trying to charge him with two strikes. In the State of California, if a person gets three strikes he or she is subject to a minimum of twenty-five to life. Derrick was sticking to his guns and not talking to the detectives. Apparently Donnie was trying to put most of the blame on Derrick for the assaults that took place at night. Donnie was just as guilty as Derrick. As far as the case with the baby, I hadn't heard any more news. I quickly gave up that they would solve it at all. If they couldn't solve the case with my daughter, I had no reason to believe that they could solve this one. The baby never ended up having a funeral. The family was too broke, and his body was in the custody of the State for so long, that they just decided to cremate him. I spoke with Derrick. Derrick's parents called occasionally, and his mother and I emailed him every day. I told her about my job, and she was updated with everything that was going on. She sent me pictures of Danielle. When I thought about leaving Derrick, I felt extreme conflict. This was only because we had a child together. It was one thing for me to leave. Derrick, but it was a total other thing to completely disregard Danielle. I knew that somehow I had to at least try to be with her. I didn't know how it would happen, but I had to try.

I got high with my friend from jail every day for the next week. I was surprised to learn that I actually liked my job. It was easy, and they switched my job to meet up with my tasks enough to where it didn't get too boring. At this point, my mom was calling me almost on a daily basis. I think that she was worried about me because she knew that I was by myself and she knew about my neighbor. I decided to take the brutally honest approach with her too. I knew that the only way to really help myself was to be honest with everyone else, and in turn I would be forced to be honest with myself. On my night off from work, the old man Lolo came over. We were bored, and he had meth. When my mom called, I went into the back room to talk to her. I was feeling guilty, exhausted and out of ideas, so I told her that I had been high for the last week. "Well, why can't you just get away from it?" she asked, not completely understanding how addiction to this particular drug manifests. "It's just not that easy. It is everywhere, no matter where I go. My neighbor has it, my neighbor's friend has it, and people at work have it. People are always stopping by here when they have it and they know that I won't say no," I confessed. "Liz, that's dangerous. You could end up dead. Those people are dangerous and unpredictable. What are you going to do?" "I don't know but all I can do is work. I don't know how to get away from it because it's everywhere. And if I know that someone has it and it's offered to me, I can't say no. It's a physical and mental addiction."

She started to understand a little bit better. "Well can't I just come and get you out of there?" she asked, and I knew that this could be my only chance to really get out. She hadn't asked me this question in a while, so I knew that when she did she was serious. "If it's okay with you guys, then yes. I don't know how to get away from this, and I think that if I just leave, it might be

504

my only chance." "Okay, Lizzy, have your stuff packed and be ready to go early in the morning. I'm probably going to leave here around 5:00 a.m." "I'll be ready. Just call me when you are a few minutes away. Love you." We got off the phone. I walked out of the back room, and Lolo was in the kitchen, crafting up some gourmet spaghetti dinner. I don't even know where he got the ingredients, because I barely had any food. He sure was creative, though. I guess he had to learn how to improvise over the years, because from what I had heard him say to Derrick, it sounded like he was living this lifestyle for over twenty years now.

The last night that I spent in Tahoe, with Tahoe being my official place of residence, was a night that I probably won't ever forget. Lolo was actually an interesting person who had once lived a very interesting life. He told me stories about his younger years and how quickly his success turned into nothing. "You should have seen me back then," he laughed. "I had the 70's Afro, I already had a house paid for, and I had a beautiful wife and a little girl." "Then, I started using drugs, and I just liked it way too much. I spent all of the money that we had saved up, and we lost everything. Of course, my wife was furious, and she ended up taking my daughter and leaving. I've tried to see her over the years but haven't been able to. Her name is Rihanna. I would do anything to see her again." This got me thinking. With all of my obsessive research I had done over the last few years, I wondered if I could find his daughter online. After doing some research for only a few minutes, I pulled up a profile picture of a woman who fit her description. I showed the picture to Lolo, and he was convinced that it was Rihanna. I sent her a Facebook message and explained who I was and why I was contacting her. I gave her Lolo's phone number and told her that he was trying to get in touch with her. Lolo took off to find more drugs, and I let him take my car. I knew that I wasn't going to need it because I wasn't going to take it to my mom's house. In the back of my mind, I knew that he wasn't going to come back in time to say goodbye.

It was already 4:00 in the morning, and the only thing I had left to do was pack and shower. My mom called me around 6:00 a.m. to tell me that she was a few minutes away. I didn't know how I was going to stay awake because I was starting to get tired. I was going to end it. I was ready to say goodbye to crystal meth. I took one last residual hit out of the empty glass pipe, and I smashed and broke it in the toilet. I flushed the remnants of the broken pipe down the drain, and I thought about how much I had lost over the drug. I can't honestly say that I let this drug into my life willingly. It snuck into my life as I was trying to find my own identity. I caved to the peer pressure by experimenting with cocaine. My heart knew that it wasn't right, and I ignored the warnings of my subconscious. The first time I ever used drugs, I thought that I was snorting cocaine. I ingested methamphetamine in extremely large quantities. Even as a recreational cocaine user, I still knew that I never, ever wanted to try meth. That was one drug that I was not willing to experiment with. I had heard the horror stories and I had seen the before and after pictures. It was never going to be a part of my life. When it suddenly invaded my body without me even having a chance to contest, it was over. While it was normal to everyone else, it was trash to me. I had allowed trash into my life and eventually that's what I had become. I lost my self-worth, my sanity, my values, my family, and most tragically, my babies. Even years after losing them, it still cuts like a knife to say that to myself. It was still extremely difficult to grasp the fact that they were no longer with me. It was unbearable. I looked at myself in the mirror, and I didn't know who I was looking at. I wasn't that young, confident mom and full-time student. I wasn't that young married woman happily taking care of her family. I wasn't that girl getting ready for her senior project. I wasn't the teenager who was in love with the idea of being in love. I wasn't the girl who spent her entire summer vacation locked up in her bedroom obsessively reading

506

the novels that she couldn't get enough of. I wasn't the aspiring musician who would spend hours teaching herself how to play songs on the piano. I wasn't the little kid getting ready for her first cheerleading competition. I wasn't the twin who was beating up her other twin in fifth grade. I wasn't the five-year-old little girl running around and screaming in excitement because she got a baby alive doll for Christmas.

I didn't know who I was. I didn't know who I was supposed to be. My babies had given me the unexpected gift of preserving and prolonging my own childhood. Although I was their mother, I was still able to live and enjoy everything about being young and innocent. I still had an excuse to buy Barbie dolls. I had a reason to watch Charlotte's Web again. Some would believe that my childhood was taken away when I became pregnant. My beliefs are much different. My happiness and childhood was given back to me when my babies came into my life. My true childhood, those years that I most vividly recall as a young person, were ripped from me when my little girls went away. That was when I lost my childhood. That was when I lost my innocence. That was when I lost my young heart and bright future. It would take a long, long time and a miracle to ever recover from the pain caused by methamphetamine. My post-traumatic-stress disorder hadn't even begun.

"How are you Lizzie?" my mom asked as she walked in to help me put my bags in the trunk. "I'm ok, just tired," I replied. She hugged me. "I'm so glad that I get to take care of you. I get my Lizzie back!" she said, patting my head. I wasn't sure how she was going to get me back when I couldn't even get myself back, but if anyone could do it, it would be my mom.

Chapter 73

I took one last look at the home that I had grown up in over the last twenty-two years as we passed through the small town and headed toward the summit. I hated this summit. It gave me flashbacks of driving to the hospital in Sacramento four years earlier. I was always going back to that dark, snowy night when chain control notified me of an Amber Alert. I had a memory of every little part of this town. Some were good, some were bad, but most were sad. I once thought that I would spend the rest of my life here. I never thought that this beautiful place could turn so ugly. As we drove up the snowy summit, I felt relief. I wasn't sad to be leaving, and I knew that this was goodbye. My mom and I stopped at a Starbucks on the way to her house. She lived about two hours away in a little town called Grass Valley.

When we finally got to her house, it was around noon. I was in a daze and starting to come down. She made us lunch, and my stepdad began to question me. I expected that I might have an interrogation coming. He knew that I had been using drugs, but he didn't know exactly what. When I told him, he shook his head, "Oh no, Liz." I was as honest with him as I was with my mom. "Well, tell me the truth, did you bring any of that stuff to my house?" "No, I got rid of all of it before I left. I flushed it down the toilet. I promise that I won't ever bring it to your house." He believed me. After eating lunch, that was probably the healthiest food I had eaten in a long time, I went back to the bedroom that I was going to be staying in and fell asleep immediately. The next thing I remember was my mom was sitting on my bed and rubbing my head, "Liz, it's okay. Wake up. Its just mom." I turned over and looked at her completely confused. I forgot that I was even there. "What's going on?" I asked her, totally confused. "Are you okay? I came to wake you up because dinner is ready, and you were fighting me while you were tangled in your blanket." "Oh, I'm sorry. I don't remember anything." In a daze, I walked out to the living room where dinner was on the table, and we sat down and ate. We talked about me finding a job as soon as I could, and I also remembered that I needed to request my last paycheck from McDonald's. I started to feel better in a few days, and I was slowly getting back to normal.

I wasn't familiar with any local clinics, and I was about to run out of my antidepressant. Because I was away from the horrible circumstances that I was living in, I thought that I would just wean myself off the antidepressant and see if I could be okay without them. I was tired for the first week that I didn't have my medication, but I quickly regained my energy. I was eating better, and my mom helped me find a church to go to. We went on Sundays and there was also a weekly meeting for people in recovery. I tried to go to the local NA meetings, but I really didn't feel comfortable, and I didn't feel like I fit in. I didn't know any of the people, and unlike the familiar group from Tahoe, it didn't seem that many of these people had very much sobriety time. One thing that I liked about the church meetings was that they always had a contemporary Christian rock band playing. Music always put me into a meditative state, and it was a good place for me to go to find forgiveness and think about my life. The more that I socialized with the real world, the less I thought about it. I didn't know what to do about it, but the thought of never seeing Danielle again broke my heart. Derrick was still in jail, so I still had time to think about my options. I was still out on bail for the accessory to a felony charge that was brought against me. I had a Court date in about four months that would determine if I was guilty or innocent. I had plenty of time to reflect on the last four years of my life and I became angry. Being around my mom and my grandparents helped me feel like myself again. I was angry that I lost myself for so long, and most important, I was angry that I didn't have my children with me.

I eventually got a job at the local convenience store. I could hardly understand the owners, but they were nice enough to hire me. After realizing that this job didn't have enough hours for what I needed, I applied for a job at the Holiday Inn. The only openings they had were for housekeeping. It paid $9 an hour and it was full-time. I didn't like the fact that I had to get up early for the job, but I knew that I was an expert at cleaning so I would probably do well. The more I worked, the more my self-esteem came back. I started to realize what I did and didn't want for my life. I went online and printed the forms that I would need to file for a divorce. I drove to Tahoe with my mom and determined that I would serve the papers during a visit with Derrick. I didn't know for sure if I was going to follow through with it, but I did want him to know that I was serious about life. His mother had been emailing me constantly, and I felt like she was being incredibly nosy. Eventually, I just had to stop responding. I needed time to think about what I really wanted. I couldn't picture myself staying with Derrick and ever being truly happy. He would just be a reminder of everything that I didn't have.

When he saw me behind the glass, his eyes lit up. He wasn't expecting me. I probably looked different and healthier and happier. When I first moved to Grass Valley, one of the first things that my mom did was take me to the local chocolate factory. Then she took me to her hairstylist and we both had our hair done. If she was trying to boost my self-confidence, she did a good job. "Look at you, all pretty and spoiled," Derrick said. "Well, it was useless for me to sit around here," I replied, feeling kind of nervous. We talked about the case, about Danielle, and about how much longer he thought he would be in jail. He wasn't sure, but it wasn't looking very good. "So I have to give you these papers. Don't get mad and don't freak out. I just want you to know that I'm serious about staying clean and not getting in trouble. I slid the papers under the glass. He took them, and stared at them. He was in shock. "I... I just don't understand. What are you doing?" "I just told you, I simply don't want to handle any pain anymore." "I know you can't. Everything will be fine once we get to Texas." He wasn't really willing to accept what I had just sent his way. I couldn't blame him since he was sitting in jail. I was happy that at least I knew that I had options. We made the drive back home, and after dinner, I sat in my room crying. I was thinking about Derrick and how lonely he must be. I suddenly started to miss him again. I didn't know what to do, so I wrote him a letter. I told him how much I loved him and that I was just so tired of all the defeat. I told him that I wanted him to get better, and that I was trying to get better at my mom's house. I sealed the envelope and I put it in the mailbox before anyone could see.

After I started my job, I started to clash with my stepdad. I was in his way and he was in my way. I went into a full-blown panic attack and determined that I had to go back to Tahoe. I threw a complete fit until my mom finally caved in and drove me to Tahoe. She dropped me off with my older sister, Lilah, because I didn't really have anywhere else to go. My sister had to work that day, so I decided to go to my old house to see what was left. As I walked in, it looked like there were squatters living there. There were old smelly blankets all over the place, and the entire house completely stunk. This was definitely not the house that I remember. Or was it? Was I really living like this? I felt

512

contaminated from just standing there. And I was worried that some people might show up. I couldn't find any of my things, so I decided that I would return to the house the next day when my mom picked me up. I was only in Tahoe for less than a day, and I already wanted to leave again. I probably just had to go there to see for myself that it would really never be my home again. My visit with Derrick gave me the closure that I needed. I didn't know what kind of closure I was even looking for, but I knew that I didn't want to spend my life visiting my husband in jail. It was no way for either of us to live. I told Derrick that I would see him the next day before I left to go back to Grass Valley and I intended to. But after leaving the jail, and realizing that it made me feel anxious, I decided not to return.

Before heading back to my mom's house, we went out to lunch with Lilah. After we ate, we returned to the house that had seen my heaviest days of using drugs. Lolo had moved in. I wasn't surprised at all. I was actually kind of glad that he was there because I wanted to know where my pictures were. He had neatly put them away in boxes for me and stored them under the porch of the house. He wrapped the boxes in plastic bags to protect the pictures from harsh weather. As I went under the porch to pull out the boxes, I immediately became worried as I saw puddles of water on top of the bags. I took the bags off, and the boxes were soaking wet. All of the pictures, albums and baby books were soaked. I was hoping that they were just wet on the outside, but the water had seeped through every single picture. My heart was broken. These pictures were the only things I had left of my babies. They were ruined. I walked away, because I couldn't handle looking at them anymore. The pictures of my daughters were gone. I was crying and wiping away my tears because I didn't want to be obvious. Lila came up to me and gave me a hug. She also cried. She must have felt the pain that I was feeling. Actually, it was more than a pain. It was an absence and a loss - almost like a death.

I spoke with my dad a few days after I returned to Grass Valley, and he told me that when he went to a job in Tahoe, he would stop by the house and pick up the pictures. He said that he was going to go through them and see if any of them were salvageable. I resumed working, and shortly after my temporary meltdown, my mom and stepdad found me my own place. It was a cute little studio that was attached to a house that had been turned into a duplex. My mom and my grandparents set me up with all the furniture that I needed and the only complaint that I had was that my television set was about 8"x8". I remembered the TV set from when I was little. My grandpa had it in his house. I loved it but it was so small that it was almost funny. My stepdad told me that he was going to pay my rent for six months. After that I would be on my own. Part of him must love me, I thought. I had a love-hate relationship with him, but it was mostly good. They were trying to teach me how to live on my own, and although I had a full time job, I didn't know if I could do it. I wasn't sure if I was ready to face the world alone.

Chapter 74

I worked every day and because I didn't have a car, I had to walk. It was about a 10 to 15 minute walk, but the summers get hot in Grass Valley. Since I had served the divorce papers to Derrick, my young mind already considered myself to be separated. I hadn't talked to him in months, and I hadn't contacted his mother either. I knew that Danielle was safe and I missed her, but I wasn't sure what I was going to do. I definitely didn't have the money to hire an Attorney to get her back into my custody. Derrick's mom said that she would never keep her from me, but I had my doubts. They had her for quite a while, and they were most definitely attached.

The best cure for my loneliness ….was boys! They were everywhere. I never knew how likeable I was until I was single! The first guy, Matt, was one I met working at the convenience store. The bad thing about him was that he reminded me of Derrick. The good thing about him was that he was a ton of fun. Nevertheless, he was still trouble. He thought he loved me, but I just couldn't handle it. He was a member of some white-boy brotherhood group, and I wasn't sure exactly what that meant, but I had a feeling it could only be trouble. The only times I called him to come over was when I was afraid that someone was going to break into my little studio and hurt me. I made him use his own blanket and stay away from me. I wasn't ready to have another relationship and just needed the protection.

The other guy that I periodically hung out with was a kid I went to high school with. We started talking on Myspace back when it was cool. He was a few years older than me, and I specifically remember him kissing me out of the blue when I was a freshman. We were both in the same P.E. class. He was still living in Tahoe, but he traveled for work. Every time he came to visit me I got super excited. It was nice to have someone around who was from the same hometown as I was. Apparently he didn't ever hear anything about my million bags of baggage either.

Then there was Jared. Our first date was amazing and we both liked each other a lot. He was a punk rocker in a band. When I saw him practice with his band, I was seeing stars. He was hot. Watching him play on his guitar like the hot guy from Blink 182 was really fun.

All of them knew that I was legally married. I told only one person my entire story after feeling he could be trusted. His name was Nate. I met him while I was hanging out at a co-workers house, and she lived just down the street from me. Her name was Ashley, and she was a few years older than me. She was from Reno, and had moved to Grass Valley to be with a guy she met. We got along great, and she was always funny. She kept telling me about a guy named Nate and how she thought we would be so cute together. Finally, out of curiosity, I had her invite him to her house when I was going over for dinner. At first glance, I thought he was gorgeous, and he had a big, bright smile. After talking for a while, I knew pretty quickly that he was someone that I could definitely be friendly with. It was very easy to be myself around Nate, and I didn't feel like I was going to be judged for anything that I said. He wasn't boring. He was outspoken just like me. I ended up hanging out with Nate almost every day for the rest of my stay in Grass Valley. I also met his mom and siblings. He made me feel young again. Despite the fact that I felt like my depression was coming back, he kept me company and made my days fun. I didn't have any money for a Dr. appointment, and I was completely out of medication. Although I should have known that it was my depression coming back, I just blamed it on feeling insecure and missing my daughter.

Once in a while, I would tell Nate that he had to go home. Sometimes I just needed to be by myself. On the other hand, it probably wasn't a good idea for me to be alone with my thoughts. Every night that I spent alone in my little studio apartment, my mind would wander off and think about Derrick. I would also think about our daughter and wonder what the best thing was to do. I started emailing his mother periodically, and I told her that I didn't have Internet access on a regular basis and that was why she hadn't heard from me. She accepted my excuse and was just happy to be in contact. By this point, I only had less than a month left of Probation providing that my upcoming hearing didn't go badly. Derrick's mom told me that her niece and her cousin applied to the university near their town. If she got accepted, she would be moving in with them for the duration of her school years. I had met her before and I liked her. At first I was excited about this, but then I wondered if I ended up going back to Texas, would be too much estrogen in one house. Derrick's mom was talking about possibly coordinating the trip out there. Meaning that instead of flying, I would ride out there with her in her car.

The big Court date had finally come. I initially thought it was going to just be for my case, but then I found out that Derrick was also going to be there, and he was going to have his sentencing as well. My grandparents drove me all the way to Tahoe because my mom was busy with school. My dad was also going to meet us at the Court to show his support and also give me the pictures that he was able to recover. I thought that it was really nice of him to do this for me, and it showed that he really cared. I was extremely nervous about going to my Hearing because I knew that it only took one decision against my favor and everything would change. I would go straight back to jail, and I would be starting all over again. I hoped that the Lawyers would see that I had left Derrick and was really making an effort to better my life. I was also nervous because I knew that Derrick was going to be there and my family was also going to be there. It was conflicting for me because I knew that my family didn't like him since he was such a bad influence on me over the years. It was still hard for me to not get upset over this, and as for myself, I didn't even know if I liked him. I loved him, but I wasn't sure if I liked him or wanted to be around him again.

I was happy to see my Lawyer standing outside of the Courtroom as I walked through the metal detector. I wanted to speak with her before anyone else could hear what I was saying, including Derrick. She asked me how I was doing, and I told her about my new living arrangement. "I don't know if it will make a difference or not, but I wanted to find out if there is any way that you can relay to the Judge and the District Attorney that I filed for divorce and left Derrick. I'd rather it not be done in front of Derrick because it just makes it really awkward." She said that she would try her best to quietly get the information to them. She told me that she wasn't exactly sure what they were thinking or what was going to happen. Based on her own knowledge, though, she said she would be surprised if they actually found me guilty of that crime.

The Judge called the case, and Derrick was sitting at the table next to me. He looked like he was so happy to see me, and he asked me how I was doing. I was extra nice to him and said that I was doing well. He looked like he was going to become emotional. The Court went over my case before they called his. The Judge ruled that what I did was more of an act of a Good

Samaritan than a crime and dropped the charge against me. I was so happy that I felt tears welling up in my eyes. I truly felt like it was a miracle and that maybe I still had hope for a good life. Derrick and his Lawyer looked over at me and congratulated me. I could tell that Derrick truly meant it, and he was honestly happy that they dropped the charge. It made me feel sad for him and what he was going through. He was not innocent of the crime, but the Court gave him two strikes and claimed that he used his fists as a deadly weapon. The Court called a ten-minute recess, and I really had to pee. They were going to call Derrick's case next, and honestly, it was just so awkward being in the same room with him that I didn't feel like I wanted to stay. I had my family with me and they were 100% sure I was leaving him. I was still unsure. I got a letter in the mail a few days after the Hearing. It was from Derrick.

Hi Honey,

It was really good to see you the other day, and I wish you could have stayed longer. I almost cried when I found out that you left for good after the break. I will always love you no matter what. You are the legs to my table, and that will never change, but if you are over me, I would really like to know. It will hurt a lot, but I need to know the truth so I can plan my future. The Court is giving me credit for time served, and I am going to be out of here in a few weeks. The only stipulation is that I have to leave the state of California forever. Before I leave, I have to do a series of Probation meetings in a weeks' time, and I also have to register my fists as a deadly weapon with the state. If I ever get into trouble again, even in the smallest amount, I'll go to prison for the rest of my life - or at least for a minimum of twenty-five years. They gave me two strikes, but I was somehow able to convince them to just let me go. I promised them that I would never be back to California and I told them that I just wanted to go live with my family in Texas. I hope that you'll still want to go there as soon as you're off Probation. The suspense is killing me. I don't pray a lot, but if there is a God, I've been praying to him lately. I love you and please, please write me back.

Derrick

As I was finished reading the letter, my tears were falling onto the piece of paper. It was almost as if I could hear him talking. My mind was not acknowledging the negative aspects of our relationship. It was only thinking about the things that I loved about him. His quick wit, his funny sense of humor, and his overall sincerity when he told me he loved me. I began to feel like I just needed to go to Texas. I didn't have the same sense of belonging that I had known for such a long time. Living alone for the first time was terrifying, and I let my fears get the best of me. I felt empty because I had three children and none of them were with me. I knew that my third baby was going to be without me, and it was going to be because of my choices. I just couldn't do that to her. I began to write Derrick's mom an email and told her that I would be ready to leave in a few weeks.

Chapter 75

When I think about depression, I think about it as an unwelcome personality. I believe that I spent at least 50% of my life living with depression, and I simply didn't know it. When I was as young as six years old, I always felt tired and weak. I never knew why. Everybody just assumed that I was having growing pains. I vividly remember my first day of second grade. I was seven years old, and I woke up feeling like I was going to vomit. Most kids are excited about their first day of school. I was incredibly nervous and didn't know how to handle it. I had a difficult time paying attention in my classes and occasionally my teachers would become frustrated with me and thought that I deliberately broke a rule when it was really just an accident. I remember my third grade teacher asking all of her students to stop doodling on their spelling tests. It didn't sink in. On autopilot, I began to doodle hearts. When I finished taking the test, she became angry me. In sixth grade, my teacher had chosen me to stand in front of the entire classroom so the other kids could give me compliments and then clap for me. She did this with all of the students on a weekly basis. She would always choose a different student. I didn't know why, but I was mortified. I started having facial spasms like I had Tourette syndrome. My face turned bright red. Mrs. Greenfield patted me on the shoulder. "It's okay, calm down," she quietly said. That's when I knew that my nervousness was obvious. I'm pretty sure that was when I had my very first panic attack. I was just eleven years old. All throughout Middle school, I felt dizzy at times, and I felt like I just wasn't in reality. Looking back on all of these strange things that happened to me as a little kid, I am now sure that they were symptoms of depression. I believe that I was born that way. Not of the fault of anyone else, but for some reason, my mind was constructed differently. I was always an intuitive child and extremely sensitive, perceptive and depressed.

I knew what depression felt like because I recognized it after we had to take Danielle to El Paso. When I got out of jail for the third time, I was broken. My psychological self just couldn't handle any more and my subconscious was trying to send me warning signals that were manifested through depression symptoms and panic attacks. When I moved to Grass Valley, my depression came back after I thought it would be okay to stop taking my meds, but it wasn't nearly as bad as it was when I was in Tahoe. I brushed it off and assumed that the only reason I was feeling this way was because I wanted to be with my husband and daughter. It was the easiest reason that I could come up with, and I knew exactly what I needed to do to fix it. Once I fixed it by moving to Texas, I knew that I would feel better right away.

Not too long after I decided that I wanted to go to Texas, I quit my job. I was tired of working, and I knew that I was going to be out of California soon anyway. Derrick's mom sent me money to pay my bills and get some groceries. I slept all day, I would get up to make dinner and watch TV, and then get in bed again and go back to sleep. My mom would stop by a few times a week and bring me homemade ice cream or give me a ride to the grocery store to help me get food. Her homemade ice cream

522

was the one thing that did cheer me up - talk about heaven in your mouth!

When I quit my job, I'm pretty sure that my mom and my stepdad were starting to realize that I was probably not going to stay there very much longer. I knew that they were both disappointed. I didn't want to disappoint them, but I honestly just didn't know how to live alone, and I wasn't truly ready to completely end my relationship with Derrick. I didn't feel like I had enough closure to do that just yet. Additionally, I knew that if I didn't at least try to go to Texas to be with my daughter, I would never forgive myself.

I was already planning my trip, and we had decided how I was going to get there. Derrick's cousin was accepted into the University in Texas. She had to go to the University to do her paperwork, and I still had two weeks of Probation left. I didn't have any more meetings scheduled with Probation. The last time I had a meeting they pretty much told me to stay out of trouble and I would be free to go on August 23, 2009. I figured that as long as I followed their rules, it wouldn't make any difference if I left two weeks early. I was already living in another town, which they knew about, so it's not like they were going to show up at my front door. We decided that we were going to take off driving in mid-August. Derrick was released from jail in early August. I was making my dinner on a Friday afternoon and watching Extreme Home Makeover on my 8" inch television set when my phone rang. It was Derrick at the County Jail. He had just gotten out of Court and told me that he was being released. I was excited for him, and I wanted to go to Tahoe right away. I wanted to see him before he left for Texas.

I had remained in contact with Casie's sister, Alicia, and she offered to come and get me. She under-estimated the length of the drive and didn't arrive until about midnight. I was frustrated because Derrick had told me that he would call me as soon as he was out of jail and he didn't. He knew that I was going to be on my way. When we pulled into Tahoe, I was livid. He knew that I had Alicia make the long drive so I could see him, and he wasn't even considerate enough to tell me where he would be. I had a feeling that I would find him at the trailer park we had lived in. When we pulled in, it was 3:00 a.m. With the headlights on, I saw the silhouette of a tall person walking out of the front door. My suspicion was spot-on. It was Derrick. Although it was dark, I could still see him pretty good because he had a white T-shirt on. He had lost a lot of weight. He almost looked like he did when we first started dating. I ran up to him and gave him a big hug. He had been in jail for around four months, but it felt as if I hadn't seen him in forever. He helped me grab my bags out of Alicia's car and I thanked her for going out of her way. I had no idea how I was going to get home after Derrick got on the bus to Texas, but I honestly didn't care. I forgot how much I missed him. I instantly remembered everything about him that I loved. I was quick to brush the bad things to the side. Although I was elated to be with him and feeling like we were dating again for the first time, a part of me wondered why he was staying in this neighborhood. I had a feeling that he had gotten high with Aaron as soon as he was out of jail. I didn't want to ruin our time together, so I never brought it up.

We walked into the house that I had lived in for just a short time but had so many memories. They were all sad memories. Unlike the last time I was there, someone had come to the house to clean it. All of the smelly blankets were gone, and it looked like it had been cleaned for new renters. "How did you get in the house in the first place?" I asked. "Oh, the backdoor was unlocked. I didn't have anywhere else to stay, and I thought that you would probably find me here, so I figured why not." Aaron had saved some of Derrick's clothing just in case he got out and needed regular clothes to wear. We walked up to our old room and Derrick was using his clothes as a pillow. The house was completely empty and it made me sad. Although the majority of time spent in this house was spent using drugs, I still made it our home. No matter what a person is going through, they still need to have a place to call home. I always valued the importance of that. It didn't feel the same at all. It didn't feel like I had ever lived there, and it didn't feel like I had ever lived in this town. Now that I was able to actually leave Tahoe, I was given a new light on life's possibilities. Tahoe was not the only place to live. It was not my only option. I'll forever be grateful that my mom helped me to realize this. It's easy to seclude yourself in a beautiful, cozy little paradise up on top of a mountain, but when I allowed myself to do this for such a long time, I didn't know what I was missing. There's a whole big, bright world out there with so many possibilities. The worst thing that I could have ever done was not try. I still think about all the locals that I knew, and I wonder how many of them were born in Tahoe and never left. It makes me sad to think that some of these people may not have ever tapped into their full potential. They simply did not know what they were missing.

Derrick and I lay on the hard floor in the empty bedroom that was once ours. We planned on falling asleep, but we had too many emotions. We were worried about getting him getting to Texas in time, we were worried about money, and we were definitely worried about where we were going to stay for the next few days. Even though we were worried about so many things, we still held each other for probably two hours. Derrick seemed like he was a little bit more serious about life, and he almost seemed uneasy about being out of jail. I thought that this was a good thing, and I hoped that it would only benefit him, and ultimately our marriage, in the long-term.

We somehow managed to survive the next few days. Derrick's mother wired us enough money to be able to eat and rent a cheap motel room. One of our mutual friends offered to give us a ride to Sacramento where Derrick would leave by Greyhound bus. Sacramento was only an hour away from Grass Valley, and I was lucky enough that she agreed to take me home. I tried my hardest not to cry as he got on the bus. I wanted to be strong for him because I knew that right now he was vulnerable and unsure about everything. He called me periodically while he was riding across the country. He made it to Texas in his allotted time and I could finally breathe. I still had a few weeks left in Grass Valley, but I was anxious to start our new lives together.

After I got home from my visit with him, a few days went by and I started to become mixed up once. Nate came and hung out with me a few times, and a part of me desperately just wanted to be a young adult and have fun. At the same time, I knew that I had a little girl waiting for me. She is the main reason I knew that I had no other option but to move to Texas.

Finally, the day came when Derrick's aunt was going to pick me up. I wanted to spend one last night in my hometown because I didn't think I would ever be back. She had wanted to go to Tahoe anyway. We were going to spend the night in Tahoe, drive to the Bay Area to kill time at her house for a day, and then head all the way up to Quincy. Ashley and I would be leave for Texas from Quincy. Ashley had offered to pick me up at my house in Grass Valley on the actual day that we would be going to Texas, but I didn't want to wait that long to leave. I just had a sense of urgency to get my life moving. Also, I thought it would be fun to sneak in one last little party - and wow, did I live it up.

Chapter 76

Aunt Cherie was going to pick me up around noon. My mom and grandparents came over to my studio apartment to help clean because I couldn't take most of the things they had given me. My mom was frustrated, and I could tell that she was depressed over the whole thing. My stepdad was angry because he probably felt a little betrayed considering that he paid six months advance rent for me to get on my feet. Now he was going to have to try to find a new person to take over the lease so he wouldn't end up wasting his money. When my family was at my studio and I was about to leave, I didn't know what to do except cry. I was sad that I was leaving and felt like I was disappointing everyone all over again. None of them wanted me to leave, but they understood why I wanted to at least try to be with my daughter. My mom made a prediction as she was wiping down the floor. "I really just can't see you ever being happy in Texas, Liz. Of course I wish the best for you, but I think you're going to get there and be miserable and Derrick's mom - she'll probably try to make you her slave," she said. "I've been emailing Derrick's mom for years now, and I highly doubt that will happen. I'll never know how it's going to work unless I try," I dryly responded. The waterworks were about to start all over again. Aunt Cherie arrived and helped me put my things in the back of her SUV. Everything barely fit. She packed so much stuff in her car that it looked like she was about to move across the country with me. She had her smelly little dog with her too. When my things were packed, I gave my mom and grandparents a hug goodbye. My stepdad wasn't anywhere to be found, and he probably wasn't in the mood to see me anyway.

We pulled out of the driveway that I would never see again, and I waved to my mom and my grandparents while trying to keep it together. I didn't know when I would see any of them again. I was mainly upset because I felt like I let them down, and the last thing that I wanted to do was cause anyone more pain. I called my dad on the way to Tahoe and told him what was going on. He was also worried, but he understood. We planned to meet for lunch the next day before Aunt Cherie and I left for the Bay Area.

We checked into our hotel room that she booked and unpacked some of our things. I somehow convinced her to go with me to the casinos that night. I wanted to live it up and say goodbye to Tahoe forever. My grief and mixed emotions were heavily sitting on my subconscious, and as usual, the best thing that I knew to do was self-destruct. At least this time though, it wasn't with drugs. I had successfully stayed away from meth for about six months. We sat at one of the oval shaped bars and ordered shots of Jaeger. They were actually Jaeger-bombs. We were served the shot glasses with the liquor along with a full cup of red-bull. We dropped the shot glass into the cup of the energy drink, made a cheer, and drank away. We were pretty drunk within just a few hours. A woman with humongous boobs and short bleached hair approached the bar where we were still sitting. Cherie knew her, and they were talking like they were long lost best friends. The three of us decided to walk around the casino for a while, and we ended up stopping at one of the lingerie stores. The store had shoes, dresses, costumes and all

528

sorts of fun things to try on. We all tried on different outfits with new shoes in the dressing rooms. This woman who was with us, whom I had never met before, seemed to be going through some sort of a mid-life crisis. She would be extremely happy and excited one minute and on the floor in tears the next. When I walked out of the dressing room with a pink backless dress on, she screamed in delight. Somehow, both of the women, along with a girl who worked at the store and whom I had gone to school with, were in the dressing room with me taping my dress to my chest, which was now sucked in and pushed up from suction-cup boob amplifiers. Before I knew it, I almost looked famous - in kind of a slutty kind of way.

We ended up dancing almost all night. At one point, a handsome man asked me if I would be his "lady luck." I had no idea what that meant. "Sure, as long as you don't try to sleep with me," I responded. I followed him to a blackjack table. He was putting down chips of $10,000. I was shocked. I secretly really wanted one of those chips. I told the man that I had to meet my friends at a restaurant in the casino for dinner. When I found them, the two of them had turned into a group of at least fifteen. I knew a few of them. One in particular was a cute guy I remembered from school. We ate, had more shots and laughed about things I don't even recall. When we asked for the bill, the waitress surprised me as she said: "The man sitting over there in the corner actually already took care of it." It was the same man who I had witnessed dropping 10k chips. I thought it was really nice of him, but I wondered why he paid the tab. He had complimented me about how beautiful I was throughout the night, but I wondered if he thought he could get me to go to his room. I wasn't about to find out.

When it was around 4:00 a.m., Cherie and I decided we better get to our room and at least get a few hours of sleep. I was flirting to no end with the guy I knew from high school. I thought it would be fun to bring him back to the room - forgetting that Cherie was Derrick's aunt. She was too drunk to notice or even care, and she actually laughed about it when she realized what was going on. When she went into the room, my friend and I went down to the hot tub. When we went back to the room, we thought she would be asleep. When we discreetly started getting busy, she drunkenly slurred, "Wrap it up!" as she threw a condom our way. It was so hilarious that I could hardly control my laughter. The entire situation was awkwardly funny.

When I woke up about noon the next day, my friend was gone and Aunt Cherie was still asleep. We ordered a pizza to help tame our hangover, and I was cracking up as I went through the pictures from the night before. I decided to post them on My Space. I wanted the world to see that I could be beautiful and popular if I wanted to, and I mainly wanted Derrick to see this. I wanted to be sure that he knew that I would always have other options, and that he should think twice before taking me for granted. Of course, I didn't post any pictures of me with the guy from high school, but either way, these pictures were a little on the sleazy side. I had completely forgot about meeting with my dad that day until my phone rang. When I saw it was my dad, I didn't answer because I had a feeling he was going to be pretty mad at me, and he was actually quite furious. "I guess you have no plans to say goodbye to me, Elizabeth and you need to take those pictures off My Space! They are sleazy!" he screamed into the message. Part of me knew that he was right, but I wasn't ready to deal with it. I wasn't ready to deal with anyone. I ignored his message and didn't call him back. I felt really bad about it, but I couldn't face my own feelings. I had too much going on and didn't want to let him ruin my good time.

Cherie and I left Tahoe the same afternoon, and we got to her house that evening around six. One of her guy friends came over that she had somewhat of a relationship with. I was still in a party mode and insisted that we all go out to a bar. I had a cute jean skirt on and a tight, white long-sleeve shirt. I was being flirty with everyone. I even convinced the D.J. to let me play with his equipment. I told the bartender that I wanted to dance on the bar that night. "I'll be really careful, I swear!" "I want to let you, but it's against our policy. If you got hurt, we could be sued," he replied. I socialized with pretty much everyone at the bar that night, and when I least expected, the manager approached me and introduced himself. "Now, we usually never let anyone dance on our bar, but you are gorgeous and your personality is bubbly and likable, so I think that if I let you dance on the bar it would probably be good for business." he said in all sincerity. "Yay! Can I pick the song?" I asked. He led me to the D.J. where he told him what was about to happen. As I was deciding on a song, he walked over to the six-foot tall bartender and informed him of what I was about to do. Of course, I chose the tackiest, most cliché song I could think of. The music started playing and Cherie and her friend had no idea what was going on. I thought it was nice of the beefy bartender to help me onto the bar. Every seat at the bar was taken. My only fear was that I was going to accidently kick someone's drink over.

Love is like a bomb, baby, c'mon get it on
Livin' like a lover with a radar phone

I very carefully busted out with my best moves. I didn't end up knocking anyone's drinks over, and by the end of my dance, I somehow got a hold of the water hose and turned this ordeal into a one-woman wet t-shirt contest, and I won. Face-palm.

Chapter 77

After my two-day party, I was tired and feeling like my hangover was going to last for the next ten years. Cherie and I packed up the next day and began the drive to Quincy, CA, and it felt like it took forever. She had a meltdown on the way there, talking about her family history and how badly she hated the drive. Like myself, she had severe anxiety. I had to convince her to take her medication, which didn't do a very good job at calming her down. We arrived in Quincy when it was dark. The cousin that would be going to Texas with me was the most conservative. There were three cousins, and they were triplets - two girls and a boy. The other girl that I had always gotten along with asked if I wanted to go into town. There was a pool hall that they went to on occasion. I went with the two sisters, got drunk (again), and by the time we got back to the house that night, I was starting to feel like a sore throat was coming on. When I woke up on the couch the next morning, I was so sick I could hardly talk. Ashley ended up having to take me to the local emergency room before we could leave the next day because I was painfully ill. The doctor gave me a strong prescription of antibiotics, and the next day we were on the road.

I spent most of the drive to Texas sleeping. I was carsick and tired from the medication, and this was my second big move in less than a year. I was overwhelmed. My self-destruction was only a temporary fix, and eventually I would be forced to face reality. Whether it would be good or bad, I would soon find out.

When we made that long and familiar drive across the country, everything was going smoothly until we were about twenty minutes away from my in-law's house where I would be reunited with my husband and daughter. We were pulled over. I was afraid and almost shaking. I was worried that if they ran my name, they would know that I was still on Probation. With my luck, I was probably going to go to jail that night. Luckily, the officer told Ashley that her headlight was out and let her go. About ten minutes later, the same thing happened all over again. This time, despite Ashley telling the officer that we had just been pulled over, this time around he was acting suspicious and shining his flashlight in the car. I surrendered to the fact that I was going to jail. Luckily, he let us go again.

We finally made it to our final destination. We pulled into the driveway and I called Derrick on my cell phone to ask him to come out to help me bring my things in. He was wearing an ugly yellow sleeveless shirt, and I was surprised at how quickly he gained his weight back. He had probably been binging on junk food in an attempt to make up for all of the junk food moments he had lost in jail.

I walked up to him thinking that he would immediately hug me and be excited to see me. He awkwardly stood there. Out of irritation, I walked toward the front door carrying one of my bags. "Don't I get a hug?" he asked in his typical, cocky manner. He was back to himself. Jail definitely hadn't scared him straight for very long. I hugged him quickly and we walked in together. On the way to Texas, I knew that I should feel bad for the way I had been acting the last few days, but I just didn't. I was still angry with Derrick. I wasn't sure if he would ever be able to make that feeling go away. If it wasn't for my fear of being alone, and the fact that Danielle was waiting for me, I probably would have never even considered moving to Texas with him. Both of Derrick's parents hugged Ashley and then me, and his mom told me that she was so happy that I was finally there to stay. Since it was late, Danielle was already sleeping. She was sleeping in a toddler bed in the bedroom downstairs which was once an office. I walked in and rubbed her head as she slept, not wanting to wake her because she looked comfortable. Derrick's mom insisted that it was okay to wake her up. When she finally stirred and opened her eyes, I thought she might cry because she didn't remember me. She sat up and once she was aware that I was in front of her, she smiled, "mommy!" I was so happy that she knew exactly who I was. I picked her up and held her until she became tired a few minutes later and was ready to go back to sleep. This reaffirmed to me that I was definitely supposed to be there.

I settled in, and within a few weeks, I told Derrick that I wanted Danielle's room to be upstairs next to ours. It only made sense. We went to the local mall got all new bedding and wall decals. Her whole bedroom was themed Tinkerbelle. When I finally had it together, she was very excited to have her own bedroom. I took plenty of selfies with my baby and posted them online for my family to see.

The first month of being in Texas went well. I don't know if it was because I was so happy to be with my daughter or if it was just the general excitement of living in a whole new place. Things started to go downhill very quickly after I put Danielle down for a nap one day while Derrick was working. Derrick had found a job that paid decent wages, but he was constantly out of town. He pretty much left me to fend for myself. I was in the kitchen making a sandwich. "Hon, Derrick's father and I were talking, and we think it would be best to just leave the custody how it is. We don't think it would be a good idea to go back to Court because it might stir up some unnecessary precautions." "Oh, you mean like, for good?" "Yeah, we're just probably going to leave it how it is." I thought that this woman was out of her mind. I quickly began to doubt every promise that she ever made to me when I was sitting in jail. After I ate my sandwich, I went out to the patio to smoke a cigarette. I called Derrick. "So your mom just told me that she and your dad are never going to give custody back?" I told him, with obvious worry in my voice. "Is this the first that you've heard of this?" I asked. "Yeah. They haven't said anything to me like that. Trust me, that ain't gonna fly." Before we hung up, he reassured me that he was going to address this idea when he got home. He came home later that week. I was upstairs watching TV after dinner when he came up to tell me that he had spoken to both his parents. "I told them that keeping custody of Danielle was not going to work for us. My dad said that they just meant that they were going to keep custody until we completely had our shit together, which is understandable." he said. I had my doubts over the sincerity of what he'd been told. I tried to make it as clear as I could that I would not stay if there were not any hope of us getting our daughter back.

After a few months, I began to notice that my panic attacks were coming back. After having a few short-term boyfriends in Grass Valley, I was more aware of Derrick and the relationship that we had built. He was rough. He was rough with everything and the way he handled everything. Even when he hugged me or playfully wrestle around with me, it always hurt. I tried to tell him this but it only made him mad. He was starting to leave for work out of town more and more. When his mother asked me to ride along with her to the store, I would dreadfully try to get out of it knowing that I would only have a full-blown panic attack. My depression was coming back worse than it ever had. I thought that when I finally got to Texas, off of Probation and back with my daughter, things would be okay I thought that my life would really begin and my anxiety and depression would have no reason to ruin my daily existence. In the back of my mind, I thought that once I got to Texas and away from the System, the change would somehow erase everything that I had been through. I would no longer be suffering from the loss of my daughters, and I could fully begin to live as a normal person. For as long as I chose to be with Derrick, I would be reminded every day of everything that I didn't have. You can take the devil out of hell, but you can't take the hell out of the devil.

I knew that I needed to get back on my medication if I were going to be able to function. We hardly had any money saved and Derrick's mom was helping us each month with rent and utilities to keep the upstairs cool. I knew that the drama was going to start when I woke up early one morning, dripping sweat. I walked toward the thermostat to turn the air conditioning on. There was a written note taped to it.

DON'T TURN PAST 74!
DAVE

I sarcastically laughed to myself. This was a joke. The handwriting was clearly a woman's handwriting. I thought it was pathetic that she had to hide behind her husband every time she wanted something her way. I also thought it was extremely inconsiderate of her to tell me what temperature to live in. She didn't know how hot it got upstairs. This was a clear sign to me that she was beginning to dislike the fact that she was now living with another woman who would be competing for Danielle's love and would have more influence over her son than she would. I certainly wasn't trying to be competitive. I went there for one reason and that was to be the mother of my child. I thought that his mother would respect this, and I was delusional for thinking that.

Chapter 78

Within just a few months, it became obvious to me that everything that Derrick's mom had ever promised was a complete lie. The only reason she wanted me to go there so badly was because she knew that her son loved me and would be unhappy if I weren't there and possibly end up leaving. I began to subconsciously detach from Danielle when I knew that the chances of getting her back into my custody for good were probably not going to happen. I could hardly stand to be there anymore. I knew that both of Derrick's parents had zero respect for me, and it was probably from the mistakes that I had made in the past. Derrick was hardly there anymore, and I was lucky if he was home on weekends. After realizing that Yoga, Valerian Root and St. John's Wort were not going to fix my depression and anxiety, I finally found a doctor who would see me for a reasonable price. He prescribed the medication I needed, and I started to feel better within about a week. I also began to realize that the method in which Derrick's mother was parenting my daughter went entirely against my personal beliefs as a parent. I knew I had failed miserably as a mother. But I still also knew that there were certain things that were just not okay. I could easily put myself in the shoes of my little girl. When her grandmother was viciously spanking her just because she was crying when Ashley and I told her that she couldn't help us move a couch up the stairs, my heart broke. I could hardly contain myself.

My daughter was only two years old at the time. Apparently the entire family thought that spanking was the solution to a child's poor behavior. At first, I brought it up carefully. I emailed Derrick's mother an article that had clear evidence that spanking did more harm than good. She didn't respond. I begged Derrick to do something about it. Not only did I know that it just wasn't the right way to do things, but I couldn't handle the fact that this was happening before my own eyes, and no matter what I said, it wasn't going to stop. Suddenly, Ashley took it upon herself to spank Danielle also. I felt as if this family were ganging up on her. She was just a little girl, and because of her age, she was curious and obviously going to be getting into things. I thought that it was more of the responsibility of the adults to keep certain things out of her sight and reach. There was a day after lunch when Ashley left her open soda can on the couch. Danielle toddled up to it, picked it up and dumped the whole thing onto the carpet. I expected it to happen. Ashley walked up to Danielle and spanked her. I intervened and picked her up and walked away.

I put her down for a nap and went outside to call my mom. Mid conversation, Wanda walked out onto the patio, reaching her hand out. "Give me your phone, now." I stood up and laughed. "Are you serious?" She walked up to me and tried to snatch it out of my hand, and I wouldn't let go. It fell and shattered on the cement. This woman was treating me as if I were twelve years old. Apparently she also thought I didn't clean up after everybody enough. I always cleaned up after myself, and I thought that if everyone did the same, there wouldn't be any issues. There were little things that caused big conflict. When Derrick came home that night, I talked to him and told him that I couldn't handle it anymore. I told him what was going on, and he stormed inside to the living room where his parents were. "Look, if you're going to just treat her like she's a kid, we might as well pack up and go back to Tahoe. What's the point of being here if you're not going to let us parent our daughter." His father was more reasonable than his mother. Somehow, the conflict was talked out, but I knew it was definitely not the end of it. That night when we were lying in bed, I gave Derrick an ultimatum. "If you don't get us out of here and into our own apartment with our daughter, I don't know how much longer I will be able to last. I can't see her being treated the way she is treated and it's literally breaking my heart," I cried. "Spanking isn't as bad as you think it is, Elizabeth. You're just going to have to deal with it. And I don't know how long we'll be here. It might be a couple years." "A couple of years?" I said in shock. A year was the most I had thought we would be there. I couldn't bare the possibility of staying any longer.

The next night I decided to go through the pictures that my dad was able to recover for me. I wanted to put what I could back into albums to keep the last memories of my daughters safe. There were a good many pictures left. I organized them into groups pertaining to which album they would go in. They were spread across the pool table in the game room that was adjoining our bedroom. I had them organized by the date they were taken. I looked down at these pictures vividly recalling the many precious moments that I shared with them. It hit me all over again - my babies were gone. I quietly cried wishing desperately to have just one more moment with them. I needed one more chance to say, "I'm sorry," and one more chance to say, "I love you." I then realized that this loss was going to hurt me deeply for many years to follow, if not for the remainder of my life. I tried to envision what it would be like to reunite with Chloe and Zoe when they became adults. I couldn't see that ever being possible for as long as I chose to be with Derrick. I was afraid at the thought of them growing up and learning that I had spent this entire time with him. Every day that I was with this man was another day that I was disrespecting my daughters. I could never expect them to understand why I was with him if I couldn't even understand it myself. That night I decided that I was going to look for a job the next day. I had no immediate plans, but whatever would eventually happen, and whenever it did happen, I knew that I must be prepared. I knew that one day God would answer my prayers and help me do the best thing. I didn't know what that was, and I didn't try to guess. I just had faith.

I was called to interview with the local grocery store that same week. I was hired full time to bag groceries, and I started right away. For some reason, I could tell that Derrick's mother was irritated that I was going to be working. It could have been because Derrick was always gone and I needed a ride to work, and she would have to take me. Truly though, I think that she wanted me to sit home all day bored and miserable like she was. She didn't want anything good for me. It would defy her assumptions of me.

On my first day of work, I went out back to the patio and called my dad. We had resolved our prior conflict when I failed to see him before leaving and I apologized sincerely. "Have you watched the news lately?" he asked. "No, not today, anyway," I replied. "Do you remember Jaycee Dugard and when she was kidnapped years ago and never found?" he asked. I was expecting to hear the worst - they had probably found skeletal remains or something. "Of course I remember," I replied. Any kid who grew up in Tahoe after she went missing knew her. Even though most of us never met her, we all felt as if she were a friend and a part of us. "They found her," my dad said. "Really?" I responded, still expecting the worst. "They found her alive!" my dad said, with excitement in his voice. I was in shock. I could hardly believe it. I almost didn't know what to say. My dad reminded me that God is good, and he does answer prayers. Most of the time I didn't know it, but I needed his reminders. I needed someone to always tell me that God was listening and would love and forgive me as long as I asked for it. With the painful eighteen-year long struggle

542

that this young girl and now a woman endured, my own situation suddenly didn't seem so bad.

The memories would always haunt me, and the pain would always hurt, but I learned again that day that there will always be hope. When it seems that life is hopeless, God will still be watching, listening, and protecting us. My belief that things happen for a reason became stronger than ever that night. Jaycee had a big purpose in life - larger than she probably even knew. As I followed the news of her case, I learned many things about myself that I hadn't even thought of before. I learned about Stockholm syndrome. I was able to evaluate my relationship with Derrick, and suddenly I didn't feel like such a sick and horrible person for being with him. All of the times that I blamed myself and felt bad about the situation that I was in were symptoms of the psychological effects of staying in an abusive relationship. I realized that all of the times I had come to his defense and became angry with people who tried to warn me, was actually normal for a person in my situation. I didn't know much about Jaycee Dugard and what amazing life purpose she would surely fill, but I did know that I began lifting pounds and pounds of hate, anger, guilt and confusion from my shoulders. For this, I'll forever see this woman as a personal hero.

Chapter 79

I began to speak with my family on a regular basis, and I was honest with them about my stressful situation. I thought that I was supposed to be in Texas to be a parent to my daughter. Wanda was refusing to allow that to happen. After rereading the book that Lilah gave me after I was last released from jail, I learned that the best thing I could do in this moment was to pray for my enemies and decipher between what I could control and what I couldn't. I knew that the only thing that I could really control were the choices that I made which would affect my future and my emotional stability. There was a lot of conflict and I no longer felt welcomed, I had a child that I was afraid to become attached to, and a husband who was never there. If I didn't have to be at work, I would sleep as much as possible. I'm sure that to Derrick's parents and Ashley, I came off as lazy and selfish. Maybe I was. As I was living my lazy and selfish existence, deep in my heart I knew that I could never learn, grow, or truly love a happy life if I were to stay.

I loved working. I loved my job. It was my escape. Eventually I was promoted to work in the bakery. I got to spend my days baking cookies and decorating cupcakes. I gladly took the direction of the managers, as I knew that it was a walk in the park compared to the wrath of Wanda. A few weeks into my new position, I went outside to have a quick break. I was sitting on a bench against the concrete wall of the store, and my attention was drawn to two men about my age who were also taking a break. I chimed into their conversation, and something about the tall blond boy wearing a hoodie had me mesmerized. He had a calm and collected aura about him. As the weeks went by, we noticed each other at work more frequently, and we eventually began talking more often. This guy, Steven, became my friend. He was really the only friend that I had. My own husband wasn't even around enough to be my friend. Ashley and Wanda had teamed up to spank my daughter mercilessly, and Dave didn't even know what was going on half the time. It got to the point that if I wasn't at work, I was hiding in my room upstairs. Once in a while after it got dark and everyone went to sleep, I'd pack up my fishing gear, and walk a short distance down to a dock that I liked. I'd sit there by myself in the quiet and stare at the stars and wonder where my life was going. Aside my new job, I really hadn't made much progress. If anything, I felt myself slipping again. Work was the only place that kept me happy, but I could only be there for forty hours out of the week.

When I was getting ready to leave work one night, Steven and a couple of his friends asked me if I wanted to go with them the next night to a nightclub. They were all my age, and I thought that it would be fun for a change. I wanted to meet new friends and feel like I had some kind of life. I accepted the invitation and when I got home, instead of asking Wanda if I could go because I was an adult, I told her that I was going to go. The next day as she dropped me off at work, she gave me her usual cowardly lies. "I asked Dave if you could go out, and he doesn't think it's a good idea." That was all that she had to say about it. She was using her husband as a source of intimidation and as a shield to hide behind because she couldn't own up to her own thoughts.

"Okay, that's fine," I said. "I'll have Ashley pick you up tonight," she said as I stepped out of the passenger side door.

About an hour before I got off work that night, I sent Ashley a text message telling her that it wasn't necessary to pick me up. I'm going out with some friends tonight and Wanda already knows. Just tell her that I'll get a ride home and not to stay up and thanks. I laughed to myself as I hit the send button knowing that her face would be red with rage after Ashley relayed the message. After work, I changed out of my work cloths and squeezed into the back seat of the car that the four of us were riding in. I was happy that Steven was sitting next to me. He was courteous and definitely a gentlemen. We had tons of fun that night. This Southern boy had a nice innocence about him that I wasn't used to. Most kids my age were more concerned with drugs. Steven and I only had a few drinks, and we sat at a table in the corner laughing at the people who were drunk and dancing. It made me wonder if I looked like that when I had a drunken urge to bust out with my signature moves. I realized that night that Steven was the first man that I had ever known who was happy to simply be my friend. He knew that I was married, and he never tried to cross any boundaries. I admired and respected him for that. Before I moved to Texas, I would occasionally fantasize about meeting a cowboy who would whisk me away to keep me forever safe and happy. I didn't truly believe it was actually going to happen, but that person was sitting right in front of me.

The boys dropped me off that night around 4:00 a.m. in the morning. I quietly snuck into the house and up the stairs. I fell asleep with a grin on my face partially because I knew how pissed off Wanda was, but mostly because I had it bad for this guy. I was going to marry him one day. The next day I woke up to a nasty email from Wanda, "Dave is pissed! Thanks for waking us up at 4:00 a.m. in the morning!

I expected it. I was surprised when she actually called me down for lunch. I figured that she wanted nothing to do with me. As we sat at the table, I found it odd that she was being nicer than ever to me. She was acting as if nothing had happened Dave was nice too. When he asked me how my night went, I hesitantly answered him and he seemed to be just fine with it. He then told me a story of when he went out with his friends when he was younger. After slurping away at my soup, it hit me. I was so mad. Wanda had completely lied, again, about her husband being pissed off at me when really...he had no idea about anything! I kept my cool and knew that if I was going to react to this, now wasn't going to be the time. I had to think about how I was going to deal with her bizarre behavior.

I went to work at 3:00 in the afternoon that day, and I was excited to see Steven. We were both working the night shift and for some reason, all of the managers were gone for the day. At the end of our shift we were on our last fifteen-minute break. We were talking about how funny it was watching the crazy dancing people from the night before. We decided to take a quick drive down the road before our break ended. We bought a small bottle of peach vodka. We figured that it would make the rest of the night a little more entertaining, and all we had left to do was clean up. We were sitting in the back kitchen area passing the bottle back and forth and laughing about how bad it would be if we got caught. It was so refreshing to be around someone that I could just talk to about almost anything.

I told him about my mother-in-law, about how Derrick was always gone and not helping me resolve the situation, and about how uncomfortable I felt every time I returned to the house.

We thought we heard other employees heading our way. "Crap!" I said, shuffling to hide the almost finished bottle. "We have to hide! Where do we go?" I quietly laughed. "This way!" he said, signaling for me to follow him. There were single bathrooms right across the storage room hall. We bolted into the women's bathroom, locked the door, and listened. We heard two women talking, but after a few minutes they were gone. I quietly peeked out the door and confirmed that we were safe to exit the bathroom. But before we did, I had to take care of something. It had been bugging me for a while. I wasn't sure what would happen, but I knew that if I didn't do this, he would never know how I felt. He was considerate of the fact that I was married. I knew that he didn't even see me as an option. As he started to walk toward the door, I surprised him. "Wait, wait just a second," I said, pushing him back toward the bathroom sink that he had been leaning against. "Whoa…what…what are we doing?" he asked, completely confused. I reached up and pulled his head toward me and kissed him. He was hesitating and quickly pulled away. "Wait, I thought you were married?" he said, more as a statement than a question. Thinking about what a joke my marriage was and how Derrick hadn't even been around to have my back like he always promised to, I replied "I thought I was too, but remember I told you I served him divorce papers when I was in Tahoe," and kissed him again. This time, he wrapped his arms around my waist and hugged me as he accepted my kiss. I can't remember how long we hid in that bathroom kissing like kids in high school would, but I was happy that I was finally able to just let him know how much I cared for him and how much I respected him.

I was worried that he might have second thoughts about me after this because he knew that I was still with Derrick. I didn't have the best history with being faithful to Derrick, either. When our shifts were over, we sat outside on the same bench where we always sat, and I thought it was important to really tell him how I felt and tell him my history. "I'm really scared right now, and you're probably confused, but I don't want to get my hopes up if my history is something that will freak you out. I don't even know how you feel about me or if you even have feelings at all." I began. He sat there quietly listening to my story. It felt like it took me forever to tell it to him, but it really probably only took a few minutes. When I was done, he pulled me in next to him and hugged me. "I'm glad you felt like you could tell me all of that stuff. You are a really strong person for going through all of that, and it makes me angry that your husband put you in those situations. I want you to know that I am here for you, and whatever ends up happening, I'll always be here for you. I didn't know exactly what he meant or how he felt, but I knew that he was being sincere. After I broke the ice, we spent as much time as we could together, and eventually I didn't care who knew. I thought it was fitting that we went together so well since he worked in the dairy department and I worked in the bakery – we were like cookies and milk!

Chapter 80

The following weekend, Dave announced he had tickets to take me, Ashley and Derrick with him to a Monster Jam show. I had no idea what that was and it sounded kind of boring, but if I didn't go, I'd be stuck at the house with Wanda. I was finishing up my early shift at work when Steven and his friends were talking about going to a truck show that same night. I was happy to find out that they also had tickets. I was also kind of disappointed because I knew there would be no way that I could watch the show with them. Still, something about knowing that Steven was going to be there made me happy.

After work Ashley and I got ready for the show. When it was time to leave, I kissed Danielle goodbye, and we hopped in the truck and headed to Galveston to pick up Derrick. He was working as usual and wanted to go but didn't have a way to meet us because he would carpool to work when they all did an out of town job. Dave wanted Derrick to be there so we left early. When he got in the back seat with me, he was actually acting like he was happy to see me. Instead of being relieved, it made me angry. He didn't even try to understand what I was dealing with and how difficult it was to try to be there for our daughter when I was forced to see her cry her eyes out from being spanked all the time. I had told him so many times,

"One day you're going to wake up, and I'll be gone." Either he simply didn't care, or he just didn't believe me.

When we got to the stadium, we walked to our seats. I quickly realized that there was probably no way in hell I would be able to even get a glimpse of Steven. Derrick brought Ashley and me a cup of beer and the show began. I was extremely bored because I didn't know what was going on. Whenever I asked Derrick a question about what I was seeing, he'd give me a partial answer and quickly resume talking to his dad. I became resentful. After all of the time he was spending away from me, it was obvious that he'd rather be with his parents and give them all of his attention. I hated how he was always on his best behavior for his parents, but he could never be that way with me. I excused myself to use the restroom when I was really about to get another beer and step outside for a cigarette. I wanted to be away from the noise and sit in peace. As I was half way through my cigarette, I got a text message that said, "Look behind you."

It was Steven. I thought there was no way he'd be able to find me. I turned around, and he was waving to me from the deck to the right. I signaled for him to stay there. I wasn't sure what kind of maze I was getting myself into, but I somehow managed to figure out where he was. I ran into his arms and I was so happy that he was holding me in that very moment. He was kind and gentle, and he listened and cared, and the best thing was that he was respectful. He was just happy to be around me. That was all that he needed. He didn't have ulterior motives. He liked me for who I was. He didn't have any preconceptions about me or any set judgment. He just liked me.

After a few minutes, I knew that I had better get back to my seat. When I was about to say goodbye, I got a phone call. Before I could even answer, Derrick was screaming in my ear, "Where the hell are you? Why did you just disappear? You are making me look bad. Get your ass back to the show – now!" he demanded.

It made me sick. He only cared about his image, and what his parents thought. He would never put me before them. He would never even consider it. I knew that no matter what, if I were to stay in this situation and continue my relationship with Derrick, I was never going to be happy. Not only did he give me panic attacks and remind me of all of the horrible things I had been through, he also reminded me of the weak, worthless person I had become and would always be as long as I chose to stay. Not only was Derrick a reminder of these things, so were his parents. It was made clear that I would never have a say in how my daughter would be raised, and his mom was no longer willing to give up custody of Danielle. Despite my constant begging, Derrick wouldn't even consider moving us into our own place so that we could possibly save our marriage, get away from his parents, and still see Danielle as much as possible. I thought of every probable solution. I thought that once I was back on my medication, things might also get better. The only thing that happened was that my mind became clear enough to realize that my life was a joke. I was trying to force something that wasn't meant to be.

"I can't handle this anymore," I said, looking up at Steven. "Let's run away together," he said. "I'm not kidding and we should," I replied. "I'll pack my things tonight. I don't know where I'll go, but I'll figure it out." "Start packing your things when you get home, and call me as soon as you're ready. Brian and I will come and get you out of there. If you change your mind, just let me know and I'll understand," he replied, hopeful but hesitant. It was going to happen. I knew that if I didn't leave that night, I would never get out. I would waste away in an existence that had no honesty, truth or integrity. I would never discover who I was. I would never have a chance to find myself. I would never, ever be capable of being a stable mother - for any of my daughters. I had to just let myself run. I had to make this choice and be brave and be willing to face the world on my own.

The drive home took forever. We drove Derrick back to Galveston, and I fell asleep with my head on his lap. It was an odd feeling. I was saying goodbye without him even knowing it, and I was doing it in the kindest way that I could. It was the only way that I could. I slept for the entire ride back to the house. As I walked up the stairs, I remembered my conversation with Steven. Without letting myself think about it any further, I sent him a text. "I'll be ready in ten minutes. Are you still coming?" Less than five minutes went by and he responded, "We're waiting outside. Do you need help grabbing your things?" If he were to get caught inside the house, it could be really bad. I opened the bedroom window and quietly called Steven over. I was on the second floor, but it was facing the street where the car was parked. It was the perfect place for me to toss out the things that I would need. I quickly bagged everything up. I grabbed the photo albums that I put together for Chloe and Zoe, but when I crossed Danielle's baby book, I became sad and unsure. I didn't know if I should take it because I didn't think I would ever be back. I wanted her to at least have access to the pictures of me holding her when she was first born and up until the time she was with us. I wanted her to know that I love her. I started crying not knowing how I was supposed to do this or how I would ever explain it to her. I did know one thing for sure though. I knew that as long as I was in a relationship with her dad, no matter how much better his life became or how much he improved, I would never improve. Any accomplishments I would make with Derrick would only be an attempt to convince myself that I was okay. It would be a way to put a nice shiny coat of sugar over a life full of sour regrets. Not long after our relationship began, every night that I fell asleep next to Derrick, I felt contaminated from the unknown. The only person that I could blame for this was myself. From the drugs slipped into my coffee, to the assault of my child, to the death of Donnie's baby, and the never-ending

554

series of traumatic events, my very existence had been lost forever.

The life that I knew and yearned to return to every moment of every day was gone, and I had turned into someone that I hated. I went against every moral and value that I ever held onto. Danielle would suffer for as long as I remained the helpless, hopeless victim I had succumbed to. I hadn't allowed myself to truly grieve the loss of her sisters Chloe and Zoe, and I hadn't even begun to grieve the loss of myself. From the day of her birth, she suffered the consequences of my adolescent choices. Even though life is sometimes tragic and unfair, there will always be beauty where there is pain. Danielle arrived in the world to represent its beauty. She was living proof that when our own little world becomes divided, life will still go on. When good meets evil, proof of heaven infinitely shines. When living becomes too painful, there's always a way to make it better. This child, who was born into a life in which she had no control and deserved no pain, gave to me the greatest lesson that life can teach. There is always a reason to live. There is always beauty beyond the dark. There is always love beyond grief. We all have a lesson to learn, and we all have a purpose to fulfill.

I tossed as many things out of the second story window as I could. I found the largest suitcase that I had and packed what was left of my life and the memories that it had created. I awkwardly bumped into the wall as I thumped down the staircase attempting to be as quiet as I possibly could and set the suitcase next to the door. It was time to say goodbye to Danielle. I didn't want to say goodbye because it was going to hurt so very much. I knew that if I left without whispering into her tiny ear that I loved her and I hoped that she could one day understand and forgive me, I would never forgive myself. It wasn't going to hurt her as much as it was hurting me because she was sound asleep in her Tinker Bell themed bedroom. I kissed her cheek and ran my fingers through her soft hair as my tears landed on her pillow. With the pain of not knowing when I'd see her again, I came close to changing my mind. Instead, I quietly turned around and walked out of the house. I was about to release my soul from the chains in which I unknowingly held the key to…all those years.

§

Epilogue

After spending a week renting a tiny room in a trailer about a block away from my job, I knew that I had to get out fast after waking up at 3:00 a.m. to my new roommate staring at me quietly in the dark. She was in her late fifties, and although she claimed sobriety, I quickly learned otherwise. Telling her that I took medication for my panic attacks was a mistake. She wanted it. When I noticed that the prescription that I recently filled was over half gone, Steven picked me up and helped me move my things back into his car. He was living with his friend and his friends' family, and I had nowhere to go. Steven wasn't going to let me be a bum alone. We moved into a motel room for the next two weeks. Initially, I was hoping that I could get on my feet and eventually go to Court and try to get custody or, at the very least, visitation rights with my daughter. I became unsure of how this was going to play out when I realized that even my job at the local grocery store wasn't enough to pay for a room in a motel every night. One night I got a strange call from a Detective who wanted to take me to the station for an interview. I figured that if I didn't cooperate, I'd be in trouble. I got a call from Derrick five minutes later. He was laughing, almost hysterically. Derrick was the Detective. It freaked me out that I honestly didn't recognize his voice. I was convinced he was possessed. I asked him if I could see Danielle to tell her that I loved and missed her. I wanted to meet with them in one of the local playground areas because I was worried about my safety. Derrick responded by telling me that the only way I could see her was if I went on a ride with them. There was no way I was going to get into a vehicle with him. I remembered the ride with Derrick to the top of the mountain in Tahoe when he was so angry and I was afraid I was going to end up dead.

Steven was going to start training at a school for Correction Officers in just a few weeks. His training was going to be paid for, and he wanted to take care of me as soon as he could. When I checked into the motel room, I told him that I wanted his company. He gladly stayed with me, and we fell in love over those two weeks. We went swimming, ate pizza, laughed about how pathetic our situation was, and purely lived in the moment while appreciating every second together. Soon enough, we were both completely tapped out of money and resources. I called my mom. "Well, until Steven starts his training, why don't you go stay with your Uncle Tony in Arizona? I'm sure he'd love to take care of you for a while," my mom suggested. It wasn't a bad idea, but I didn't want to leave Steven, and I knew that I had to try to see Danielle as much as I could. "Liz, if you go stay with Uncle Tony, I'll buy you a plane ticket back to Texas whenever you're ready." She convinced me. Steven agreed that it was probably our only realistic option. Before taking me to buy my Greyhound bus ticket, he took me to a sporting goods store and bought me a small bottle of pepper spray for my safety.

As Steven stared at the ground with his head hanging low, I hugged and kissed him one last time. I left most of my things in his car, knowing that I would soon return. He promised he would take care of them. I boarded the bus and had a lump in my throat as I watched him from the window of the crowded bus. He sat in his car waiting for the bus to get on the road. I knew at this point how unpredictable life was, and I hoped I would be back in his arms sooner than later.

I woke up on the third morning from riding on a bus for what felt like a million mile journey. As the sun rose, the mountains and cactus looked so perfect to me. I was tired and missing Steven and my baby, but I was also hopeful. The tall Southern man who I'd met just a few months earlier was my angel in disguise. The guy working in the dairy department showed me what it really felt like to be cared for. He showed me what I forgot could exist. He showed me a way. He saved my life.

The driver announced over the intercom that we'd be arriving at the Phoenix Greyhound station in less than twenty minutes.

I felt free. I felt as if I were breathing in new air. Air which was sustaining my heart and soul. Air that felt pure, clean and fresh. I realized that God was with me all along. He was listening to my prayers. He was keeping me safe. Most importantly, he had forgiven my sins and he was blessing me with a chance to start new.

I was only twenty-two when I arrived in Phoenix. I felt as if I had lived over a hundred lives. The morning sun was peeking through the tinted window as I rode down the interstate. The dark was gone. As quickly as the lightning struck the ground of my world, I was stepping back into the light that I hadn't seen in over four years. I was crossing into a new chapter, and I knew that it was safe to turn the page. I was finally going to begin the life of healing I so yearned for, and find the real Elizabeth that had been lost for so long. I smiled with tears of relief. I knew that my struggle was over and my life was just beginning.

"I hold it true, whate'er befall;
I feel it, when I sorrow most;
'Tis better to have loved and lost
Than never to have loved at all."
-Alfred Lord Tennyson

Long was the line
An abrupt walk of fate

Blue was the time
The long years left to wait

Line was the life
So blessed to create

LONG
    BLUE
        LINE

Gabriella, Madeline and Danielle,
I'll always love you and I'll never stop waiting. Please come back to me.

Love Always,
Mom

If you enjoyed this story, please let us know by submitting your Amazon review.

*The author asks you, the reader, to please consider the book as a whole rather than considering her moral choices when submitting your review. Feedback on moral choices are not conducive to her works as an author which she lives to grow as today and in the future.

Don't forget to visit
Poemaboutlife.blogspot.com
to sign up for updates on current and future publications by E. McNew

About the Author

Elizabeth McNew is a dynamic professional whose publishing acumen has resulted in amazing success for her clients. In addition to her roles as freelance writer, blogger, best-selling author and web design specialist, she has helped over one hundred aspiring authors launch and sell ebooks in nearly every genre as the Founding Member of Ebook Marketing Company. She's also invested in website and domain sales.

While life is certainly treating her well, it wasn't always so cordial. Formerly known as Elizabeth Jeter, she grew up in the small town of South Lake Tahoe, California. During her youth, Elizabeth struggled with substance abuse, teen pregnancy, domestic violence, child custody loss and hardships in the California court system. Her ultimate passion has always been writing and she candidly recounts her challenging journey in the controversial book, Long Blue Line-which is available on Amazon.com.

It wasn't easy, but she persevered in the end and is still going strong. Her ambition is clearly evident in each project she assumes and her impeccable reputation is something new and existing clientele have learned to depend on.

30708213R00361

Made in the USA
San Bernardino, CA
20 February 2016